Americans at War
in Foreign Forces

ALSO BY CHRIS DICKON

The Foreign Burial of American War Dead:
A History (McFarland, 2011)

Americans at War in Foreign Forces

A History, 1914–1945

CHRIS DICKON

McFarland & Company, Inc., Publishers
Jefferson, North Carolina

LIBRARY OF CONGRESS CATALOGUING-IN-PUBLICATION DATA

Dickon, Chris.
Americans at war in foreign forces :
a history, 1914–1945 / Chris Dickon.
p.   cm.
Includes bibliographical references and index.

ISBN 978-0-7864-7190-4 (softcover : acid free paper) ∞
ISBN 978-1-4766-1537-0 (ebook)

1. Foreign enlistment—United States—History—20th century.
2. Mercenary troops—United States—History—20th century.
3. Americans—Foreign countries—History—20th century.
4. United States—Armed Forces—Foreign service—
History—20th century.   5. World War, 1914–1918—
Recruiting, enlistment, etc.   6. World War, 1939–1945—
Recruiting, enlistment, etc.   I. Title.
UB321.D53 2014   940.4′1208913—dc23   2014023633

BRITISH LIBRARY CATALOGUING DATA ARE AVAILABLE

On the cover: American volunteers for French forces
in Paris, August 1914 (Library of Congress / *New York Times*).

Printed in the United States of America

*McFarland & Company, Inc., Publishers
Box 611, Jefferson, North Carolina 28640
www.mcfarlandpub.com*

Table of Contents

Preface

This book covers a topic that is mostly unknown in the history of American participation in the two world wars of the twentieth century. I did not learn about it myself until a fine spring day in 2009 at the Brookwood American Cemetery outside of London. I was researching my book *The Foreign Burial of American War Dead*, about American military members buried abroad since the Revolutionary War, and the assistant director of the cemetery was giving me a tour.

At one point, we stopped amid the headstones of members of U.S. forces who had rested at Brookwood since World War I, and he pointed to a patch of grave markers away from the main cemetery, at the edge of a wood. "Those are all Americans, too," he said, "but nobody seems to know about them." We walked to the very neat rows of stones, which were designed and placed differently than those of Brookwood's official American burials. They told of service in the Royal Air Force Volunteer Reserve, the Royal Canadian Army Service Corps and similar forces, but, with a few exceptions, they did not note that the deceased were American citizens.

I went on to learn and write about the approximately 3,500 such Americans buried in Commonwealth Graves Commission cemeteries in more than 25 nations on five continents. But the larger questions remained: who were these Americans, why were they there, what was their experience, how were they perceived by their own country, and what were their circumstances after returning from war?

The answers follow, and the narrative they tell may add an extra dimension to the understanding of American participation in the two world wars. The French Foreign Legion plays a substantial role in its full context, more than might be presumed based on typical stereotypes of the legion.

The stories of the aviators of the Lafayette Escadrille in World War I and the American Eagle Squadrons in World War II are familiar to many, and those of American ambulance drivers and medical personnel less so. But they are only a small portion of the unknown number of Americans in foreign uniforms, probably in the range of 75,000, who participated in the wars, mostly as Canadians. Beyond their service in those wars, many played a role in related skirmishes around the world in the first half the twentieth century. And the actions they took influenced national and international politics and diplomacy during nearly 50 years of world conflict.

As in all works about war, this one will take us from small towns to burned villages, from diseased trenches to vast battlefields, war at sea to dogfights in the clouds, misery to exaltation. More than that, it is a work about those who go to war though they are not required to. And much of it is in the context of the common history of two nations that don't fully know each other though they share the world's longest single border. It begins at the time of the American Revolution, and with perhaps the first person in American history to fight a war in a uniform that was not that of his own nation.

With thanks to my best reader and editor, Dr. Frances Beck.

ONE

The French American

Never in my country will the American volunteers of the Great War be forgotten.—Jean Jules Jusserand

In 1824, Marie Joseph Paul Yves Roch Gilbert du Motier, the Marquis de Lafayette, had occasion to bring his beloved American friends full circle in their understanding and appreciation for their revolution of 1776. He had first come ashore in America, at South Carolina, on June 13, 1777, at the end of a clandestine journey from France. Now it was an October day 47 years later in Charlestown, outside of Boston. Citizens, military attachments, musical bands and city officials were there to greet him.

"Permit us, beloved General," spoke a committeeman of the town, "again to welcome you to our borders; to express our ardent hopes, that your valuable life may be prolonged to the utmost limits of earthly happiness; that the land which has been enriched with the dew of your youth, may be honored as the asylum of your old age; that the country which now blends your fame with the mild luster of Washington, may henceforth hail you as a citizen of Washington's country; and that during the residue of your years, you may live amidst the attentions, as you will forever live in the hearts of a grateful and admiring people."[1]

This was not just undisciplined rhetoric, but a true telling of the American heart where Lafayette was concerned. He responded to the committeeman in kind, and spoke of the blood that had been spilled in the revolution.

> That blood has called both American continents to republican independence, and has awakened the nations of Europe to a sense, and in future, I hope to the practice of *their* rights. Such have been the effects of a resistance to oppression, which was, by many pretended wise men of the times, called rashness; while it was duty, virtue; and has been a signal for the emancipation of mankind.[2]

Lafayette's sense of duty toward the emancipation of the oppressed had grown in a child of privilege and a young man of great wealth and opportunity, and was fired by the idea of a country trying to free itself from tyranny. "The moment I heard of America," he wrote at one point, "I loved her; the moment I knew she was fighting for liberty, I burnt with desire to bleed for her."[3] And so, he had taken action, as many men had taken before and would again, especially in the case of the long, shared history of the United States and France. He left his own country and joined the army of another.

Lafayette disguised himself—some accounts say as a woman—to escape France (which had other ideas for his talents), and went to Spain. He hired his own ship at San Sebastian, crossed the ocean, and soon appeared in Philadelphia where he was able to take on a com-

George Washington and the Marquis de Lafayette, Mount Vernon, 1784. **The painting, 1859, by Thomas Pricard Rossiter and Louis Rémy Mignot depicted a friendship between the two men that was familial (Metropolitan Museum of Art).**

mission as major general of the Continental army. A few days later he became aide-de-camp for Gen. George Washington. It was the beginning of a relationship that some would observe as that of father and son.

More than just a volunteer in a foreign army, Lafayette became a benefactor of the revolution. He purchased clothing and arms for the cause, and gave George Washington a direct donation of 60,000 francs.[4] Promoted to major general, the Frenchman was badly wounded with a shot to the leg during the Battle of Brandywine at Chad's Ford, Pennsylvania, in September 1777. The event satisfied skepticism about his intentions that was held by some, and led to his command, in November, of Continental army troops as they sent the forces of British general Cornwallis into retreat near Gloucester, New Jersey. By February of 1778, the tacit support of France for the American Revolution had evolved into an alliance for mutual support against the British, and by July, ships of the French fleet had arrived in American waters.

Lafayette was by now a hero of the American Revolution. He had received a message of appreciation from the U.S. Congress in September, to which he had replied with the words about burning "with the desire for bleeding for her, and," he continued, "the moment I shall be able of serving her, in any time, or in any part of the world, will be the happiest of my life."

The young marquis had not been the only Frenchman drawn to fighting with America during its revolution, but he was the most visible, and it seemed to be sensed as a deserved respite in his life when he was called back to France for an accounting of his actions in a foreign land. King Louis XVI had not been pleased, and upon Lafayette's return to Paris he was placed under house arrest for two weeks. In a subsequent meeting, however, the two formed an alliance that would further the American cause. With the counsel of American ambassador Benjamin Franklin, he was able to return to America and Gen. George Washington with the promise of 6,000 more French troops and five French frigates. He was met with great celebration and affection, and spent the rest of the war in command positions. Another return to Paris on America's behalf culminated in collaboration with the French fleet to bring about the British surrender at Yorktown in October 1781.

Lafayette, however, was not done with his work on behalf of America. He returned to Paris, now a hero of both nations, and worked with Thomas Jefferson and Benjamin Franklin to secure America's political and economic place in the world, and commuted back and forth between the two countries in following years. Eventually he was able to bring the potential of the American Revolution to his own country with the introduction of the Declaration of the Rights of Man and of the Citizen to the National Assembly. Inspired in part by the American Declaration of Independence, it became a core document of the French Revolution.

French-American history continued on from that point and endured some rocky years, including the so-called, and seemingly half-hearted, Quasi War from 1798 to 1800. The two countries would not come together again until the American entrance into World War I. And the Marquis de Lafayette contributed mightily to his nation's fortunes during the post–Revolutionary War years of turmoil, a few of which he spent in prison. By the time of his final return to America in 1824, however, all seemed calm and reflective. "After the lapse of half a century," said the mayor of Boston, "you find the same people prosperous beyond all hope; and all precedent; their liberty secure; sitting in its strength; without fear and without reproach."[5]

Lafayette returned again to France, and kept up his busybody ways, fighting against slavery wherever it existed, and for Polish independence from Russian tyranny, among other things. He died in May 1834, and, fulfilling the marquis' wish that he be buried in American soil, his son, George Washington Louis Gilbert du Motier, spread American earth (in some accounts it was from Mt Vernon) on his burial place in Picpus Cemetery in Paris.

In the following century, on the evening of September 6, 1916, the Marquis de Lafayette was very much on the minds of 800 prominent Americans drawn to a dinner at New York's Waldorf Astoria Hotel. The event was in honor of the French ambassador to the United States, Jean Jules Jusserand, but it was the marquis who gave the energy to the evening's celebration. France had been struggling against Germany's aggression for two years. The American government would not enter the growing war in Europe until 1917, but individual Americans had been supporting France since 1914.

"Never in my country will the American volunteers of the Great War be forgotten," said Jusserand. "Serving in the ambulances, serving in the legion, serving in the air, serving liberty, obeying the same impulses that brought Lafayette to these shores, many young Americans, leaving family and homes, have offered to France their lives. America has shown tonight that she doesn't forget; France will show that she remembers."[6]

The sentiment of the evening also extended to the former common foe of the United States and France. "Today, America's independence Day [*sic*] is almost as much of a national holiday in Great Britain," asserted F. Cunliffe Owen, chairman of the France-America Society. "George Washington is looked upon in Great Britain as an English national hero, as one who fought for those rights dear to every Briton, as they are to all Americans and Frenchmen.

Something over 2,000,000 British soldiers are now in France, fighting shoulder to shoulder with their heroic French comrades, to rid the soil of France of the horrors of German invasion—a task in which they have, I know, the heartfelt sympathy of all present, and at least 80 percent of the American nation."[7] Whatever the true percentage of Americans who sympathized with the French, thousands of Americans were already unofficially numbered among the British troops in France. And they had been preceded by those described by Jusserand in the ambulances, in the air, and in the French Foreign Legion.

The legion was created in 1831 by King Louis-Phillipe expressly to recruit foreign nationals into the cause of enforcing French colonialism. A subtext of the legion was that its members were often loners, or those who lived on the edge of society, sometimes troublemakers and revolutionaries. The legion was gritty and loosely structured, just the place for soldiers of fortune, those who just wanted to escape somewhere, true believers or the obsessed.

In 1918, Minnesotan John Bowe published an account of his experience in the legion that was at once sentimental and detached, a narrative of common men traveling through an uncommon landscape. *Soldiers of the Legion* opens with the view of a Frenchwoman that Americans were extraordinary and complicated. In the first weeks of German pillaging, death and destruction, she told the author, those Americans living in Paris just ran about "like chickens with their heads cut off."[8] They thought only of themselves and had no sympathy for the grief that had come to France.

"But," she continued, "the same ship that took these people away brought us other Americans. Strong and vigorous, they did not remain in Paris. Directly to the training camps they went; and, today, they are lying in mud, in the trenches with our poilus.

"Now, we should like to know, if you please, which are the real Americans—those who ran away and left us when in trouble, or those who came to help us in time of need. Are you goers or comers?"

Those Americans who came to join the Foreign Legion were described respectfully by their fellow John Bowe as basically disobedient and reluctant to subordinate themselves to authority, but always prepared to stand up for what was right. They were courteous to strangers but quick to fight among themselves. "They would never patch their clothes. They did no fatigue duty they could dodge. They carried books in one pocket and grenades in another, and only saluted officers when the sweet notion moved them."[9] They were seemingly perfect for the French Foreign Legion, and in Bowe's estimation an "aggregation of automobile racers, elephant hunters, college students, gentlemen of leisure, professional boxers, baseball players, lawyers, authors, artists, poets and philosophers"[10] that acquitted itself with superb effect in the fight against Germany.

Of the unknown number of American members of the legion, many would be killed in action. Some would be killed, but live on in history. Some would move on to other fighting forces in the war, especially aviation. A few would eventually end up in American forces after U.S. entry into the war in April 1917, and a small handful would go on to play a role in the world war that was yet to come after the supposed "war to end all wars" that was World War I.

Among those who would begin their journey through the war in the legion was Kiffin Yates Rockwell. "I came to pay the debt we owe to Lafayette, to Rochambeau," Rockwell is quoted as saying at one point, though variations of the phrase were heard in public meetings throughout the country as America entered World War I.[11] Rockwell, born in Newport, Tennessee, had been a student of the Virginia Military Institute and gone on to work in advertising in Atlanta. He and his brother Paul were spurned in an attempt to join the French army, but were accepted into the Foreign Legion in August 1914. They found themselves in the trenches by October, and Kiffin was wounded in December. After convalescence, he was wounded again in Morocco, this time to an extent that jeopardized his effectiveness as a fighting man, but offered a turn of fortune that would take him into the sky. Paul Rockwell was wounded also, but went on to work diplomatically between the two nations, marry a French woman and work administratively in the General Headquarters of the French army.[12]

Of those who would live on in history, Alan Seeger was perhaps the most emblematic of the young American man marching to his own drummer into the uncommon paradigm of the French Foreign Legion. He was a Harvard graduate and a poet, and his every writing seemed to lead with confidence to the fact of his death at a young age. The most famous of his war poems, *I Have a Rendezvous with Death*, is excerpted:

> God knows 'twere better to be deep
> Pillowed in silk and scented down,
> Where love throbs out in blissful sleep,
> Pulse nigh to pulse, and breath to breath,
> Where hushed awakenings are dear ...
> But I've a rendezvous with Death
> At midnight in some flaming town,
> When Spring trips north again this year,
> And I to my pledged word am true,
> I shall not fail my rendezvous.[13]

The references to the making of love were an expression of his love of France and French women, but the rendezvous with death was just as elemental in the life of a soldier fighting for what was right. After Harvard, Seeger had moved to New York's Greenwich Village to lead the life of the poet, then to the Quartier Latin in Paris. On August 4, 1914, Germany invaded Belgium, and by the end of the month had reached into northern France. On August 14, Seeger was in Bruges, Belgium, by now behind the German lines as they advanced southward. He took a boat from Bruges to Paris and enlisted in the legion on the 24th. For Seeger, the German invasion was a moment when everything had changed, a time when the duty of those who loved freedom had become clear. "Being without responsibilities and no one to suffer materially by my decision," he wrote to his mother, "in taking upon my shoulders, too, the burden that so much of humanity is suffering under, and, rather than stand ingloriously aside when the opportunity was given me, doing my share of the side that I think right."[14]

As of 1920, Alan Seeger was just one of 360 known Harvard students, alumni and officers known to have participated in the struggle against Germany. Thirty of them had died before the U.S. entry into the war, and their statistics offered a good example of the cross currents of who people were and whom they fought with at that time in American history. Of the 30; 19 had been born in the United States, four each in Canada and Great Britain, two in France and one in Italy. How they fought in the years leading up to American entry into the war was not necessarily related to initial citizenship. The two Frenchmen joined the French army, but eight of the group joined Commonwealth forces directly, three were Americans who joined Commonwealth forces through Canada, nine joined the British Red Cross and various ambulance services, five joined the French Foreign Legion, and, of those, an unknown number went on to join the American aviation corps in the French army, the American Escadrille. One joined the Escadrille directly, and one was killed in the German sinking of the RMS *Lusitania* on May 7, 1915.[15]

Others of the Harvard group who joined the Legion included the first of them to die in the war, Edward Mandell Stone, born in Chicago in 1888. His father was second vice-president of the Chicago, Burlington and Quincy Railroad in Illinois, and then the president of the Chicago Telephone Company. After graduation from Harvard, Edward served in the Diplomatic Corps in Argentina, and then returned to Harvard Law School. Like Alan Seeger, he had been living in France before the German invasion and enlisted as a private in the legion in August 1914. Wounded in the trenches at the front, he died in February 1915 and is buried in a small military cemetery at Romilly-sur-Seine.

The draw of the legion reached into the most varied corners of American life. John Joseph Casey was an artist and newspaper illustrator who joined the legion in the fateful month of August 1914. He wrote and illustrated an article for a monthly magazine published by the *New York Times*. "It is an astounding, appalling admixture, the legion, of all manner of breeds and men and rakehells, of professions honorable and proscribed, of virtues and fatuities."[16] He fought with the legion until 1918, when he tried to join the American Expeditionary Forces, but was turned away as too old.

Bob Scanlon of Mobile, Alabama, was a professional Negro boxer who had bested a number of the most important boxers of the day. He was known in the legion as a man of extraordinary luck against injury and death, and, like many members of the legion, moved on to join the 170th French Regiment. His left hand was severely wounded at Verdun in May 1916, and his boxing career ended. Another of those who moved from the legion to the 170th Regiment was Eugene Jacobs of Pawtucket, Rhode Island. A butcher by trade, he carried a carving knife on the end of his rifle.

American members of the French Foreign Legion in an Argonne trench. The African American pugilist Bob Scanlon is at the far upper right-hand corner (Library of Congress/*New York Times*).

Christopher Charles, a Brooklyn mechanic of French descent, found himself vacationing in France in 1914. There was no question that he would get into the fight, but, as an American, he could not join the French army. He had heard the stories about the French Foreign Legion, but decided that he would find out for himself if they were true. What he came upon at first was a legion scrambling to get up to fighting condition. "All of our officers were former Paris firemen," he remembered. "They were pretty good officers, but too many people complained about having firemen for officers, but we later got regular Foreign Legion officers. There was not enough equipment."[17] He enlisted as a machine gunner in the Third Marching Regiment of the Moroccan Division, but there was only one machine gun in the whole regiment.

Charles was wounded in the Battle of Horseshoe Wood in the Second Battle of Champagne in September 1915. He recovered, and the legion itself was given the Cross of St. George by the Russian czar for its heroism, though the offensive by France had ended inconclusively. By the time of the Battle of the Somme in July 1916, Charles was writing long and very human narratives of his experiences in the war. He had watched the opening of the battle from an orchestra seat in the machine gun emplacements:

> It was great to see the boys crossing the hill. The Germans were about eight hundred metres away. The boys walked at an easy gait until they were within two hundred yards of the enemy. They were within good range of the German rifles and rapid-firers and they began falling fast.
>
> When the boys saw their friends falling, they got mad and went forward like a cyclone. In five minutes they had taken the German trenches and more than two hundred prisoners, the enemy not resisting vigorously when at close quarters. My section reached the trenches before the fighting was over and had a hand in it. We took a few minutes' rest in the captured trenches, while the prisoners were being taken to the rear.[18]

The Franco-British forces pushed through the village of Belloy-en-Santerre, the fellows of the legion, in Charles' telling, first lying down for a little rest before rising with a shout and storming German positions. It seemed to be all about pacing oneself to do the work that had to be done. They pushed further, took some casualties, ran out of ammunition, charged forth with bayonets, took prisoners and enemy arms with which to prevail once again, then

> at midnight other sections relieved us and we returned to the second line, where we found a hot meal. Believe me, we suddenly discovered that we were a hungry lot of men. We surely did eat. We had done a good day's work, and everybody was happy and contented. The boys in the first line also had a hot meal, for that night the rolling kitchens went right up to the firing trenches, and dished out "eats" and wines. For here it is realized that a man must eat to fight well. The Germans counter-attacked three times that night, but there is no regiment in all Germany which the Legion cannot stop.[19]

Among those Americans who would go on from the legion to play a continuing role in both world wars, perhaps the most important was Charles S. Sweeny. A West Point graduate, he quickly rose through legion ranks to captain. He suffered a head wound in 1915 and was decorated with the Legion of Honor and the Croix de Guerre. Upon American entry into the war, he was made a major in the U.S. army, but it was just the beginning of an extraordinary career that took him into the sky and extended through the years of the gathering of World War II before American entrance into the war in December 1941.

(Note: Charles Sweeny will be a recurring subject in the pages that follow. Different histories and newspaper articles variously spell his last name as Sweeny or Sweeney, and readers who look for more information about him should use both spellings. This narrative will use the former. Further complications with the name will be noted in Chapter Thirteen.)

Whomever they may have been individually, a report in the *New York Times* of August

26, 1914, described the first of the new recruits of the legion to leave Paris for training in Rouen as an impressive group.

> First to arrive at the Gare St. Lazare were the 150 Americans to strains of "Marching Through Georgia." They created a great impression upon the crowds, mostly composed of women as is natural at the present time, for it must be admitted that they were by far the finest body of them all. Strapping, athletic young fellows, mostly students, they came in for a considerable amount of hugging by the warm-hearted spectators, many of whom were in tears.[20]

For the most part, American members of the legion were divided into two foreign regiments with the goal of keeping the Americans together. With deaths, wounds and reassignments, the two regiments were eventually reduced to one, then subsumed into the full legion. All Americans, like Bob Scanlon and Eugene Jacobs, were then given the opportunity to join the 170th Regiment of the French Infantry. So successful was the 170th that it gained the nickname "Swallows of Death," or, in the German version, "The Chimney Swifts of Death."

There was no typical experience for the American member of the French Foreign Legion. The very popular autobiography of Albert Depew, published in 1918 as *Gunner Depew*, told just one story. It can be seen as an important popular culture story of the legion and the war in Europe, but it contains a confounding puzzle that seemed, unaccountably, not to have been noticed at the time of its publication.

As his best-selling book told it, the writer was born of French heritage in Pennsylvania in 1894, moved to Yonkers, New York, and set out to sea on sailing ships at age 12. At sixteen he joined the U.S. Navy, eventually working his way up from fireman to first-class gunner,

Albert N. Depew (left) sits with former American ambassador to Germany James W. Gerard, who helped Depew during his imprisonment by Germany. Depew's book *Gunner Depew* told of his adventures in the French Foreign Legion and French Navy before America's entrance into the war. As a best-selling book and through newspaper serialization, it gave many Americans their first extensive knowledge of the war that was being fought in Europe (Library of Congress).

gaining the nickname Gunner Depew. He left the Navy in 1914 and, like many others with military inclinations, was drawn to the stories of German atrocities in Belgium and France. Impatient with the U.S. reluctance to enter the conflict, he signed on as a water tender to an American steamer that had been chartered by the French government and set sail from Boston to St. Nazaire. He wanted then to enlist in the Foreign Legion but his tearful French grandmother convinced him not to, and he worked the ship back to Boston. In Boston, however, he regretted the decision, and worked the same ship back to France.

Overcoming his grandmother's continued importuning, he set off this time to enlist, but was met with suspicion by legion recruiters. He was not sure why; perhaps he seemed too young, or a German in disguise, though he knew that Germans already in the legion were the hardest fighters. He was finally accepted as a gunner on the first day of 1915, and ended up on ships of the French navy. It was a much more civil experience than that of the U.S. Navy, and, like many who fought for France in the early years, Depew became enamored of the French people. "I have never met one of this nationality," he wrote, "who was not anxious to help you in every way he could; extremely generous, though not reckless with small change, and almost always cheery and there with a smile in any weather."[21]

After time at sea, Depew took the uniform of an infantryman and moved by train and truck to the front at Flanders, Belgium. The trip was marked by station stops in which French women, young and old, fed the men and would tend to their needs as "a mother and a sweetheart all at the same time to any hairy old ex-convict in the Legion and do it in a way that made him feel like a little boy at the time and a rich church member afterwards."[22] In other cases, however, men of the legion were often preceded by their stereotypes and feared in the small towns along the way.

In Flanders, the fighting was in the trenches (that would later come to be called the Trenches of Death) and bayonet to bayonet on the battlefields. Depew saw the Germans use women and children as shields and sacks of dead rats as ammunition. Some men died with grace, and some without. Wounded in fighting at Dixmude, he was sent, after convalescence, to Brest where he set sail in French uniform on a dozen trips delivering war matériel to the Dardanelles strait in Turkey for the fighting on Gallipoli. On one of those trips, a French officer pulled Depew aside to ask if he knew any other ex-navy gunners in the United States, and would he write to them to ask that they come to fight with France. The need was dire and Americans were prime recruits, but he did not have mailing addresses for those he knew.

On his last trip in the convoys, Depew was drawn reluctantly into three weeks of trench warfare on land. He had had quite enough of it before. The trenches were as chaotic with death and blood as they had been in Flanders, and he noted that they were curiously lonely places with scarce friendships that often ended in blood and dismemberment. The culmination of the fighting on Gallipoli would take place at Sedd el Bahr where Depew volunteered for a communications mission that would take him through the most intense fighting and the most difficult trenches. The mission completed, he was ordered to return to a beachhead where he was put on a 14-inch gun and destroyed a key enemy warehouse. Upon return to his ship, the French frigate *Cassard*, he was told that he would be awarded the Croix de Guerre for his actions on land, and he set sail once again for Brest. The *Cassard*, however, became caught up in a battle with German cruisers that led to the deaths of nearly 100 of its crew. Depew was caught in the premature explosion of a shell in a gun turret and permanently blinded in one eye. That and other injuries put him in a hospital at Brest where he received great attention as the only American in residence. There, a French officer presented him with the Croix de Guerre.

When he had pinned the medal on, he said he thanked me from the bottom of his heart, for the French people, and also thanked all the Americans who had come over from their own land to help a country with which most of them were not connected. He said it was a war in which many nations were taking part, but in which there were just two ideas, Freedom and Despotism, and a lot more things that I cannot remember. He finished by saying he wished he could decorate all of us.[23]

During a month of convalescence, Depew was visited frequently by the American consul at Brest, who eventually convinced him to leave French service and return home. As the story continued, he set sail with three trunks of souvenirs and pictures, but his ship was attacked and sunk and he was converted to slave labor in an intolerable environment on another German ship. A number of his comrades were driven to madness and death. By the time he and others were taken to a German prison camp, Depew's identity as a member of the French Foreign Legion had long since been erased, but, though the United States had not yet entered the war, he was not seen as a neutral by the Germans who complained of American assistance to the British and French though it had not declared war. During months of travel in freight cars and imprisonment in prison camps that seemed to foreshadow the German concentration camp system of World War II, Depew met just one other American, evidently one of the first of those citizens of the United States who were beginning to enter the war through enlistment in Canadian forces.

At one point in Depew's internment in the prisoner of war camp at Dülmen, the camp was visited by the American ambassador to Germany, James W. Gerard. Gerard had spent much of his effort in Germany trying to bring light to the horrendous conditions of the camps, and to trying get the Germans to alleviate them if he could. His visits were great morale boosters to the prisoners. By Depew's account, Gerard heard of the lone American in the French barracks at Dülmen and sought him out against the protest of prison guards. They talked at length, and Gerard promised that Depew would hear from him again in three weeks' time. It would be longer than that, and Depew was moved to the prison camp at Brandenburg. He was visited there at one point by someone he described only as "a war correspondent named Bennett from a Chicago newspaper,"[24] probably James O'Donnell Bennett of the *Chicago Tribune*.

Bennett was a controversial reporter in Europe who asserted that claims of German atrocities were lies created by the British and French. The *Tribune* often printed his dispatches with the disclaimer that the newspaper neither supported nor denied his reporting, but that it deserved to be read. His dispatches were often part of a collective reporting by correspondents traveling through the war together, in which the view that German atrocities were fiction was mutually supported.

Always on our march the facts relative to the German atrocities evaded us. Always it was "in the next village" that a woman had been outraged, a child butchered, or an innocent old man tortured. Arriving at that "next village," we could get no confirmation from the inhabitants.[25]

Bennett's reporting along these lines was often vitriolic and voluble. At a time of debate about American involvement in the European war, it presented Germany in a sympathetic light, and the British as censors of the truth. As reported by Depew, their meeting was in keeping with Bennett's sentiments.

When he came to our barracks, I told him I was an American and asked for the news. Instead of answering, he began to ask all sorts of questions. Finally, after I had told him I had been in the French service, I asked him if be could help me in any way. He answered that I had only myself to blame, and that it served me right if I had been in one of the Allied armies....

... when he began smoking a cigarette, it almost drove me crazy, and I could not help asking for one. He refused me, and said I should have stayed in my own country, where I could have plenty of cigarettes.[26]

Whether or not Bennett's view was indicative of a sentiment in America at the time, Albert Depew eventually returned home and became a famous man. Ambassador James Gerard was kicked out of Germany in February 1917, but it seemed he had been able to negotiate the release of 69 Americans from German prison camps, Depew among them. Depew returned to New York in July 1917 and took up the life of a penniless hobo until his story was uncovered by a Chicago newspaper reporter, leading to the publication of his book a year later.

Gunner Depew was published in March 1918, and became part of the popular culture consideration of the war. The book was much purchased and well advertised as "the first great war story by an American sailor who fought on land and sea—with the Foreign Legion—on the French battleship *Cassard* at the Dardanelles."[27] It served to give the general public a gritty viewpoint of the war that had begun three years before their own country had gotten into it. It was serialized in newspapers across the country and Albert Depew went on a speaking tour. His speeches were especially promoted and reported upon in small town newspapers, and they continued well into the 1920s. In the 21st century, the book is still sold, sometimes as collector's copies, and transcripts are available from a number of Internet sources.

Another claim in the book and its advertising presents a conflict with the truth that seemed never to have been addressed in the years following its publication:

Gunner Depew is the only war book which describes the capture by German raider *Moewe* of the S.S. *Georgic* and *Yarrowdale*—the only book which describes the famous cruise of the *Yarrowdale*, with its cargo of human wretchedness, around the north of Iceland into Germany.[28]

In the book, Depew sets out on the SS *Georgic* on a trip from Brest, France, and west across the Atlantic toward home. A full chapter tells the story of a mid-transit attack on the *Georgic* by the German SMS *Moewe*, a raider disguised as a lumbering, neutral merchant ship. The date was December 10, 1916. The *Georgic* was sunk and its passengers were taken upon the *Moewe*, some having to swim to it through torrential seas, in Depew's account of his own actions. The book's description of the *Moewe* was lengthy and specific in details about the ship, including a drawing of its deck plan. After a time, the *Georgic* passengers were put on the captured British cargo ship *Yarrowdale* and taken back to captivity in Germany.

In the history of warfare in the North Atlantic during World War I, the sinking of the *Georgic* by the *Moewe* is well known, but the actual circumstances of the confrontation are the opposite of Depew's account. The *Georgic* had been launched in 1895 as a livestock carrier of the White Star Line. During the war, she was a key supply line for American horses sent to Europe. On December 10, 1916, she was traveling east from Philadelphia to Brest with a load of 1,200 horses attended by a crew of veterinarians and horse handlers. Though the captured crew tried to convince the Germans to take the horses back to Europe as a prize, the *Georgic* and its cargo were sent to the bottom of the sea.

The *New York Times* reported the sinking of the eastbound ship on January 18, 1917, and subsequent history confirmed the event as reported. Among the 66 American crew taken, the *Times* named as one of its horsemen Albert Depew.[29] That Albert Depew can be traced in documents from capture on the ship heading toward Europe to his eventual return to Ellis Island from Barcelona, according to immigration records, on April 21, 1917, on the ship *C. Lopez y Lopez*. In the book's telling, he arrived home on the same ship from Barcelona, but in July. That arrival is not found in the records, either in the name of Albert Depew or in the name of the ship, which did not land in New York during that month.

Once both the eastbound and westbound Albert Depews were back in America, however, their stories seemed to re-converge and take the young man through at least 15 years of fame. In the effect of his book and its serialization, Depew became a fierce advocate for the war against Germany. As early as December 17, 1917, before the book's publication, he was reported by the Fort Wayne *Journal* to have appeared at the Methodist church in Huntington, Indiana, the previous evening to speak in support of the Red Cross in France, and described German atrocities in Europe and in its prison camps. The church choir sang "La Marseillaise" and other patriotic songs.[30] After the book's publication, the same newspaper and many others across the nation reported at length on Depew's treatment at the hand of the Germans, including his harrowing survival of the capture of the *Georgic*. Published reviews of the book retold that story and pushed images of the horror of German atrocities further into the public eye. Other accounts told of his lecturing in small towns about America's failure to ally itself with France on the day that Belgium was invaded in 1914.

In January 1920, it was reported that Gunner Depew had been murdered in Arizona by Mexican bandits. According to an account in the *Chicago Tribune*, after sales of his book began to slow down he had spent all of his royalties and gone to Los Angeles to become an actor, then to the Southwest to become a prospector. The following month, however, Depew re-emerged very much alive, telling the press that at the time of his supposed murder he had actually been visiting with the playwright Harold Bell Wright in Tucson, and was on his way to New York where a second book was being published, and then to Los Angeles where he would be writing movie scenarios for D.W. Griffith. A second book was never published, and occasional reporting on Depew showed up throughout the 1920s. In one story, he had been caught in Elyria, Ohio, attempting to receive assistance from the Red Cross under false pretenses. "It has later been learned," reported the Lorain County *Chronicle-Telegram*, "that he is wanted both by government officials, as well as the Red Cross officers for wearing the French, Austrian and United States Uniform without authority."[31] But that event had been preceded in 1920 by a warning to all Red Cross chapters to be on the alert for a Depew imposter seeking the same kind of assistance. Gunner Depew last appeared in the American press in the notice of the filing of an alienation-of-affection suit on the part of his wife against a Seattle socialite in 1934. In all of those years, the mystery of an otherwise historically accurate and detailed book, premised on an event that anyone could have shown not to be true, never came up.

Fourteen years before he would become the 31st president of the United States, Herbert Hoover had been casting about for a way to use his wealth, gained as a mining engineer, for public service. As the war began in 1914, it was the suffering of the Belgian people under German occupation that most captured the sympathetic attention of those who followed the growing turmoil in Europe. Among other problems, the people of Belgium were on the brink of starvation.

During the first skirmishes of the war, more than 100,000 Americans found themselves stranded in Europe and suddenly without resources to live or return home. Hoover was living in London at the time and led an effort to keep them fed and to give them the cash needed for passage to America. That, in turn, led to his chairmanship of the Commission for Relief in Belgium. Belgian Relief, as it came to be called, developed a structure in the country, and in northern France, that effectively managed the welfare of the region for the duration of the war through means that were extralegal to the German occupation.

The effort involved the actions, provisions, matériel and ships of a number of nations, but, for the most part, it was an American operation under Hoover's leadership and it set a tone of volunteerism for some Americans as the United States officially stayed out of the war. Hoover saw it as a duty particularly suited to America.

> Not only was it our duty, but it was our privilege. It was our purpose to forfend infinite suffering from these millions of people, to save millions of lives, and it was our opportunity to demonstrate America's ability to do it in a large, generous and efficient way, befitting our country; but far beyond this, it was our opportunity to demonstrate that great strain of humanity and idealism which built up and in every essential way saved our Republic. We could throw a gleam of sunshine into the sweltering dungeon into which Europe has been plunged.[32]

The American volunteer workforce for Belgian Relief was largely drawn from academia. A number of Rhodes Scholars at Oxford University in England were the first to show up in Belgium. Harvard University was represented, of course, as was Yale University. Two of the Rhodes Scholars were from Princeton University. One was Gilchrist B. Stockton who began his work in 1915 as a courier between Belgium and the Netherlands. Eventually he undertook inventories of warehouses and mills and created methods of inventory tracking that enhanced the effort. Stockton and Hoover became friends and Stockton was appointed special assistant to the U.S. ambassador in London in 1916, an aide to U.S. Navy Admiral William Sims in 1917, and Chief of Mission of the American Relief Administration in Austria in 1919. Hoover appointed him as Minister to Austria from 1930 to 1933. He retired in 1945 as a Rear Admiral in the naval reserve.

In 1916, the American writer Owen Wister referred to Herbert Hoover as "the Godfather of Belgium," and to the early years of war in Europe as "the great convulsion." Wister, author of very successful fiction based on the American West, would be an important voice in the national debate of the years to follow. In the year before America would see its way clear to get into the war, he contrasted the work of Hoover and others to an American failure, "the stain which was cast over all Americans when we were invited to be neutral in our opinions while Democracy in Europe was being strangled to death."[33]

The sentiment was found in Wister's preface to a book recounting a young man's experiences in the French Red Cross. Edward Dale Toland's *The Aftermath of Battle* was an autobiographical journey from American privilege and innocence into the heart of the "convulsion" in Europe. It was an expedition into the death and dismemberment of the war that would be taken by many young Americans.

A Princeton graduate in 1908, Toland had worked in banking, but when the New York Stock Exchange was shut down for four months in 1914 he decided to take the fallow time to travel to Paris as a tourist, "simply to see the excitement and the French people in wartime."[34] His intentions were perhaps naïve, but they were pure. He set off in a steamer from New York as a passenger in steerage. Many of his 600 steerage mates were British subjects returning to join the war effort. In London, he found his passage to Paris blocked by the conversion of Channel ferries to troop transports. After several days' wait, and a very long journey by passenger ship and train, he arrived in Paris, and, for reasons that aren't explained, took himself to the Cooper-Hewitt Hospital on Ave. Bois de Boulogne.

The trip had been intended as a holiday after years of college and working, but Toland was immediately drawn into the strange drama of a Paris that seemed to him to have been deserted while tragedy played itself out on the fields and in the villages of the surrounding countryside. For the most part, in his view of things, the wounded were left to lie where they fell without medical assistance from the army, and if they were to be treated it fell upon volunteers to go out into the battleground and bring them back to Paris. The fields were full of the wounded, but the hospitals of Paris were empty. Toland immediately fell into assisting the ambulances as they delivered their wounded passengers.

"I am not accustomed to this sort of the thing," he wrote, "and in five minutes I was *groggy* and the first thing I knew, I had fainted. When I had got my head clear, I took a walk for a few minutes in the air, had a drink of brandy and then came back."[35] From that moment, Toland became, like many other Americans, a tireless cog in the grueling middle ground between life and death. Though without medical training, he became an orderly at the Cooper-Hewitt Hospital. The hospital was associated with the French American Committee for Men Blinded in Battle and supported by Lucy Cooper Hewitt, wife of the American inventor and scientist Peter Cooper Hewitt.

If the hospital heard of a train of the wounded bypassing Paris—sometimes whole trains of freight cars with the wounded lying in straw—a car, bus or truck would be commandeered to meet it and bring back the worst of them. Guile and flirtation would be used to get through guards and buck the system. Toland found himself working endless shifts and participating in amputations, whatever needed to be done to alleviate suffering. In the seeming absence of French policy and practice for dealing with its wounded, all was in chaos. When the French Red Cross could get into the mix, the Germans often shot at its ambulances.

Eventually the hospitals were able to move their operations closer to the battlefront, often in old chateaus and homes of the countryside, but the chaos continued. The press of the wounded seemed never to stop, and the shifting battle often placed the hospitals in range of German guns. Airplanes fought above, and bombs fell without distinction for those who had perhaps suffered enough. The wounded were increasingly men from different parts of the world, different cultures and languages; even the German wounded were brought into the mix. And Toland increasingly found himself in the company of more Americans who had come to do what they could.

Among the growing number of American volunteers in France were the ambulance drivers whose lives were often as much in danger as the soldiers they transported. The need for transportation of the wounded described by Dale Toland was partly met at first by a combined effort of the American Red Cross, alumni of Yale and Harvard and the Ford Motor Company. Seventeen Ford automobiles were sent to France in wooden boxes that were then converted into ambulance bodies and attached to the automobiles. The alums were often their drivers. One of them, W.P. Clyde, Jr., wrote in a letter to the *Yale Alumni Weekly*:

> We carried wounded, we carried those gone mad from shell-shock, we carried the dying, even the dead. Among the thousands of wounded in our cars were some Germans, and they received from us and in the French dressing stations and field hospitals the same care as the others. For the Allies do not hate the poor, half-starved, bullied, and driven German Yokels who now compose the bulk of the German soldiery. Even we whose work is a work of mercy have come to have the greatest hatred for the Heads of the Huns and all that Hundom stands for; besides helping the wounded it is a great satisfaction to every member of our corps to feel that, as perfectly good Americans, we are doing more than just "watching and waiting" by helping the Allies defeat for all time the attempt of the Hun to enslave the world.[36]

The ambulance services developed by American interests became integral to the fight before America actually entered the war. The Norton-Harjes American Volunteer Ambulance

Service in the French army was an outgrowth of the Red Cross effort. Richard Norton was an eminent archaeologist, member of an historic Harvard family and friend of the American authors Edith Wharton and Henry James, who supported him in the development of the ambulance corps. He had gone to Paris to become a war correspondent, but, like Dale Toland, was drawn into the chaos of care for the wounded. Henry Herman Harjes was an American banker in Paris who had been brokering loans for the Allied cause, and become head of the American Red Cross in France. Now the cars and buses that could be commandeered for a tenuous retrieval and care of the wounded were replaced by convoys of ambulances driven in a formation that brought an organized response to the human damage of war. And the ambulance services began to engender their own medical services and hospitals. Among the Norton-Harjes drivers was the American writer John Dos Passos, and, over time, more American writers would inform their own work with experience driving for ambulance corps. They included Ernest Hemingway, Somerset Maugham, E.E. Cummings and Dashiell Hammett, among many others.

One of the volunteers to arrive in France in 1915 was A. Piatt Andrew. He had been a Princeton graduate in 1893, an assistant professor of economics at Harvard until 1909, followed by two years as Assistant Secretary of the U.S. Treasury. By the time of the American entrance into the war in 1917, he had developed what would come to be called the American Field Service (AFS), an ambulance corps of 300 cars driven by American volunteers and attached to various divisions of the French army. Another 150 cars and drivers were in the pipeline.[37] In the well-recorded history of the AFS, it was present at all the significant fronts

The Norton-Harjes American Volunteer Ambulance Service was associated with the Red Cross. Many of its ambulances were Model T Fords. They were shipped to Europe, not fully assembled, in wooden boxes. Upon final assembly of the vehicle, the box was then converted into the ambulance body (American Field Service).

of battle, including 120 cars at the height of the fighting at Verdun. After the American declaration of war both Andrew and Norton received the French Croix de Guerre (Harjes had been honored earlier).

A few of the American ambulance drivers were killed in action and many were wounded. Among the first to die was Richard N. Hall, a student at Dartmouth University. He was the son of a Michigan doctor, and was recruited into the service at the AFS American headquarters on the top floor of 14 Wall Street in New York. He was reported to have given as his motivation for the journey the value of friendship as demonstrated by George Washington and the Marquis de Lafayette, France and America. It was an idea that had been passed down from his parents.

Until Hall's small detail of AFS ambulances arrived in the town of St. Maurice at the headwaters of the Moselle River near the Swiss border, farm wagons and mules had been used to move the wounded up and down the mountain roads. The first deployment of 10 ambulances, likely Packards or Fords, took on the mountains with strength and vigor. A description of Hall's daily travels by one of his colleagues offers a concise re-creation of the environment in which the ambulance drivers worked.

> ...Hall calmly drove his car up the winding, shell-swept artery of the mountain of war,—past crazed mules, broken-down artillery carts, swearing drivers, stricken horses, wounded stragglers still able to hobble,—past long convoys of Boche prisoners, silent, descending in twos, guarded by a handful of men,—past all the personnel of war, great and small ... past abris, bomb-proofs, subterranean huts, to arrive at the postes de secours, where silent men moved mysteriously in the mist under the great trees, where the cars were loaded with an ever-ready supply of still more quiet figures (though some made sounds), mere bundles in blankets.[38]

The outbreak of the war in Europe in 1914 quickly led to the development of American-based ambulance services in France and Belgium. The American Field Service, based in Boston, actively recruited American volunteers for a service that was fully in place upon the American declaration of war in 1917 (American Field Service).

Hall was described as unflinching, thorough and calm, sleeping wherever and whenever the opportunity arose. On Christmas Eve 1915, Hall set out on the two-hour journey to the front. In one telling, the next

American to follow the route found Hall sitting at the steering wheel of his stopped ambulance, his hands still on the wheel in a driving position, dead, most likely the victim of a stray shell. A picture of his destroyed ambulance, however, shows damage so extensive that there would have been no seat and steering wheel left to allow that description.

He was buried with the Croix de Guerre in the valley of St. Amarin, and spoken over by a French chief surgeon.

> Driver Richard Hall, you are to be laid to rest here, in the shadow of the tri-colored flag, beside all these brave fellows, whose gallantry you have emulated. You are justly entitled to make one of their consecrated battalion! Your body alone, gloriously mutilated, disappears; your soul has ascended to God; your memory remains in our hearts- imperishable!—French men do not forget!
> Driver Richard Hall—farewell![39]

"The man who favored war must be a fool," Dr. M.J. Sheehan told the *New York Times* upon returning from the struggle in France early in 1915. Behind the American ambulance drivers had come American doctors and nurses. Dr. Sheehan and his wife had been volunteers in the French army for half a year, and were glad to be home. The most terrible place to be in the war, he told the *Times*, was not at the frontlines, but behind them. Trainloads of the wounded arrived nightly, parts of their bodies shot away, with compound fractures of their bones, often blinded in both eyes.

Dartmouth University student Richard Hall was a quiet though persistently brave and resourceful driver for the AFS. His death on Christmas Eve 1915 was followed by a memorial service and burial with a Croix de Guerre in the St. Amarin valley of France (American Field Service).

"It made a man no matter how often he saw such cases and steeled his nerves to the shock, realize the awfulness and the crime of war, and in the doctor's case made him an advocate of world peace."[40]

The Belgian Relief effort had easily sparked the intentions of those in the healing arts to leave the comforts of home for places that could only be imagined. American women volunteered for work in France in all of the traditional occupations of women, but mostly through nursing, and most of those with the Red Cross. American medical personnel ended up in the far-flung corners of the war.

Thirty-five nurses and nine doctors arrived with supplies in Stockholm, on their way to Petrograd, in September 1915. In response to an appeal by Queen Eleanora of Bulgaria, herself a former Red Cross nurse, a training school for Bulgarian nurses was set up by Helen Scott Kay, superintendent of a suburban Chicago hospital. In addition, four women were brought from Bulgaria for training at the Presbyterian Hospital of New York. Wealthy patrons could sponsor American women who lacked their own resources to travel to the war, and patrons were openly sought in response to immediate needs. The needs of a chateau hospital near Compiègne, France, that was run by a New York socialite were described in a letter to the editor of the *New York Times* on March 29, 1915. The hospital had just sent a cable asking for another nurse.

> One has been engaged who is preparing to sail either on April 3 or 10. A very considerable amount of supplies may be sent with her baggage directly to this hospital without the usual delay and risk. Cotton and gauze are particularly needed. The chateau is within a few miles of the trenches. Fighting in the neighborhood has been almost continuous since the war began. An enormous amount of good work has been done there. Much more must still be done, it is feared. This is an unusual opportunity for those who wish to co-operate in direct and effective aid.[41]

In September 1914, a letter from Queen Mary's secretary thanked the American Women's War Relief Fund in London for its part in obtaining a Red Cross ship with doctors, nurses and supplies. "Her Majesty feels sure that this friendly action on the part of the American ladies will receive the deep gratitude of the people of this country." The return letter to Buckingham Palace was grateful for the acknowledgment, but unflinching in its description of dire circumstances. "We have 42,000 wounded in this little corner of Brittany alone," it said. "One morning last week, before 6 o'clock, 380 wounded men were brought in here without warning. We all went to work at once, but there were so few doctors that some of the men did not get their wounds dressed until the following day, and they had been traveling for four days. Some died."[42]

The Red Cross aside, other efforts were organized to inject American medical personnel into the European war. The development of the American Ambulance Service in France included the operation of two hospitals that would be staffed by highly selected personnel from American teaching hospitals. The experience that could be gained in what were, for the most part, intense three-month tours was a primary motivation. The first of the nurses known to have died in service was Margaret Hamilton of Indianapolis, Indiana and East St. Louis, Illinois. Having attained the highest ranking in the examinations of the Indiana licensing board, she was appointed leader of 75 nurses who traveled with 35 surgeons from Chicago to France to treat British and French wounded. Once there, she established herself in a 1,000 bed hospital as a nurse whose treatment was so effective and caring that patients talked of committing the treason of refusing to return to the front so that they could stay in her care. Unfortunately, she contracted meningitis and died within 36 hours. "On October 22 [1916]," wrote her commander, "a dark cloud of sorrow and sadness enveloped our camp."

Margaret Hamilton was buried with full honors in the section of a Commonwealth cemetery reserved for officers. The casket was draped with flowers and carried on a two-wheeled carriage preceded by trumpeters. "Many eyes were dimmed by moisture that had been strangers to tears for years. Convulsive sobs and freely flowing tears, blended with thoughtful, serious consideration, that opened up new views of past, present and future. Who will say that there was one present that did not go away strengthened, fortified, purified?"[43]

It would be another six months before the United States would officially declare itself in the unfolding war, but Americans were already dying. In the following years some, like Hamilton and Richard Hall, would be honored in their time; others would slip away under identities not fully their own.

TWO

World War I

*That is the law, boys; but if I was young and stood in your shoes, by God
I know bloody well what I would do.*—Myron T. Herrick

The American ambassador to France in 1914 was former Republican governor of Ohio
Myron T. Herrick. Though he had lost a bid for re-election, he was a Republican star and
was appointed to the ambassadorship by President William Howard Taft. He loved France,
and France loved him. He stayed there after his appointment ended with the election of
President Woodrow Wilson and until the end of the war, and was reappointed ambassador
in 1921. He died in that office in Paris in 1929. He had been awarded the cross of the French
Legion of Honor in his lifetime, and a Paris street was given his name after his death. His
remains were ceremoniously returned to the United States on the French heavy cruiser
Tourville.

Herrick was known and appreciated as a man who did not worry too much about the
disciplines of his craft or what was appropriate vs. what was obvious. In 1914, it was his
response to the influx of Americans in Paris who wished to fight with the French Foreign
Legion that almost seemed to give an official seal to a policy that would touch tens of thousands of Americans and remain variously ambiguous through two world wars.

A group of young men had come to him at the embassy to ask if, as Americans, they
had the right to join the French Foreign Legion.

> They filed into my office with that timidity which frequently characterizes very courageous
> men, more afraid of seeming to show off than of any physical danger. They came to get my
> advice. They wanted to enlist in the French army. There were no protestations, no speeches;
> they merely wanted to fight, and they asked me if they had a right to do so, if it was legal. That
> moment remains impressed in my memory as though it had happened yesterday; it was one of
> the most trying in my whole official experience. I wanted to take those boys to my heart and
> cry, "God bless you! Go!" But I was held back from doing so by the fact that I was an Ambassador.
> But I loved them, every one, as though they were my own.
>
> I got out the law on the duties of neutrals; I read it to them and explained its passages. I really
> tried not to do more, but it was no use. These young eyes were searching mine, seeking, I am
> sure, the encouragement they had come in hope of getting. It was more than flesh and blood
> could stand, and catching fire myself with their eagerness, I brought my fist down on the table
> saying, "That is the law, boys; but if I was young and stood in your shoes, by God I know bloody
> well what I would do."[1]

In light of American reluctance to enter the war, Herrick saw these young men as "the
saviours of our national honour, giving the lie to current sneers upon the courage of our

21

nation."[2] But the law saw them as potential ex-citizens of the United States—maybe. The controlling Citizenship Act of 1907 prescribed the loss of American citizenship when the individual took actions that signaled "the intention of relinquishing United States nationality."[3] But "intention" was a subjective term. Some would hold that joining the fighting forces of a foreign government was an act of intention, while others (perhaps Myron Herrick) would see it as a simple act for a simple goal of fighting a just war and nothing else. The ambiguity of the law was compounded by President Woodrow Wilson's proclamation of U.S. neutrality in the conflict, given August 4, 1914. It asserted that under the Penal Code of the United States a number of acts were forbidden, including:

> 2—Enlisting or entering into the service of either of the said belligerents as a soldier, or as a marine, or seaman on board of any vessel of war, letter of marque, or privateer.[4]

(Another consideration undertaken by British and Canadian authorities who imagined Americans in their forces was the U.S. Foreign Enlistment Act of 1818. Though it dealt with American individuals who might fight for belligerent forces, it was mostly intended to address the fitting of foreign warships in American ports. Its application to the events of the following

Former Ohio governor Myron T. Herrick was the American Ambassador to France 1912–1914 and 1921–1929. His was the most important American face and voice in France during those two decades, especially in relation to the French Foreign Legion. Upon his death in 1929, his body was returned to the United States with French honors on the heavy cruiser *Tourville* (Library of Congress).

American volunteers in the French Foreign Legion cross the Place de L'Opera Paris on August 25, 1914, headed for Rouen. The flag is carried by Rene Phelizot of Chicago. Among those following were Alan Seeger of Boston and Dennis Dowd and Ferdinand Capdevielle, both of New York (Library of Congress/*New York Times*).

century seemed open to interpretation. Initially, the interpretation was that the act would prevent American enlistment in their cause, but eventually, the act seemed to disappear from the conversation.)

Views of the question from abroad offered interesting perspectives.

The Hague Conventions of 1889 and 1907 sought to create a body of law undergirding international conflict and war. In its view, a citizen of a neutral country could not be treated as neutral "particularly if he voluntarily enlists in the ranks of the armed force of one of the parties."[5] Nor could he be treated more harshly by one of the belligerents because he had broken neutrality. But it was not permissible for one of the belligerents to set up a recruiting effort within a neutral country.

For its part, the French government sought to simplify things by holding that one was not required to declare allegiance to France when joining the Foreign Legion, for example, but only to the legion itself. And Germany, without which these matters would not have needed to be considered, made the assertion as the war began that the Foreign Legion would not be considered a legitimate military body. Further, members of the legion who were not French citizens would be considered non-combatants and treated without the rights of normal soldiers. It would not be the last time in the two world wars of the century that Germany would attempt to define who its enemy combatants should be and how they should be treated.

Myron Herrick's way through the confusion of it all had been to answer the question posed by young men wanting to join the fight from his gut. Ultimately, the decisions made by many Americans would come from the same source, and they would escalate the effect of their presence in the foreign war. As the United States debated the declaration of war that would not come until April 1917, newspaper reporting on Americans in the French Foreign Legion brought the stories of the war into the forming of American attitudes pro and con. But the legion was still an abstract kind of notion about soldiers of fortune, outsiders and romantics. Poet Alan Seeger was most visible among that group, and was found dead on July 4, 1916, in fighting at Belloy-en-Santerre. His prediction was fulfilled, though it occurred in the daytime and not at midnight in a flaming town. Some reporting suggested that, finding himself mortally wounded by a German shell, he finished the job with a shot through the temple from his own his gun.[6] It would have been in keeping with the supposed legion ethos.

At that time, many Americans had already migrated from the French Foreign Legion to the regular French army, further blended into a war that their country saw officially as the problem of others on the other side of the sea. But the American prewar presence in France finally became more interesting to the public as American fighters took to the new battlefront of the sky.

It made sense that airplanes could be used in war, but it was not yet clear exactly how. In the Punitive Expedition to Mexico that preceded America's entrance into the European war they had been used with mixed success for reconnaissance. The Expedition was undertaken to ferret out Pancho Villa and his revolutionary forces and to stop their menacing of the U.S.–Mexico border, but the frail wood and canvas flying machines were no match for the mountains, winds and heat of the Mexican desert. The European environment was more hospitable to the airplane, but the work that they could do in effective support of either side was yet to be determined.

Most industrialized countries and their air and sea forces had started to work with airplanes after the first Wright Brothers flight in 1903. They were joined by the few established airplane manufacturers, including the Wright and Curtiss companies. Flight was taken seriously, and the development of its technology and the training required to use it was intense and open-ended. The uncharted territory of the sky was particularly appealing to Americans, especially to some of those who had already gotten a leg up on the war through service in the Foreign Legion, and France was a leader in the implementation of the rigorous training required to fly an airplane in combat.

Among the boys who had come to Ambassador Myron Herrick to seek advice on their participation in the legion, he recalled that three of them had eventually gone on to their deaths as members of what would come to be called the Lafayette Escadrille. The Escadrille was a product of an evolution of American participation in the air war that was perhaps best exemplified by the short career of American Victor Chapman.

Victor Emmanuel Chapman was another son of privilege and a 1913 graduate of Harvard University. Like a number of young men of his upbringing, he was familiar with Europe through previous family experience and continuing education. From Harvard, he had gone immediately to Paris to study architecture and prepare for entry into the École des Beaux Arts. Like Alan Seeger, who became his friend, he seemed to live in his own detached and dreamy world. His father, John J. Chapman, wrote a candid preface to a book of his son's letters published posthumously in 1917 in which he described the young man as living with "a sort of poetic aloofness that hung about him and suggested early death in some heroic form."[7] It was injustice and danger that brought him to life, and he preferred "roughing it" to comfort. Against the advice of his father, he had diverted his energies from the French School of Fine Arts to the French Foreign Legion in the fall of 1914, but he found the legion frustrating. Most of his time was spent sitting in trenches waiting for something to happen rather than actively taking the fight to the enemy.

An increasing number of restless Americans, mostly in the Foreign Legion and ambulance services, wanted to move into the air, and the French army was interested in having them do so. Norman Prince had been one of the boys mentioned by Myron Herrick, and is loosely credited with the idea of forming an all–American flying corps in France. As it developed, it was supported by the French army and French business interests who assisted Americans in making the transition from ground based fighting to various existing and developing aerial units. Victor Chapman entered the corps from the Foreign Legion in September 1915, first worked in dropping bombs from the sky, and, with training, became a pilot the following February.

The most significant body of American pilots in France was initially made up of seven eager volunteers, including Chapman and Norman Prince, and came together as the Escadrille Americaine in April 1916. It was sent to the front at Luxeuil-les-Bains under French command and celebrated its first success against a German reconnaissance plane on May 13, 1916. In June, Chapman flew into what his fellows saw as an inevitably fatal encounter with a bullet wound to his head and damage to his plane. But he held one of the plane's stabilizers together with one hand while landing with the other. Once his wounds were dressed and his airplane was repaired, he was off again.

On June 23, his head still wrapped in bandages, there seemed to be a lull in the battle, so Chapman set out on a mission to deliver eight oranges to a comrade in a nearby hospital. Instead, he fell into a fight with a group of German planes, and was seen to fall toward the ground, his propeller at full speed. He was the first of the young Americans who had come

Founding members of the American Escadrille. Left to right, Kiffin Rockwell, Capt. Georges Thenault, Norman Prince, Lt. de Laage de Maux (sometimes spelled de Mieux or de Mux), Sgt. Elliot Cowdin, Sgt. Bert Hall, James R. McConnell and Victor Chapman, undated (Library of Congress).

to fight for France to be killed in an airplane. The dramatic nature of his death resounded throughout France. The French author André Chevrillon wrote of the power of Chapman's death to John Chapman, who had by now become a critic of American dithering about its participation in the war.

> The death fight of Victor Chapman touches our imagination with fire. Be assured that his name will stand forever in France.... That name will become a new symbol, and far more moving than any of the old links between our nations, and the name of America will partake of glamour. Morally the sacrifice more than makes up for all that you resented so much in the attitude of your present government. You may indeed be proud of your son. In those last minutes of his life he rose to the front rank of what we call here our Saints: he carved his own statue; it has the essential simplicity of the supremely beautiful.[8]

Chapman's death, and the subsequent adventures of the Escadrille would serve to bring thinking about America's place in the war further forward in the American mind. And, when the U.S. finally did declare war, the Escadrille had helped to put the beginnings of an American air force already in place. But among the first orders of business for the Escadrille Americaine was to bow to the continuing complaints of the Germans about Americans fighting in a war that America had not declared. It brought the matter up directly with the United States, and in December 1916 the name was changed, calling upon the memory of the central figure of French-American history, to the Lafayette Escadrille.

The first known black American aviator to fight in war, though not for the United States, was Eugene Jacques Bullard. His family's origins were in the complicated mixture of ancestries that created black America. His father traced back to the French culture of Martinique, West islands and slavery in Haiti, and his mother was a Creek Indian. He was born in Columbus, Georgia, in 1894, but ran away from the racial oppression of the South at the age of eight after his father had nearly been lynched. William Bullard had always spoken to his son of France as a place where black men were free, and that was where Eugene set his sights, though it would take him years to get there. He spent four years traveling in the shadows of the Southeast, and living with gypsies for a time. In Norfolk, Virginia, he stowed away on a German freighter and arrived in Aberdeen, Scotland, at age 12. He worked in Glasgow and Liverpool on the edges of criminal enterprise, on the docks and in the warehouses, and was drawn to the sport of boxing. He was short and slight, but he excelled in the ring and became a protégé of a famous British boxer of the time, the Dixie King. Finally, he landed in Paris as a dancer and comedian with a group called "Freedman's Pickaninnies" until establishing himself there as a boxer. He loved France and the equality he found there. "It seems to me," he said, "that the French democracy influenced the minds of both white and black Americans there and helped us all to act like brothers as near as possible.... It convinced me too that God really did create all men equal, and it was easy to live that way."[9]

At the outbreak of the war, Bullard joined the French Foreign Legion. As a boxer, he was well suited to the bayonet fighting that would carry him through the most vicious action of the following year. In October 1915, he joined the French army's 170th Infantry, the Swallows of Death, and took as his nickname The Black Swallow of Death. Wounds received at Verdun in March 1916 removed him permanently from fighting on the ground with the result that he looked to the sky. He received combat training and a pilot's license and was accepted into the Lafayette Escadrille. He was immediately successful, but went off track when he tried to join the American Air Force after the U.S. entered the war. The application went nowhere, as did his subsequent place in the Escadrille, and he returned to non-combat duty in the Swallows of Death, though he came out of the war as a French hero. That status served him well. He married and later divorced a French countess, and became part owner of a Parisian nightclub that was popular with the literati in the 1930s.

In its full history, the Escadrille was the core group of American flyers in France until it was converted into the American 103rd Aero Squadron in February 1918. The romance of the Escadrille was fodder for American media and led to a growing number of American men who arrived in France to meet the challenge of the sky. The overflow of applicants was addressed by the development of the Lafayette Flying Corps as an umbrella organization. Precise numbers are difficult, but the Escadrille Memorial Foundation listed 269 pilots in the full corps. A book edited by members of the corps listed 65 dead from all causes,[10] but the list of burials in the Memorial Foundation's crypts in the Paris suburb of Marnes-la-Coquette numbers 68.[11] Among the living and dead were many others who would become household names of their time: Raoul Lufberry, born in France to an American father; Kiffin Rockwell of Newport, Tennessee, the first American to shoot down a German aircraft; Bill Thaw of Pittsburgh, Pennsylvania, who distinguished himself early in life by flying a small airplane under the four bridges of New York's East River; Clyde Balsey of Carbondale, Penn-

Above: **Eugene Bullard of Columbus, Georgia, took the nickname "The Black Swallow of Death" in the 170th French Infantry Corps, and became the first known black American aviator to fight in the war, in the Lafayette Flying Corps (U.S. Air Force).** *Right:* **Raoul Lufberry was born in France of an American father and French mother, and served both in the Lafayette Escadrille and the United States Army Air Service. In May 1918, he fell from the sky in combat and was impaled on a picket fence (Library of Congress).**

Kiffin Rockwell of the French Foreign Legion, left, in the trenches, December 1914. Wounded in the Foreign Legion, Rockwell joined the American Escadrille, where his success in air combat earned him the nickname "Aristocrat of the Air." He was considered one of the most accomplished American fighters in World War I (Library of Congress/*New York Times*).

sylvania, the first of the corps to be shot down (and to whom Victor Chapman was taking the eight oranges). James Norman Hall of Colfax, Iowa, and Charles Nordhoff, born in London of American parents, became co-authors of the classic book *Mutiny on the Bounty*. Bert Hall of Higginsville, Minnesota, was either a hero or a fraud depending on his biographer, and a movie director and actor who played himself in the 1919 movie *A Romance of the Air*.

The German invasion of Belgium and declaration of war against France on August 3, 1914, was the beginning of a sometimes romantic, though violent, engagement of Americans in the struggle of the invaded against the Germans. But it was the declaration by England of war against Germany on the following day that began the first footsteps of what would become a virtual migration of Americans into British forces over the next three years. It began with the largely unobserved travel of individual Americans across the Canadian border and into Commonwealth forces.

As in France, however, Americans in the sky had more visibility. By the time the United States entered the war in 1917, an estimated 300 Americans had joined, or were yet to join, England's Royal Flying Corps (RFC) or Royal Naval Air Service (RNAS).[12] The Royal Flying Corps had been created in 1912 as an army and navy effort to explore the potential use of aircraft in war. It eventually split off a second organization, the Royal Naval Air Service. Starting with the German invasion in 1914, the RFC struggled to keep up with needed aircraft and pilots until it attained 27 squadrons and at least 400 usable aircraft by July 1916. It continued to expand as the war progressed, and its needs for men and matériel were always pressing. By the end of the war, the RFC and RNAS had grown to a force of 290,000 personnel and approximately 22,000 aircraft. Their work on all fronts of the war would be considered decisive in the ultimate success of the Allies.[13]

Drawn into the war by the same mix of adventurousness and/or sense of duty as their counterparts in French aviation, most American recruits in the RFC were trained in Canada before being sent to England for more training, and then to the front. Ten percent of the group was able to reach the status of "Ace," which was variously defined as having attained five or more kills. A reading of the circumstances by which some of them moved from their American lives and into the British flying services offers a representative sample of the paths that would be taken into air and ground fighting by tens of thousands to follow.

Frederick Libby was a native of Colorado working in Canada as a cowboy in 1914. Like many, his first move was to the ambulance services in France. When recruiting papers for the Royal Flying Corps began to circulate in the trenches, Libby jumped at the opportunity. He became a machine gunner, placed in front of the pilot in the planes of the 23rd Squadron. To avoid shooting the propeller, the gunner was required to stand up into the wind as the plane flew toward its target. There were no safety belts, and the gun was the only thing to hold on to. In this manner, he shot down 10 enemy planes and was awarded the Military Cross for what was demonstrably "Conspicuous Gallantry in Action."

Libby returned to England for training as a pilot, and his subsequent fighting was equally as distinguished. Like many, he remained in British service after the United States entered the war, but eventually changed uniforms as the war progressed. He was recruited into the United States Army Air Force by General Billy Mitchell, a lion for the development of air forces in war, and returned briefly to the United States to reaffirm his American citizenship and use his fame in support of the Liberty Loan drive. At that point, though, his health failed and he was never able to fly again. He died in 1970, considered an American Air Ace though he had never flown an American plane.

Frederick Ives Lord was born in Manitowoc, Wisconsin, either in 1897 or 1900. In the version of his story based on birth in 1900, he joined the U.S. army in 1917, but was discharged when it was determined that he was too young. In response, he went to Toronto with an altered birth certificate to join the Royal Flying Corps. He foreswore his American citizenship to join the corps and quickly became responsible for the downing of 11 enemy aircraft and one balloon. In one instance, he single-handedly chased a formation of German planes from the skies over London, shooting down two of them in the process. He received the Distinguished Flying Cross and rank of squadron commander before his 20th birthday. After the war he went on to fly as a soldier of fortune for the White Forces in the Russian Civil War and the Republican side of the Spanish Civil War. His last service was with the British Air Transport Auxiliary as it ferried aircraft transatlantic between war and factory in World War II. His death came at the hands of a vagrant in Apple Valley, California, in 1967.

The American-Canadian border in the early 20th century was made porous by the economy of the time. Many families lived and worked where money could be made, irrespective of nationality. Emil John Lussier had been born in 1895 and raised in Chicago, but at age 15 he followed his father to construction work in the westward expansion of Canadian railroads. Though he was American by birth, he enlisted in the Royal Flying Corps from Medicine Hat, Alberta, and was flying Sopwith Camels in France in March 1918. By September he had attained Ace status and the King's Award of the Distinguished Flying Cross. Post-war he took up farming in Maryland.

When the United States finally entered the war, the training programs in place for the RFC were used for the development of American air forces. Americans entering the RFC and RNAS before April 6, 1917, had gone initially to Camp Borden, Ontario, then on to facilities across the Atlantic. After the declaration of war some went to a training camp in Texas to avoid the Canadian winter, but overseas training continued in the United Kingdom. In the early days of American participation in the war, two of the American squadrons were assigned to fly under the command of Royal Flying Corps.

The American reluctance to join the war that was raging in Europe led another group of citizens, or citizens-to-be, to seek their own path into the fighting. The mostly young men who had sought adventure or the righting of wrongs in the French Foreign Legion or battlefields in the sky were one thing. But immigrant populations that saw their homelands affected by the war were another. Depending on how things turned out, the outcome of the war could bring devastation or liberation to the families they had left behind.

More than a year after the American entrance into the war, *Harper's Magazine* of July 1918 published a lengthy, though unsourced, article on the prevalence of immigrants in the country's military. Author Fred Ringhe, Jr., secretary of the International Committee of the Y.M.C.A., asserted that the nation held 15,000,000 foreign born residents and 20,000,000 more of foreign parentage. One of the conclusions of the article was that 3,000,000 of the alien population were draft age but not eligible because they were not naturalized, and that steps ought to be taken in social services and education to help bring them into eligibility.[14] Ringhe also suggested that the same problem applied to thousands of Americans in the armed forces who were too illiterate and uneducated to function effectively.

Immigrant population in turn of the century America reflected growth from the time of the Civil War and during the so-called Second Industrial Revolution. Attracted to perceived economic opportunity in the growing factories of America, the wave of immigrants started from Western Europe and eventually moved eastward. The full census of 1910 showed who was living in America in the decade that the country would go to war in Europe. In that year, 258,737 immigrants, the largest number, had come from Austria-Hungary (including Poland), 72 percent of them male; 215,537 from Italy, including Sicily and Sardinia, 78 percent of them male; 186,792 from the Russian Empire, 67 percent of them male; 98,796 from the United Kingdom, 58 percent of them male; and 56,578 from British North American possessions, 67 percent of them male. In all cases, the 1910 arrivals had added to significant immigration from those sources since 1860. The notable exception to the trend was the German Empire. It had been the source of the largest immigrant group, 5,351,746, since 1820, but in 1910 was among the smallest with just 31,283 members.[15]

As might be imagined, opinions about the European war as the decade progressed were varied in this group of immigrant aliens and Americans. In 1914, more than 2 million people made up the National German American Alliance. German communities were strong and activist, with influential newspapers, and they advocated for continuing American neutrality in the war. Further, they took political action to prevent non-combat related American support of the Allies. And, though they were Democrats by inclination, many worked against the reelection of President Woodrow Wilson in favor of the Republican candidate Charles Evans Hughes. Their focus on the perceived depredations against Germany by Great Britain brought them into common cause with the Irish community. The Irish had formed the second largest immigrant group after those from the German Republic. From 1820 to 1910, 4.2 million Irish had taken up residence in the United States. Though they did not want to see America supporting the Great Britain they saw as an oppressive colonial power, they were conflicted by the need to continue on a path toward acceptance in American society. They bridled at the country's perceived lapses in neutrality that favored the British, but they wanted to remain patriotic. In the end, as America formally entered the war, the mainstream of Irish and German populations fell in with the rest of the country.

The challenges and opportunities given to world Jewry by the war were complex. At the outset, emigrant and in-place German Jews were loyal to Germany. Germany also received the sympathies of most non–German Jews opposed to czarist Russia. Russian Jews were initially loyal to Russia for the most part. International Jewish organizations like the World Zionist Organization tried to remain neutral at first, but saw the potential for the establishment of a Jewish state in Palestine at the end of the war. That would require the agreement of Great Britain, which came in the form of the Balfour Declaration of November 2, 1917. The Declaration solidified growing Jewish support of the war. It also factored into the British effort to bring America into the war. President Woodrow Wilson was key to that decision, and his two closest advisers, Felix Frankfurter and Louis Brandeis, were active Zionists.

If the shifting alliances and strategies of the evolving war were difficult to track, there was one certainty in the mind of Vladmir Jabotinsky. As a Jew born in Odessa in 1880, and a star Russian journalist in adulthood, he had seen enough oppression of the Jews in his country. He advocated for proactive development of Jewish culture as a response, and the use of self-defense fighting units when necessary. With the outbreak of the war in 1914, Jabotinsky left journalism and took up the cause of a proposed Jewish Legion that would fight with the British against Turkish forces on the Palestinian front. Though Jabotinsky and other Jewish leaders continued to serve with British forces in the following years, the Jewish Legion was not fully realized until August 1917 as the 38th Battalion of the Royal Fusiliers. A 39th Battalion was added in April 1918, made up mostly of volunteers from the United States and Canada.

A general operating premise had developed in the course of the prelude to American participation (and stayed loosely in place after American entrance) that un-naturalized immigrants in America could enlist in the Allied armies of their home countries. Without a country of their own, Great Britain was the natural partner for the Jews, and the recruiting effort in America was thorough and well publicized. Saturday, July 6, 1918, as an example, saw open air rallies in various neighborhoods of Boston, as well as appeals in the city's synagogues. It was part of an organized effort throughout New England.

The recruiting drive for the Jewish Legion was loosely paired with England's own effort to bring British subjects in America and Canada back to their home country for service in the war. On February 28, 1918, a British tank with eight crew was found roaming New York City. It threaded through the streets and avenues, in and out of the pits of construction sights, and stopped occasionally to allow recruiting speeches from its outside decks. The appeal was both to British expatriates and American Jews. The previous day, 150 recruits into the Jewish Legion had assembled at the British and Canadian recruiting office at 220 West 42nd Street and "paraded through 42nd Street to Fifth Avenue, and down the avenue and other streets to the Fall River Line pier, North River, from which point they embarked on their way to the war."[16] They would meet up with another group in Boston and head to Canada for training in Windsor, Nova Scotia, followed by a sea journey to England and arrival in Palestine on June 1. Major Brooman White, in charge of all British recruiting in the United States, estimated that 50,000 American residents were with British forces in Egypt as of June 1918,[17] but various accounts of the actual number range upwards from 2,000 to 5,000 as the most often mentioned number. The number said to be killed in combat in Palestine is also various. The *New York Times* of December 28, 1918, published a "Complete List of Casualties Suffered in Palestine Fighting." It included the names of just 41 legion fighters from all nations.[18]

The recruiting of non-draft eligible American Jews carried with it the understanding that those who wished would be allowed to settle in Palestine with government assistance if they succeeded. Their fighting in the wresting of Palestine from Turkey helped to bring that about, though many returned to their lives in the United States. Polish refugee Roman Adolph Freulich, as an example, had been in New York's Union Square when the British tank made a recruiting stop. In 1920, he returned to America and moved to Beverly Hills, California. He became head photographer first at Universal, then Republic Studios, and went on to win four Academy Awards for his work.[19]

Other immigrant groups saw opportunities for their people and homelands in the European war, and worked to change American neutrality. Occasionally, reporting on the war would mention an American immigrant found fighting in the uniform of his home country, particularly in the combined legions of the Czechs and Slovaks.

In January 1914, a report from the *New York Times* bylined in Petrograd asserted that private interests in Warsaw were forming a Polish Legion that would join with the Russians against Germany. It would consist of all classes of Polish society from the aristocracy to the working class, and include a large contingent of Poles "expected to arrive from the United States."[20] Activity in the country's Polish communities leading up to April 1917 was intense. Its leaders were those Poles who had come to America since the turn of the century and found livelihoods in the industrial cities of the Midwest. Its international symbol and voice was the pianist and composer Jan Ignacy Paderewski.

The territory that had once been known as Poland was partitioned into surrounding nations before the war. It existed only in the minds of its people who saw an opportunity to reconstitute the country after the war if Germany could be defeated. Paderewski was more than 50 years old in those years, and a regular visitor to an America that met him with standing room only audiences. Starting in 1915, his recitals were often accompanied by a fundraising speech about the struggles of the Polish people. But by 1916, critics began to see weariness in his performances. "There was a haunting sadness about it all," wrote a critic in the *Indianapolis Star*.

> The Paderewski we heard last evening was not in many respects the Paderewski we have known in the past. We know that Paderewski is suffering, suffering over the cruel fate which it has been

the misfortune of his beloved Poland to encounter over the last three years. It has, it is said, become almost an obsession with him. so [*sic*] perhaps it was not imagination that led me to believe that this suffering was reflected last evening in his attitude and his playing.[21]

The Polish government in exile was based in Paris, and Paderewski began to seek American Poles as volunteers in a Polish army in France. A force of 50,000 or 100,000 Americans seemed a possible number. In March 1916, he was invited to dine with President Woodrow Wilson, after which the president agreed with the need for an independent Poland. A presidential speech given to the Senate in January 1917 was based largely on a memo written by Paderewski. It endorsed Polish independence and would carry that goal into the April declaration of war. Contemporaneously, the French government issued a decree calling for the formation of the Polish army in France, and the British government secured a dedicated training camp in Niagara-on-the-Lake, Ontario, Canada.

With war declared, however, Wilson could not allow American Poles to join the Polish army. It was agreed, however, that Poles in America who were not yet naturalized would be allowed to join the fight through that outlet. The effort was endorsed by the War Department and operated under the National Department of the Polish Central Relief Committee of Chicago. Initial training would take place in the camp at Ontario. Paderewski's recruiting appeal to eligible Poles reminded them of the role of France as a defender of the oppressed in "this struggle of light against darkness," and concluded:

> Go, so the world may know that in your breast the knightly valor of your forefathers has not been stilled; that the fearless bravery of the Poles of old has not vanished.
> Go, to give testimony that the American Pole is a worthy heir the glory of Polish arms.[22]

Under the restrictions set by the War Department, the American contingent of the Polish army was able to reach just under 23,000 members. Recruiting for the army reached deep into the American heartland. In March 1918, as an example, the newspaper in Rhinelander, Wisconsin, reported that 14 young Polish men had departed the town for training in Canada and transfer to France. In addition, four young women would soon be leaving for service as Red Cross nurses with the legion, and $500 in donations had been received. It had all been the work of John Deptalo of the Polish recruiting station in Stevens Point, who "is an eloquent speaker and possesses rare descriptive powers. He has participated in real fighting in the trenches and was once injured while in action."[23]

The Polish Legion had been the largest of the groups of immigrant Americans to enter the war under foreign flags. But many Poles had not waited until 1918. They, and Americans of all status and motivation, had been entering the war through Canada in much larger numbers since the German invasion of 1914.

THREE

An American Legion

No country or flag can be mine except the United States, but if I could go to this war as a citizen of the world, I would pray to be allowed. — Edwin Austin Abbey

On January 20, 1916, James Frederick Kennedy of Princeton, West Virginia, wrote to his mother at 108 College Avenue in Princeton on a piece of paper provided by the YMCA of Canada. The letterhead pictured three Canadian soldiers ready for battle and identified the writer as "With His Majesty's Canadian Forces on Active Service ... For God, King and Country."

Dear Mother,

Rec'd your letter yesterday and am very sorry to know that it worried you to know that I had enlisted, for that is right. I'm in the Army, but I can't see why you should worry. Please don't. You must not think it is so rough as you seemed to, as I like it more every day, and we don't have to lie in tents or sleep on the ground. We are living at the exhibition grounds here, quite a nice place.

By 1916, the Toronto exhibition grounds had become the point of conversion for Americans into members of the Canadian Expeditionary Force. James Frederick Kennedy was typical of the largest number of them, though the actual numbers of who they were could never be precisely known. A 1927 memo from the Department of Soldiers' Civil Re-Establishment gave figures that could be considered official, but ambiguous.

Enlistments into Canadian Units through the British Canadian Recruiting Stations at various points in the United States: 31,000

Enlistments through the same medium into British Units: 13,000

In addition to the above there was one regiment of the C.E.F. concentrated in Toronto which was recognized as being composed of Americans.

Furthermore, there were a large number who drifted across the line and joined various Canadian units.

It would be a moderate estimate to say that the total embraced above reached 40,000. However a considerable proportion of these were doubtless British, that is English, Scotch, etc., who lived in the United States.

The official figure of men who on enlistment in the C.E.F. gave their birth places as United States or Alaska is: 35,612.[1]

Though this was the most official document about American enlistments in the C.E.F. that can be found in Canadian records, the true numbers would be variously reported and speculated upon during the war, and impossible to know definitively in any examination.

34

The Canadian Expeditionary Force in World War I totaled approximately 620,000 members over the years 1914–1918. By a word search examination of all enlistments, 53,000 of those carried American connections in their enlistment records. In the absence of a person-by-person accounting, a random, non-statistical, sampling of one percent of the list can only be a suggestion of basic numbers.

Fifty-nine percent of the sample was born in the United States. Of that number, 35 percent were born in the U.S. with U.S. next of kin, and 59 percent were U.S. born with Canadian next of kin.

Ten percent of the sample was born in Canada, but listed family in the U.S. as next of kin. Of that number, 62 percent were a mother or father, who may or may not have been born in the U.S. and, if so, thus passing American citizenship on to their child. Twenty percent were wives, and the remaining were sisters, brothers, aunts or uncles living in the U.S.

Thirteen percent of the sample was born in the United Kingdom, but listed family in the U.S. as next of kin. In this case, 47 percent of those were wives, 35 percent were a mother or father, and the rest were sister, brother, aunt, uncle, daughter and friend.

Eighteen percent of the one percent sample was born in Canada with Canadian next of kin, or the United Kingdom with UK next of kin, or in some other combination of countries, but enlisted from American addresses.

Whatever the nature of their American origins, they were joining a war that the United States could not agree to enter in its first three years. All parties to the conflict had been signatories to the Hague Convention of 1907 setting down the rules of warfare, including the rights of neutral territories. The German invasion of Belgium in August 1914 and Germany's treatment of Belgian citizens and commerce were the first of the German violations of the Hague Convention that would follow in the war. In September of 1914, the French government drew up a document outlining atrocities that had been committed by the Germans in Belgium and France, and communicated it, with a special emphasis, to "the powers who signed The Hague Convention, the United States being one of them."[2] In the United States, however, the official view of the nature of Germany's violations wasn't as clear. The American signatory to the convention in 1907 had been President Teddy Roosevelt, a man who believed in proactive and vigorous response to injustice and conflict. The president in 1914, however, was Woodrow Wilson, whose principles were rooted in deliberation and diplomacy. Roosevelt had run against Wilson in the 1912 election as the Progressive Party candidate and lost, though he had received more votes than the Democratic candidate William Howard Taft.

In 1914, Roosevelt was a much-respected, indeed beloved, figure worldwide and in the United States, but he was also mindful of the protocols that existed between presidents and ex-presidents. He could say at the very least, as he did, that the U.S. should have protested the invasion of Belgium diplomatically, but he could not advocate for a military response. A result was a seeming ambiguity in American attitudes about events in Europe leading up to its final declaration of war, by Woodrow Wilson, in 1917. As might be expected, those already embroiled in the war watched the United States with great interest and anxiety. It seemed inevitable that America would declare itself, but the path to that declaration was confusing and tortuous. The reporting and editorializing in British and Canadian newspapers were constant.

In January 1915, the *Toronto Star* reported on an editorial in the London *Daily Chronicle* supporting Roosevelt's call for diplomatic response on the part of the United States.

President Woodrow Wilson, pictured at Arlington National Cemetery in 1914, held the United States in neutrality while a growing number of Americans entered the war through service in foreign forces. Events in Europe finally led to an American declaration of war on April 6, 1917 (Library of Congress).

Those of us on this side of the water who for many years have been striving constantly to get a fair hearing given to the United States, and a fair construction put upon its policy, would be no true friends if we concealed from American opinion the new difficulty which her Government's abandonment of The Hague conventions has created for us.[3]

The following month, the *Toronto Star* published its own editorial premised on an editorial in the *Detroit News* which noted that both sides of the neutrality debate were unhappy with America's stance in relation to the war and took that as a sign that it must therefore be a correct one. The *Star* disagreed.

There is surprise and disappointment that the American Republic should have preserved not only neutrality but a silence that suggested indifference when a small neutral country like Belgium was invaded and wrecked merely because a great nation deemed it easier to go over than around it in order to attack another great nation. It was not expected that the United States would find in this a justification for going to war. It was expected that the American Republic would have a vigorous opinion to put on record.[4]

The American government may have been dithering, in the view of some, but a portion of the American people were beginning to put together what would become the first of three distinct and unrelated organizations

Theodore Roosevelt, photographed in 1915, was U.S. president from 1901 to 1909, and remained an important voice in American life until his death in 1919. Outspoken against American neutrality in World War I, he was seen as a possible leader of Americans who had joined the Canadian Expeditionary Force (Library of Congress).

called "The American Legion" in the 20th century. And it was something that Teddy Roosevelt could support without reservation.

On February 28, 1915, a group of military and civilian leaders announced the formation of an American Legion. It would recruit former military members into a reserve force of 250,000–300,000 men. Its Executive Committee would include the most distinguished of Americans—"several former Secretaries of the army and navy, former United States senators, college presidents, former governors, leading newspapermen, magazine editors, &c."[5] It had received the unofficial endorsement of Major General Leonard Wood, the much decorated former army chief of staff. Wood had been a leader of the Preparedness Movement designed to strengthen the military after the German invasion, which led to his replacement by President Wilson in 1914. Teddy Roosevelt shared leadership in the movement, and offered a full-throated endorsement of the American Legion as a ready force to enter the war when and if America made that decision. The legion would be open only to those not already in the U.S. military. Though American citizens only needed apply, it was modeled in some respects on the French Foreign Legion and divided into two distinct kinds of forces. "The Line" would include those who had fought before whether as regular military or of the roughrider sort. "The Specials" would be civilians with experience in the necessary supporting vocations of war like medicine, bridge building and mule packing. The national headquarters of the new legion were to be housed on Governor's Island in New York Harbor. Legion recruits would have to pay annual dues of 25 cents to support administrative costs, but they would not receive payment themselves.

The public response was explosive. Sacks of mail began to pile up in the legion's offices. An old army major in Minnesota offered three troops of retired cavalry members ready to go, and mentioned donations already promised to him of a supporting car and an airplane. Others offered their own newfangled automobiles with themselves as drivers, and Captain Gordon Johnston, speaking for the legion, noted the importance of that kind of volunteer. "If any trouble came automobiles, thousands of them, would be in instant demand and we would need drivers to operate them. They would be needed for transportation, for ambulance work, for messengers' service, and for many other branches of military operations. This is a feature which we wish to emphasize."[6] An offer of 50 aviators and their own airplanes was received. A contingent of Negro soldiers was ready to go, according to an Ohio minister. The Junior Order of American Mechanics, a white Christian group whose members needed not to be juniors or mechanics, said that it could provide at least 8,000 members, and perhaps as many as 65,000. Donations of money were received from all quarters, but were declined.[7]

The legion was controversial, however. It's most vocal supporters saw it as a sadly needed organization in light of the actual state of American preparedness for a foreign war. In the matter of translators, as an example, supporters pointed out the problems faced by countries that went to sudden war with an enemy whose language could not be understood (the British military could communicate in its colonies of India and Africa, but not with its neighbors of Germany and France). The legion would maintain a file of bilingual members of The Line and The Specials, and would be ready to go in all other fine points of war.

In other quarters, however, the legion was suspect. Was it just an extension of Roosevelt's Progressive Party? Would it be an extra-military militia organization? Pacifists wanted to know if it was an indication of a new militarism in society, and, indeed, if it was intended just as a lever to push an official American declaration of war. United States Senator George Earle Chamberlain of Oregon, chairman of the Senate Military Affairs Committee, feared that such an organization, with a strong leader, "could kick up quite a revolution.... I regard the proposed American Legion as a menace to the peace and safety of the United States."[8]

But the most important skepticism came from the War Department. Major General Leonard Wood, whose split with President Woodrow Wilson was by now more institutionalized, seemed to give the army's imprimatur to the legion. And it was his aide, Captain Gordon Johnston, who seemed to be the spokesperson for that advocacy. Secretary of War Lindley Garrison wanted to know what was going on and received a response from Wood.

> It has no connection with the army up to the present time ... activities in connection with it have been purely unofficial. He [Johnston] simply aided them [the legion's founders] with suggestions concerning their list of special qualifications and talked the matter of the organization over with them. He appreciates fully the fact that he cannot take any official position in an organization of this sort. He has tried to steer them into a line of procedure which would fit in with the War Department plans. This has been purely in an unofficial and personal way.[9]

Garrison's response was lengthy but definitive. The kind of preparatory work being done by the legion was already underway and in the purview of the War Department, and "I consider it undesirable for officers of the army to have any connection with organizations outside of the War Department which are dealing, or contemplate dealing, with the same subject matter."[10] Eventually, Garrison ordered Wood to remove all vestiges of the legion from all army offices. Then, and for decades following World War I, the antagonisms between Wilson and Roosevelt, Wood and Garrison, neutrality and engagement, and pacifism and preparedness would remain controversial and passionate. The first American Legion of the century lingered for a while, but it was asked for assistance only once when the War Department needed to move 100 trucks to the Punitive Expedition against Pancho Villa's incursions across the Mexican border. Drivers were quickly enlisted from the legion's file of Specials.

It would be the second American Legion that would actually go to war.

When the United Kingdom declared war on Germany on August 4, 1914, the job of recruiting soldiers for the British ranks fell to Lord Herbert Horatio Kitchener, the Secretary of State for War. Contrary to the wisdom of most of his peers, Kitchener predicted a long and difficult war. His recruitment of a volunteer force for the war was aggressive and successful. By its very nature, it swept non–British men into the war, including American men already in Europe and some who came from the U.S. to join up. The recruitment of Americans was not an afterthought. In September 1914, First Lord of the Admiralty Winston Churchill sent a memo to Kitchener and Prime Minister Sir Edward Gray. Churchill's premise was that "nothing will bring American sympathy along with us so much as American blood shed in the field."[11] He recommended that the word should go forth that Americans who went to Canada or England to enlist would be given every support, including transportation, and would be formed into units in which they could fight together. "The problem is how to set up the rallying flag in Canada and so indicate where those who wish to help us can go to join."[12]

Among those Americans who answered the call was James Norman Hall, who would go on to join the American Escadrille and co-author *Mutiny on the Bounty*. In *Kitchener's Mob*, a book recounting his experiences as an American in the British army, Hall recreated the outlook of the British fighting man with a deft and humorous ear. The war itself seemed at once necessary, brutal and inevitably humorous. The book ended with a tribute to his fellows, and a chuckle.

> The intimate picture of him which lingers most willingly in my mind is that which I carried with me from the trenches on the dreary November evening shortly before I bade him goodbye. It had been raining and sleeting for a week. The trenches were knee-deep in water, in some places waist-deep, for the ground was as level as a floor and there was no possibility of drainage. We were wet through and our legs were numb with the cold. Near our gun position there was a hole in the floor of the trench where the water had collected in a deep pool. A bridge of boards had been built around one side of this, but in the darkness a passer-by slipped and fell into the icy water nearly up to his arm-pits.
>
> "Now, then, matey!" said an exasperating voice, "bathin' in our private pool without a permit?"
>
> And another, "'Ere, son! This ain't a swimmin' bawth! That's our tea water yer a-standin' in!"
>
> The Tommy in the pool must have been nearly frozen, but for a moment he made no attempt to get out.
>
> "One o' you fetch me a bit o' soap, will you?'" he said coaxingly. "You ain't a-go'n' to talk about tea water to a bloke wot ain't 'ad a bawth in seven weeks?"
>
> It is men of this stamp who have the fortunes of England in their keeping. And they are called, "The Boys of the Bulldog Breed."[13]

Hall had enlisted in England in August 1914, posing as an Englishman with a wink of the eye from his recruiter. A member of the Ninth Battalion Royal Fusiliers, he had fought as a machine gunner in the Battle of Loos, lost by the British. His true identity was discovered before the end of 1915, and he was forced to leave the service.

Another American who joined Kitchener's Army was Harry White Wilmer of La Plata, Maryland. His course through the full war was typical of many who entered the fighting in advance of his own country, and he ended his service with full honors in an American cemetery. A graduate of the University of Maryland, he was employed by the Fidelity Investment Company of New York when he traveled to Kingston, Ontario and joined the 21st Battalion of the Canadian Expeditionary Force (CEF) on November 7, 1914. Though he correctly listed his father in Maryland as next of kin, he noted his occupation as a lumberman and his religion as the Church of England. He was shipped out from Montreal to Devonport, England, where he attained rank of lance corporal, but wasn't ready to move to the front until September 1915. His battalion was inspected by Lord Kitchener and King George V, and sent off to France "to do our little part in the great struggle and honestly I can't wait to get there. We all feel extremely bitter towards Germany on account of her many unpardoned atrocities, and I know when the time comes we shall go at them with all the strength we possess."[14]

Wilmer was wounded by shrapnel in trench fighting near St. Omer, France, in June 1916, but was not able to recover sufficiently to return to fighting. He was discharged from the CEF in January 1917, but joined the United States army in October of the following year. He returned to France as an observer in the planes of the 20th Aero Squadron, but he was shot down on October 10, 1918, and buried in the American cemetery at Suresnes, France.

Philadelphia native Joseph F. Smith also took that kind of journey through the forces of various countries. In August 1914 he was a self-described not very good cowboy on a ranch deep in British Columbia, and his only goal in life was to make enough money to go to San Francisco to see the upcoming Panama Exposition. The first confirmation of the rumors of war he had heard on the range came to him from an Indian who told him "England's big white chief was going to war, or had gone."[15] The Indian said he would be enlisting and asked if Smith would do the same. By Christmas he was in training in Vancouver. He had enlisted by giving his birthplace as Canadian instead of American, but it was a misstatement also driven by his love of Canada and disgust with Germany.

By Smith's account, it had been the Second Battle of Ypres, opened on April 22, that had converted the Canadian view of the war from poetic and romantic to an absolute and aggressive necessity. It had been a battle for the strategic town of Ypres in Western Belgium, and one of the first instances of the German use of gas as a weapon. The Canadian army distinguished itself in the fighting, but had suffered 2,000 deaths and 4,000 casualties by gas, which killed immediately or wounded permanently. In retrospect, Smith said that April 22, 1915, was the day that Germany lost the war that would continue for three more years, and by May, he had left Halifax for France.

Smith was charmed to be in France and among its people, many of them in mourning black for those of their men already lost. But as he and his fellows moved further into the country towards Flanders in Belgium, more and more ruined villages appeared on the horizon. Military flares seemed like shooting stars, and trenches honeycombed the land. The fighting began here for Smith, and within a few days and nights of it he had arrived in another place. "We have discovered that there are worse things than Death and many a one of us has had abundant cause to envy our first pal to 'go west.'"[16] From there, the void of battlefield territory between the two enemies that was yet to be taken came to be known as "No Man's Land," but was eventually named "Canada" as statement of the success yet to come.

In August 1916 Smith was commissioned from the Canadian army to the Royal Scots

Battalion of the British army, which moved the fighting to Greece and the Macedonian front against Bulgaria. Before the war was done he would wear the American uniform.

Perhaps the thought process of an American making the decision to join the war through Canada was no more thoroughly demonstrated than in the letters of Edwin Austin Abbey, published after his death at Vimy Ridge on April 10, 1917. Like many others of the time, Abbey was an American of multi-geographic origins. He had been born in Scotland, but grown up in Philadelphia in a family that had become American. He trained there as a civil engineer and found work in Canada in 1915. Like so many Americans, his part in the war, or preparation for the war, was set by the sinking of the British passenger liner RMS *Lusitania* off the coast of Ireland on May 7, 1915, by a German submarine. "The dishonor to the flag is great'" he wrote from Sudbury, Ontario, "but it seems to me more a dishonor to manhood and humanity."[17] Germany, in his view, was "a terrible menace, and she is just beginning to feel confidence in her own resources to defy the world."[18] He ended the letter with a statement that many in the foreign legions that had preceded him and the Americans in Commonwealth forces that followed him would utter to themselves or to others in one way or another.

> No country or flag can be mine except the United States, but if I could go to this war as a citizen of the world, I would pray to be allowed.[19]

Abbey continued his civilian employment in Canada, but told his superiors that if his America declared war he would be gone at once to fight it. The resolve had pre-empted his ability to plan for his own future, and he asked that his parents, at this point in his life, give him their confidence in whatever course he pursued. The sentiment was returned from them in a subsequent letter, and he set about his path to the war.

America, thought its immigrant son Abbey, had failed in its reluctance to fight but succeeded in placing its spirit strongly in the middle of the conflict starting with its very important work in Belgium in the first days, and in subsequent actions. He felt that the same spirit would resound powerfully if Americans entered the fighting. He wished for the young men of America the chance to prove themselves for a just cause as they did in the Civil War, and he longed to be in Europe with that job in front of him. But it would not come soon enough for him, and in late July of 1915 he found himself in Toronto. He described city streets with storefronts festooned with recruiting banners. "Enlist Now," they said, or "For King and Country," "Remember the Lusitania." A decorated streetcar traveled the city full of recruiting officers ready to sign up the random pedestrian. It was all parades, marching bands and mass meetings.

> They are letting up a little bit in the physical requirements. The men with defective teeth are taken in and turned over to special dentists, who make them new sets free of charge; but I have heard nothing about the eyes.[20]

Abbey had a problem with his eyes and, though recruiters in Canada were almost desperate to sign up more men, they were being stringent about physical problems, eyes included. Abbey was discouraged. He continued to hold out for an American call to war, but his frustration only grew with each passing month. Finally, in October 1916 he returned to Toronto determined to join up, and was accepted into the Second Canadian Pioneer Battalion, an engineering corps. He did his work at the Flanders Front in March 1917, and moved on to Vimy Ridge in April.

Vimy Ridge became, and would remain, the central event in Canadian military history. In the minds of many it was, indeed, the central event in all of Canadian history, in which Canada solved a problem that no one else could, and with exceeding determination and

A recruiting streetcar coursed the streets of Toronto in 1915 promising a free and easy trip to Europe. Any Americans who might have been in Toronto were welcome to get on board (City of Toronto Archives).

valor. It shocked what had historically been a national identity that was as scattered and unrealized as its territories and wildernesses into one that was centered on a vital military success that all could share, and which distinguished the country as a strong nation within its own rights in the larger Commonwealth.

Vimy Ridge, in Pas-de-Calais, France, commanded a strategic dominance over some of the most important battlefields of the war. Germany had taken it in the course of its first invasion of France, and it seemed impossible to take it back. The French had tried and failed twice in 1915 with a toll of 150,000 casualties. Early in 1917, Allied forces gave the job to the relatively untested Canadians. The full Canadian force of nearly 100,000 would be concentrated on the effort, with the supplement of soldiers and equipment from the British Fifth Infantry. The Canadians took an unconventional approach to the problem that began with gaining as full an understanding of the battle space as possible. They used balloons and microphones to find gun placements, and tunnels to place mines beneath the German front. A scale replica of the space was created and used for planning and information for those who would fight on it. They opened the battle on April 9, 1917, after a week of heavy shelling to soften up the enemy.

By this time, Abbey was an officer in the Fourth Canadian Mounted Rifle Battalion, and in charge of a post forward of the trenches intended to limit German access to the ridge. It was deemed to be too dangerous to be held in daylight hours, but Abbey convinced his superiors to allow him to stay with it. Upon doing so he came across a wounded man who could only survive if returned to the trenches. After four hours of movement from shell hole to shell hole up a 300-foot slope, Abbey had returned the wounded man. After a few hours

A memorial service is held for the men of 87th Battalion of the CEF who fell at Vimy Ridge in 1917. The Battle of Vimy Ridge would help to turn the course of war, and to fix Canada's place firmly in the ultimate Allied victory (Canada Dept. of National Defence/Library and Archives Canada).

rest, he led his men back toward the advanced posts, signaling them to stay back as he explored forward. Apparently, he lost his bearings and arrived at the lip of a German trench where he was shot in the heart. He was one of 3,598 Canadian dead.

Found in his backpack was an unsent, final letter to his parents, excerpted:

> It is my greatest comfort that I know you two will gladly give all that is asked, and live on happily doing all that can be done, grateful to God for his acceptance of our sacrifice. Tuesday the news came to us that the United States had joined the Allies, so I go with happy consciousness that I am, and you are, fighting for our dear flag, as thousands of American have before us in the cause of Liberty.[21]

Edwin Austin Abbey is buried in the Commonwealth Graves Thelius Military Cemetery in Pas de Calais, France.

The American entry into the war at the time of Vimy Ridge had come after the luxury of years of national deliberation. But it was a luxury not available to America's neighbor to the north. Canada was a dominion of the British Empire. It could control its own domestic affairs without interference, but on foreign affairs it was bound to follow the lead of England. The operating principle, as stated in 1910 by Canadian prime minister Sir Wilfrid Laurier, was that "when Britain is at war, Canada is at war. There is no distinction." There was little disagreement with that sentiment in Canada, and the country officially offered its assistance to England. The offer was immediately accepted. But the nature and extent of what that assistance would be was quite another question.[22]

By 1914, Canada and the United States had shared nearly 150 years of good and bad history. The opening battles of the American Revolution had included an invasion of Quebec by the Continental army with the goal of converting the French Canadians to the American side against Britain. The Québécoise joined the Battle of Quebec on both sides, though England ultimately prevailed. As the war proceeded, the liberation of Quebec remained a secondary agenda for many in the 13 colonies, though it would never receive the effort that had gone into the original Battle of Quebec. Nova Scotia, then including present-day New Brunswick and Prince Edward, was actually considered the 14th British colony in North America, but it was too small and disconnected from the other 13 to become an active part of the war.

When the United States once again declared war on Great Britain in 1812, the occasion was seen by some as another opportunity to bring Canadian territory into the American fold. Once again, however, an expectation that the British subjects of Canada would join the American side wasn't realized. The War of 1812 came to an end in 1814 almost by virtue of a loss of interest on the part of its participants, but it had the important result of establishing once and for all a relationship between the U.S., Canada and Great Britain that was productive and enduring. In 1867, Canada obtained its own status as a self-ruling dominion of the British Commonwealth. And the border between the two North American neighbors would continue to be refined. Though it was never significantly disputed, it was occasionally the subject of squabbling, especially between the two world wars.

When the American Civil War broke out in 1861, Great Britain determined to remain neutral in the dispute between the Northern and Southern states. That stance was occasionally troubled mostly by incidents that involved ships and shipping within the prickly triangle of Union vs. Confederate vs. British interests in shipbuilding and seagoing commerce. Both sides in the Civil War used British ships and crew, and each side sought both to engage England on its own behalf while fighting against perceived British alliances with the other side. For its own part, Great Britain had to act in its own, and Canadian (technically British North American, as the Dominion of Canada did not yet exist), interests as it prepared for an indeterminate outcome of the war. And at various times in the conflict, the potential of a Union attack across the border had to be considered and dealt with.

In Canada itself, opinions about the war were mixed. Those who disagreed with slavery were likely to support the Union cause, and Canada was an important destination for escaped American slaves who traveled the Underground Railway. The proximity of Canada to the Northern states further increased an affinity between the two. But the more conservative and Catholic East tended to support the Confederacy. Both American sides in the dispute had connections and suppliers in Canada, and internal struggles within the country over independence for its eastern and maritime regions engendered natural sympathies among them for the secessionist states to the south.

The Civil War was emblematic of the American melting pot. By one of many accountings, the largest immigrant group to sign up with either side was German (est. 200,000 in the Union army; 10,000 in the Confederate army), followed by Irish (est. 144,200 Union; 20,000 Confederate), British (est. 60,000 Union; 10,000 Confederate), and Canadian (est. 53,500 Union; 10,000 Confederate).[23] In the absence of verifiable figures, all estimates were subject to challenge,[24] but whatever the true number of Canadians it was partly a result of the cross-border economic and social life of the two neighbors. In the case of the Civil War, there was a questionable side to the economics of participation by Canadian men. American Union law allowed escape from the draft by hiring someone else to take one's place, and many Canadian men took the job. Others were "crimped," or lured across the border with promises of employment and then tricked or induced to enlist in the Union army. Stories about Canadian men plied with drink and dragged south to servitude were popular in the media.

The proportion of Canadians who sold their service, were crimped or kidnapped to those who joined the Civil War out of more pure motivation is as unknown and controversial as the actual number of men involved. In 1861, an estimated 247,000 Canadians or British North Americans lived in the Union states beneath the border. An estimated 80,000 of them would be military aged men.[25] The numbers were further complicated by the porous border in both directions.

While the number of Canadian immigrants in America was measured at 1.2 million in 1900, American emigration to Canada from the time of the Revolutionary War through the two world wars could only be estimated for the most part, but was significant. The first group to arrive in Canada was 50,000 British loyalists from 1781 to 1790, followed by a larger portion that included Quakers and Mennonites seeking exemption from military service, then by those drawn to free or inexpensive land. That movement was considerably reduced after the War of 1812 amid lingering animosities between the two nations. Post-Civil War through 1910, an estimated 588,000 Americans emigrated to Canada. Following opportunities in the Canadian east and expansion in the west, they were businessmen, laborers and farmers. The latter group was the most significant, adding perhaps half a million to the American immigrant community in Canada between 1896 and 1914. They responded to an overt attempt by Canada to bring American and Canadian expatriate farmers in the U.S. into the Canadian West. The recruitment extended to Europe and Great Britain, but it was the Americans, and unnaturalized immigrants living in America, who came in large numbers. They were close by, and the economic limitations of many American farms and farm labor encouraged many to look for new horizons.[26]

It was particularly this group that embodied the complexity of figuring out who was who when talking about Americans who joined Commonwealth forces through Canada in World War I. Some of those who were listed as having come from America to Canada were actually just returning to their home country after time seeking opportunity on the other side of the border. And the same kind of back and forth had occurred with Canadians in America. A 1911 census of Canada determined, for example, that there were 167,000 native-born Americans in the three western provinces. Half of those were said to be Americans born of British origins, if that could be seen as a true indicator of their backgrounds. Some of them were black and Indian, and, in the laws of the time at least, of ambiguous background and not enthusiastically received, if at all. More telling, perhaps, were naturalization figures that showed 74,000 Americans given Canadian citizenship between 1902 and 1914.[27] For purposes of discussion, were they Americans, Canadians or dual citizens?

During the war years of 1914–1918, Americans emigrated to Canada at an annual rate of 40,000,[28] but the true meaning of that number was equally as ambiguous. Some were those seeking to avoid the American draft for personal or religious reasons, and some had the opposite goal of getting into the war by whatever means of self-identification necessary. Not all were who they seemed to be, but whatever their origins and motivations they were much needed in Canada. When the Dominion declared war, as was its duty to do as a member of the British Commonwealth, it had a standing army of just more than 3,000 troops and a navy supported by a handful of ships that had been hand-me-downs from England. Within just a few weeks of the declaration of war, however, 32,000 men had been assembled at a training camp in Quebec in preparation for a convoy across the Atlantic as the Canadian

Expeditionary Force. The first of them to move on to combat in France were known as the Princess Patricia's Canadian Light Infantry, or the Princess Pats.

The Princess Pats were the product of foresight on the part of Canadian army Captain Hamilton Gault. He had been watching events unfold in Europe and, from his perspective as a supporter of the British-Canadian relationship, predicted the eventual need for a response from Canada. He was also a wealthy man and, before the British declaration of war, proposed that he fund and organize a horse regiment that would be ready to go when needed. The war was soon declared and, as the regiment was evolved from a cavalry into an infantry unit, the Princess Pats were advanced enough in development to hold their first formal parade on August 23, 1914. It was marshaled by their namesake the Princess Patricia of Connaught, granddaughter of Queen Victoria and a very popular woman in Canada. The Princess would go on to live a much-storied and sometimes controversial life as a member of the Royal Family, and the Princess Pats would distinguish themselves in Canadian military history into the 21st century.

One of the most storied members of the Princess Pats in World War I was the American soldier of fortune Tracy Richardson. Conflicting records give his birth years as 1892 or 1899 in Broken Bow, Nebraska, from which his family moved to Lamar, Missouri. He left home as a young teenager and went on to a remarkable life as a soldier, pipeline worker, writer, friend of many of the famous of his time, fugitive from justice, prospector, and prohibition agent, among other pursuits. His military experience started in the Missouri National Guard and went on to the rebel army in Nicaragua, and revolutions in Venezuela and Honduras. A stint in the Mexican Revolution led to a price of $10,000 put on his head by Pancho Villa, and stories of a showdown between the two in which Richardson prevailed by sticking a gun in Villa's belly and demanding an apology when Villa challenged general American manhood. The apology was allegedly received as Richardson backed out of a cantina and disappeared into the night. Years later, he would come out of World War II as a lieutenant colonel in the U.S. army, but in 1914 he traveled to Canada and caught the first boat out with the Princess Pats. From there he seemed to disappear, and, with no word about him, his friends could only assume that he had been killed. Then came a few letters from a convalescent hospital in England. An expert with machine guns, he had come to be known as the "Machine Gun Man of the Princess Pats." But now he was only frustrated and "full of holes," waiting to get back into the fight. His description of the trench warfare that had gotten the best of him in the Second Battle of Ypres was indicative of the reporter he was yet to become in one of his many occupations.

> All around you, men, or what had been men, were to be seen. Some of these poor chaps you had known for months and had come to have a great affection for, and yet not one thing could you do for them. In some places my heart was sickened at the sights I saw. In some of these "places of the dead" the bodies of our poor fellows were piled four and five deep. I passed a machine-gun platoon—that is, the ghastly wreck of what had been one of the most gallant machine-gun sections of our force. The gun had been destroyed, and about it lay the men, most of them dead, and a few left, but badly wounded. But I could do nothing, and I moved on.[29]

The Princess Pats had been largely made up of those with prior military experience and motivation, but in the larger universe of Canadian men fit for war the going was slow. The shortage of farm labor in the west, for example, was not much better in the east. In Ontario, many men had already been drawn to the cities and rural labor was no longer sufficient to a national imperative to improve its agricultural output. The Toronto *Star* editorialized that "it would be foolish policy to allow the recruiting officer to cripple agriculture by withdrawing men from the farm, while other men in the towns and cities are eager to enlist and are not being enrolled."[30]

Bureaucratic problems and regional quotas hampered the enlistment of volunteers in the cities, but, until the draft finally came to Canada late in 1917 after angry national debate, the raising of an army was plagued by more complex problems than the differences between urban and rural. The first response of the Canadian public to the declaration of war was one that would seem to overcome the natural divisions in the country between English and French heritage. There was a common ally to support, Great Britain, against a common enemy, Germany. But the differences between immigrant-based populations in the country soon began to reappear. Two-thirds of the first contingent of 32,000 Canadians to head off to the war, including the Princess Pats, had been born in England. Conversely, just 1,000 were French Canadian.[31] The French felt no particular allegiance to England, though the war was ultimately in defense of France. But they had never had the mother country relationship with France that English Canadians had with England. Ultimately, only an estimated 15,000 French Canadians would volunteer for the war before the advent of conscription.

Nor did native-born Canadians ultimately volunteer in proportion to their numbers in the population. After the initial burst of enthusiasm for the war, enlistments fell off and the search for volunteers became more intense. The first period of recruitment had been fueled in part by a general lack of employment in the country, but employment opportunities increased as the war progressed. A solution was to break down the national effort to regional and local levels and allow governments, towns, affinity and ethnic groups to create and underwrite their own battalions. There were, as an example, two battalions made up of men beneath five feet two inches in stature, another made up of teetotalers. As this method of recruitment proceeded, it was successful, though it could not keep up with the demand. The goal for July 1915 was a force of 150,000, but that number was already jeopardized by heavy losses in battle. Just three months later, the goal was extended to 250,000, and would double in the following year.[32]

The Canadian Minister of Militia and Defence was Colonel Samuel Hughes. In retrospect, Hughes was one of the most colorful figures in Canadian history, but by the time he had reached the position of Militia Minister he was a basket of controversy. Born in the west in 1853, he had been a newspaperman, infantryman, teacher and parliamentarian. By his own lights, he had been a hero of the Boer War and deserving of a Victoria Cross that he would never receive. On the other hand, he had been fired from that war for military indiscipline. He had foreseen the World War years before it began, however, and, when made Minister, began to prepare Canada for its role. King George V would knight him for that work in August 1915, but it was about that time that problems of recruitment and training began to get out of control. He had told the Toronto *Star* in April of that year that recruitment was going exceedingly well. "We have never recruited by advertisement the same way as Great Britain. We didn't have to. We can get all the men we want. It is but proper that men should only be put under arms and trained when they are found to be necessary."[33] At that time, 101,000 Canadians were in service, but the need for 150,000 was just three months away, to say nothing of what would be required to meet the number of 620,000 that would serve in the Canadian Expedition Force by the end of the war, a half million of those as volunteers.

A continuing resistance on the part of a strain of French-Canadians to any participation on their part compounded the problem that Hughes faced. In the most notorious example, Hughes offered the command of a French-Canadian battalion to militia Colonel Armand

Lavergne and was publicly rebuffed. It was Britain that should be defending Canada, said Lavergne, not the other way around.

> I consider it unwise and more than criminal to place Canada in danger of a war in which we have not had, have not and will never have any control whatever. I will ever oppose any contribution of our country of one man, one ship or one dollar, until England believes it just that we should participate with her, not only the dangers, but also the full control and responsibilities of the affairs of the empire.[34]

Lavergne went on to say that if Canada imposed the order to fight on its French citizens it would be tantamount to the imposition of Germany on France, though, as a good soldier, he would, of course, fight for England if so ordered. Many in the press declared him a traitor, but in the fullness of Canadian history his importance as a politician was more important. He had led the creation of one of the first laws to require French as the official language of Quebec, and he fought for the rights of French-Canadians until his death in 1935.

Eventually, Sam Hughes would look toward America to solve his recruitment problems, and that would follow on the work of an American Unitarian minister, C. Seymour Bullock. In his youth, Bullock had been pointed toward education at West Point, but at some point he came under the influence of the evangelist team of preacher Dwight Moody and singer Ira Sankey. Moody's words and Sankey's voice convinced thousands across the country to seek their comfort in a return to God, salvation and the promise of heaven. Bullock's military ambitions were re-directed toward faith. He graduated from Northwestern University as a clergyman in 1889, and served as an army chaplain in the Spanish American War. Before the rumblings of World War I, he was most noted as a supporter of physical exercise for disadvantaged children. In 1913, he was supervisor of playgrounds in New London, Connecticut, where he also first became a Unitarian minister, and often reminded people that the state spent more on prisons than on playgrounds. He traveled the country in support of the life lessons of supervised play for children, especially in rural areas.

> Nowadays when this country-boy leader goes from his rural home to the city he brings with him a fund of vitality and physical strength. But, he himself, narrow and ill-poised, is often borne by his own surplus energy and love of excitement into the worst of the city's temptations.[35]

As a member of the Unitarian Universalist Conference of the middle states and Canada, he had a voice in the Unitarian debate over the topic of women's suffrage in 1915. The conference took a position in favor of suffrage, but Bullock argued against it; not on the merits of the suffrage argument, but asserting that suffrage was not a moral issue and thus not of concern to Unitarians. He was also the great nephew of Robert Livingston, the ambassador to France at the opening of the 19th century and collaborator with Robert Fulton in the development of the steamboat. One hundred years later, Bullock was considered the country's leading expert on steamboats with the world's largest repository of steamboat pictures and ephemera. He gave popular lectures on the topic, and impersonations of Robert Fulton in period dress.

Bullock had been in Germany at the opening of the war in 1914. He made his way to London and was drawn into Herbert Hoover's effort to assist stranded Americans in Europe, and was put in charge of the search for those stranded on the continent. In 1915, after a similar stint in Chicago, Bullock became the Unitarian minister in Ottawa, Ontario. His world view was both American and Canadian while Canada was at war and the United States was not. The Unitarian view of the war was not resolved, and much debated. In May 1915 a national meeting in Boston of the Unitarian Fellowship for Social Justice seemed to take on every possible debate of the day. It concluded with resolutions that were: supportive of President Wilson's conduct in the current international crisis; supportive of the Anti-Enlistment League, which sought to preempt an American declaration of war by working against enlistment in its armed forces; supportive of Prohibition, equality between men and women, and condemnation of the racist film *Birth of a Nation*. The nation's churches and philanthropies were criticized for not doing enough for the needy, and there was discussion of the plight of the scrubwomen of Boston in seeking an increased wage.

By far, the largest debate in Boston was over the American response to the war in Europe. Unitarians were inclined to disfavor war in favor of other alternatives, but this war was particularly brutal for the innocent. The arguments for and against American participation were led mostly by Unitarians with German ancestry who demanded that American war munitions not be sold to the Allies. Seymour Bullock led arguments for the opposite position. The convention could arrive at no firm conclusion on the matter and debate was shut down by the presiding officer upon his exclamation that he would have to be removed from the meeting on a stretcher if it was not.

Bullock's motivations regarding the war in Europe probably began with his time working in London after the German invasion of Belgium. By the time he got to Ottawa, Canada had been long at war and the sinking of the *Lusitania* was hardening resolve against the Germans. Of the 1,198 civilians lost, 128 were Americans. The sinking was met first by shock, then resounding anger in England and America, and in Canada, where Bullock took to the pulpit in Ottawa two days later and sounded anything but a gentle Unitarian, or a happy American. Among the arguments about the war in the United States was the conviction held by many that if the country was going to benefit financially from the sales of armaments and matériel in Europe, it had better take a stake in the fighting. Bullock referred to the Bronze Star he had received in the Spanish American War.

> But I have laid it aside, and shall not wear it again until it shall have been demonstrated that my country in its passion for dollars has not lost sight of its honor. I feel confident that the right thing will be done, but I shall not again hail that flag nor touch that bit of bronze until not only Germany, but the whole world, shall have been brought to see that every cannon on every American ship, every gun in every American fort, every musket in the American army, and every dollar of America's wealth stands for the rights of every American citizen, either at home or abroad.
>
> Better to be a man without a country than be the citizen of a country in which one cannot be a man. Better to have no flag that simply waves in the dead air of a national atmosphere that has lost the ozone and oxygen of self-respect.[36]

With that, Seymour Bullock took up the role of traveling the country to raise funds for the support of Canada's military families, and to recruit more families into the war. And, traveling near the border in the complex economic and social mix of Canadians and Americans, it seemed natural to develop the idea of an American battalion for the Canadian Expeditionary Force. Back in Ottawa, he proposed the idea to Minister of the Militia Samuel Hughes. Despite a warning against it by the Canadian adjutant general, Hughes did not hesitate. He set up the 97th Overseas Battalion of the British army, to be known as the American Legion. Seymour Bullock would become captain of the 97th, and its chaplain—the only American Unitarian clergymen to serve in the British army.

At the time of the creation of the American Legion in Canada, the American Legion in the United States began to lose its energy, though the two organizations had no relationship to each other. By the end of 1916, the directors of the U.S. legion, including Teddy Roosevelt, sent a letter to members telling them that the organization would become unincorporated on January 1, 1917. Information about 24,000 of its members would be turned over to the Council of National Defense as a fulfillment of the goal of creating a ready reserve. It was suggested that those wishing to do so contact their local Red Cross affiliate for volunteer opportunities. The letter closed by saying that "the work of the legion could not have been done but for the financial support of one generous and patriotic citizen, not a member of the board, whose identity the Directors are not at Liberty disclose."[37]

FOUR

Canada

If you are a real man, come overseas with us. —Canadian poster recruiting Americans

Canadian newspapers of 1915–1916 followed America's involvement with the war in Europe on two parallel tracks. C. Seymour Bullock had not been alone in his barely contained anger over American dithering, "a country in which one cannot be a man." Teddy Roosevelt remained popular in Canada, especially in light of the perceived failings of President Woodrow Wilson. There seemed no doubt about what Roosevelt would have done in reaction to the sinking of the *Lusitania*, and no small amount of ridicule for Wilson's reluctance to move forward. "Has there ever been such a sexless, soulless, spineless occupant of the White House in Washington," wrote T.M. Campbell of 1463 King Street West, Toronto, in a letter to the editor of the *Toronto Star*.[1] Editorial pages were barely more tempered. The same newspaper reflected on the Hague Convention.

> The United States is concurring in the German view that the signed convention between nations is only another scrap of paper, and that the signature of the United States affixed to it means nothing and gives the document no importance before the world nor in the opinion of Washington herself. Germany has ignored that signed convention. By her silence the United States ignores it, too.[2]

On the other track, the newspapers reported on the growing presence of Americans in Canadian forces and the development of the American Legion. In November 1915, the *Star* passed along speculation that Teddy Roosevelt would affirm his convictions about war with Germany by volunteering for a leadership role in the Canadian Expeditionary Force. It noted that several thousand Americans "have joined the Canadian expeditionary forces since the war began, and there is still a steady influx of recruits from across the line. Were Colonel Roosevelt to accept a command with the Canadian forces there is not doubt that many thousands of his fellow countrymen would follow his example and ask to serve under him."[3] Such a move on his part was already, and perhaps fancifully, anticipated. The *Detroit Free Press*, an American eye into the Canada that sat across the Detroit River, reported in November 1915 that the 33rd Canadian Infantry Battalion formed in London, Ontario, contained many Americans from Detroit and other cities. The city of London would be willing to offer its resources to the development of an American battalion there, and other Americans already in Canadian forces would eagerly transfer to the battalion if Roosevelt were to take its command. The offer was telegraphed to Roosevelt, but was refused.

The citizenship implications for Americans in Canadian forces was not yet resolved,

Enlist Now!

WHAT IN ?

American Legion, C. E. F.

WHERE ?

RECRUITING STATIONS AT
FERRY DOCK SARNIA, BRIDGEBURG, WINNIPEG, CALGARY
AND WINDSOR

CANADA NEEDS YOU TO-DAY

It was not legal for recruiting of Americans into the Canadian Expeditionary Force to take place within the United States. But recruiting posters and flyers were plentiful, especially along the U.S.–Canadian border (Imperial War Museum).

but all agreed that Roosevelt's participation would do much to answer the question. But Roosevelt himself squelched the speculation as his secretary passed word that he would not be attending, nor had he agreed to attend, an American Legion recruiting event in Toronto on December 11, 1915. Another account, in the *New York Times*, quoted Roosevelt more directly. "I cannot speak in Toronto until the war is over. I cannot trust myself, for I would certainly say what would be unwise to say."[4]

With or without Roosevelt's presence, the Toronto event was a foundation stone in the legion and served as a first introduction to Americans of the formalization of the enlistment of their countrymen in British Commonwealth Forces. As reported upon in the *New York Times*, its primary speaker was the distinguished Canadian Judge William Riddell. A jurist and writer, Riddell specialized as a historian in U.S.–Canadian relations. Upon his mention of Col. Roosevelt, the attendees roared their approval and waved American and British flags. Roosevelt, he said, had called America's failure to follow through on denunciation of Germany with action "disgraceful," and he directed his words at the Americans in the audience. "If you young men do not enlist as a result of this meeting, then you disgrace yourselves."[5] Twenty-one Americans signed up at the event and it was seen as a good first step in the goal of 1,100 members of the legion by the beginning of 1916.

In the same article, the *Times* reported on a letter it had received from "G. [*sic*] S. Bullock, Chairman of the American Citizens' Recruiting Committee at Toronto."[6] Adventurous young Americans, said Bullock, were showing up at all points in the border and being sent on to Toronto, where they were welcomed with open arms. They were coming from West Point, Annapolis, Harvard, Yale, Princeton, Cornell, the University of Pennsylvania, various military academies and regiments of the National Guard.

> The caliber of the men is excellent, and it looks as if the legion is going to give a good account of itself when it comes to grips with the enemy. We Americans up here are proud of them. We who are of them are proud to do our bit in the great fight for right.[7]

The *Times* article went on to quote an editorial in the *Toronto Globe* of a few days earlier that referred to a previous war.

> The tables are turned. A half century ago, in the awful tragedy of the civil war in the United States, many thousands of Canadians crossed the line, enlisted in the American regiments, and fought for freedom and humanity on the great battlefields of the Republic. Today a new battalion is being organized in the Dominion, the Ninety-Seventh of Canada, composed wholly throughout all ranks, of men born within the United States.[8]

It was not the case that all were born in the United States, but the complex origins of those who lived in, or had immigrated back and forth between, the two countries seemed a fine point in the basic story that Americans were coming to Canada to fight in the war. Their progress was closely followed in the Canadian press. On November 28, 1915, the first members of the legion took up residence in the livestock building at the Toronto fairgrounds as better quarters were being prepared and instructors were being trained. By the first days of 1916, the group was in fine shape. Samuel Hughes himself had made a surprise visit to the camp and commended the men of the 97th for their drill and soldierly appearance.

The American press took less notice of the legion, but it was hard to find reporting and editorial opinion that was critical of Americans going off to fight in British Commonwealth Forces. In a day when small town newspapers were still the important media of their communities, the Middletown, New York, *Daily Times Press* editorialized at length on the announcement from Canada that it was recruiting Americans. The context of history was an important factor, it said, and pointed to the Civil War. It was certainly the case that many Canadians had gone below the border to get into it for financial reasons, "But the great mass of Canadians who joined the Union army fought for the Stars and Stripes with as much zeal as they would have fought for Great Britain had occasion required.... It is not strange that Canada is enabled to send a full regiment of unhyphenated Americans to help the motherland in what appears to be the hour of her dire necessity."[9]

In England, the formation of the legion was only lightly noted at first. It was introduced in an article in *The London Times* about the mood in Canada at the beginning of 1916. It noted that Canadians were neither critical of the British war effort, nor of the American tactic of diplomacy. It reported, slightly tongue in cheek, that Canadian prime minister Sir Robert Borden had been successfully representing the Canadian cause in New York.

> As a son of Nova Scotia speaking to the Pilgrims he emphasized the intimate relations between New England and the eastern Provinces of Canada which he could fairly have described as the common nursery of letters and statesmanship on this continent, recalled that many thousands of Canadians had fought for the North in the Civil War, and rejoiced that an American Legion was forming in Canada to go oversea with Canadians in the defence of freedom and civilization.[10]

Early in 1916, the force size goals had increased to 5,000 by mid-year and 10,000 by the fall, and Sam Hughes had authorized Seymour Bullock to extend the range of recruitment from Ontario to all provinces of Canada. Offices were to be opened in Vancouver, British Columbia; Calgary, Alberta; Saskatoon, Saskatchewan; Winnipeg, Manitoba; Fort William, Ontario; Montreal, Quebec; St. John, New Brunswick; and Halifax, Nova Scotia—all to be funneled into training in Toronto, where recruitment was also expanded.

The 211th Infantry Battalion was known as the Alberta Americans, though just 218 of its 628 members were listed in the company's roster as born in the United States. Of those, 116 noted next of kin with American addresses, 99 with Canadian, and three in the United Kingdom. Some of those included a family of four men from Ames, Iowa, the Chenette brothers. In 1916, Stephen Edward Chenette was the director of the city's band, and his

Major General Sir Sam Hughes arrives in Boulogne, France, undated (Canada Dept. of National Defence/ Library and Archives Canada).

seven brothers were also musicians. Stephen Edward, Clate, Eugene Dow and Tec Clate traveled to Vancouver and became members of the 211th band. Their positions were maintained as the battalion was quickly merged with others to form the Canadian Railway Troops in March 1917.

On the evening of February 27, 1916, Seymour Bullock could be found on the stage of the Walker Theatre in Winnipeg. He recalled what he had seen in Germany at the outbreak of the war, and his journey back to London. The 212th Battalion of the CEF was now forming in Manitoba, and all Americans or those of American parentage were asked to join. Most thinking Americans, he said, supported Canada against tyranny and the legion was designed to accommodate those American men who felt it their duty to join the fight. "Altogether," reported the *Manitoba Free Press*, "his talk was most absorbing, and made a profound impression on the audience which packed the theatre."[11] In April, the *Winnipeg Telegram* published a lengthy article after a discussion with 212th Commander Major B.C. Pittman. Since the German invasion, he said, thousands of Americans who wanted to fight the Germans in American uniforms had come to Canada instead. All were true Americans, and their travel to Canada signaled no loss of love for their country; rather, the upholding of its ideals. It was not legal for the legion to recruit within the United States, and it had to rely on word of mouth or happenstance to gain the interest of the young men south of the border. But once they arrived at any point in Canada, they could approach any border agent or recruiting officer and be taken directly into the service. An American donor could reimburse those who had to borrow money for their travel to the border. Those with further questions were assured that if they wrote to him "in care-of American Legion, Winnipeg" they would receive a quick response.

The 213th Battalion complimented the 97th in Toronto, and moved to England where it was absorbed into the Fourth Reserve Battalion. The 237th Battalion was formed under Seymour Bullock in Sussex, New Brunswick, then disbanded into the 97th Battalion. Most other battalions of the Canadian Expedition Force held small numbers of Americans: 30 in the 100th Battalion; 18 in the 101st; 20 in the 159th, and so forth. The comings and goings of the Americans became part of the daily life of Toronto and were reflected in the newspapers. They told stories of notable recruits like U.S. Navy Petty Officer John Daly of New York City. The Spanish American war veteran had been aboard the USS *New Jersey* in Nor-folk, Virginia, received a discharge from service and come to Toronto in search of the 97th Battalion. Not all Americans went into the so-called American Legion battalions, and the 134th Highland Battalion of the CEF saw Daly first, but he insisted that "I have come to join the American battalion.... Every man who loves freedom should be fighting against Prussian militarism."[12]

If new recruits committed crimes they were reported in the crime blotters, including desertions from the forces. Marriage engagements and social events involving the Americans were reflected in the social columns, as were the many social events held in their honor. The Society column of the *Toronto World* of April 18, 1916, promised the delights of a Thursday evening American Cabaret performance at the Toronto Arena, a fundraiser for the legion. It would be one of the largest evenings of entertainment ever staged in the city, with performances by the most famous of Canadian and American musicians and actors.

If there was resentment in Canada over the American presence in its armed forces, it

An undated Canadian poster seeks American recruits to the 237th Battalion of the American Legion (Library of Congress).

was difficult to find. But one event quickly came to cast a curious shadow over the good feeling of the time.

In the dark, early morning of February 16, 1916, three distinct explosions seemed to blow outward from the heavy walls of the American Club at 17–19 Wellington Street West. The former bank building had become the Toronto headquarters of American interests in the city, and had served as the birthplace of plans for the American Legion. A few days previously, it had been the location of a rally in support of the Entente Allies of Britain, France and Russia, and supportive of Canada's part in the war. Many had been asleep in the building at the time of the explosion at 2:30 a.m. One, P.I. Hairston, a Texas mining broker and developer of the American Legion then living in Ontario, was killed, and several were injured, including the club's president Captain Asa Minard. It was quickly determined that the explosions were purposely set, probably in an empty third floor bedroom.

The crime was never solved, and eventually the fact that it was purposeful would be questioned, but it was determined by leadership of the American Club to have been an act of war, and that members of the legion would attend Mr. Hairston's funeral in honor of a victim of war.

By March 1916, the first of the American Legion members were ready to go to war. They were reported to be tired of life in their barracks in the Machinery Building of the Canadian National Exhibition, and "in a state of eager expectation."[13] They had been given their heavy marching equipment, a sign of imminent departure, and strategic exercises among officers were underway.

Two months later, the foundation of the American Legion in Canada was fully formed and ready for wide exposure in the American press. At the time, *The Outlook* was one of the country's most popular weekly magazines. Teddy Roosevelt had become an associate editor after leaving the presidency, and, on May 3, the magazine published a lengthy article about the battalion, prefaced by what it called the legion's hymn, excerpted.

> Not because our homes are threatened
> Or our country calls to the fight
> We're fighting because we want to,
> Because we love both Fight and Right[14]

"They are interesting fellows, these men," the article began, and went on to describe who they were and who they were not. They were not boys, dime novel readers, or hotheaded adventurers. A few were soldiers of fortune, to be sure, but they were basically sober, hardworking Americans with convictions. Many came from colleges, some from West Point, "and there are also frontiersmen from the beaches of Alaska and the hills of Mexico who 'ain't had no chanst at learnin'."

Among them were:

Tom Longboat, a Native American professional runner who had trotted 80 miles from his home in New York State to enlist in Toronto. He was assigned to the 213th Battalion, but tried to smuggle himself into the 97th when he learned it would be the first to go to France, and "was arrested for his excessive patriotism."

Tracy Richardson was mentioned in his caricature as the "human sieve." He was a captain in the legion and idolized by many of his men. Lieutenant R.E. Smith was a child of England, but a resident of Rochester, New York, where he had built and flown the first airplane ever seen in that city.

W.H.S. Taylor of Port Huron, Michigan, was a veteran of the Spanish American War who had seen the surrender of Santiago in 1898 and was "grizzled till he looked perilously near the upper age limit. But the recruiting officers will strain a point for an applicant who carries himself with the unmistakable 'set' of the knight of many battles."[15]

Indeed, the article considered a comparison between these men and the knights of the Crusades. "Instead of fighting for the recovery of the Holy Land," it asserted, "they are fighting for the recovery of land just as holy and more wrung by the grip of the oppressor than Palestine ever was ... instead of fighting for a concrete and narrow creed and the promised reward of spiritual salvation they are fighting for an abstract idea of justice and the satisfaction of their own consciences."[16]

Notwithstanding all of that, however, the writer told of the poster he had come across upon crossing the border into Canada, typical of many different pitches made to young American men who made similar journeys.

If

You believe in fair play
You really love liberty
You want to fight for right
You are a real man
COME OVERSEAS WITH US

If a man must fight for a living from a material standpoint he could not do better than join the American Legion. In the first place, the Canadian army is the highest paid army in the world. Privates in the ranks get $1.10 a day, as against a shilling a day in the British army, $15 a month in the United States army, and much less than that in the armed camps of Germany, France, Russia, and the other countries of the world.

Reference to other countries, including Germany, was meant to address the soldier of fortune, and those who might otherwise choose to fight for their country of origin. The poster went on to say that the wife of each recruit would receive a stipend of $20 per month, plus $5 for each child. Later in 1916, it was announced that under a land colonization program of the Canadian Pacific Railway those married Americans who could show service in the British army or navy would be eligible for free land, financial assistance and equipment assistance in the West.

Recruits had to be of good physical and moral health, of American birth, parentage or residence, and between the ages of 18 and 45. The legion asserted that the oath given by each recruit was only to King George V and not to an alien country, and the courts had already decided that those Americans who enlisted in Canada would not lose citizenship, though the claim was yet to be fully proved true. Nor was American neutrality in jeopardy because recruiting happened only in Canada.

A state-by-state accounting of the origins of the first 875 recruits in the 97th Battalion was both predictable and surprising. As expected, most came from states immediately bordering Ontario, but almost all of the states were represented.

New York 187
Michigan 140
Illinois 60
Massachusetts 58

Above and opposite: **The full 97th Battalion of the American Legion posed in panorama in Toronto, undated (courtesy Glenn Hyatt).**

Pennsylvania 51
Ohio 50
Minnesota 29
Washington 27
Wisconsin 20
Missouri and Indiana 19
California 18
Iowa 15
Alabama 14
Montana 12
Rhode Island, Oregon and Nebraska 11
North Dakota and Connecticut 10
Virginia and Texas 9
Vermont and Colorado 8
Tennessee, Kentucky and Maryland 6
Idaho, Maine, Louisiana and Kansas 5
Florida and New Jersey 4
New Hampshire 3
Oklahoma, D.C., Arizona, Mississippi, North Carolina,
    South Dakota, Georgia, Wyoming and Utah 2
Arkansas and West Virginia 1[17]

Their average age was 30, and 62 percent of them were said to have previous U.S. military or state militia experience. By mid–1916, the 875 had increased to 5,000 recruited into the American Legion. General, unsourced estimates claimed that another 11,000 Americans had enlisted in other battalions and fighting units. In late May, the legion was the subject of a feature article in the Sunday *New York Times* that perhaps served as its first substantial introduction to the American people. With a brigade badge of George Washington's coat of arms laid over a Canadian maple leaf, it said, the battalion of 5,000 would be heading off to join the war in Flanders, and not without first bringing shame to those able-bodied Canadian men who had not yet signed up. Their training, meetings and parades in Toronto had offered a stark contrast to idle Canadian men, "for the plight of the able-bodied Canadian of fighting

age who is not in khaki is almost pitiable, at least in Toronto. He is ignored by young women, hooted by small boys."[18]

The recruiting success of the legion thus far, the *Times* reported, was an extension of the rush of Americans across the border in the first weeks after the German invasion. They had been submerged unseen into the battalions that left Canada after the British declaration. As reporting of the movement first appeared in American newspapers along the border, more American men followed suit, and by the time the legion was forming there were more than enough Americans in Canada to fill its 1,200-man battalions. They were said to be aware of, but unconcerned about, questions that might arise about their American citizenship. It was a matter of some tension: the American consul in Vancouver warned that any American joining the Canadian army would lose his citizenship, while the consul in Winnipeg held an opposite view. And there was a situation yet to be resolved in Detroit in which German Americans in the city insisted that a Michigan man who went to war with Canada and returned with wounds "be deported on the ground that he was an alien physically unfit to support himself."[19]

As proof of the general acceptance of the legion within America, the President Emeritus of Harvard University was said to be set to write the preface to a religious guide for the battalions. John Philips Souza was composing a legion march, though the spirit of the legion was ultimately only included in his postwar *Comrades of the Legion*. One of the enlistees was a Boston shoe manufacturer N.L. Francis, son-in-law of a late Supreme Court justice. Upon becoming an officer in the 237th Battalion, he received letters of congratulations from ex-President William Howard Taft and Supreme Court Associate Justice Holmes, son of the patriotic poet Oliver Wendell Holmes. Other examples were given of recruits from West Virginia and Michigan who arrived in Canada with letters of recommendation from their U.S. senators and representatives.

No matter their background or recommendations, every American joining the legion entered as a private and rose in the ranks by virtue of experience, accomplishment and character. In the latter regard, the *Times* reported that they were all teetotalers and that when they rose at each evening's meal to toast King George it was with cold water instead of wine. Seymour Bullock was said to have on file a letter of resignation from each man, to be used if he was to be discovered with alcohol. Sir Samuel Hughes was known to believe that a man who drank was not fit to be responsible for other men in his command. The legion also operated under an order first given to American Revolutionary troops in 1779 and repeated in the orders of the day in Canada:

DON'T SWEAR
...For the sake, therefore, of religion, decency, and order, the general hopes and trusts that

officers of every rank will use their influence and authority to check a vice which is as unprofitable as it is wicked and shameful.

GEORGE WASHINGTON[20]

By this time, Bullock had been given the rank of lieutenant colonel and supervisor of all the battalions. Command of the 97th Battalion was given to Lt. Col. W.L. Jolly, a Philadelphia construction tycoon born in Conway, Iowa, and captain in the Spanish American war with experience in the Chinese Boxer rebellion. Lt. Col. B.J. McCormick was made commander of the 213th Battalion. He was a citizen, and veteran of the National Guard, of Michigan, but working as the Industrial Commissioner of Welland, Ontario, at the beginning of the war. He enlisted in the CEF, and went on to become a British major. He became an expert in defense against gas warfare and was credited with helping to neutralize its effect on Allied troops. His son, Lt. Arthur McCormick, was also with Canadian forces in Flanders, and both would be fighting together as American citizens. Officers of the battalion would come to include experienced military men from Alabama, Indiana, Illinois, New Jersey and New York.

Nova Scotian Captain Asa Minard, of the American Club in Toronto, took a lead in the 237th Battalion, accompanied by his two sons, Asa and Basil, who were both born in Massachusetts. Though he was captain of the officer's mess in the 97th Battalion, Alexander Rasmussen was one of the most colorful of the battalion's personalities. He was an American citizen born in Denmark with next of kin in Oregon. His military career in the U.S. Cavalry had begun in the Spanish American War, but at the time of the German invasion of France he had been high in the Yukon Territory prospecting for gold. His mother was French and

The 97th American concludes training at the Toronto exhibition grounds before leaving for Halifax, Nova Scotia, and Europe in late 1917 (Library of Congress/*New York Times*).

her experiences in the Franco-Prussian War of 1870–1871 prompted her son to travel quickly east to Ontario and sign up for the fight against Germany.

The article in the *New York Times* did not sit well with elements of the German American community. As in the case of the complaint against the wounded American veteran of Canada in Detroit, Germans in the United States were vigilant about trying to keep American sensibilities and actions neutral in relation to events overseas. Rudolf Cronau was a Prussian writer and artist who had moved to the United States in 1880 and become an important German voice in the country. In 1916, he published the lengthy book *German Achievements in America*, dedicated to "the millions of children, born by German parents and raised in German American homes, the Hope and Future of our United States...."[21] An immediately previous book had been *England, a Destroyer of Nations*. The creation of the American Legion, he asserted, had come of pro–British propaganda in the nation, and the *Times* article was indicative of "the demoralization that has taken place among our people."[22]

Much of the article was reprinted without comment, but it was the raising of cold water in a nightly toast to King George V that most symbolized the problem with the legion. It was even worse than the hiring of Hessian soldiers by King George III to fight against Americans in the Revolutionary War.

> It was left to our 20th century to witness the much more shameful spectacle that free American citizens voluntarily hire themselves to King George V., to fight his mercenary battles and help to crush a friendly nation, which is struggling heroically for its existence.
> And these men wear a badge showing the coat of arms of George Washington![23]

Rudolf Cronau's view of things did not immediately prevail, though the idea of it would gain some traction later on. The men wearing the badge were responding in part to Canadian recruiting posters that asserted that Germany was the enemy of the liberty, civilization and the welfare of humanity that were the values of all Americans, to say nothing of the possibility of "a line of German forts on what is now the peaceful border-line between the United States and Canada."[24] Increasingly, the question of German influence in the American discussion about the war was mixed into a growing debate about "preparedness." Should the U.S. be more prepared to enter the war? Would preparation for war make it easier for those who advocated for an American declaration to actually get into it? It was the chief topic of national debate in May 1916, and it focused on the wills of two American icons: Teddy Roosevelt and Henry Ford.

By 1916, the Ford production line was making and selling almost half a million Model Ts annually, and Henry Ford was a man of great influence on an international stage. He was a pacifist in regard to World War I, a position that was confused by his own growing anti–Semitism. He was famously quoted as saying in 1915 "I know who caused the war—the German-Jewish bankers!"[25] Ford's views were expounded after the war through his ownership of the newspaper *The Dearborn Independent* in 1919 and following years in which articles and headlines were clearly anti–Semitic, ranging from warnings about Jewish control of financial systems to "Jewish Jazz—Moron Music—Becomes Our National Music."[26]

In early May, it was announced that Roosevelt would be coming to Henry Ford's Detroit as part of a national tour in support of preparedness in general, and to take on Henry Ford where Detroit was concerned. "He is ready for his invasion of the city," the *Detroit Free Press* reported, "where Henry Ford lives and where 'peace at any price' [Ford] may expect to hear him tell them Friday night what he thinks about pacifism."[27] It was also a prelude to his unsuccessful attempt to gain the Republican nomination for president that year, for which

WAKE UP, AMERICA! ❧ By LOUIS RAEMAEKERS

This was done to Canadians by the Huns. Will America wait to see it done to her soldiers before waking up to the entire earnestness of the war?

Louis Raemaekers was a controversial Dutch artist whose political cartoons depicting German brutality caused Germany to offer a reward for his death or capture. This drawing, ca. 1917, depicted America as drawing away in horror from the sight of a dead Canadian hanging from a tree (Library of Congress).

Ford was also a minor candidate. "Colonel Roosevelt," the *New York Times* reported, "is determined to go to Detroit and tell the voters there just what he thinks of the question of national preparedness. He has no intention of mincing his words or attempting 'pussyfooting' methods."[28] The trip was met with great anticipation, with regular news dispatches of the location of his train, and expectations of what he would say upon his arrival.

Roosevelt arrived in Detroit at 7:10 a.m., and was met at the train station by a crowd of 1,000. A melee was reported outside the filled Opera House as hundreds had to be turned away. The speech was predictably fiery. He asserted that influential Germans in America were driving pacifist and anti-preparedness forces to make Germany strong and keep the United States unable to join the war. As for Henry Ford, he had nothing but praise for the man and his accomplishments, but suggested that if he and his cohorts had been present at the time of the American Revolution they would have prevented it from becoming a nation. They were compromisers, and sometimes, in the face of world cataclysm, it was just not possible to compromise.

> There is only one way to oppose a policy that is inherently wrong and that is by opposing it with every ounce of earnestness, every ounce of energy that man possesses. The only kind of faith to have in any policy is 100 percent faith. If we believe that the most certain way for us to insure peace is to be prepared for war, and to have it known that we are prepared for war, then let us wholeheartedly advocate such a policy, not a little, not with tremors and gaspings, but fully and absolutely.[29]

It was not Germany, he asserted, that was most responsible for the loss of American lives in the sinking of the *Lusitania*, but the weak ultimatums given to Germany from the position of American neutrality at the outset of the war, followed by no action. And he ended the very long speech with a hand extended to Americans of German descent as good people in a time of difficult decisions. "Preparedness" needed to be accompanied by "Americanism ... a matter of the spirit, not of birthplace or descent."[30]

Lt. Col. Charles Seymour Bullock of the American Legion displays one of the legion's American flags that was presented by him to Queen Mary at Buckingham Palace after the war (Canada Dept. of National Defence/Library and Archives Canada).

Both the Ford and Roosevelt camps had voiced friendly intentions to effect a meeting between the two during Roosevelt's visit, but the problem of whose turf would be used was unsolvable, and the meeting did not take place. Ford's response to the Roosevelt event was to rightfully respect him as an ex-president, though "antiquated" in his case, and not in tune with modern times. And, said America's most important industrialist, "The trouble with this whole Detroit demonstration is that the armament and munitions crowd are too prominent in it. I know this crowd, and I know that it is not all patriotism."[31]

Roosevelt had visited Detroit not on his own initiative, but at the invitation of a group of city leaders of all mainstream political parties and beliefs. What they wanted, said the *Free Press*, was the thinking of an important American voice on a difficult American choice. And that, according to the newspaper, was what they got.

But, as the choice hung in the balance, a growing number of Americans prepared to go to war for Canada.

FIVE

Trenches and Clouds

It is a land of death. It seems every trip safely made is a feat.—William
T. Martin, ambulance driver

As German soldiers enforced the occupation of Belgium in 1914, they faced a kind of asymmetrical warfare that had nettled their determination in the Franco-Prussian War of 1870–1871. They could prevail in confrontation with regulars of the occupied nation, but it was the irregulars that plagued them. The aggressive actions of a random citizen with a rifle were a dangerous nuisance, and, further, such people had the temerity to operate outside the traditional rules of war. During the Franco-Prussian War the Germans came to call these people franc-tireurs (free-shooters) or mavericks. In 21st century parlance they might have been called guerrillas. In Belgium, the Germans found that the franc-tireurs were increasingly trained sharpshooters, and their response to the problem led to atrocities in which whole villages could be destroyed on the suspicion of one such irregular among the population. Innocent civilians could be lined up and shot. This German response was credited with the revival of the use of the pejorative term "Hun," which derived from the excesses of Attila the Hun in the fifth century. Kaiser Wilhelm II had anecdotally reprised it in his command to his troops in the Boxer Rebellion to seek out vengeance: "Let the Germans strike fear into the hearts, so he'll be feared like the Hun."

As it became aware of the American Legion developing in Canada, Germany responded with the same peevishness it had demonstrated in regard to the French Foreign Legion and its members of international descent before the war had begun. In April, *The Fatherland*, a magazine published by the German American George Sylvester Vierick, and believed to be financially assisted by Germany, laid out what could be the basis for a theory of vast conspiracy between England, Canada and certain American officials—if there was a wish to find one. "While, on the one hand," he wrote, "treasonable Tories delude young Americans with false representations, to cross the Canadian border and enlist in British regiments, that march to their doom, as they did in the Dardanelles, in Mesopotamia and Flanders, [J.P.] Morgan, England's war agent, finances the campaign ... the bankruptcy of Canada, the death or mutilation of thousands of American dupes, mean nothing to the men who are engaged in this profitable traffic in human blood."[1]

Vierick's anger extended from the young American men of wealthy families who could do "gentlemen's service" in airplanes that flew high above the trenches full of "London Hooligans, French Apaches, Senegal Negroes, Maori savages. Turcos, Hindoos, and the other riffraff of the armies in Flanders."[2] It was bad enough that Norman Prince of the Escadrille had not been arrested for treason when he returned to the U.S. after its formation, but he was the son of a Boston banker and Wall-Street financier. As for the American Legion: "...in Canada capitalists can no longer coerce men to go to war, and it is only here that the attempt to gather cannon food for England's army is being pressed with despairing efforts as the last hope and resource for the dying Empire of Great Britain."[3]

Germany had already tried and executed a civilian British sea captain, alleged to have rammed a submarine with his ship, on franc-tireur charges in July. In August, American newspapers reported a letter of obscure origin that had first appeared in a German newspaper that said, in part, "We are waging no war with the United States, but North Americans whom we encounter with arms in their hands ought to be treated as franc-tireurs and shot."[4] Whatever their origins, the words were taken seriously enough that they could be ridiculed by Captain Asa Minard of the 237th Battalion. "He must first catch his fish before he fries it," he said, adding that the legionnaires would have no qualms about taking their chances with "Fritz."[5]

Despite that confidence, the story of the legion would not go smoothly in the following months. A question of its identity seemed to set the tone. At the time the legion was preparing to leave Canada for Flanders, the American government suggested to England through diplomatic back channels that the battalions should not have the name "American Legion." And certainly it should not appear on the insignias and badges they would wear to war. The American government was neutral in the conflict in fact and in name. The suggestion from America was converted into an order from Great Britain to the militia in Canada that the term be removed from the lexicon of American volunteer recruitment. Henceforth, the American battalions would be known officially only by their numbers. Unofficially, however, the name lingered in common usage well into the war and would continue to be used as a recruiting tool to assure Americans that they would joining with their own countrymen.

James Frederick Kennedy wore the original version of the American Legion badge. It depicted George Washington's coat of arms laid over a Canadian maple leaf. Subsequent versions would have to remove the name "American Legion" (courtesy Glenn Hyatt).

As the legion/97th Battalion developed in Toronto it became occasion for the joining of other kinds of forces from Canada and the United States. In early April, it was reported that the Toronto Arena would hold what was described as the Great Moving-Picture Ball, hosted by the Motion-Picture Exhibitors of Toronto. Its featured guests were the American silent movie stars and romantic partners Beverly Bayne and Francis X. Bushman. Guard of honor for the two was to be provided by a squad of fifty members of the legion, which would also perform an exhibition drill. With dancing and other entertainments, the Arena's 6,000 seats were expected to be filled, and its boxes would hold political and military dignitaries.

By May, the New York Times reported that 16,000 Americans were already at the front and scattered about in any number of Canadian units, and the rate of American enlistments was accelerating.[6] But, as always, the specific number of Americans in the CEF would remain elusive. In the same month, other aspects of the American Legion story brought forth the number of Americans involved as 6,000. Canadian engagement in the war had been accompanied by the development of the Canadian Patriotic Fund devoted to assistance for military families, and the fund noted that financial aid would be sent to the American families of 6,000 men. In June, the 213th American Legion Battalion in Toronto put forth a plea to the government for financial assistance to be used for recruiting. "We gave the United States aid during the civil war," said Captain (the Rev.) D.B. Nelson of the 213th, "and now they are trying to pay back the debt. We have only 6000 Americans in the Canadian army."[7] In June and July of 1915, the 213th managed to enlist more than 300 Americans, noting that none had been actively recruited from the American side of the border and all had paid their own expenses to get there and join up.

It was certain, though, that some recruiting within the U.S. was taking place. As the summer progressed, more recruiting offices opened in smaller Canadian cities, often targeted at the populations of close-by American locations. In June, a Canadian army captain was indicted in Seattle for recruiting for the legion in contravention of neutrality laws. It followed on a dust-up involving the *New York Sun* and the *Raleigh News and Observer* earlier in the year. The Raleigh paper, owned by Navy Secretary Josephus Daniels, had published a full-page advertisement calling for Americans to cross the border and join the legion. Daniels learned about the ad in an article in the *Sun*, and sent off a blunt telegram to his managing editor: "I am astounded that you should ever have permitted such a thing to appear. Never let such a thing happen again."[8]

Vague reporting of the defections of newly minted legionnaires also confused the numbers. In July, the *Toronto Star* reported that scores of Americans were crossing back over the border to fight in the ongoing Punitive Expedition, but were being refused by U.S. army recruiters in Niagara Falls. In September, a number of them showed up at the border with the complaint that they were badly treated by Canadians in the 213th Battalion who attributed to them the same qualities they attributed to an America that wouldn't join the fight. "I ran away," said Medical Sergeant Clarence Warner of Detroit, "because the Canadians were always yelling 'too proud to fight, and peace at any price' at us Americans and always despising us generally."[9] Warner also complained that promises to be sent to the front were not being fulfilled and many thought that they ought to be back in America where they could be more effective. Some deserters were described as opportunists who had gone to Canada to find shelter in a military camp over the winter months, now leaving in the warmer months, and especially before they were sent off to fight.

These kinds of problems would continue for the legion and eventually prove fatal. But in August of 1915 most had been moved to Nova Scotia for training in Digby and the militia camp at Aldershot. An appeal for recognition for the men came in a letter to the editor of the *New York Times* from a citizen of Maine.

> They have no home towns to fall back on for little comforts, as do the Canadian regiments, and not enough Americans know of the work to send them sums for tobacco, chocolate, or even for yarn to be knitted into warm things while in the trenches. If any of you readers who care to help out with this work will communicate with Colonel Charles Bullock, Digby N.S., 237th Battalion, I am sure they can find out more to interest them. At present the battalion is striving to raise a sufficient sum to have a band to take overseas with them. If you were to die for a cause would you not wish sweet music as you did the job? I would.[10]

In September, Germany spoke up again about the legion, but this time in a more philosophical manner. The *Toronto Star* reported on a taunting editorial in the *Koinische Zeitung* of Cologne. It noted the legion with a strength of 6,000 and soon to be 20,000 and said that if there were to be such a thing as the legion, accompanied by munitions sales to the Allies, the U.S. "should carry their opinions to the logical conclusion and take the field against us.... We hope to see the Terrible Teddy Roosevelt in command, otherwise the American Legion will be incomplete."[11]

Halifax was the northernmost port in North America. A few years earlier it had been the source of heroic work upon the sinking of the RMS *Titanic*, and in 1917 it would be nearly destroyed in the most devastating man-made explosion in history up to that point. In September 1916, its streets were filled with soldiers and sailors waiting there for the ships that would take them east. It was described as a cheerful town, but it was fortified for any eventuality and its harbor was fully mined. A submarine net stretched across the harbor entrance, and heavy guns lined the coastline. The British White Star Liners that had once taken passengers and immigrants from England to New York and back were now painted gray and moving between Halifax, Liverpool, London, Le Havre or Bordeaux every 17 days. The four-stack RMS *Olympic*, sister to the *Titanic*, for example, was now *Transport Twenty-Eight Ten*. Each of those trips that fall and early winter carried various numbers of the 97th, 212th and 237th Battalions. One of them, described in a report that was syndicated in American newspapers in December, held 7,000 men including one full battalion (by Canadian military standards) of 1,250 Americans, an unnamed, retired U.S. military officer second in command, and proud to be so.[12]

As the American Legionnaires were beginning their journeys to war, the Americans of the French Foreign Legion and the American Escadrille had long since distinguished themselves in battle, suffered their losses and received the continuing honors of their allies.

Late in 1915, James E. Kelly of New York City began a public search for his son Russell, also known, through letters home to his parents published in the *New York Sun*, as "Kelly of the Foreign Legion." Kelly had set off from New York to France on a horse transport ship in November 1914. He told his parents that the 600 horses destined for the French army had been better treated and fed than the crew of 30, of which he was one. From the ship's landing in Bordeaux, he and three of his fellows made their way to the offices of the Foreign Legion. After a rigorous physical examination, he was given five francs—the equivalent of one dollar—and a ticket to Lyons.

The days began with Reveille at 5:30, a cup of coffee, and drilling until a heavy lunch at 10:30. That was followed by potato peeling and more drilling until 4:30. Dinner was next, followed by free time until inspection and lights out at 9:30. Eventually, the training was sufficient that the call went out for those who would volunteer for the front, but Kelly was turned back because he had not had the four sequential and difficult inoculations against a severe form of typhoid that was lethal in the trenches. Kelly described the social life of the post as free flowing, with an expected development of friendships and conflicts between men from various stations in life, countries, cultures and languages. The official language was French, and those who did not understand it had to figure things out for themselves, or with the help of friends.

In February 1915, the move began to the front and the corps was divided by groups of nationalities. Kelly's group included Americans, Belgians, Swedes, Romanians, Italians, British and one Egyptian. Rations included one glass of wine each day. Time spent in the intermediate stop of Noisy-le-Sec was good and the place was pleasant. But the sound of battle could be heard from the other side of a nearby mountain range. Life in the region was good but hard. The most able-bodied men were gone and it fell to the women, children and elderly to tend the vineyards and farms. Then, in March, the men of the Foreign Legion were marched into the war, through torched countryside and towns that had been reduced to dust and rubble, and into the trenches. They were uncomfortable, but not much fighting took place, and, after a time, the group was marched back to Noisy-le-Sec for R and R. 'Well, mother," wrote Kelly, "I am nearly a full-fledged soldier now. You would be surprised to know how glad I am to be where I am."[13]

So it went. Return to the trenches and return to "repose," as he called it. Highlights of the time, at least those he reported to his parents, were an Italian fellow who ate carefully cooked trench rats electively rather than out of necessity, and a bath he was able to take in April. He had befriended another American, Kenneth Weeks, and the two of them were able to meet local families that would invite them for family meals. In May, the legionnaires moved on to Arras and into more dangerous territory, packed up in freight cars for a 24-hour journey toward the Second Battle of Artois. The action was intended to begin the recovery of Vimy Ridge from the Germans, and to keep them occupied so that they would be less effective on the Russian front. Fighting became trench-to-trench and death came in larger numbers, immediate and randomly. Artillery fire was ceaseless. The squad lived without water for two days. All of the officers were killed or wounded.

In June, Kelly and the others, including six Americans fighting with him learned of the sinking of the *Lusitania* the previous month. In his last full letter home, Kelly wrote "We would like to see the United States keep out of the war if it can."[14] A brief postcard dated June 15 from a place unknown said that all was well and he would write soon. Then he disappeared. The letters home stopped. He did not show up on the rolls of the dead, and the legion could not account for his whereabouts.

At the time of his enlistment, Kelly's father had warned him of the claim by Germany that any captured member of the Foreign Legion who was not a citizen of the country they were fighting would be executed. His advice to his son was to not state his nationality if captured, and to claim the right to speak with the American Ambassador in Paris. Because Kelly was a public figure through the publication of his letters in a New York newspaper, interest in his disappearance, and in the stories of Americans in the Foreign Legion, was intensified.

The date of Kelly's last postcard was a day of extraordinary preparation for the attempt to take a strategic hill—number 119 near Souchez—in the Second Battle of Artois. The legionnaires were each given 100 extra rounds of ammunition to complement the 250 rounds they carried on their belts. New underwear and shirts would lessen the chance of contracting tetanus if they were wounded. A special mass was held for the Catholics among them, and time was taken for the writing of special instructions and letters in the event of their deaths. Kelly's postcard was a product of that effort. When opened after death, at least one such sealed letter of instructions would reveal its writer's true identity and name, and address of his wife. Due to deaths by friendly fire earlier in the battle, many knapsacks were replaced by pieces of white muslin sewn to their uniforms to distinguish them from the enemy.

Kelly's First Regiment included several other Americans, a few of whom had already distinguished themselves as young men, including Kenneth Weeks, a graduate of the Massachusetts Institute of Technology, architecture student at the Beaux Arts Paris, and writer of several plays and volumes of poetry. Paul Rockwell of Asheville, North Carolina, the brother of American Escadrille flyer Kiffin Rockwell, would become a commander of the French Legion of Honor, recipient of three French Croix de Guerre for valor in both world wars and the Rif War between Spain and France and Moroccan Rifs in the 1920s. He would end his military career as a colonel in the U.S. Army Air Force.

On the morning of June 16, 1915, the regiments rose out of their trenches on ladders. Kelly's battalion was the first to go. Meeting machine guns and rifles, a large number fell before reaching a first line of previously abandoned German trenches. After reorganizing, they charged to the second line of occupied trenches. Many were lost and those that had gotten through would have to engage in hand to hand fighting. It was here, or in the next advance, that Kenneth Weeks was lost, and Kelly received a wound to the shoulder that was not deemed to be serious. The trenches were captured and those remaining set out for the third line of trenches, which was also captured. Past the trenches, the regiments of the legion pushed along the road to Arras and took the hill on the southern outskirts of Souchez. Then they fought a mile east of Souchez, toward Givenchy, but the Germans were able to surround them and cut off their reinforcements. An initial group of 500 was able to hold out against surrounding fire until the next day, but those remaining were finally captured. Each of their officers was killed, but they had advanced two miles. Kelly's name was listed at first as a casualty of Givenchy, but later reports said that might not be the case.

A result of the battle was an increased public awareness of the extent of American participation in the French Foreign Legion, the descriptions of who these men were, and utter confusion as to which of them were, dead, alive, missing or captured. The task of sorting it all out fell to a growing number of people and organizations on both sides of the conflict, ranging from the American embassies in Paris and Berlin to the German War Office and the International Red Cross. It wasn't until six months after the fact that everyone who had been lost was ultimately found either dead or alive, except for Russell Kelly. It was believed that he had been captured, and his father's fear was that he had been executed.

It was then that the small human scale of war emerged in a letter from a woman in England to the Kelly family in America. She had received a letter from a relative that told of four soldiers, including Kelly posing as French, who had been hiding within the German lines since the battle of Souchez. Kelly carried a bad head wound, and they were being supported and fed by French peasants. The woman was credible and there seemed to be corroborating evidence for the story. Then, in January, an officer of the legion reported that he had seen Kelly as a prisoner in Belgium. He was missing a leg and guarding his true American identity, in keeping with a supposed plan by all Americans in the legion to destroy all uniform markings, abandon all printed materials and assume false names if they were in danger of capture.

Kelly's appearance in Belgium might have followed another scenario. Those few legionnaires who survived the battle at Souchez then ended up in the Second Battle of Champagne in September in which nearly 150,000 French were lost. In mid–January, James Kelly received a letter from the French government telling him that "your son is honorably missing. Was seen in German trench with bullet in shoulder." It was reported that the letter was seen by James Kelly "as sufficient evidence that his boy died as an American should."[15] His military record showed him still missing in May 1917, and he was never found living or dead.

Whoever they really might have been, and whether they were dead or alive, the French government took a number of occasions throughout the war to honor Americans who fought on behalf of the French people. The deaths of the American Legionnaires at Souchez, Givenchy and Champagne did not go unnoticed and on May 30, 1916, the American Memorial Day, a memorial service was held on what is now Rue de Lubeck in Paris, halfway between the Eiffel Tower and the Arc de Triomphe.

The relationship between the Marquis de Lafayette and George Washington had long been celebrated in Paris in Le Place des États-Unis with a statue of the two shaking hands beneath a stand of their two flags. The statue had been commissioned from Frédéric Bartholdi by the American publisher Joseph Pulitzer, and, on this day, was covered in Garlands of flowers. In attendance, along with dignitaries of both nations, were Lt. William Thaw, representing the American Escadrille, and A. Piatt Andrew of the American Ambulance. Legion member Alan Seeger was to have read a poem he had written for the event, but had not been able to attend, and it was read by someone else.

"Ode in Memory of the American Volunteers Fallen for France," excerpted:

> Ay, it is fitting on this holiday,
> Commemorative of our soldier dead,
> When—with sweet flowers of our New England May
> Hiding the lichened stones by fifty years made gray—
> Their graves in every town are garlanded,
> That pious tribute should be given too
> To our intrepid few
> Obscurely fallen here beyond their seas.[16]

The American poet Alan Seeger left behind a literature of the duty of war and sacrifice in the face of aggression. He died in battle July 4, 1916, perhaps at his own hand after receiving mortal wounds (French Foreign Legion).

The names of 11 Americans who had died in the fighting thus far were read, including those of Russell Kelly, Kenneth Weeks and John Earl Fike, whose instructions to be opened upon his death had changed his true identity from "John Smith."

Six months later, a less symbolic but more thorough consideration of the role of Americans in the war was held in the amphitheater of the Sorbonne. It was intended as "the first of a series of meetings which will carry through this country to civilians and to soldiers at the front the story of what America has done for France during the war."[17]

Former war minister Alexandre Millerande reminded his audience of American generosity, and the sacrifice of time and life by hundreds of Americans fighting for France.

> There will forever remain sheltered, under the mingled folds of the Stars and Stripes and the red, white and blue of the French flag, and preserved in the annals of the two countries the names of the young American heroes who have fallen gloriously on the field of battle as aviators, as soldiers of the Foreign Legion or in succoring the wounded.[18]

The list given of American and French organizations working together for France went on endlessly, and the names of prominent Americans who gave their support to the alliance by letter to the meeting included Teddy Roosevelt, Thomas Edison and Mrs. W.K. Vanderbilt. But the focus of appreciation was given to those same men of the legion and American Escadrille who had been honored at the Place des Etas Unis, to which now was added the name of Alan Seeger. He had not been able to obtain leave to read his poem on Memorial Day, and died near Belloy-en-Santerre on the Fourth of July.

By that time, the American Escadrille was receiving the same attention to its name that had led to the loss of the name American legion for the 97th Battalion. The American State Department cited the same fact of American neutrality in suggesting to the French Foreign Office that the name be changed. It placed the United States in an "embarrassing position."[19]

Germany was once again complaining about Americans in a war not yet declared by America—or perhaps not. The press from Germany was contradictory. Many German newspapers decried the name as an indication of the crumbling of American neutrality, but the more official German Overseas News Agency, perhaps in keeping with German taunting of America to get into the war, said that the government did not see a problem with it.[20] In any case, it did not seem difficult to find a new name for the organization and, in December, it became the Lafayette Escadrille.

At the same time, the Escadrille moved to the Somme from the Verdun front. In November 1916, it had arrived from fighting at Verdun, and was working now with the French army on the Somme. The fighting at Verdun had begun in February, and the Escadrille flew into its skies in late April. Twenty-two kills of enemy planes had followed at the cost of three pilots lost, Norman Prince, Kiffin Rockwell and Victor Chapman.

The Battle of the Somme was an offensive on the part of the Allies meant to severely damage the German lines. Correspondents for both the Associated Press through the *New York Times* and the London *Times* arrived at the Escadrille headquarters near Cachy in early November to find 14 Americans eager for battle by air. Their accounts were at some variance, but a synthesis is possible. The weather was bad and the clouds were low, but the French Nieuports headed out to take advantage of probably limited fighting to give their pilots the lay of the land. "They all looked to me an extraordinarily useful set of men, as fearless as the young lion cub which has been adopted as the corps' mascot, and far more modest,"[21] wrote the *Times* of London. The reference was to two lion cubs named Whisky (spelled as Whiskey in some accounts) and Soda who traveled with the Escadrille, which tended to live ostentatiously when it could, in part to mock the pitiable lives of the enemy. The Associated Press story talked of two other animals: a lion named Verdun, and "an understudy in the form of

An informal picture of the Lafayette Escadrille, ca. 1917, included the lion cubs Whisky and Soda, in a lap third from the left and standing beneath the American flag.

a big wolfhound and the two are inseparable companions."[22] At Cachy, according to the London *Times*, the fliers found themselves in a barren and drafty barracks but did their best to make it habitable with hammers and nails. And they sought out a talented French chef to prepare their meals. In the *New York Times* account, they were comfortably housed in large huts with separate bedrooms and were attended by enlisted servants.

The flyers practiced their loops and dives, and skimmed the treetops, just out of reach of the puffs of smoke on the horizon that indicated German attempts to shoot them down. The article described the flying strategies of the two opponents. If the German flyers targeted the important French observation planes and their protective layer of chaser planes, they would fly above them in two layers. The Escadrille flyers would then rise above them all to bear down on the Germans, "a formidable, if small, addition to the air-strength of our Allies."[23]

Escadrille commander Lt. Vol. Georges Thenault described a code of battle:

1. Never attack without looking behind you.
2. Attack a single seater from behind and above, then break the combat by a "chandelle [180 degree turn while rising]," and *always maintain a superiority of altitude.*"
3. Attack a two-seater by getting under its tail in the "dead" angle formed by the stabilizator, and stay there to prevent him taking you unawares.
4. Fly always waving around and break combat when expedient by a clever "renversement [rising up from rear attack to get ahead of the target and turn to face it for re-engagement]."[24]

The daily drill for the flyers, weather permitting, was two two-hour flights. Takeoffs were at 30-second intervals until all had reached an altitude of 10,000 feet for patrol above the French lines. Their mission was restricted to fighting rather than participating in observation and reconnaissance.

The Escadrille did not have much opportunity to use its skills at the Somme. The following winter allowed little flying, and by February 1917 Germany had withdrawn back to the important Hindenburg Line. But the flow of Americans to France to join the air war continued, and those who were qualified were accommodated by the creation of a larger Lafayette Flying Corps.

The honors given by France in the two Paris events of 1916 also included American ambulance drivers who arrived with their new vehicles in a constant flow to French seaports. They traveled deeper into the country in convoys, past farmers in their fields and abandoned trenches. Occasionally they encountered enemy fire or gas. The roads they took were either nicely paved or impossibly rutted. At bridges and railroad crossings they had to stop and show authorization. At night they formed tight parking formations in farmyards and slept in the stretchers that would carry the dead and wounded. The convoys served to cement égalité between Americans and the French troops and civilians.

One of those drivers, William T. Martin of Burlington, N.J., had received the Croix de Guerre for one tour of service, and returned for another that he described in the *New York Sun.*

> It is a land of death. It seems every trip safely made is a feat. From the base the road leads among innumerable shell holes. As they are filled up by troops fresh ones are made. Shells of all sizes burst in front of the cars, behind and on both sides.... Through them and on runs the road. It is a steep hill. No military vehicles are allowed to go further. The only cars now allowed to proceed are the ambulances of the Americans. They go up the hill in low gear. Their progress is slow and laborious.[25]

The path leads to the top of the hill and a stretch beneath shells that are still flying back and forth between the combatants. Past the blackened sticks of burned trees, "dead men's woods," the scores of dead men and horses are unreachable under ceaseless firing, the road leads to a fort surrounded by trenches, stone gates and bridges that have been repeatedly shelled into pieces and rebuilt. The press of bodies of those who had been protecting the fort grows larger. The final turn leads through a tunnel.

"When the driver finally arrives here he feels he has reached safety with an overwhelming sense of relief. All the way up it has been his consuming idea to get here. He now finds himself worrying about how to get back."[26] But there is a relatively unprotected courtyard to get across, then another tunnel. The ambulance arrives at its front while the injured flow from the trenches into the back. The blasts of nearby shells often let loose percussive waves within the tunnels. Needed artificial light comes in the form of smoky gasoline fires that mix with the smell of damaged bodies and powerful anesthetics. If the return to base is driven by night, it is steered by memory and surrounding sound and the occasional flash of light from exploding shells.

William T. Martin's descriptions of driving through battlefields for the American Field Service offered a stark narrative of fear that could only be ignored if one was to save lives (American Field Service).

As the 97th Battalion sailed away from Halifax toward fighting in the Somme it became, at least, better covered in the American press, but with reporting that it had become "lost" on one hand, and mired in scandal on another. Then a legal decision was made that, by leaving America for war, its members would be expatriated.

Newspaper headlines seemed to imply that the 97th had literally disappeared, but the term "lost," as it was applied to a group of Americans in another uniform who had gone off to fight a war undeclared by their own country, was more abstract. Among those who defected from the battalion before it would leave Toronto for war was one unidentified American who got the attention of the press by calling the group a lost legion "composed of tramps who deserted wholesale when it came time to sail."[27] The term stuck as the battalion crossed the ocean and seemed to fulfill the expectations of those who waited to fight alongside them on the other side. Nor did their arrival seem to be gloriously received, and they passed their first weeks in tents burdened by rain and built on muddy ground.

At the same time Captain Asa Minard, who had taken charge of the legion's financial affairs was accused of embezzling its funds. The charges came from another American who had worked into the British command through deft self-promotion as a wounded officer. It was soon learned that his wounds were the result of an accident while showing off his gun in his London flat, and the charges disappeared. But the effect of the two lies took its toll on the perceptions of the former American Legion from without, and of morale from within. Then an old, nagging question arose once again: were the members of the former American Legion still Americans?

The moves to erase the American references from the names of the legion and the Escadrille had come of "suggestions" by the American government, but they were related to a more problematic decision by the United States State Department. Theodore Marburg, Jr., was a prominent young man of Baltimore and son of the former U.S. Minister to Belgium. Theodore Marburg, Sr. was generally not in favor of American participation in foreign conflicts, but in the matter of the German invasion of Belgium he was vehement. "The cruel way in which devoted little Belgium is being trampled to death simply because it lay in the path of a war-mad government makes one's blood boil," he had written in a statement issued upon stepping off the *Lusitania* and a return trip from Europe.[28]

> Only force will avail. She must be beaten to her knees to stem this flow of barbarism, to free the German masses from the grip of the bureaucracy and ruthless class, and to arrest militarism itself.... What we have witnessed is as nothing compared to what is to come if Germany wins out. And America will not only share the added burdens which will be placed on the shoulders of all nations, but will be open to the dangers of actual attack by men of boundless ambition and inhuman callousness. England is fighting our battle.[29]

His son agreed. He was attending Oxford University at the time, and entered the Royal Flying Corps at the outset of the war. One of his first missions was observation photography over the German lines, but mechanical failure crashed his plane on the way and he lost his leg. After convalescence in Baltimore, he set about to return to the Flying Corps, but the State Department refused to issue him a new passport. The Department maintained that Americans who had taken an oath of allegiance to the British Crown had broken their allegiance to America and, in fact, had expatriated themselves. It was not possible for State to issue passports to non–Americans.

The tortuous path to a correct answer to the question of American citizenship for those who fought with foreign forces was only more confused by Marburg's case. It seemed to be a bureaucratic response to an overriding human impulse to fight in war for various reasons, and it contained exceptions. Members of the French Foreign Legion would only have the burden of proving they had not taken an oath to another nation before being allowed to continue citizenship. The Foreign Legion oath was more ambiguous than what had been required of Americans who wished to fight with the British, including members of the American Legion and the thousands then fighting in other parts of the Canadian and British forces.

Further, the State Department said it would not issue passports to those wishing to go to the war, and it added a nail to its ruling. Those Americans who had expatriated themselves would only be received back in the country as alien immigrants. They would be deported if they could not support themselves, or receive the help of relatives, and if they had contracted a contagious disease.

In his own way, Marburg ignored the question of citizenship that had come to all American volunteers abroad to various degrees. He had the resources and the connections, and the papers of the Royal Flying Corps as an entrée. He returned to Europe, probably on a Holland-America ship. Steamship lines of neutral nations did not require passports of passengers who were willing to waive all risks in the crossing. In April 1916, he married his first wife, the Baroness Geselle de Vavario of Belgium at Southampton, England. In February 1922, while visiting his ranch at Magdalena, Sonora, Mexico, he shot himself in the head for unknown reasons and lingered for a week before death. His father went on to become a founding force of the League of Nations after the war.

The younger Marburg was buried in the family plot at Druid Ridge Cemetery near Baltimore, Maryland. A monument holding the statue of Icarus, who, in Greek mythology, flew too close to the sun, holds a memorial to Marburg with the crest of the Royal Flying Corps and the words:

Follow the Flag

Too long it has been absent from that line in France where once again an Attila has been stopped. And yet though not visible to the eye, it is and has been there from the beginning. It is there in the hearts of those fifty thousand American boys who saw their duty clear and moved up to it.[30]

SIX

Splendid Work

Lafayette, nous voici!—Col. Charles E. Stanton

Whatever their actual number, citizenship status and sworn allegiances, the American boys who went to war while their own country remained in place at the western shore of the Atlantic Ocean suffered all the hardships of war and sometimes made the ultimate sacrifice. For the most part, their stories were little known in their own time and surprising when discovered in the following decades.

One autumn day in 1999, military historian Glenn Hyatt was rummaging through a weekend flea market in the southwestern Virginia town of Dublin. Hard up against the Thomas Jefferson National Forest and the West Virginia line, Dublin is about 60 miles on a path that partially follows the New River through the town of Narrows, Virginia, from the town of Princeton, West Virginia. At the time of World War I, Princeton was a coalfield and railroad town on the route between the coal piers of the East Coast and the markets of the inland west.

In Dublin, Hyatt purchased an old trunk full of papers and military miscellany that had come from Princeton. He found the World War I history of a family that had long since disappeared from its address in West Virginia, and the letter written by James Frederick Kennedy to his mother on the letterhead of the Canadian YMCA. Its assurance to his mother that he would be fine would not prove out in the end, but his path from Princeton to its conclusion would mark him as just another young man trying to find his way in the world as it was, and with a measure of grace, eventually to be forgotten.

Kennedy lived with three brothers and a sister at 108 College Street in Princeton. His father, Steven, was a machinist in the railroad shops, but his health wasn't good and the work wasn't steady. His sons learned the same trade in the shops, and, in 1915, James headed out on his own to find work that would help support his family. He carried with him a letter of reference from his superintendent at the Virginia Railway Company listing his skills with the conclusion, "We have found him while to be in our employment, very attentive to his duties and a capable man."[1] He was 19 years old. The work was hard to find and eventually he ended up at the confluence of wartime Canada and neutral America: Detroit, Michigan, and Windsor, Ontario, which faced each other across the Detroit River.

Living at the Detroit YMCA, he was able to earn $0.35 an hour making cannon shells. Though he was injured on the job at one point, he managed to send money home. As Canada's part in the war figured increasingly in the social and economic life of Detroit-Windsor, Kennedy crossed the river and enlisted in the 97th Battalion on January 8, 1916,

James Kennedy's position at the center of this photograph was noted in pencil near the bottom by his mother (courtesy Glenn Hyatt).

volunteering as a machine gunner. He listed his birthplace as West Virginia, his residence as Bay City, Michigan, his mother as next of kin and his religious denomination as the Church of England. His signed oath was to "be faithful and bear true Allegiance to His Majesty King George the Fifth, His Heirs and Successors." He was on the troop ship carrying the 97th when it left Halifax, and among the figurative "lost" after it arrived in Europe. The scraps of newspapers about the "lost legion" found in the trunk from Princeton showed that his mother was playing close attention to the fortunes of her son.

The 97th Battalion was never actually "lost," and it wasn't too long before it was "found." The young war correspondent J.W. Pegler, who would become the controversial columnist Westbrook Pegler during World War II, was perhaps the only named journalist of the war paying attention to the American Legion. Both in his own name and in an un-bylined dispatch from the United Press he reported in late November 1916 that the legion had been found both in Germany and in England. In Germany, "Two drafts of real Americans already are at death grips with the Germans on the Somme."[2] But in England, the men waited beneath tents in rain and mud for deployment in the war and mulled over an enemy they had left behind in Canada.

> The men enlisted to fight Germans—but if any survivors ever get back to American they will settle a grudge with a deserter who gave his pals a black eye in the American newspapers. The correspondent found in the camp a determination to find the ex-legionnaire and beat him within an inch of his life.[3]

As presented by Pegler, the men in England couldn't get over the betrayal by one of their number who had deserted and publicly referred to them as tramps, "A yellow parlor soldier." But the battalion seemed ultimately unable to overcome the slander, combined as it was with the loss of its American name. Though its members would hang together loosely in the fighting to come as an American Legion they found themselves subject to other needs of the Canadian Expeditionary Forces. They would soon be scattered to the Princess Pats, the CEF 38th Battalion, and the Royal Canadian Regiment, among many other destinations.

By early 1917, American newspapers were already telling the stories of American Legion members returning wounded to their hometowns, though they may have been applying the legion name to any American fighting with the British. The *Renwick (Iowa) Times* of January 25, 1917, told of F.G. Petersen of Des Moines who had returned from 22 months with the British army in Belgium, Verdun and the Dardanelles. His left leg and hand had been shot away and he was blind in one eye. "He declared that reports of the war are exaggerated— that the fighting is not nearly as fierce, nor the fatalities so great as reported."[4] The same newspaper reported on two Iowans preparing to go to France for service in the American Ambulance.

A February article that was widely distributed in American small-town newspapers estimated that 40,000 Americans were fighting in Europe at the time but that their true number and their deeds abroad would probably never be fully known. Unlike most reporting on the subject, however, the article was quick to point out that there were some Americans fighting on the German side, and there would probably be more if they could get through an effective British blockade. Most of the Americans abroad were in the Canadian Corps, and, the article asserted, there may have been more Americans than Canadians in the first contingent sent to war. "They died by the score when the Germans used gas for the first time—in the so-called second battle of Ypres."[5]

In February, *The United Press* asked Lord Northcliffe for an assessment of Americans fighting in France. Alfred Charles William Harmsworth, First Viscount Northcliffe, was among the most influential of British voices during the war, the appointed Director for Propaganda, a founding force in tabloid journalism, and publisher of the London *Times*, which carried his account of the Americans fighting with the Canadian army in France.

They were comparable, in Lord Northcliffe's estimation (and perhaps keeping in mind his position as Director for Propaganda), to the American contributions to warfare by the invention of the Wright Brothers' airplane, the Lewis machine gun and Boston Baked Beans. That the world was topsy-turvy, according to Lord Northcliffe, was demonstrated when he saw them marching back from the trenches singing "My Country Tis of Thee," and "The Star Spangled Banner." German complaints about the Americans as hired guns were noted, along with the "princely" salaries of $1.25 per day designed to attract the best of American men, graduates of its best universities and sons of its richest families.

Those preliminary observations made, Northcliffe offered perhaps the most succinct description of what these American men brought to the spirit of the war against Germany.

> While most of the newspaper dispatches from the French and English newspapers are full of the word "peace," these husky young American citizens will not hear of it. "To h— with peace talk," said a bright-eyed boy from Kansas City, "while those slantheads across the line there are enslaving French and Belgian women and children. There would be none of this peace business at home if the people there knew the facts." On New Year's Day the Boche soldiers put out boards saying, "Why not have a peace talk?" The reply of the whole Allied line was an artillery bombardment which clenched the question.[6]

The reference to peace was to a German refrain for an end to the war now that it had accomplished its goals, and a consideration of the idea by some in the Allied countries. That sense of determination on the part of the Americans, along with their British and French comrades, was described under the sub-head AN ARMY THAT THINKS.

> They had brought to the stock of vitality and knowledge embraced in the wonderful citizen Armies of France and England the qualities inherited by the generations which have spanned the North American Continent with its railroads, chained Niagara, linked up the world's cities and armies by telephone, lit the dugouts with incandescent lamps, cheered then with canned music, and brought a thousand other mechanical ideas to perfection.
>
> If you take a map of the United States and go up and down the American lines in France, you will find no city, great or small, which has not sent a flying man, a bomber, an artilleryman, a sniper, or dispatch rider to help to destroy Prussian despotism.[7]

The article by Lord Northcliffe was followed in the newspaper column by a separated small dispatch reporting the death of Second Lieutenant George Clement Winstanley, aged 36, whose father had preceded him in death Omaha, Nebraska (though records of the Somerset Light Infantry, of which he was a member, showed his birthplace as London).

In March, the article was followed by an event in London that was addressed by Northcliffe and the American journalist Isaac Marcosson, a biographer and supporter of General James Wood, who he deemed "The Prophet of Preparedness."[8] The gathering was said to be the largest ever in the history of the American Luncheon Club at the Savoy Hotel, with 500 in attendance representing both nations and meeting with the tacit expectation that America would soon be entering the war. Lord Northcliffe referred to the time spent with Americans he had reported upon in the February article, and asserted that their prowess and achievement had gone too little remarked upon. The claim was met by the cheers of the room, and followed by yet another estimate of how many Americans were involved.

The great fact is that more than 50,000 young Crusaders have crossed the Atlantic to join an Army in which they are not fighting for King or country, but against what they realize to be the curse of the world at this moment—the attempt of the Germans to dominate Europe and then America. (Cheers.) In seeing these Americans one gets some idea of what the American Army in being would be like.[9]

At the time, there were many in America who thought of peace with Germany though their country was not officially at war, and the drumbeat for an American declaration of war was getting louder, as was the anticipation of what that might mean for Americans already fighting in Europe. Public sentiment began to turn toward war, and, in some respects, the American Legion, still referred to by its old name, was already in place as a bridge between neutrality and war. And the notion of a debt owed to France was still in active in the discussion.

In February, the newspaper of the mid-sized Ohio city of Massillon editorialized about the friendship with France that had been opened with the treaty signed by Benjamin Franklin in 1778 and continued with its unselfish assistance in the Revolutionary War.

We have never repaid that debt. We could never repay it ...
    Different as we are in temperament and culture, we are alike in our instinct for freedom. "As soon as the soldiers of Washington and Rochambeau met, they understood one another." [Quoting words of the World War I French ambassador to the U.S. Jean Jules Jusserand] It has been like that with our American Legion that is fighting in France today. It will be like that if we send new legions over.[10]

On April 1, 1917, a newspaper of America's largest city editorialized for an end to the debate and a firm decision to go to war. The *New-York Tribune* likened the decision to that made by the forefathers to fight for independence from the British. The issues involved, in its view, were no less than those that informed the American Revolutionary and Civil Wars and the French Revolution. But American leadership and its statesmen had fallen short of the challenge in the present situation, so the decision must be made individually.

The decision is the decision which each American citizen must make for himself. Patriotism is, after all, personal. The stream will not rise above the source, nor the nation above its people. What America does to-day depends now upon what we are.[11]

The same *Tribune* page imported a short editorial from the *Philadelphia Inquirer* that estimated 26,000 American boys had enlisted in the Canadian army through the American Legion and other battalions. The officer corps of the United States military was not prepared for war, in its view, and it would be beneficial if the British and Canadians released the best of the American Legion to be commissioned in the U.S. army. They would bring training and experience worth more than four years at West Point. A transaction between the United States and Canada had been concluded: 20,000 Canadians had served in the U.S. Civil War and now a similar amount of Americans had fought for Canada. Now "the need of officers is great, and the American Legion boys have had the finest education in the world for present emergencies."[12]

As America got closer to war, the same voices that had preached preparedness in the past were speaking loudly once again. On the evening of March 20, 1917, the Union League Club of New York City heard from former President Teddy Roosevelt, Nobel Peace Prize winner Elihu Root, 1916 Republican candidate for president Charles E. Hughes and others that America was already at war, but with a dearth of trained men to fight it. "We are terribly unprepared," said Roosevelt, "but we must prepare at once a great army of a couple of million men, so that if the war lasts for a year we will be able to be the decisive and controlling factor in it." American diplomat George Choate warned that just as the nation was already at war with a Germany that had sunk its ships and murdered its citizens, it wasn't prepared to defend itself. "If we go to war with Germany our only real protection will be the ships of the British and French navies, and our own navy, which is undermanned."[13]

At the same time, an American conflation with British forces was seemingly rounded out with the announcement of the creation of a British brigade to be created in the United States. Modeled in part on the American Legion and headquartered in the Hotel Collingwood on New York's West 35th Street, it would sign up British citizens living in the U.S. for mobilization upon the expected declaration of war. Its potential members were characterized as British with history and family in America, anxious to show allegiance to the American flag.

The brigade was the ambition of Lt. Col. Ivor Thord-Gray, one of the more colorful characters in British military history. By the time he had arrived in New York in 1917, he seemed to have been involved in every large and small war and conflict everywhere in the world since his birth in Stockholm, Sweden, in 1878. He joined the British army with the rank of major in 1914, and was on sick leave from the British Expeditionary Force when approached by British expatriates living in New York and asked to create a brigade that would reach out to all British in America. The goals of the brigade were set forth in a number of New York papers, but the story seemed to quickly disappear from attention and history. It was said, but could not be confirmed, that Thord-Gray had consulted with Teddy Roosevelt and wanted to name the brigade in his honor, and that President Wilson would not allow such an organization to be formed in the United States.

It was actually the case, however, that Thord-Gray was mistakenly believed by England's MI5 to have been a German spy during this time, and that one late night in a Manhattan restaurant he challenged a group of American marksmen to a competition between their guns and his bow and arrow, and subsequently won the match.

Among those Americans of the 97th Battalion who had arrived in England only to be scattered into other fighting units was James Frederick Kennedy. When the battalion was still thought of as the American Legion, Kennedy became one of 35 members of the machine gun crew, all of them American. They were sent into the battle late in 1916 and, by the account of one of Kennedy's best friends in the group, Pvt. J.J. McMahon "we did splendid work, several of the boys winning medals and commanding praise for their work. Jimmy was the life of the regiment and the pet of the section."[14]

Kennedy and the others became members of the Royal Canadian Regiment (RCR). The RCR was (and remains) among the oldest of Canadian fighting forces. It saw its first action in the North-West Rebellion of 1885 in which a northwest aboriginal Canadian group, the Métis, rose up against perceived abuse and exploitation by the Canadian government. Eventually, with the help of the RCR, other military and police forces and the Canadian Pacific Railway, the government prevailed. In World War I, the RCR distinguished itself in the battles of Ypres of 1915 and 1917, and by the time the Americans appeared in its ranks it had just come out of the Battle of the Somme, which was designed to hold German forces in check near Arras and wear them down. The RCR's assigned task had been to attack Germany's large Regina Trench, but it suffered too many casualties and withdrew from combat. After the Somme, the RCR moved on to the battle of Vimy Ridge.

Kennedy's family did not hear from him during this time, but it can be assumed that he and his machine guns fought with continued "splendid work" through this most important of Canadian offenses. The Canadians had followed extraordinary preparations for the battle and softening up of the enemy. Their execution was forceful and effective, and surprising to the Germans. The RCR was at the leading edge of the attack and helped to attain the first goal of a 700-yard advance. The fighting intensified, with more casualties on both sides. It was the next day before the objective of Hill 145 was attained at the cost of 56 dead, 155 wounded and 65 missing (just within the RCR; total Canadian losses exceeded 3,500 dead), but the RCR had met all of its objectives and helped to win the battle. The Canadians, and presumably most or all of the Americans within their ranks, had brought about a turning point in the war, and a turning point in Canadian history. In the budget of war news, however, the Battle of Vimy Ridge, begun on April 9, had to share space with the expected American declaration of war on April 6.

The final American determination to go to war had come about as a result of all of the debate and maneuvering that had preceded it, but was precipitated by the revelation of the so-called Zimmerman telegram. The telegram was an intercepted diplomatic message from Germany to its ambassador in Mexico directing that, if it appeared the United States was about to enter the war, Mexico be promised an alliance with Germany in its continuing border conflicts with America, and the gaining of American territory when Germany prevailed in the war. Germany's goal was to divert American effort and matériel from the Allies in Europe to its own problems on the border, while Germany stepped up its submarine warfare in the Atlantic and along the American coast.

Mexico dismissed the idea. President Woodrow Wilson revealed the contents of the telegram to the American public at the same time that Germany was beginning to follow through on its plans with the sinking of several American merchant ships. The declaration of war seemed inevitable.

But now what? Despite the best efforts of those who had spent more than two years arguing for preparedness for war, the American inventory of men and matériel was limited. The U.S. army was comprised of 210,000 men, some of them occupied in Mexico, with an additional 97,000 in state reserve forces. By contrast, the Battle of the Somme earlier in the year had produced estimates exceeding 600,000 casualties on each side. Less than 20 officers were in place at army headquarters in Washington. The troubles in Mexico had already taxed resources, and the arsenal consisted mainly of 890,000 Springfield rifles. The Navy was more prepared, with almost 40 destroyers and six battleships in place by the end of the summer.[15] General John J. Pershing was sent from his command in Mexico to lead the effort in France, and, after an assessment there, he reported back that the army would need 1 million American men in France by the end of 1918—at minimum.[16] By June 1918, setbacks in the war led to an increase in Pershing's needs to 3 million men by mid–1919.[17] The number of Americans already in place upon the declaration of April 6, 1917, was minuscule by comparison, but at least they were there and, in effect, on the ground running.

July 4, 1917, American Independence Day, would be eventful in France. It had been preceded in London on April 19 with the celebration "America Day" in honor of the American declaration of war. Elaborate ceremonies and parades had flown the Union Jack and American flag in tandem. The king himself had attended, and could be seen joining in the singing of the Star Spangled Banner inside St. Paul's Cathedral. Also in attendance were Americans of the Canadian Expeditionary Force, 100 of them brought from convalescence in the hospitals of London.

The celebrations of July 4 in Paris were described by a French reporter as "the first time in the world's history the national holiday of one nation was feted in another as it was the other's own."[18] The Place des Invalides was full of the older French soldiers, "poilus well past life's meridian."

> About them, standing upon three sides of the court, stood a battalion of the Sixteenth Infantry, U.S.A., khaki-clad, youthful, sunburned, bright-eyed, typical of the energy permeating their land across the sea, typical of the great army of which they are the vanguard, of the millions that will fight the cause of France in the near future.[19]

One and a half million spectators flowed out of the Place des Invalides near the Eiffel Tower, across the bridges over the Seine and up the Champs Élysées. One of every three, by the reporter's estimate, waved an American flag, large or small, new or tattered. The American contingent of officials included General Pershing and an international businessman representing his nephew Norman Prince, the first American to be killed in the Lafayette Escadrille.

The course of the day brought the common history of France and America full circle. At Les Invalides, the lineal descendants of the three great generals of the American Revolution, Rochambeau, DeGrasse and Lafayette, offered pennants to General Pershing. A large, silk American flag was offered to the general by the residents of the town of Puy, the birthplace of Lafayette. The pastor of the American Episcopal Church in Paris presented to Pershing the American flag that had been carried since 1915 by Americans in the French Foreign Legion, "a veritable flag of history, a banner that had been baptized in blood upon thirty occasions."[20] It would remain at Les Invalides into the 21st century.

At the conclusion of ceremonies, the newly arrived Americans marched five miles

General John Pershing salutes the Marquis de Lafayette at his tomb in Paris. Though Pershing himself did not utter the words, the visit on July 4, 1917, was defined by the phrase "*Lafayette, nous voici!*" (Library of Congress).

through Paris to the old Picpus Cemetery. Their path was lined with singing children, wounded soldiers at attention, and "300 old ladies, occupants of the Etienne Home for the Aged, added their feeble heartfelt cheers."[21] They arrived at Picpus covered in roses and posies. There, as many as could be accommodated in the small cemetery gathered at the burial place of the Marquis de Lafayette. Speeches were given, and, in a statement often incorrectly attributed to Pershing, Col. Charles E. Stanton, an aide to Pershing, said "Lafayette, nous voici." Lafayette, we are here![22]

The long awaited American declaration of war had been made and acted upon, but its implications for the 15,000, 25,000 or 50,000 Americans who were already fighting the war were unclear. By some accounts they were an indeterminate number of expatriates and no longer relevant, by others they were "50,000 young crusaders." To most people they were unknown and unconsidered.

There was no ambiguity about the former "American" now "Lafayette" Escadrille, however. At the time of the American-prompted change of name for the organization, a group of women at the U.S. Treasury Department in Washington, led by the Treasury secretary's wife, had begun to sew together a new flag for the flyers. It was presented to them in a grand event on July 7, 1917. At the ceremony, the French demonstrated the esteem in which they held the Americans with a version of their army's longstanding tradition of demonstrating prominence in battle. The new American flag was surrounded on one side by the flag of their Balloon Corps and on the other by the standard of the Aviation Corps, by which placements the Americans were made the flag squadron of the French army. The ceremony was brief, and apparently a surprise to most of the Americans who were still in their flying uniforms after a recent mission. The lion cubs Whisky and Soda were described as vying for Raoul Lufberry's attention during the event before being chased away by a large police dog.[23]

The Americans of the French Foreign Legion also welcomed the American declaration with anticipation about their own roles. In early 1917, the legion had distinguished itself, particularly in the offensive in the battles of Aisne and Champagne. It had operated as "A marvelous regiment, animated by hatred of the enemy, and the highest spirit of sacrifice," in the words of the French government's award to the legion for gallantry.[24] They had fought continuously for six days and six nights, and were said to have fallen asleep standing when the battle was finished. Several Americans in the force were awarded the Croix de Guerre, and reporting asserted that every American involved wanted now to join the American army. While America was neutral, said one, they had been forced to join the legion. "Now that America is a belligerent, we all want to fight under our own flag."[25]

Another organization that returned to light with the American entrance into the war was the American Ambulance. Started in 1914 to do a job that the French army could not do well for itself, it had cared for more that 400,000 of the wounded by April 1917. It was still a service of volunteers who had to buy their own round trip fare between New York and Paris, buy their own uniforms and pay their own incidental expenses. A new ambulance, including shipping, cost about $1,000 plus operating expenses of $600 annually, an easy expenditure for civic organizations like Rotary clubs. A full section of 20 ambulances required an investment of $30,000 plus half that again for maintenance. Sections were often donated to the cause by governments and universities, like Boston, St. Louis, the state of California, the Universities of Wisconsin and Chicago, Northwestern University and Cornell University in New York.

Recruiting for the American Field Service continued without pause after April 6, 1917, and with the full endorsement of the War Department. In England, the American service was determined to be the most effective of all of them, and France had bestowed 76 Croix de Guerre on ambulance drivers. Like the other groups of Americans already in place and prepared to join the forces of their own country, the Field Service declared its readiness to join the American army. "The American ambulance field service," said one of its leaders, "is absolutely prepared and willing to lose its identity immediately and place itself under the control of the War Department of the United States."[26] Recruitment for the corps continued. The requirements included American citizenship with proof of American birth and parentage, and the references of "five or six persons of standing."

To the average American who had been fighting in the Canadian Expeditionary and British Commonwealth Forces, some since 1915, the American declaration was welcomed and long overdue. The news was said to have electrified a training camp near London where 700 American Legionnaires were in attendance. From an unnamed location in the trenches of France, a 97th Battalion soldier, Harry Norton, described his fellows as a contingent of "madmen" when they received the news. Such was their excitement that they spontaneously leapt over the top of their trenches and ran toward a German position with American flags attached to their bayonets. The enemy was surprised and off guard as the Americans jumped into German trenches and re-emerged with 50 prisoners and valuable intelligence. "The Americans were dirty and disheveled and some were very bloody from slight wounds, but they were all happy—very happy to think they had done something real to welcome Uncle Sammy into the great war."[27]

The attack was met with the cheers of their Canadian fellows in the battalion, and Norton concluded his report.

> There is a burning desire among the Canadian troops that United States troops fight alongside them. Everywhere the hope is expressed that they may stand shoulder to shoulder with the men of the Uncle Sam's army, but nowhere is the desire more keenly felt than among what is left of the American Legion.
>
> We have heard stories of how the Germans treat American prisoners. If the Americans happen to have the Stars and Stripes tattooed on their arms, the Germans cut out the tattoo marks.[28]

The question of the status of the Americans in Commonwealth forces now that America was entering the war was inevitable. The discussion had begun as soon as it became apparent that the American declaration was at hand and one of its starting points was within the Canadian army. In February 1917, the commander of the 211th Battalion, Lt. Col. W.M. Sage, wrote a letter to the 14th Canadian Infantry Training Brigade and General Headquarters suggesting that the effort be made to keep together and strengthen the 211th as a distinctly American unit. It would enhance the feeling that "they were fighting for their own country as well as for Britain, and their friends and relations in the United States of America would feel that they were fighting for them."[29]

Lt. Col. Sage pointed out in the letter that the battalion included "an all American band of professional musicians under the leadership of Mr. Chenette, a graduate of the conservatory of music and acknowledged as the finest band which has ever left Canada."[30] The reference was to one of the four members of the musical Chenette family who had enlisted in the CEF from Ames, Iowa.

A similar proposal came from C. Seymour Bullock "with the aid of influential Americans—on a scheme to transfer all Americans now fighting with the allied armies into one American fighting unit."[31] Bullock described to reporter J.W. Pegler a Canadian army unit that would wear American uniforms and carry the American flag. It was an expansion on the practice that had been in place since the beginning of the American Legion of placing an American flag pin on the inside of one's tunic. He asserted that all Americans were eager to enact such a plan, and the next step was to seek congressional support in lifting legal barriers. He also sought the return of identification of the new unit as the American Legion or something similar. In Bullock's terms, the Americans were now called the American Legation to Canadian Forces, and he reminded Pegler that the Legation had fought at Vimy Ridge with great distinction and many casualties and were "regarded by British and French alike as first class soldiers."[32]

The efforts of Lt. Colonels Sage and Bullock appear to have come to naught. But at the same time, and without much fanfare, doors were opened that would allow American men in Canadian service to transfer to American service. The Canadian Associated Press, in mentioning the American Legion standards that would be placed at St. Paul's Cathedral in London, seemed to put the information in the context that Americans were free now to leave the Canadian army for service in the American army through application at an American embassy. The permission, seemingly approved from London, would be granted to officers and infantry alike. Then, in July, the question of repatriation for these men entered the deliberations of Congress.

It was the National Geographic Society that most effectively broached the subject in a bulletin related to the war. "Are the men who have dedicated their lives to the cause which their own country has now enlisted to be barred perpetually from the privilege of American citizenship?"[33] The bulletin went on to say that the exact number of those involved could not be known, but could be estimated up to 55,000, and it pointed out the extenuating circumstances involved for some. Italian-born Americans, for example, had received notices from the Italian government that if they did not return to Italy and enlist they would be named as deserters. The confusion was the result of vague treaties between the two nations, and the challenges presented to those who received the letters were not only moral and legal, but involved with one's own self-identity.

There were many proposals in Congress, none reported to be other than compassionate, about the choices facing these Americans—or former Americans. A bill from Rep. John Jacobs Rogers of Massachusetts seemed to give a core to the argument for repatriation. Rogers referred to the challenge presented to the State Department by the Theodore Marburg case in the previous year. In his estimation there were between 40,000 and 50,000 Americans fighting with France, England and Canada who would be treated like Ellis Island immigrants when they returned to the country. The situation was "intolerable and absolutely unnecessary."[34] The Rogers bill was assumed to have the support of the State Department. It was accompanied by a bill submitted by the only woman in Congress at the time, Rep. Jeannette Rankin of Montana, that would repatriate American women who had lost citizenship by marrying foreign nationals.

What was eventually agreed to by Congress and signed into law by President Woodrow Wilson on October 5, 1917, seemed to resolve the matter fairly for all parties. Men who had enlisted in Canadian, British and French services before the U.S. declaration would still be seen as aliens, but needed only present themselves to a U.S. consulate, explain their situation and take an oath of allegiance. Seymour Bullock asserted that the law would affect 32,000 men as an official estimate. Men who joined the French Foreign Legion were not in jeopardy of loss of citizenship because they had not sworn allegiance to a foreign government. Those men who enlisted in foreign services after the declaration were not considered to be aliens because it was not legal for an American citizen to relinquish nationality during time of war; therefore they had not done so.

An undated cartoon depicts the dilemma faced by Canadian men who did not want to go to war after the official American declaration of war in April 1917. The two countries worked together to support each other's enlistment efforts (Toronto Public Library).

During the months between the final determination to go to war, realization of the dire need to develop a fighting force and quick federal action to welcome Commonwealth Forces Americans back into the national fold, a battle of another sort was unfolding somewhere on the fields of Canada and in a movie studio outside of Philadelphia. One evening in a trench in France, Captain Edwin Hesser of the 213th Battalion happened to read in a French newspaper the story of a French army officer whose wife persisted in visiting him at the front against the rules, and so had shot her dead. Hesser was a writer, producer, director of films and a famous photographer of nudes and movie stars, and head of recruiting publicity for the brigade. His commanding officer suggested that he produce a movie based on the story.

By the time the idea had been turned into a movie, it would be distributed by Goldwyn as a "patriotic spectacle," based on the story of the American Legion and grandly titled *For the Freedom of the World*. Filmed in Canadian training camps, it told the story of a wealthy young American who had joined the legion, fallen in love and married a bride who could not bear to be apart from him. She then assumes the identity of a Red Cross nurse and follows him to France, but another man who loves her turns them in and sends the star-crossed couple to certain death by firing squad for breaking the rules. To save his wife from the terror of the firing squad the young man shoots her himself, hears her profession of eternal love, and embarks on a mission that will be certain suicide. It doesn't turn out that way, of course, and the wife remarkably recovers from her wounds. They live happily ever after. Advertising for the film promised "feats of human courage almost beyond credence—how your American youth and manhood behaves under fire—how your Canadian neighbors to the north of you mobilized and went into action on behalf of the Motherland."[35] The press release also promised the most stunning night fighting footage ever to be seen on film.

The more practical intended purpose of the film was to match a time that required engagement of Americans in the fight with the story of Americans who had already been there, and heroically so. Said Hesser:

> I feel that it should set at rest for all time the argument regarding why we are in the war. I want it to show the American public that we are at war with a people whose brutality and barbarism, the result of their governmental system, is something that everyone of us must hate and do our best to stamp out.[36]

SEVEN

Whisky and Soda

He groveled against the wall of the trench, nauseated by the din. He seemed to be alone in a universe of incredibly brutal noise.—Raymond Chandler

In advance of the U.S. declaration of war in 1917, correspondent Kenneth MacDougall of the International News Service published a lengthy assessment of the nation's ability to join the war. By his accounting, about 7,000 men of officer caliber were ready in the nation's military schools and academies. The civilian population had a healthy number of engineers and builders to help the army to establish itself in battle, as well as those suited for the Signal and Aviation Corps. New York state alone already had 310,457 automobiles, half of which might be recruitable along with those who drove and understood them. Red Cross nurses would be in plentiful supply, and the American ambulance efforts already operating in Europe were a large asset. And he noted that, though disbanded, the American Legion was still intact, with large human assets to draw from. But he was talking about the American Legion that had been created in the spirit of preparedness, then disbanded at the prompting of the U.S. army. There was not a mention of the American Legion, now in the form of numbered battalions, already fighting the war in Europe. He did, however, single out the Boy Scouts of America "who I am sure would rise to the emergency in the same lucky manner as their little brother scouts have done in every country in Europe."[1]

The Canadian military historian F.A. McKenzie took a more inclusive view. The opening of the war in 1914, by his telling, had included an American invasion of Canada. They were former U.S. army officers, ranch owners, cowpunchers, adventurers, engineers, schoolteachers, bankers, sailors and lumberjacks. Now they were scattered in the many Canadian battalions, made officers in the British army, had earned great glory and died by the hundreds. Asked about the Americans in his charge, one British commander replied that "we had scores of them, but you will not find them here. You will find their graves on the Somme."[2] On June 30, 1917, one of the sons of Asa Minard, of the legion's founding leadership, was killed. Asa Minard, Jr., was reported only to have been shot in the head, arms and legs somewhere in France. Killed with him in what was described as a successful raid on a German trench were legion members from Charleston, West Virginia, and Buffalo, New York. Among the injured were men from Detroit and Traverse City, Michigan, New York, Kentucky, Washington state and Cornell University.

J.W. Pegler could be expected to comment on the legion through his reporting, and his contribution included the exploits of various individuals. Major Alexander Rassmussen had led seven other Americans in a successful raid of a German trench and a return with two prisoners of war, one of them a former waiter in a New York hotel. Major ___ Pitcairn of Kansas City had described the shelling of his sector of trenches as "a thousand express trains running abreast 60 miles an hour, all blowing up at the same time."[3] Lieutenant Maurice Burbank of Maine won fast promotion to major soon after arriving in France, and worked together building railroads with Lieutenants Thomas Haven of Minneapolis and ___ Davis of Columbus, Ohio, a former professor at Ohio State University. Captains F.H. Burr of Columbus and John Manning of Florida had told American Secretary of War Newton Baker of their willingness to move from the Canadian to American armies, but only after they had finished their responsibilities in the trenches. Lieutenant Allen Allenback of Scranton, Pennsylvania, served on the front with the Royal Canadian Rifles/Regiment.

RCR commander Lt. Col. C.H. Hill told Pegler that the Americans had fought so well in France that he only wanted more of them. Among those under Hill's command was James Frederick Kennedy. From the success at Vimy Ridge the RCR had moved on to other skirmishes intended to extend the effect of that battle, and gave its effort to the rebuilding of roads and reclamation of still useful war matériel. The Germans were effective in menacing the effort, and, in June, the Canadians created a ruse that led to German fire upon their own troops as they refilled trenches previously held by Canada. The next objective was Hill 70.

In July 1917, the industrial and mining town of Lens, in northern France, became an essential holding for both sides. Germany needed its access to rail networks, and England needed its access to coal. The fight for Lens would also distract Germany from other pursuits in France. Canada was asked once again to take on a daunting challenge, and the job fell to the command of Lt. Gen. Arthur Currie. Currie was as controversial as was his plan to take Lens. He was a former real-estate magnate in British Columbia who had been knighted by King George V, but later found to have used government funds to resolve personal debts. His orders were to attack Lens frontally, but he determined that those orders were misdirected. The British command predicted that his alternate plans would fail, but approved them nonetheless.

Lens was surrounded by higher ground, and Currie supposed that he might be able to take it, but would not be able to keep defending it against surrounding forces. He proposed to take Hill 70 that was north of the city and an excellent defensive position for whichever side possessed it. It offered high ground and a honeycomb of underground mines and pathways. The Canadian effort to take it from the Germans would be one of the dirtiest—though little known in history—battles of the war.

Preparation, softening up and modeling of the battlefield was as extensive as it had been at Vimy Ridge. At dawn on August 14, three divisions and 10 battalions spread up the hill and took their first objectives immediately. They filled the German trenches with burning oil, and flames cascaded down the hillsides. Low-flying aircraft scouted out the most effective targets. It took five hours for German troops to begin an effective response with high-powered shells and the use of mustard gas. The need to cover themselves in heavy clothing and wear gas masks, combined with the very hot day, led to death by heat prostration. Those who were forced to remove their protective gear were subject to immediate internal and external burns. Eventually, the heavy use of arms and shells reduced the fighting to bayonets, but the Canadians gained and held their line.

The Royal Canadian Regiment did not participate in the battle for Hill 70, but it became integral to holding positions in its aftermath. The Germans were more than usually angry about the loss, and their bombardment of the line was continuous. On August 23,

Members of the 15th Battalion of the CEF take leave for rest after fighting at Hill 70 near Lens, France, in August 1970 (Canada Dept. of National Defence/Library and Archives Canada).

James Kennedy's machine gun unit was holding the line in the former German trench line known as Nun's Alley. In the early afternoon, the Germans had been shelling the trench for a couple of hours without effect. James Kennedy told a friend that he wished that "Fritz" would just show up in the trench in person when a 5.9 shell fell into the machine gun nest and seemed to kill him instantaneously. A friend reported his face to be peaceful and without a sign of pain. He was buried quickly, his grave registered and a white cross was planted at its head. His friend Charles Thompson wrote Mrs. Kennedy months later about James Frederick "he was buried properly. I was present when the ceremony was performed and the place was marked so that he shall not rest in an unnamed grave, but have a cross erected to show that he made the supreme sacrifice for the cause which we all believe to be just."[4]

The American declaration of war did not end the movement of Americans into Canadian and Commonwealth forces. There were still many men in the United States with Canadian and/or British and/or American origins, parentage and citizenship, and there seemed to be no impediments in the way of their enlistment. One of those who crossed to Canada was a young man who had been born in Chicago in 1888 of a family with British origins. The Chandlers of England and Ireland were Quakers who had come to America with William Penn in the 17th century.

Raymond Thornton Chandler was born into a Chicago that was roiling with railroads, stockyards, politics and labor unrest. His father's alcoholism led his mother to move to her Irish family in Nebraska, then to London in 1900 where Chandler's life became distinctly British. He was enrolled in Dulwich Academy, which also produced the writers P.G. Wodehouse and C.S. Forrester and a handful of others who would ultimately find themselves working in Hollywood. After Dulwich, Chandler traveled in Europe with the support of an uncle. By 1907, he became a naturalized British citizen in pursuit of civil service employment, but soon left that behind to attempt to establish himself as a writer. He moved to San Francisco in 1912 as part of a general migration to the state at that time, and, with his mother, to Los Angeles in 1913. There, he began to see the city's environment in ways that would support his Philip Marlowe books of the 1930s.

By 1917, though, Raymond Chandler was not nearly the success he had hoped to be in Los Angeles, and he was restless. Like many other young men at the time, he looked to the war in Europe as a solution. He traveled north to Victoria, British Columbia, and enlisted in the Canadian army on August 14, 1917. His attestation papers showed the difficulty of determining the actual origins of those who came from America to enlist in Canada. His birthplace was identified as Chicago, his address as 127 South Vendome Street, Los Angeles, and his mother as next of kin at the same address. A random note written on the record, as if as an afterthought, simply said "Naturalized British Subject."

Chandler's enlistment also shared a decision process that was similar to that of others who had gone to Canada. Though naturalized as British he seemed to still think of himself as an American citizen by birth (if not by law; he returned to legal American citizenship in 1956), but with strong pro–British feelings and comfortable in a British uniform.[5] But when it came down to it, his financial situation was not good and his mother was now his dependent. Canadian pay was higher, and it would include necessary dependent support. By November of 1917, he was training in Sussex with the British Columbia Regiment, and in March 1918 he was in the trenches near Arras, France. His battalion had suffered great losses since 1915, and he ran quickly up the replacement chain to a non-commissioned commander of 30 men. Years later, he wrote to one of his fans:

> Courage is a strange thing. You can never be sure of it. As a platoon commander very many years ago, I never seemed to be afraid, and yet I have been afraid of the insignificant risks. If you had to go over the top somehow all you seemed to think of was trying to keep the men spaced, in order to reduce casualties. It was always very difficult, especially if you had replacements or men who had been wounded. It's only human to want to bunch for companionship in face of heavy fire. Nowadays war is very different. In some ways it's much worse, but the casualties don't compare with those in trench warfare. My battalion (Canadian) had a normal strength of 1200 men and it had over 14,000 casualties.[6]

The letter was rare for Raymond Chandler. Like many men, he did not like to talk much about the worst of his experiences in war, and he barely wrote about it. He was prompted to try as a result of his final experience in France. A round of German shells killed everyone in his unit except himself. A concussion sent him to convalescence in England where he trained to be a pilot for the Royal Air Force. Though the war ended before he would ever fly, it was during this time that Chandler took up the drinking that would haunt him for the rest of his life, and an unpublished piece of writing about trench warfare predicted the style of writing he would develop in the 1930s as his detective Philip Marlowe plied his trade in noir Los Angeles.

> As he pushed aside the dirty blanket that served for a gas curtain the force of the bombardment hit him like the blow of a club at the base of the brain. He groveled against the wall of the trench, nauseated by the din. He seemed to be alone in a universe of incredibly brutal noise. The sky, in which the calendar called for a full moon, was white and blind with innumerable Very lights, white and blind and diseased like a world gone leprous.... Time to move on. Mustn't stay too long in one place.[7]

With America now in the war, the mission of Americans already in the Canadian forces took on another dimension. In mid–September, J.W. Pegler found himself at the U.S. army headquarters in France where he reported on a grand reunion. Alexander Rassmussen and Jock Manning, former U.S. army officers who had been fighting as members of the Canadian Expeditionary Force, were allowed now to bring their experience in the war to the training of new American forces. Pegler reported good feelings all around as the American-Canadian officers instructed the "Sammies" in what they had learned about fighting the Germans, particularly in counteracting German firefighting. The two men were attached to the U.S. First Division as combat officers, but they were exceptions to the rules in late 1917.

It wasn't until the turn of 1918 that the American War Department could come to reliable conclusions about the transferability of Americans in the CEF to American forces. In this case, the estimate was that there were 25,000 to 30,000 Americans in the CEF, "and perhaps half as many more scattered through other British contingents in France, Mesopotamia, Palestine and elsewhere."[8] The War Department determined that they would only be allowed to transfer in special circumstances that were clearly in the national interest.

The reasoning was conciliatory and practical. Those Americans who had enlisted in Canada had demonstrated patriotic motives. It would not matter which flag they followed since they were fighting for the same cause. And the removal of Americans from Canadian fighting units might be too disruptive to their effectiveness. Less magnanimously, the Department pointed out that the motivation of some transferees might only be to gain better pay and benefits in the American army. (The question of relative earnings in the U.S. and Canada was not possible to answer. The Canadian Pay Book for Active Service listed a range from $1 plus $0.10 field allowance per day for the lowest ranks up to $6 plus $1.50 per day for a colonel.[9] But different job skills could produce different rates, and compensation to dependents was determined by various factors. American Expeditionary Force pay ranged from $30 to $90 per month with varying allowances.[10])

An enlisted man in the CEF would have to obtain a letter from his British commander saying that the transfer would be in the interest of the United States, and present it to the military attaché at the American embassy in London. Those of officer rank would have no special advantage, and they would also have to appear in person at the embassy to argue their case. Those granted a transfer would be required to travel to the American Expeditionary Force headquarters in France at their own expense. There are no definitive lists of who and how many may have undergone the process and made the move.

The French Foreign Legion contained a smaller group of Americans, but it seemed that those few who moved to U.S. forces tended to exhaust themselves in the work of the legion before moving on. The legion had been in the toughest of battles, and no less so since the American declaration of war. In August 1917, the French launched an attempt to improve on the results of the Battle of Verdun of 1916. The fight for the city on the Meuse River was one of the longest of the war, not successful for the Germans, and produced more than half a million casualties. The Second Battle of Verdun resulted in the French recapture of lost ground, and a number of Americans of the legion were key to that success. None were killed, but a number were wounded.

Arthur Barry of Boston was hospitalized in Lyons with a wound to the back. Grenadier Ivan Nock, a mining engineer from Baltimore, was hospitalized with a leg wound. Others included Oscar Mouvet of Brooklyn, and P.A. Ringfield of San Francisco. Jack Moyet, who had joined the legion at age 17, was unhurt, as was Algernon Sartoris, grandson of General Ulysses S. Grant, because he was on sick leave. A Brigadier Bergey of the American Field

Service was killed in the same battle, and several other members of the ambulance corps were wounded. They convalesced at the French estate of Vanderbilt heir Elliot Fitch Shepard.[11]

One of those legion members who came through the Second Battle of Verdun without wounds was Christopher Charles of 619 de Kalb Avenue, Brooklyn. His well-written narratives of life on the lines since the Somme in 1916 had continued through the battles of Champagne and Aisne. The Second Battle of Aisne had begun just a few days after the American declaration of war, and when Charles and his comrades were finished with it they began to think about their place in the coming American effort. They were soon returned to the trenches, however, in a holding action at Berry-au-Bac. They wrote a letter to President Woodrow Wilson, asking a question that seemed logical to them, but not so to the president. It asked for his "intervention in order that we may obtain our liberation from said regiment to enter our own service."[12] The Americans of the legion, it said, had gained a great reputation for valor. Others of the Allied countries had taken their legion members into their own armies.

> The experience and training that we have received in this regiment will undoubtedly render most of us of great and inestimable service to our own countrymen still unused to modern warfare. Since our country has taken part under your wise leadership in the great struggle for liberty and humanity we, who are, so to speak, the advanced guard of the American forces, respectfully bring your attention to the need of immediate action toward our liberation, and we claim our right as American citizens to fight under our own flag. Therefore, we rely on your own patriotic spirit to see that we obtain this right without delay.[13]

If the message seemed both like a sales letter and a demand, the response seemed a rebuke, and came from an adjutant general. Dated June 29, it said, simply, that the War Department had no interest in accepting Americans from Allied armies, except in special cases. "The cases in question are not believed to be of such a character as to warrant the War Department in making such a request."[14]

It was not an answer that the Americans were prepared to accept, but they received no satisfaction from continued efforts to talk with American military officials, often in person at the American embassy in Paris. Some felt that they were unfairly tainted by a mistaken impression of the French Foreign Legion as an assembly of misfits and malcontents. When the American flag that had been carried by legion members was presented to the July 4 ceremonies in Paris, the June 29 letter from the War Department may have been on the mind of American clergyman Dr. Samuel Watson as he addressed General Pershing.

> General, it is my privilege to transmit this banner on behalf of the first Americans soldiers who fought for France, our American Legionnaires, who in 1914 enrolled themselves in the Foreign Legion to fight for France and liberty, who gave all they had to give, who are proud to have been the pioneers of that great American Army which now arrives under your leadership to take up the task they laid down. Your flag now replaces their flag.[15]

Watson did not let up on the idea in a subsequent statement to French general Gustave Léon Niox, Governor of Les Invalides.

> How prophetic has this banner been, the first American flag to float over the heads of those who fought on French soil for ideals represented by the Star-Spangled Banner, which have been the life and soul of France! It was not permitted our brave men in the Legion to carry the flag openly, as the pennant of the chief leading his soldiers to the assault, but they carried it none-the-less. One after another wore this flag draped around his body as a belt—the life belt of his soul. One after another was wounded or killed, and thus the American flag has received its first baptism of blood in this combat, where now it has its appointed place.[16]

Some of the American members of the Foreign Legion would go on to find acclaim in their own country and service in their own army despite the disinterest of the War Department. But, even in the words of the American Samuel Watson, the American Legion that had drawn tens of thousands of Americans to Canada well before their own country saw fit to go to war had disappeared into the description of Americans in the French Foreign Legion as "American Legionnaires."

Another of the French Legionnaires found himself back home just after America decided to enter the war. Ferdinand Capdevielle, born in New York of French distraction, had gone to Paris in August 1914 to join the legion. With many of those other Americans who distinguished themselves in the legion, Capdevielle fought through the first battle of Champagne and went on to join the 170th Infantry Regiment, the Swallows of Death. At Verdun in early 1916, he was awarded the Croix de Guerre, and received a promotion to sergeant after the Battle of the Somme. After the French offensive at Champagne, he received a further promotion and, as further reward, was granted three weeks leave to return to New York where he received a hero's welcome. The war was just beginning for America, and Capdevielle was asked to share his knowledge at West Point and a number of army training bases.

Upon his return to France, the American army tried to recruit him with an offer of the rank of captain, but he replied that he started the war as a French soldier and would finish it that way. As he led his brigade into battle at Arcueil, France on October 3, 1918, he was shot in the forehead, and believed to have been the last American volunteer in France to be killed in a war that ended a month later.

Among those who did eventually make the move from French to American forces was Eugene Jacobs, a butcher from Pawtucket, Rhode Island, from sergeant with the French to private with the U.S. army. Another was David King, who ended the war in American counterespionage and would become an important member of the intelligence and Air Force efforts in World War II.

Some Americans who might have fulfilled the Foreign Legionnaire stereotype as not quite from the mainstream did not always succeed post–Legion. Those who were "liberated" from the legion still had to be accepted by the American Expeditionary Forces in Paris. Some were too old, but managed to end up in non-combat positions. Others were not healthy enough, and one of those, Algernon Sartoris, descendant of Ulysses S. Grant, was to be released from the AEF until a shortage appeared in an inventory for which he was responsible. He was to be court-martialed if he could not return $100 to the army, but he pleaded that his service in the Foreign Legion had left him penniless. Finally, a friend of the grandson of a former American president put up the necessary hundred, plus another hundred so that he could buy himself decent clothes. Sartoris subsequently tried again but failed to receive a commission in the U.S. army.

Christopher Charles, after valiant service and narration on the battlefields, was taken into the 23d Engineers Battalion and given an office job. Others of his closest comrades in the legion were given similar jobs in the same outfit. Charles was described as indignant. "I shall ask to be put where I can hear the whistling of those old shells once more," he wrote. "If we could only get a bit of credit for our three and a half years of hardships I would be pleased to go back to the game I was made for."[17] He and some of his friends were eventually assigned to the 18th Infantry and heavy fighting with the First Regiment. At war's end, Charles remained in Paris for three years, working as a machinist. He finally returned to Brooklyn and became a streetcar conductor, then a tool and die maker.

In 1966, Charles was the subject of a newspaper article in St. Petersburg, Florida, where he had retired. His picture was that of a bent old man, and the writing recounted some of the experiences he had written about a half century earlier. He didn't really want to talk about them. "'Please don't make a big thing out of this,' he asks sincerely, "I didn't do anything worth remembering."[18]

In early February 1918, there were an estimated 300 Americans flying in French air forces. They included members of the Lafayette Escadrille, the Lafayette Flying Corps and those scattered through lesser-known units. Many had come from the French Foreign Legion and American Ambulance Corps. They were separate from Americans in the aviation branch of the U.S. Army Signal Corps, though training for all aviators took place in French schools. On February 18, the Escadrille itself was converted to the First American Pursuit Squadron, S 103, and other Americans in the French services eventually found themselves to be officers in the U.S. army.

The transition did not come naturally. The men of the Escadrille, in particular, were at first conflicted when the U.S. army began to recruit them in the summer of 1917. Though Americans in identification, they were French in every other respect. The French had spent thousands to train each of them. They flew French airplanes and worked with French comrades to whom they felt an understandable allegiance. Also, they weren't made entirely confident that they could be as effective in the American forces as they were in the French. The American army seemed to be having problems getting itself into the field, and the development of the proper equipment for flying was problematic. In the fall, however, they came to the decision to offer themselves to their home country as a unit. The French Government released them from service in January. They took to the air the following February as the army's only effective air squadron. Other American flyers became impatient while waiting in Paris between their French and yet-to-come American service. Three of them re-enlisted in the French army though they had American commissions, and two of those were killed in French service.

By the fall most American airmen were in place, and their work was intense. Raoul Lufberry, an Ace in the Escadrille and a recruiter of the lion Whisky into their fold, became commanding officer of the 94th Aero Squadron and instructor to new pilots like Eddie Rickenbacker. In combat on May 19, 1918, he fell or jumped out of his burning plane and died, impaled on a metal picket fence. When his comrades went to retrieve his body, they found it lying before the altar of a village church covered in flowers, and many of the villagers kneeled in prayer. He was eventually buried, with others at the Lafayette Escadrille Memorial outside of Paris, and was inducted into the American Aviation Hall of Fame in 1998.

Escadrille Ace William Thaw, also credited with ownership of the lion, ended the war as a lieutenant colonel, with American, French and British medals for valor. Frederick Zinn, who had traveled to France from Battle Creek, Michigan, in 1914 had been twice wounded in the Foreign Legion, then moved on to the French Air Service in 1916. By his own enterprise, he advanced the art of reconnaissance photography into methods that would be used by both sides. After the war, he was put in charge of the search for the bodies of allied airmen who had fallen behind enemy lines.

By the account of Paul Ayres Rockwell in his book *American Fighters in the Foreign Legion*:

> One hundred and eighty American pilots in all flew at the front in French uniform. They served with ninety-three different French pursuit, observation, and bombardment squadrons. Fifty-one were killed in action; six were killed in school accidents; and five died of illness. Fifteen

were taken prisoners; ninety-three transferred to the United States Air service and twenty-six to the United States Naval Aviation. Thirty-three remained by their own choice with French Aviation until the end of the war. The American volunteer pilots were officially credited with the destruction of one hundred and ninety-nine German aeroplanes.[19]

Rockwell himself had served in the French Foreign Legion with his younger brother Kiffin Rockwell. Kiffin had gone on to be shot down as a flyer for France, and Paul would live to play an influential role in pre–World War II France, and as an American officer in the war that followed.

Upon the end of the war, the commandant of the U.S. Army Air Service acknowledged what had occurred in the first years of military aviation in General Order Number 17. It asserted that the Lafayette Escadrille had helped the American people to understand "the basic issues of the war."[20] It predicted that its pilot's names would have the same meaning to the French people just as the names of Lafayette and Rochambeau were meaningful to the current generation of Americans. The Escadrille's conversion into the 103rd Aero Squadron had brought that valor into the American army. "While giving this generously of its experienced personnel to new units, the standard of merit of this Squadron has never been lowered. No task was too arduous or too hazardous for it to perform successfully."[21]

Whisky and Soda ended their days in the Paris Zoo. Soda died of rheumatism in May 1919, and, by July, Whisky seemed headed toward the same fate when he was visited by former Escadrille commander George Thenault. It was reported to the *New York Times* by special cable from Paris that Thenault had entered the zoo with full war decorations calling the lion's name. Hearing the voice, Whisky jumped up from the corner of his cage and licked Thenault's caressing hands through its bars.

Thenault made the observation that the rheumatism had probably been contracted in the drafty wooden hut the airmen shared at Cachy. And it had been compounded by the inability of the zoo to heat its cages postwar.

> When Thenault went away Whisky stood looking after him for a moment, then limped back to the corner where he spends all his time listlessly huddled.[22]

EIGHT

Some Come Home

"The King commands me to assure you of the true sympathy of His Majesty and The Queen in your sorrow."—From a condolence received in West Virginia.

The opening of the Battle of Amiens on August 8, 1919, marked the first day of the Hundred Days Offensive in which Allied forces would bring Germany to defeat. For its part, Canada had arrived at the Amiens battlefront with its reputation for valor intact since Vimy Ridge. The British prime minister, Lloyd George, was famously said to have offered after the Battle of the Somme:

> The Canadians played a part of such distinction that thenceforward they were marked out as storm troops; for the remainder of the war they were brought along to head the assault in one great battle after another. Whenever the Germans found the Canadian Corps coming into the line they prepared for the worst.[1]

The Hundred Days Offensive would come to be known in Canadian history as Canada's Hundred Days. By the evening of August 7, the Canadian troops had been moved quietly into position, traveling there under cover of night and ordered to move quietly until they were fully mobilized in the area of Gentilles Wood, southeast of Amiens. They were at full strength in men and matériel, and satiated by the grace notes of tea, biscuits and cigarettes. The horses' bellies were full of hay.

As at Vimy Ridge and Lens, the coming attack upon the unsuspecting Germans had been fully planned in days of calculations and the study of maps. Each shot fired was to have an immediate effect. The night was described as clear. "From out a velvet sky the stars looked down on the hosts waiting to go into battle at the first flush of dawn along a twenty-mile battle front that stretch from the river Avre to the Ancre."[2] Australian troops sat at the ready to the left of the Canadians, French to the right. At precisely 4:30 a.m., the Allied line roared into life and its assorted infantries began their charge against an enemy that was, by all accounts, surprised and unprepared. A thick mist hung in the air and prevented communication with German back lines.

The assault continued with troops, tanks and low-flying aircraft. The trenches were captured in an hour and, no matter their effort, the Germans could not gain the momentum to fight back. The first Allied objective, a place to stop and reconnoiter together, was reached five minutes before its 10:20 a.m. schedule. As planned, the horse battalions came charging from behind infantry lines at noon, hearing the cheers of the infantry and returning the salute as they ran ahead. By nightfall on the 8th, they had advanced nearly eight miles, taken

The Canadian Cavalry rests in a wood before its roaring advance in the Battle of Amiens, August 1918 (Canada Dept. of National Defence/Library and Archives Canada).

6,000 prisoners and suffered very few casualties. They were able to rest, and even receive their daily mail, brought up from Gentilles Wood.

On the fifth day of the advance, the Canadian commander, Lieutenant-General Sir Arthur W. Currie, posted what would become a Special Order commending his troops at length. Things had come a long way since those first uncertain days of Canada's declared alliance with England in 1914.

> Canada has always placed the most implicit confidence in her Army. How nobly has that confidence been justified, and with what pride has the story of your gallant success been read in the homeland. This magnificent victory has been won because your training was good, your discipline was good, your leadership was good. Given these three, success must always come.[3]

Though the rapid success of the first days of the advance on Amiens was increasingly slowed by supply problems, the Allies had moved about 12 miles into German positions by August 13. From that point, the Canadians turned their attention toward the Battle of Arras, with the capture of significant numbers of prisoners and enemy arms, and to the Drocourt–Quéant portion of the heavily fortified Hindenburg Line. Drocourt–Quéant had last felt the footfall of Allied forces in 1914, and the Germans presumed it to be impregnable. It was a complicated series of five trench lines that had taken two years to build, but the Canadians crossed it in an hour on September 2.

By the end of a full month of their advance, a writer for the Overseas Ministry of Canada, Fred James, offered an accounting of their success. Twenty thousand prisoners had been taken, including 262 officers. Nearly 2,000 arms of various sorts had been captured.

They had put four divisions of the enemy out of business and had captured the equivalent of 140 square miles of land.[4] Their casualties for the period amounted to more 14,000.

The breaking of the Drocourt-Quéant line allowed an advance toward the Battle of Canal du Nord in Nord-pas-de-Calais during the last week of September. Part of a combined effort of all Allies along a line from Verdun, France, to the Belgian coast, a breach of the canal could lead to the capture of the important German-held marshaling city of Cambrai. As part of the British First Army, the Canadians had once again surprised the Germans by stealth, building bridges and crossing the canal by night.

"One wag said today," wrote James, "that the reason 'Fritz' is trying to stop us crossing the Canal is because he knows Canadians like to have a wash and swim, and he hates people who appreciate either cleanliness or Godliness."[5] The canal was taken, and, at Cambrai, the Canadians breached the Hindenburg Line for a second time. By October 2, they had arrived at the outskirts of Cambrai. Canadian railway troops had built track and supply networks along the path of the advance, and the doctors, nurses, chaplains, the YMCA and transport services were all fully engaged behind the lines. The German effort to stop them was to no avail.

Cambrai was entered at 1:30 a.m. on October 9 and by 6 a.m., the Scheldt Canal had been crossed by pontoon bridge and the southeast portion of the city had been secured. The advance was preceded by intentional German destruction of the city they would now be losing. Troops and engineers tried to limit the destruction, but without much success. In another Special Order, Lt. General Currie added to the notation of prisoners, arms and territory

Retreating Germans did not expect that the Canadians would be able to overcome their destruction of the bridges over the Canal du Nord at the Arras front, but a new bridge was constructed overnight (Canada Dept. of National Defence/Library and Archives Canada).

captured the assertion that the Canadians had "defeated decisively forty-seven German divisions—that is nearly a quarter of the total German forces on the Western front."[6]

In the happy telling of Fred James of the Overseas Ministry, it was the Canadian capture of Cambrai, and the subsequent taking of Cateau, that vanquished all hope on the part of Germany that it might yet win the war. Whatever the truth of that assertion, it was now generally agreed that the Great War was in its last days. The Canadians continued to take back small villages and key sectors within their scope, and rebuild infrastructure in their wake. They were met in most places with great celebration, but had then to assume the task of feeding and caring for the newly liberated French.

From Cambrai, the Canadians embarked on what would come to be known in Canadian history as "The Pursuit to Mons." The first meeting of the British and German armies had taken place in the Battle of Mons, in Belgium on August 23, 1914. History was never able to come to a firm conclusion as to which side won or lost the battle, but, as the war was ending, Mons became the prize that would close its final chapter. It was especially important to the British. The assignment was given to the Royal Canadian Regiment, and, once again, stealth was the key. On the evening of November 9, they began to work in the dark and a heavy mist, crossing a strategic canal with improvised bridges. By the time the mist was burned away by the morning sun, they had arrived at the city's northern perimeter where they found a strong German defensive force. The fighting was slow and steady, but the regiment managed to move forward. Regiment Company B, however, lost five members as it crossed a partially destroyed bridge in another northern sector of the city. They would be the last RCR soldiers killed in the war.

Canada's "Hundred Days" enters Cambrai on October 9, 1919 (Canada Dept. of National Defence/ Library and Archives Canada).

At the same time, RCR Company A had advanced to a few hundred yards from Mons' southern limits where they were required to work patiently through strong machine gun resistance. Company B persisted in its movement from the north, and, as the night of November 10 turned into the morning of November 11, German fire receded. It was gone by 5 a.m., and, coming upon the city's police chief, a contingent of troops was directed to the Hotel De Ville at the Grande Place where it was welcomed by the mayor and assorted dignitaries. Lt. W.M. King of RCR 5 Platoon was offered a glass of wine and asked to enter the name and regiment of the first soldier to liberate the city in the Golden Book of Mons, on behalf of all Canadian brigades and battalions involved. Armistice, and the end of the war, came a few hours later, at 11 a.m. Paris time.

Canada's Hundred Days, according to Lt. General Sir Arthur W. Currie, had brought the capture of 31,537 prisoners and almost 4,000 arms. It had marched 170 miles, liberated 500 square miles, including 228 cities, towns and villages, and defeated 47 German divisions. "To the normal difficulties of moving and supplying a large number of men in a comparatively restricted area were added the necessity of feeding several hundred thousand people, chiefly women and children, left in a starving condition by the enemy."[7]

The Hundred Days had created 42,000 Canadian casualties, an unspecified number of them killed in action. In the full war, Canada had contributed 620,000 men from a population of 8 million people. It had suffered 66,000 dead and 173,000 wounded. Though the number of Americans included in the force was in the tens of thousands, it could not be

The Mayor of Mons calls for three cheers for Canadians, November 1918 (Canada Dept. of National Defence/Library and Archives Canada).

exactly known. What could be measured more generally, but not specifically, was the approximate 2,700 of American birth, next-of-kin or address who lay in the cemeteries of the Commonwealth forces, or were named on its memorial tablets, after the war. Almost 11 percent of all Canadians had been killed; 2,700 American dead would be 11 percent of just more than 27,000.

Whatever their actual number, the Americans had no aggregate identity in the Commonwealth forces by the end of the war. The legion had been converted to the 97th Battalion; the 211, 212, 213 and 237 battalions had been absorbed into the 97th and other battalions; then the 97th was disassembled into the Canadian Expedition Force. When the full list of the 2,700 American-related dead was merged into the burial records of the Commonwealth forces, just two of them would be noted as members of the original battalions. Ninety-seventh member Private William Denning of Corning, New York, died of pneumonia on February 23, 1916, and was buried in St. John's Norway Cemetery in Toronto. Private Francis J. Russell of Centralia, Washington, died of an unspecified cause in the 213th Battalion on September 15, 1916, and was buried in the Toronto Necropolis. Neither would have seen combat.

The concepts and names of the legion and the 97th Battalion, however, had lingered through most of the war. May 5, 1918, was Canadian night at the New York City Hippodrome, a fundraiser for "the relief of the families of the Canadian soldiers, as well as the dependents of Americans who fought or are still fighting in Canada's army, who are residents of the United States."[8] The official program for the event continued:

> Thousands of red-blooded Americans—also Canadians and Britishers making their homes in the United States—early in the war, fired by the brutal treatment of Belgium and France, enraged at the sinking of the Lusitania, and seeing the freedom and liberty of the world assailed, rushed across the border to join the Canadian forces, many forfeiting their citizenship, others using subterfuge, hiding age and physical defects in their anxiety to be accepted.

A prophesy was made that would not prove out to be true:

> When the history of the part the United States will have played in this war is written, the story of the "30,000 honor legion" will be a tale of heroism, patriotism and devotion to ideals not surpassed in the annals of human events, and will furnish one of the brightest pages in American history which no single subsequent event of the war can dim.[9]

It would not prove to be the case, at least, in the dramatic end to the journey of the RMS *Mauretania* in the early spring of 1919. When the ocean liner/troopship left the piers of Southampton England on March 31, the biggest story of her departure was the impending return to America of Vice-Admiral William Sowden Sims. Upon the American declaration of war, Sims had moved from leadership of the Naval War College, and strong advocacy for a modern navy, to the command of American naval forces in England. His anti-submarine warfare, in close partnership with his counterpart in the British navy, was viewed in England to have been heroic, and his victory lap back across the Atlantic would return him to a Navy Department which he had felt free to criticize as being almost neglectful in the support it had given him and his sailors during the war. Sims' return had begun outside U.S. naval headquarters in London where the streets were reported to have been filled with cheering crowds and the ringing of cowbells. The send-off continued at Waterloo station, with fond best wishes from the lowliest of common citizens to the highest of naval and government dignitaries. At Southampton, the city's mayor escorted him from the train to the docks, and the ship sailed west with Sims, many of his subordinates, and a distinguished passenger list including Samuel Gompers, British-born founder of the American Federation of Labor. Reporting on the send off noted, almost as an afterthought, that the ship also carried 2,000 returning American soldiers. But that wasn't the full story.

While still far off the coast of Long Island, the *Mauretania* was met on April 7 by a flotilla of the American navy. Airplanes darted among the dirigibles that hung in the sky. After a brief quarantine, the entourage moved up the harbor and, from the smaller ships that accompanied the *Mauretania*, the admiral could be seen smiling and regal high up on the ocean liner's bridge. The arrival at Manhattan's 13th Street pier was a grand occasion, and Sims was followed off the ship by the 2,000 American soldiers, noisily happy to set foot once again on American land. What followed, however, would reveal a conflict not yet fully resolved and cause some of the nation's most influential newspapers to say something that perhaps still needed to be said.

After immigration agents had processed the returning American troops, they found yet another 2,700 men waiting to disembark. These were Americans who had preceded their countrymen to war through Canada and England, but in the eyes of the authorities they were deemed, in the characterization of the *New York Tribune*, as aliens to be imprisoned. They had been discharged by the British and given free transport back to America, but the *Mauretania* had not arrived with the proper manifest for these passengers. While American and British officials argued over the mistake, the men were eventually marched off the ship and taken to holding camps on Long Island and in New Jersey. Reporting and editorials on the problem bordered on the sarcastic and the cynical. And the incident revealed information about these Americans that had not been known before.

A headline in the *Tribune* proclaimed that "U.S. 'Tommies' Are Held as Aliens on Arrival Home."

> Many of them were among the first Americans to see service. They are the men who, when the arrogant German hosts were menacing the gates of Paris, chafed at their country's delay and slipped over the border to Canada, or overseas to Britain, in answer to civilization's call. Monday night on the *Mauretania* they came back to what they supposed was home—came back 2,754 strong, men who had fought under Maude in Palestine, had faced the Turkish guns and the fevers at Gallipoli, and who during the days of diplomatic note exchanges, swept the skies with the British Air Service, men who wallowed in Flanders' trench-mud in the uniforms of Scottish units because they could not then have born a share there in the khaki if the U.S.A. Others had been turned down by American army medical officials after this country's entry into the war and, rather than be "out of it," had gone into the British service, where the medical tests were less rigorous.[10]

The *New York Times* reported that there were "300 negro troops among them, who, before joining the British forces, used the Southern dialect, but who today have a decided cockney accent."[11] Another report noted that the group contained 600 Jews who had set off for the Palestinian army of General George Allenby, but ended up in regular British forces, "and another 600 West Indians, colored, who were employed in restaurants, hotels and other work in this country and responded to the call for recruits from the British Government."[12]

The detained men were described as ranging from being philosophical about it all to enraged about another battle to be fought. "We've been fighting for you in France, and been through a hell on earth for four years, and now you want to stop us from going to see our families."[13] Immigration authorities continued to claim that they had no way of being sure that all of those who had returned claiming to be Americans were actually so. Some of the men were reported to have sent a wire to the King of England complaining that they had received a "rotten reception." When the Red Cross arrived at the dock to feed men who had foregone ship's food for expected meals ashore, it was not allowed to take the food aboard.

The matter was resolved within a few days, and all who had returned legally were allowed to go on their way with a ticket home and 28 days pay courtesy of Great Britain. The question of allegiance of the men to America while serving with foreign forces was not reported as a part of the problem, and did not come up in editorials seeking relief for the returned Americans.

The most striking examples of the diaspora of Americans in Commonwealth forces at the end of the war could perhaps be found among those who did not return on ships like the *Mauretania*. They remained behind in fact or in name in Commonwealth cemeteries. Among the largest of them was Tyne Cot Cemetery, northeast of Ieper, Belgium. Tyne Cot absorbed the largest portion of its inhabitants after the Armistice as the dead were brought from surrounding battlefields in Passchendaele and Langermarck, and from temporary burials in smaller cemeteries of the region. It portrayed the full tragedy of the war with 11,956 memorial names or burials, 8,369 of the latter unidentified.

Seventeen of the known burials are American-related. Their names are listed in the format used by the Commonwealth Graves Commission, and other information from attestation papers is added.

BILLARD, Private, J, 30582, Sixth Bn., King's Own Yorkshire Light Infantry
　　... wife living in Roanoke, Virginia; birthplace unknown.

BROOKER, Private, H, 241069, Second/Sixth Bn., Lancashire Fusiliers
　　... chauffer; wife living in Kennebunk, Maine; born in New Brunswick, Canada.

BROWN, Private, HULBERT PERCY, 892334, 52nd Bn., Canadian Infantry (Manitoba Regiment)
　　... mechanic; parents living in Dalton, Pennsylvania; born in New York City.

CANNING, Lance Corporal, A H, 129826, 72nd Bn., Canadian Infantry (British Columbia Regiment
　　... parents living in Plainfield, Connecticut; birthplace unknown.

FISK, Private, JOHN KNOWLTON, 489852, Princess Patricia's Canadian Light Infantry (Eastern Ontario Regiment)
　　... student; parents living in Chicago, Illinois; born in Chicago.

FITZGERALD, Private, E P, 207834, 85th Bn., Canadian Infantry (Nova Scotia Regiment)
　　... wife living in Bellingham, Washington; birthplace unknown.

LESLIE, Private, FRANK, 133253, 85th Bn., Canadian Infantry (Nova Scotia Regiment)
　　... hospital attendant; parents living in Lynn, Massachusetts; born in Scotland.

MARTIN, Private, WILLIAM, 11900, Third Bn., Canterbury Regiment, N.Z.E.F. [New Zealand]
　　... mother living in Rochester, New York; birthplace unknown.

McCRUDDEN, Private, J, 241284, Fifth/Sixth Bn., Cameronians (Scottish Rifles)
　　... wife living in Philadelphia, Pennsylvania; birthplace unknown.

McLEAN, Private, GEORGE WALTER, 812095, 50th Bn., Canadian Infantry (Alberta Regiment)
　　... farmer; wife living in Calgary, Alberta; born in California.

OUNSTED, Private, ALFRED JUDGE, 760743, Second Canadian Mounted Rifles Battalion
    ... messenger; parents living in Vancouver, British Columbia; born in Tacoma, Washington.

PARKER, Private, W C, 267691, Fifth Bn., Canadian Infantry (Saskatchewan Regiment)
    ... wife and parents living in Smithland, Iowa; birthplace unknown.

POPE, Corporal, F G, 8201, Seventh Bn., King's Shropshire Light Infantry
    ... parents live in Lakeland and Syracuse, New York; birthplace unknown.

ROBBINS, Private, MORTIMER GIBERSON, 709331, Fifth Canadian Mounted Rifles Battalion
    ... carpenter; mother lives in Nahant, Massachusetts; born in Bath, New Brunswick.

SMITH, Lieutenant, D E, 20th Sqdn., Royal Air Force
    ... parents live in Cambridge, Massachusetts; born in Dundee, Scotland.

SMITH, Lance Corporal, N C, 307670, Second/Eighth Bn., Lancashire Fusiliers
    ... mother lives in Newburgh, New York; born in Radcliffe, Manchester, England.

WOODCOCK, Lieutenant, FRANK FREMONT, Eaton's Motor Machine Gun Bty., Canadian Machine Gun Corps
    ... engineer; parents live in Princeton, Minnesota; wife lives in Medicine Hat, Alberta; born in Minnesota.

The Tablets of the Tyne Cot Memorial list 28 men of American origin. Fourteen name wives, 11 name parents, and one names an aunt living in the United States as next of kin. One enlisted in the United States, though next of kin were in England; and one was described as an official of the Pennsylvania Railroad with parents living in England. All were in different fighting units.

Many of the Americans who died in service with Canada were not found and were not buried. More than 500 of their names were engraved in the Memorial tablets of the Commonwealth forces. One of them, placed on the Vimy Memorial in Pas de Calais, France, was that of James Frederick Kennedy of Princeton, West Virginia. Soon after his death as a machine gunner in Nun's Alley, care had been taken to bury him as carefully as possible and to mark what would be a temporary grave. Friends had witnessed the burial, and his mother had received assurance from them that he would not be lost. Ultimately, however, the burial site was ground down and lost forever in the aftermath of the devastation at Lens.

The aftermath of Kennedy's death had brought about a bureaucratic response from England and Canada that may have seemed rote and hard-edged, though it was delivered with a velvet glove. A lengthy typewritten letter had been received from one of his officers that was otherwise laudatory and sympathetic, but referred to him repeatedly with the name Frank. A month after his death, a letter was received from the Minister of Militia and Defense for Canada. It seemed to have been pre-typed en masse with spaces left for the later inclusion of the name of the person to whom it was addressed, the name of the decedent and his relation to the addressee. Thus it opened:

Dear **Mrs. Kennedy,**
I desire to express to you my very sincere sympathy in the recent decease of **your son,**
    No. 2017418, Pte. James Frederick Kennedy,
Who in sacrificing his life at the front in action with the enemy, has rendered the highest services of a worthy citizen.

A sense taken from a reading of the full letter is that it was intended, as might be expected, for Canadian citizens. Though the question of citizenship for Kennedy and his American peers may still have been confused, there seemed to be no acknowledgment of the decedent's sacrifice as an American. The letter from the Canadian Minister, signed with a rubber stamp, was followed by a piece of mail from the British Secretary of State for War. The small piece of paper was topped by a coat of arms, and said "The King commands me to assure you of the true sympathy of His Majesty and The Queen in your sorrow."[14]

Kennedy had left Princeton and traveled to Detroit, then enlisted in the American Legion for financial reasons that were important for many families of the time. Upon his death, Kennedy's mother received a copy of the will he had drawn in Canada, leaving her his full estate, which subsequently consisted of his few personal effects and a check in the amount of $279.20.

In 1920, Mrs. Kennedy (her given name does not show up in any document) wrote to the Board of Pension Commissioners in Ottawa asking if there would be any compensation available to the family he had left behind. "I can establish the fact," she wrote, "that up to the time of entering the army we were depending on his help, altho not entirely, and if he were still living would still be helping as there are four girls not yet old enough to support themselves [the only indication in the available history of the family that James Frederick had sisters]." A Canadian comrade of James' supported her in the appeal. "The lad was a good clean cut young fellow, a friend of everyone who knew him," wrote C.A. Iverson of Toronto, "everything that his mother would have him be."[15]

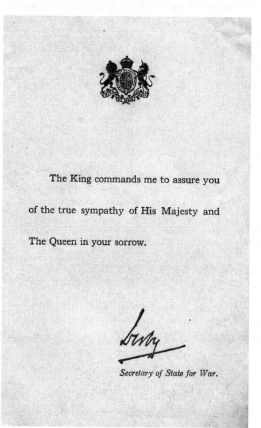

The King commands me to assure you

of the true sympathy of His Majesty and

The Queen in your sorrow.

Secretary of State for War.

King George VI of England sent this printed condolence to the mother of James Frederick Kennedy (courtesy Glenn Hyatt).

As it related to Mrs. Kennedy's application, Canadian pension regulations applied to a mother if she was a widow, or if the deceased would have been the sole support of a parent, and if there were not dependent children or a widow involved. The response from the Secretary of the pension board was gracious and unfulfilling. "I have the honour to inform you," it began, and continued with a denial of benefits because her husband was still earning the sum of $150 per month, "considerably in excess of the maximum pension provided for parents of deceased soldiers who held the rank of private."

In August 1921, Mrs. Kennedy received a letter from an officer of the Navy League of the United States. It evidently responded to a letter sent to the League previously by Mrs. Kennedy telling the story of her American son in the Royal Canadian Regiment. She was thanked for the information, and asked if she knew more about others from West Virginia who may have served in a similar way. It seemed evident that the identities of these men were not easily found. "I have been in France endeavoring to obtain complete lists of Americans who were in the French Army and will later go to London where I hope to obtain the names of many of those who were in the English Army," wrote Lydia S.M. Robinson. "I know much about the glorious deeds of the Royal Canadian Regiment and am proud to think how many of our countrymen had a share in making it famous."[16]

Ascertaining the full identities of those Americans actually buried in Commonwealth cemeteries would be just as difficult. More than 5.5 million members of the Allied forces were killed in the war, and 4.1 million were missing. The fate of the bodies of American forces derived out of the country's experiences during the Civil War. The number of deaths among Americans on both sides was so large that effective policies and methods of dealing with all of the bodies seemed forced into being. There had to be systems of maintaining records of who they were, and where they were. Medical advances into embalming and advances in transportation technology now allowed bodies to be returned home or taken to designated and central burying places. Eventually, the work became the physical and bureaucratic mission of the American Quartermaster General, and, by World War I, American policy about the disposition of its war dead was firm and generally well practiced.

The families of those American war dead who could be found and identified were given the options of requesting that their family member be returned home for burial in a family or national cemetery, or that he be left in one of the American cemeteries of Europe for burial near where he fell and with his fellows. It took years, however, for everyone to end up where they were wished to be. A body could be buried in and disinterred from a succession of smaller temporary cemeteries before it arrived at a larger American cemetery or a point of shipment home. And in some cases, politics and bureaucracies held up the process. Most notably, France was reluctant to allow Americans buried in its soil to be removed and returned. It seemed that the nation that so honored the Americans who fought on its behalf was equally reluctant to give them up. As exasperated American families begged for their return, their government found itself in a diplomatic two-step that sought to reconcile what seemed to be a plausible French problem with an American law. There were 1.7 million French dead buried in their own country, and the French people demanded that they be the first to be sorted, before the effort that would be needed to disinter and return the Americans. And France worried further that other nations with soldiers buried in France would follow the demands of the Americans. Some in America asserted that it was all a French ploy, and that France wanted to retain the (well-tended by the French people) fields of American burials as tourist attractions to help rebuild the French economy. It took some time, but eventually everyone arrived where they were supposed to be.

The operating principle of the Imperial War Grave Commission (IWGC)—later the Commonwealth War Graves Commission (CWGC)—was the opposite. The Commission had been founded in 1917, and put under the supervision of Sir Fabian Ware. Ware had been a British luminary since the turn of the century, and was commander of a mobile Red Cross Unit until the Prince of Wales appointed him to the IWGC. The lessons of the American Civil War had crossed the ocean by World War I, and Ware understood the extraordinary need for proactive management of the saddest result of war. Indeed, he thought, respect for the dead was perhaps the only thing that those at war could agree upon together, and he fostered a strong ethic and aesthetic for their treatment. The Commonwealth cemeteries and memorials—eventually totaling more than 23,000 worldwide—would be simple but welcoming in design. The director of the British Museum was enlisted to make them so, and the language of the tombstones and memorials became the responsibility of the writer Rudyard Kipling. The operation and ethical missions of the cemeteries was thoroughly articulated, and the quality of experience for those visiting their beloved dead was an ultimate goal. The dead themselves were in all cases to be treated as equals, irrespective of rank and station, in the quality and placement of their graves.

Where Commonwealth and American practices differed was in the matter of return. The American operating principle was that the dead and their families had the right of return to America, supported by the government. The Commonwealth principle was that the dead would be left near where they fell, and with their fallen comrades. They could not be returned, whether with government assistance or by the private effort of their families.

There was some grumbling about the policy in the Commonwealth nations, but it was generally accepted, though often appealed. On November 18, 1919, Sara Smith of Leeds penned a letter in perfect handwriting "To His Majesty King Albert," on behalf of "many who like myself, [sic] have suffered loss in the War." She reminded the king that every English family saw their dead as belonging to "them alone," to be put "in the family vault here so we could visit and tend to the graves ourselves.... We pray and beseech your gracious majesty that the right which has ever been the privilege of the bereaved may not be denied us."[17] Those who wrote letters of the sort to the king received gracious response in return from the private secretary to the king, and later the queen, saying that their request had been forwarded to the War Graves Commission.

The response of American families to Commission policies was similar: general acceptance, but with notable exceptions. When families of American forces servicemen had been given the option of leaving their family members buried in Europe, more than 40 percent had agreed to do so. Presumably, a similar number of American Commonwealth families would come to the same kind of conclusion, but even if they weren't in agreement there was nothing to be done about it and no way to join together in common cause. Many who crossed borders to fight the war had acted on their individual initiative. Then they had been spread to the winds over the course of the war, and, by another policy of the Graves Commission applying to all of the dead, their gravestones contained no reference to their national origin. There could be no common advocate for all of the American dead.

An individual effort to bring home the body of one American rests in the archives of the Commonwealth Graves Commission in Maidenhead, England, outside of London, though predominantly in drafts of letters and memos that aren't found in their final form. It persisted over nearly a decade and seemed to lead to a continuing discussion within the Graves Commission about whom the dead were and how they should be treated, especially if they had come to the war from America.

Leonard Sowersby Morange was a member of the Yale University graduating class of 1918, but, like many young men, he had left college upon the U.S. declaration of war and entered military service. In May 1917, he arrived in the Officers Training Camp of the U.S. Forces at Madison Barracks, New York. He was anxious to get to the front and, after training in field artillery, he asked for and received an honorable discharge so that he might take the entrance exam for the Royal Flying Corps. At the time, there was an open channel between American flyers and British aviation similar to that of Americans and the Lafayette Escadrille in France, and training of Americans for the RFC took place in Canada and Texas. In early 1918, Morange was a student of what came to be known as the "Gosport course," a revolutionary method of flight instruction at the time. Remarkably, previous flight instruction had usually told aviators what to do with their airplanes while in flight with little reference to the reasons why, which lay in the complicated laws of aerial physics. The Gosport method, named after the flying school at Gosport, near Portsmouth, England, added the teaching of basic physical laws to flight instruction which, in turn, led to a better ability of new pilots to understand their own mistakes, and more effective standards for judgment of the work of their instructors.

Morange, now a lieutenant, was an exemplary graduate of the course and became an instructor of advanced training and aerial acrobatics. Finally, on August 11, 1918, he was ordered to combat at the front, but collided with one of his students during a training flight and fell to the ground, dead. He was eventually buried in the military section of a church cemetery in Shotwick, Shropshire, England. In 1919, his father, Edward, contributed to the catalogue of an aeronautical exposition held at Madison Square Garden with a tribute to his son and his fellows, excerpted:

> To you, hovering twixt youth and man's estate,
> You clear-brained, gentle-eyed boys
> Who, like eaglets with untrained pinions
> Sprang from your sheltered nests
> To stay the vulture's claws
> To you, conquerors of the air,
> With man-made wings,
> Who paid the price,
> That right should prevail ...[18]

The senior Morange seemed a sensitive, but persistent man. His burden, shared with his wife, would be made heavier with the death of Leonard's brother. Irving Morange had also been a flyer, but for the United States Air Service. He had been wounded on a reconnaissance mission and received the Croix de Guerre, only to die in 1926 of the after effects of mustard gas inhaled in the war. He would be buried in Kensico Cemetery near the family home in Bronxville, New York.

Leonard's death in 1918 was well recognized in Bronxville. He had been the first citizen of the city to be killed in the war and a memorial stone would eventually be placed in his honor. But Edward and his wife wanted their son back with them, and he wrote to the War Graves Commission in England requesting that the body be returned. The ensuing exchange of memos and letters within the Commission struggled with core considerations about a man of one country fighting in the forces of another. A draft of a form letter to be sent to all such applicants stated that the request could not be fulfilled, and tried to explain why.

> It was decided when first the question was seriously discussed, not to allow the remains of any soldiers serving in the British Forces to be exhumed and returned to their own country. When coming to this decision the Commission were aware of a pathetic desire in a small number of cases that this should be permitted, but the reasons to the contrary appear to them overwhelming. To allow the removal of a few individuals would be contrary to the principle of equality of treatment which must, you will agree, be the foundation of their policy; on the other hand to arrange for the removal of all, as the United States has done, was unfortunately an impossible task in our case—how impossible you will appreciate when I remind you that great as were the American losses ours were ten times greater. The British Empire gratefully accepted the offers made by the governments of France, Belgium, Italy and Greece and of all countries in which British Troops have fought, to provide land in perpetuity and "adopt our dead." I hope you will share the view of the overwhelming majority of the relatives of our dead, that a very high ideal

is embodied in these war cemeteries in foreign lands, where those who fought and fell together, officers and men, lie side by side in their last resting places, facing the line which they gave their lives to maintain.[19]

The request from Edward Morange occasioned a review between the Graves Commission and the British Foreign Office of the origin of the policy as it applied to Americans. Immediately after the war, such returns were allowed as exceptions though it appeared that few had taken place. By the end of 1920, however, the requests had become too numerous to accommodate in light of the Commission's stated policy and the practical reasons behind it. In April 1921, Sir Fabian Ware told the head of American Graves Registration, Colonel Charles Pierce, that it would not be possible to continue to allow those exceptions. In June, the Quartermaster General of the United States fully agreed to the right of the British to determine final outcomes for the bodies of Americans who had served in Commonwealth forces. The Morange request had arrived too late, but it was at least considered in good faith.

One line of inquiry within the Commission took up the complicated matter of the citizenship of these deceased. Those Americans who had enlisted in Commonwealth forces under the Citizenship Act of 1907 might be seen as having given up their American citizenship. A smaller group, including Morange, had enlisted under later determinations made in the press of war that they retained American citizenship. Thus, the argument could be made that, of all of those buried in Commonwealth cemeteries, Americans who had not given up their citizenship were exceptional to the rest who were Commonwealth citizens or subjects. The families of the former, who had given up American citizenship, should not begrudge the desires of the families of those who had not. Not apparent in any of the discussion found within the CWGC archives was the fact that those of the former who gave up citizenship would now have been allowed to regain it if they wished, but had died before the opportunity was available. In any case, the request to exhume the body of Leonard Morange, although he had entered the war as an American citizen, was ultimately denied.

The decision seemed to be accepted by Edward Morange in 1922. The Commission had assured him that a permanent headstone would be placed over his grave, and he was allowed to write its inscription. But when his second son died of delayed war injuries in 1926, he and his wife now had two sons killed as the result of their common service as Allied airmen in a common war, but buried on opposite sides of an ocean. It appeared to be a dilemma for the couple. He was more understanding of the Commission's notions of equality and ultimate rest with one's fellows in war. The ideas appealed to his wife as well, but not as strongly as did her sense that the two boys needed to be buried together. The decision was made to try once again for the exhumation and reburial of Leonard, and this time it was accompanied by a plan. On April 1, 1927, a representative of the American Express Company informed the Commission that the agency had been hired to obtain all of the formal papers required in England to exhume a body. Mr. Morange would be coming to England to seek the Commission's consent, and oversee the return of his son. The reply that was received was that the policy of the early part of the decade was still in place. It was suggested that he take up the matter with the American ambassador to the United Kingdom in whose office the matter had been previously resolved between the two countries.

Instead, Morange appeared in the London offices of the Commission on April 13. The results of that visit are told from a variety of unattributed and undated papers found within the CWGC archives (none of which refer to Mr. Morange without respect for his mission).

On his visit in 1927, Edward Morange's "object appeared to be to satisfy himself as to the Commission's policy in this matter, and accordingly the reasons for it and for applying it to the case of burials in the United Kingdom as well as those in the War Cemeteries overseas was very fully explained."[20] Morange asked for and was "shewn" correspondence between Americans and the British in which the commission was granted full authority over the American burials.

Then the following corrected paragraph appeared in the draft account of his visit:

> It was made clear to Mr. Morange that the Commission could not be expected to give official consent or encouragement to his plan, ~~but he was confidentially and unofficially given to understand that they could not go out of their way to stop its execution if he found a way of carrying it out without their official cognizance.~~[21]

Ultimately, the full paragraph received a strike mark. The following paragraph described a meeting with Morange on May 26 in which he renewed his request for official authority to exhume his son's body with his own resources, and repeated the Commission's statement that it could not "countenance that proceeding, ~~but would take no steps to prevent it.~~"[22]

An apparently later, undated document seemed to bring the issue full circle, then start it on yet another. It stated openly that the result of the May 26 meeting was to tell Mr. Morange that the Commission "would refrain from doing anything that would prevent him from having his son's remains exhumed and removed from England, but was advised to use every effort to prevent the knowledge of the exhumation and removal from being brought officially to their attention. Since his son was officially enlisted by the British Government, having been given an honorable discharge for this purpose by the United States Government, it is distasteful to him to be asked to bring back the remains surreptitiously, or even as those of a civilian."[23]

The memo then quoted at length a letter the commission had received from Edward Morange on May 15, 1928. It was now nine years after the war, but the father's integrity about the nature of his son's service perhaps summarized a view that could be taken of all Americans who had gone off to World War I under the flags of other countries.

> I claim that the conditions under which the United States released my son was but for a temporary service for the duration of the World War and according to the laws of our country he remained an unexpatriated American, entitled to the same privilege of return to the land of his birth, even though deceased, as those Americans ... who survived and returned to America with the official consent of both Governments...[24]

The matter continued on, but it was never resolved. Edward Morange had received all the documents and permissions to return Leonard to America, except for the official approval of British policy on the matter. It would be disrespectful of his son to remove the body under subterfuge, even though it would be quietly agreeable to all official parties. In 1929, the boy scouts of Bronxville, New York, attending a Jubilee in the United Kingdom, appeared in the churchyard at Shotwick to place a metal plaque in his honor beside his grave. Leonard and his memorials remained in place into the 21st century, near where he had fallen in war, under the adopted care of the Pritchard family of Chester, Cheshire County, England.

Almost everything that had preceded in the "War to End all Wars" would be repeated in the war that would soon follow.

NINE

A Troubled Respite

... we, from Canada, your northern neighbor, come with our nation's tribute to those who were, in the truest sense, our brothers in arms.—
J.L. Ralston, Canadian Minister of National Defense

Not long after the armistice ending World War I was signed in France, a number of Americans who had fought the war as members of U.S. Forces were back in Paris and commingling with those who had not yet left the country. As war veterans, they believed they had a platform to promote peace, and to advocate for their own welfare after a bruising fight. Veterans' organizations in England and France took on similar goals, and all three talked about eventually combining their forces in an international organization to prevent future wars.

The three-day meeting in Paris concluded with the election of an executive committee, and the determination to form common cause with a similar group also organizing in St. Louis for a national convention to be held on the anniversary date of the Armistice, November 11, in Minneapolis. It was suggested that the group of veterans take on the name "The American Legion." Thus, the third, and most enduring, American Legion of the century was born. By September 1919, membership was 400,000 in 4,000 posts in all 48 states. The initial membership goal of 1 million was pursued in welcome-home-to-veterans carnivals across the country, slides and talks in movie theatres, and cars driven about with American Legion signs and their mufflers removed.[1]

The previous American Legion, broken up into various other British fighting units of the war, had no place in the origins and concepts of the new organization. There seemed to be no postwar discussion of the role of Americans in British Commonwealth and other forces, and in following years the subject only showed up in occasional papers and military journals. One of those was undertaken by the Canadian military historian Ronald Haycock, and offered a nuanced look at the intricacies of the relationships between imperfect men.

History saw Sam Hughes, the Minister of Militia and Defence who created the American Legion, as willful and uncooperative with others in government who may have had other ideas, as well as a bad manager. He was forced to resign from the post in 1916, and died five years later. A memorial to him in his hometown of Linsey, Ontario, took the somewhat extraordinary step of referencing his controversy: "Differences with his colleagues and subordinates forced his retirement from the Cabinet in 1916."[2] C. Seymour Bullock, who perhaps tended to overstate his own accomplishments, ended the war as a traveling educator within the military on the subject of venereal disease. He died in South Bend, Indiana, in 1942. Other notables in the story of the legion presented other problems and inconsistencies, and, in retrospect, some of the American enlistees may have been less savory than Hughes and Bullock—and George Washington—would have liked.

"In its brief history," wrote Ronald Haycock, "the American Legion had been a military, political and diplomatic embarrassment to all concerned. It demonstrated many of the faults which marred much of Sir Sam Hughes entire war administration on a large scale. Nevertheless, it was also an interesting episode in Anglo-Canada relations. When the American Legion scheme collapsed, most British and Canadian leaders must have been relieved."[3]

Whatever the judgment of history, the story of the American Legion was at the center of an extraordinary response by tens of thousands of Americans to what they saw as a just war, in advance of their own country's decision to join the fight. Canada understood it that way, and, in 1925, Canadian prime minister McKenzie King proposed to American president Calvin Coolidge that his country build a monument in their honor in their own country. Coolidge agreed, and the construction of a Cross of Sacrifice was planned for Arlington Cemetery, outside Washington. The Cross had become the central feature of the larger cemeteries developed by the Imperial War Graves Commission. Designed by the British architect and author Sir Reginald Theodore Blomfield, it was a Latin cross formed in limestone and faced with a Bronze sword pointing down to an octagonal base.

The Arlington Cross was dedicated on Armistice Day 1927. Attendance at the ceremony on Farragut Drive, near the Tomb of the Unknown Soldier, ranged through the leadership of three countries including England, soldiers in kilts and fatigues, and assorted adults and children. They heard a succession of lengthy encomiums to the relationship between the United States and Canada. Said the American Secretary of War, Dwight F. Davis:

> Canadians and Americans speak the same language, read the same books, think the same thoughts. Jointly they occupy the largest area of the earth's surface where a single language is spoken.
> No unfriendly rivalry mars the even tenor of their intercourse. The calamity of one is the calamity of the other; and the attack upon one is an attack upon the other. They are jointly engaged in the greatest work of settlement and civilization known to mankind.[4]

J.L. Ralston, the Canadian Minister of National Defense, remembered the Americans in U.S. forces who had fought side by side with Canada.

> But that was not all. We remember today that your brothers in blood in our own forces, and shoulder to shoulder in the ranks with our own men, endured the toil and conflict, and we, from Canada, your northern neighbor, come with our nation's tribute to those who were, in the truest sense, our brothers in arms.[5]

The decade of the 1920s proceeded, but the memory of the American sacrifice did not recede in the national expression of France. The graves of those Americans who remained buried in France by the choice of their families were still well tended by the French people, and the French government seemed only to escalate the old sentiments of the Marquis de Lafayette.

The American Memorial Day of May 1923 saw the dedication of a memorial to American soldiers and civilians in the cloister of the American Cathedral in Paris. The event was led by French Marshal Ferdinand Foch, a hero of the war, and American Ambassador Myron Herrick, still involved in the lives and deaths of young Americans who fought with France. French president Raymond Poincaré was in attendance. The memorial was to include the names of those who fought with both U.S. and French forces, including Americans who had joined the war through Canadian and British forces.

King George VI places a wreath on the Canadian Cross of Sacrifice at Arlington National Cemetery in Washington, June 9, 1939. The cross was erected by the Canadian government in memory of United States citizens who served and died in the Canadian Army during World War I (Library and Archives Canada).

Two months later, on July 4, the nation's attention was drawn once again to the Place des États Unis in Paris, where there now stood a "Memorial to the American Volunteers." It had been built with public donations, and designed by Jean Boucher who had been inspired in his work by Alan Seeger. A statue of a French and American soldier shaking hands was accompanied by the names of 24 Americans who had died in the French Foreign Legion, and excerpts from the poem that Seeger had not been able to read in person at the same site on Memorial Day 1916, and which now applied to him, *Ode in Memory of the American Volunteers Fallen in France.* A statue of Seeger stood atop the monument.

Speaking on behalf of the French people, Premiere Poincaré thanked God that there was no longer a need for the volunteers, but seemed to warn against what was to come in the next decade. Volunteers were still needed to "fight with tongue and pen to combat the German propaganda which distorts our thoughts and actions and travesties our whole intention."[6] Marshals Ferdinand Foch and Philippe Petain were in attendance, as were representatives of thousands of schoolchildren who had donated small sums to the monument's construction. As ever, Ambassador Myron Herrick was there to honor the young American men of the Foreign Legion.

Once again, the memory of Lafayette was invoked, and Alan Seeger was quoted by French general Charles Mangin.

> It was those young heroes "who kept their rendezvous with death" in the uniform of France who spread the contagion of their heroism through the great western continent till it poured its wealth out in charity, and in blood on the battlefield, until victory was won.

On a rainy day in Paris one year later, a similar event took place at the Place des États Unis. It was part of what the *New York Times* described as "the greatest Fourth of July fête ever held in the French capital."[7] Flags and bunting throughout the city were "wet and bedraggled," and raincoats and umbrellas were severely challenged. This time, the march to visit Lafayette at Picpus Cemetery was led by the color guard of the American Legion Post Number One of Paris, followed by the Sons of the American Revolution. At the Place des États Unis flowers and wreaths were placed on the (incorrectly described) "tomb of Alan Seeger" and the statues of Washington and Lafayette. This event, too, seemed to point toward an unease that might eventually lead into a Second World War. At another event nearby, French Premier Édouard Herriott remarked upon the help America had given to France in the war. "He invoked," according to the *Times*, "the words of Pershing that America sent a million men and then would send a second million and, if necessary, a third million. Then he said that France still needed the help of America, as her fight for justice is not ended, and only with American help could she hope to win it."[8]

Paris had also been the site of another discussion that might have led to yet another organization with American Legion in its name, the American Legion of Poland. As the Great War was settled, it seemed that the dreams of Jan Ignacy Paderewski and the Polish Legion had been mostly fulfilled. Poland had reconstituted itself into a second Polish Republic and land had been gained through the course of the war and its ongoing settlement. But, as always seemed to be the problem, that land lay between Russia and the rest of Europe, and always in the center of ideological, economic and cultural conflict. Russia saw Poland as an obstacle in the way to a defeated Germany and Western Europe beyond, while a Communist movement was developing in post-war Germany that could seek closure with Russia. In between the two, Poland saw the time as an opportunity to firm up and perhaps expand its own borders eastward. The Polish-Ukrainian War of 1918–1919 and the Polish-Soviet War of 1919–1921 were a result.

Whether they were an extension of World War I, as some saw it, or separate events, their importance seemed pretty clear to many of those who had just been through a war that had pitted freedom against tyranny. Russian designs on Poland needed to be stopped in their tracks.

In 1919, Paris had seemed to be the center of the universe in matters of war. The Armistice had been signed there the previous November and the Paris Peace Conference was underway to determine the terms of agreement (and future conflict) among its participants. There were also enough Americans left in France to help form the new American Legion, and enough of them still in fighting mode that they seemed to be natural candidates for participation in yet to be solved conflicts. Many members of the Polish Legions of Americans that had entered the war in 1918 were still in place, and many more Americans of both the CEF and AEF forces, to say nothing of Canadians and Britons, were still in Europe and open to enlistment in the cause. Paderewski had not taken the opportunity to rest on the occasion of the Armistice. Instead, he approached the American Secretary of War, Newton D. Baker, with the idea that all American forces of Polish extraction be discharged so that they might join the Polish army. The number of such men was estimated at more than 200,000, but Baker and President Wilson denied the request out of fear that the Americans might be drawn into a pursuit that was more nationalistic than defensive.

At the same time, a similar effort was reaching out of Chicago to the Parisian Polish National Committee, but it, too, ultimately failed. Then a discussion took place in Paris about the formation of a contingent of former Allied forces, including a specific group that might be called the American Legion of Poland. Paderewski remained in the thick of the various efforts to bolster the army of his now established country. From Poland, he wrote to an advisor to Woodrow Wilson, describing the desperate fight in the country, and asking for help in slightly faulted English.

> My country appeal to the best, most generous friend asking for help, for salvation in this tragic hour. This barbarous movement will certainly be stopped in its further progress if fifty thousand Americans, one division of British troops and one French are sent immediately with necessary material for large Polish Army. Our entire civilization may cease to exist if action is delayed. The establishment of barbarism all over the Europe may result from the war.[9]

The appeal had no effect with the Wilson administration, but the continued effort to enlist Americans in the Polish fight began to reach into members of the American military still in place. In the view of Polish general Tadeusz Rozwadowski, based on friendships with American military officials, "a strong agitation is developing now in the American army, which is still in Europe, for whole units to enlist in the Polish forces in the event that we face battle against the Germans."[10] But he noted that the American government was opposed to the notion, and was quickly demobilizing troops in Europe so that they might not have the opportunity to make that kind of decision. Finally, an aide to Rozwadowski presented American General John Pershing with a direct question about the formation of an American Legion in Poland. That led to a considerable discussion over several weeks. It took the question seriously, speculated on practical problems that might be involved, including language differences, and suggested options for making it work that included using the French Foreign Legion as a model. As discussion seemed to turn to planning in June and July of 1919, the intricacies of its geopolitics became more complex, and ultimately it failed. However, that was not the end of it.

Among the many Americans who had flown the war in American, French, Canadian and British Air Corps was Captain Merian C. Cooper of Jacksonville, Florida. His service had been with the AEF, starting with the Punitive Expedition in Mexico, but it was typical of the resilience of many flyers in all services who would occasionally fall to the earth, take care of their wounds and leave the earth once again for more of the same. In September 1918. Cooper had brought his flaming airplane safely down behind German lines, and received the Distinguished Service Cross while a prisoner of the Germans. Eventually, he had made it back to a Paris hospital, and was soon back in the sky. Like a number of the distinctive flyers of the war, Cooper's military and executive skills kept his fighting life in a tension between non-combat work like intelligence and the constant itch to get back in an airplane and shoot the enemy out of the sky. Eventually he brought both skills to the fore in bombing runs behind the lines in which he was able to direct his combined flying and intelligence skills toward effective targeting.

On the return from one of those bombing runs, however, Cooper fell back to protect a comrade with mechanical problems, and received fire from enemy planes. One of the bullets made a strategic hit through the body of the observer with him in the plane and into the fuel tank. His plane on fire, Cooper's immediate plan was to jump, though he had no parachute. As he started to climb out of the cockpit, he saw signs of life in his observer and decided to try to land the plane. He climbed back in, but his hands and arms were badly burned and useless, so he crossed his arms against his chest and operated the stick with his elbows. He put the plane into a dive that succeeded in blowing out the fire, landing with a minor crash. Both he and the observer survived, but were taken prisoners for the rest of the war. At one point, German doctors urged that one of his arms be amputated, but he resisted and was able to make a full recovery before his return to Paris one month after the Armistice. There, he determined that there was more to be done.

Those few years as an airman in World War I were just a small portion of the remarkably American story of Merian Cooper. It had begun during the Revolutionary War in a correlative of the story of Lafayette and Washington. Merian's great grandfather, John, had served in that war alongside the Polish nobleman Kazimierz Pulaski. Pulaski was one of a number of Poles who had come to the Revolution, along with Tadeusz Kosciuszko and others. Kosciuszko had simply moved to the U.S. at the outset of the war, quickly become a colonel in the Continental army, and received a promotion to brigadier general before returning to Poland. Pulaski's life story had taken him, for a time, to a debtor's prison in France in 1775, but two years later he met both Lafayette and Benjamin Franklin who recruited him into the war in America. Arriving in Boston on July 23, 1777, he wrote to Washington, "I came here, where freedom is being defended, to serve it, and to live or die for it."[11] Upon meeting Washington, he advocated for an enhanced cavalry and was eventually able to prove his beliefs in the Battle of Brandywine. The battle would not be won by the Americans, but Washington ordered Pulaski to manage a least damaging retreat. His actions were judged to have saved the U.S. Cavalry from disastrous losses and to have saved Washington's life.[12] They also helped to give him the historical marker as "the father of the U.S. Cavalry." As brigadier general of the cavalry, he went on to a number of successes against the British until he was mortally wounded on October 9, 1779, and died at sea on the USS *Wasp* two days later. He was held in a regard similar to that given to Lafayette, and, as late as 2009, was proclaimed an honorary American citizen by the 111th Congress of the United States.

In Merian Cooper's family lore, it was his grandfather John who had transported the wounded Pulaski to the *Wasp*. The story had been told through the generations and was foremost in Cooper's mind when he returned to Paris amid the turmoil of Poland's continuing problem. He also learned of the work of Herbert Hoover's American Food Commission in that country. Poland's continuing fight for independence was undergirded only by poverty and starvation. There was not enough coal for basic heat, and firewood was rationed. It was not until mid–1920 that the Hoover Commission could attain a level of daily meals for 1.3 million Polish children. The city of Lwow, subject to continued Ukrainian attempts to take it by force, was among the most imperiled of places. Cooper volunteered with the Commission on February 12, 1919, and he was in Lwow a few days later to take charge of its mission. By that time, Poland was gaining victory over Ukrainian aggression, but Chief of State Joseph Pilsudski saw that as an opportunity to expand the country's borders, and the conflict evolved into the Polish-Soviet War.

Among the few spoils of war gained by the new Polish Republic were a few hundred German and Austrian airplanes that had been left behind in retreat. They formed the first Polish Air Force, operating from Lwow, in 1918. It did not take long for Merian Cooper to find a new calling in Lwow. The need for an experienced use of those planes was obvious. Cooper traveled to Warsaw and proposed that he continue on to Paris where he would recruit American pilots still in Europe. His first recruit there was Cedric Fauntleroy, who then became commander of the squadron. Fauntleroy was an American from Natchez, Mississippi. His career had begun with the French Foreign Legion, one of many that then continued into the Lafayette Escadrille, then into the American Expeditionary Force. In the AEF, he had flown with Eddie Rickenbacker's notorious "Hat in the Ring Squadron."

According to Kosciuszko Squadron lore, Cooper and Fauntleroy then set off on a tour of Paris cafés in search of unemployed American pilots. Among the first they found were Kenneth O. Shrewsbury of Huntington, West Virginia; George M. Crawford of Wilmington, Delaware; Edward C. Corsi of Brooklyn, New York; and Carl H. Clark of Tulsa, Oklahoma.[13]

Once the squadron was fully formed in Paris, it was reviewed in the garden of the Ritz Hotel by Ignaz Paderewski, who was by now the premier of Poland. The pianist offered the men $35,000 of his own money to offset their expenses, but the offer was refused. It was then that the squadron received the name of Tadeus Kosciuzko, friend and ally of George Washington.

By 1920, the small Polish air force had added some of the leftover planes of the European allies. Eventually, the squadron was composed of 21 American volunteers and saw its first service in the Kiev Offensive of April–June 1920. The offensive was seen as an attempt to establish an independent Ukraine on Polish terms, and the opening of the Polish-Soviet War. At the war's outset, the most important Russian advances were made by the First Cavalry Army, but they were most effectively counteracted by the squadron's strafing runs at low altitude. The Russian Cossacks seemed ruthless as they cut across the land on powerful horses, but they were no match for hand-dropped bombs from 600 feet followed by strafing at near horse-top level. The American aviators were described by their Polish leaders as exhausted pilots who fought like madmen. "Without their assistance," said General Antoni Liskowski, famously, "we would have gone to the devil a long time ago."

The results of the Polish-Soviet War included borders that would hold until World War II and an abeyance of Soviet ambitions in the region. Fauntleroy, who became Chief of Aviation of the Second Polish Army, had been wounded in July 1920 and received Poland's highest military honors from Pilsudski. He returned to America in October of that year and became involved in the recruitment of men and airplanes for the effort until its conclusion in March 1921.

Merian Cooper had flown 70 missions until he was shot down on July 26, 1920. He ended nine months of captivity as a Soviet prisoner of war by running from a work detail on the railroad tracks outside Moscow and, with a fellow prisoner, traveling 400 miles through the Russian winter to safe harbor in Latvia. The imprisonment had given him the occasion to start the next phase of his life with the writing of an autobiography, *Things Men Die For.* The book contained information about someone who may have been an illegitimate daughter in Poland, and, though it was published under the pen name "C," Cooper thought better of its revelations about her, and succeeded in buying back most of the 5,000 copies initially published in 1927. His postwar writing also included an unfulfilling period as a reporter for the *New York Times*, from which he escaped as a writer and photographer for a journey around the world on a sailing ship. That, in turn, led to experiments with film and documentary production, and the eventual production of two documentaries that were formative in the history of American film. *Grass* followed a nomadic tribe through a man-against-nature journey in Turkey and Iran, and *Chang* portrayed the struggles of an impoverished farmer in the jungles of Thailand. The films helped to open up an audience for other stories of man and wild nature, including the *Tarzan* movies of the 1920s.

In the late 1920s, Cooper took time off from his films to refocus on aviation. His experiences in Poland had made him severely anti–Communist, and he advocated for the development of civil aviation as the foundation for military aviation that would be needed in the future. His investments and public expression involved him in the formation of manufacturing companies and airlines, most notably Pan American Airways where he served as a board member. Then the producer David O. Selznick called him back to Hollywood. Selznick needed help with financial and technical issues for the film company RKO, and Cooper took the opportunity to develop a new idea for a film. It would involve a giant gorilla and use the new technologies of image production. Cooper's production of *King Kong* in 1933 became an epic milestone in the history of American film. In its most fantastic scene Merian Cooper and his co-producer Ernest Schoedsack, also a veteran of the Polish-Soviet War, could be seen as the pilots of the small biplane that finally shot the large gorilla from the top of the Empire State Building.

It would not be the last shot from Merian Cooper, especially in matters of war and Communism.

As seemed always the case, American aviators got more press than American soldiers. While the Kosciuszko Squadron caught the attention of American newspapers, the continuing story of Americans fighting for Poland on the ground went on fairly unnoticed. Official attempts to convert Poles in the American Forces to Polish Forces at war's end were never realized, but the Polish Legion developed by Paderewski in 1917 had remained in place. It was sometimes called the Blue army, after a design element in its uniform, and sometimes Hallers' army, after its leader at the end of the war, General Jozef Haller. As the Great War ended and the Polish-Ukrainian War commenced, many of the Americans of the legion stayed to fight and many other Americans joined the effort despite attempts from Washington to discourage them. Like the estimates and guesses of the numbers of Americans in Commonwealth forces, the number in Polish forces was reported variously to be 20,000, 70,000, or somewhere in between, but probably in the range of 20,000 to 25,000. The 70,000 figure of "American born or naturalized Americans" was given in a short *New York Times* article in February 1920. It reported that the Polish army was receiving 100 freight car loads of matériel purchased from the U.S. army. "A new levy of 300,000 men is being outfitted almost entirely with American army uniforms, including overseas caps. A half-million pairs of American Red Cross socks and a quarter of a million sweaters were distributed in December. American uniforms are being worn by most of the Polish Army at the front."[14]

Many of the Americans in the Polish army had come out of the French Foreign Legion. Most notable among them was Charles S. Sweeny. The son of a millionaire, the young man from Spokane, Washington, had gone from West Point to Mexico where he fought on the side of the reformer Francisco Madero against the dictatorship of Porfirio Diaz. Then he had moved to Belgium and married a daughter of that country, only to see the German invasion of 1914 and join the French Foreign Legion in response. Rising to the rank of captain, he was wounded in the battle of the Marne after he had single-handedly captured a German machine gun nest, and led the troops under his command across the German trench line. Following a period of convalescence in a French hospital and receipt of the *Croix de Guerre*, he returned to America just as the country had finally entered the war.

Sweeny's reputation had preceded him as he returned, but all that the bureaucracy of the American army would allow him was a teaching position at Ft. Myer, Virginia, accompanied by plenty of the grunt tasks given to new recruits. He put up with it all, but asserted his true value at the same time. The *New York Times* later described his predicament in dramatic terms (in an article written by the poet and fiction writer Steuart Emery; see note about the spelling of Sweeny's name in Chapter One).

> Sweeney of the Legion had seen many a gray dawn lighten a field wrecked by shellfire and strewn with quiet figures; he was a past master of the art of combat in the maws of the black trenches where every corner meant a new bomb; he knew the creeping midnight patrol of No Man's Land, the white flare of dropping lights and the malignant rattle of the searching machine gun. He saw no particular reason why he should be instructed by officers who had learned their battle out of the pages of a manual. He announced that fact in explicit terms.[15]

At one point, and almost overnight, Sweeny's true value was realized and he was promoted to major. He led a newly-formed 80th Division of Pershing's army back to France and stayed with his men on the front lines until he finally had to be removed to a Paris hospital just before the war was ended. He claimed that the knowledge of what his men had accomplished was enough satisfaction, and he did not need to be present at the final triumphant moment.

In Paris, he met Ignacy Paderewski and became caught up in the continuing struggle of Poland to reestablish itself between Germany and Russia. He assured Paderewski of his assistance if need be, and the moment soon arrived. Again, he worked the front lines with his men, and the *Times* reported the closing of a circle between man and machine that would open up yet another era in postwar Europe, and in Sweeny's career. "Sweeney of the Legion was Brigadier General Sweeney of the Polish army. Out ahead of his lines were going the fast planes of the Kosciuszko Squadron manned by former members of the immortal Lafayette escadrille. The little group of fighting Americans had come into their own again."[16] He had always been a foot soldier while many of his contemporaries had taken to the sky. After the Polish-Soviet War, there was yet another war seeming to be waiting in line to be fought, and Sweeny would push through this one in an airplane.

In November 1921, the *New York Times* offered a stray piece of reporting on a subject that was otherwise little known. Thirteen Americans under the age of 26 had shown up in the city claiming to have escaped cruel treatment as members of the Spanish Foreign Legion. Spain had been neutral in the Great War, and in 1920 it saw an opportunity to consolidate and perhaps expand some of its holdings just across the Straits of Gibraltar in Morocco, North Africa. Spanish forces were not well trained and equipped, and were met with resistance from the Moroccan Jibala and Rif tribes. The following years of conflict came to be called the Rif War. Riffian forces were equally as well prepared for war, but came from strong fighting traditions and were motivated to defend their own lands and homes. Members of the French Foreign Legion with nothing else to do seemed drawn to the formation of a Spanish Foreign Legion, and it was some of its American members that arrived in Paris seeking respite. Aside from the treatment they had received from the Spaniards, they claimed, this war was not like fighting the Germans, "a comparatively mild pastime compared with campaigning against the Moors."[17]

British Premier Lloyd George had written to Spanish officials protesting the treatment of all British subjects in the legion, and 53 of them were released from service as a result. It was sworn to the Spanish that the Americans among them were Canadians, and therefore British subjects. Though they left 21 of their fellow Americans behind in Spanish hospitals, the 13 described unfulfilled promises in pay and living conditions, barbaric medical treatment without the use of anesthetics, and food cooked in olive oil, which was intolerable to American and British digestive systems. The American Red Cross and the American Legion post in Paris took care of the men, who hoped that the U.S. Government would give them passage home.

By 1924, the Rif War had seemingly entered a new phase with the introduction of chemical weapons from the Rif side and the entrance of France on the Spanish side. It had also gained increasing international attention. The French, who also had interests in Morocco, brought 300,000 troops to the battle and lost an estimated 12,000, but the war dragged on. Airplanes were added to the Spanish side late in 1924, and in July 1925 the Escadrille Americaine was formed. Its name quickly evolved into the Escadrille Chérifienne, and it included a number of the flyers of the Lafayette Escadrille, including Paul Rockwell. Other Americans of the legion volunteered as machine gunners and observers. The fearless foot soldier Charles Sweeny emerged as its commander. The Escadrille was not popular with the American government, which, at one point, threatened to replace citizenship with imprisonment for its American members. And the Rif war became increasingly unpopular with the French people. The Escadrille flew only for seven weeks. Lacking an opposing air force, the largest danger for its pilots was to be shot down from the ground, or to fall for mechanical reasons, and be taken captive with the prospect of certain death by torture. That never happened, however, and, in 470 missions, it suffered no loss of life.

France won the war in 1926, and the Escadrille Chérifienne went pretty much unremembered in its aftermath. Charles Sweeny, however, still had decades of service to come.

And the Lafayette Escadrille that had served as the model for American flyers in two wars following the Great War was given its due in 1928, with the opening of the Lafayette Escadrille Memorial in the Paris suburb of Marnes-la-Coquette. Funded initially by private donors and families of some of the flyers, it became the Escadrille Memorial Foundation under the leadership of American lawyer and philanthropist William Nelson Cromwell in 1930. The bodies of 49 of the Escadrille's 68 fatalities rest in crypts beneath a memorial arch.

TEN

Spain and China

They were professional murderers and they took
Their blood money and impious risks and died.
—Hugh McDiarmid

When the luxury liner *Normandie* set off from its Manhattan pier and down the Hudson River on November 10, 1936, it was heading for a Europe that was once again on its way to war. The Treaty of Versailles, ending World War I, had not reconciled Germany to its defeat, and economic and social dislocation had only made the problem worse. In response, the country had begun to reassert itself under the leadership of Chancellor Adolf Hitler in 1933. By 1935 it had become a totalitarian state, with all energy devoted to German primacy, and that led, in turn, to the beginning of thinly disguised German aggression against its neighbors. In March 1936, Germany quietly re-militarized the Rhineland, west of the Rhine River. It seemed to meet no resistance from surrounding Belgium, the Netherlands, Luxembourg and France. France, in particular, was occupied with its own internal political and economic problems and could not devote much attention to a move by Germany that was seen by some to be understandable these many years after the war.

Among the notable passengers of the *Normandie* as it headed east was the "daredevil flyer" Bert Acosta. Born in San Diego in 1885, he had taught himself to fly and was designing airplanes in 1910, apprenticed to Glenn Curtis. In 1915, he was one of those who made the trek to Canada, becoming a civilian flight instructor for the Royal Flying Corps as it evolved into the Naval Air Service. He joined the American Air Service as an instructor when his own country declared war in 1917.

It was after the war, however, that Acosta came fully into his own as an almost incorrigible aviator. He seemed to break all rules of physics and aerial decorum at will, flying beneath bridges, and buzzing Manhattan skyscrapers, while his womanizing and drinking on the ground were no more redemptive. But he helped to map the first domestic air mail routes, and, in 1921, he set a new speed record of 197.8 mph. In 1927, he set a new endurance record with a fellow pilot, and that was followed by the first airmail flight from New York to France in a co-piloted heavy tri-motor just a month after Charles Lindbergh had made the same trip.

The *Normandie* was headed to Le Havre, France, but Acosta would be going on to Madrid Spain. He denied a *New York Times* report of the Spanish destination by saying he was meeting with a French airplane developer, and had sought anonymity by registering on the *Normandie* as "B. Acosta, ballet dancer." Four other American flyers were traveling with him, among them Edward Schneider of New York City who had set several transcontinental

The first successful coast-to-coast air mail delivery in an all-metal Junker F 13 airplane was noted with this picture at Durant Airport, Oakland, California, undated, 1920. Eddie Rickenbacker is second from left, and Bert Acosta is fourth from left (Oakland Public Library, Oakland History Room).

speed records, his first before he had turned 21 years of age, and Major Frederick A. Loyd of New York, who had gained Ace status in the Canadian Royal Flying Corps. Whatever Acosta's pretense to ballet, he and his friends had come to Valencia, Spain, to fly for the Loyalists in the Spanish Civil War.

Spain's neutrality in the First World War would repeat itself in the second, but the years after the first had not gone peacefully. The Rif War had ended to Spain's advantage, but by 1930, the country was broke and unsettled. The year 1931 saw the advent of the Second Spanish Republic, which took a liberal view of social, civil and religious rights and liberties, but it was not able to solve the country's problems and was met by opposition from those who held to more traditional mores of Spanish life. The differences became heated, and the elections of 1933 changed the course of government from liberal to conservative. In October 1934, conflict came to a head in a general strike that was most symbolized by a miners' strike in the province of Asturias. The strike took on the actions of a rebellion, and was crushed by army forces led by General Francisco Franco. Nationally, Spain seemed set on a violent course from which it could not recover, and which evolved into the Spanish Civil War of 1936–1939. Internationally, the Civil War became a proxy for sometimes violent passions across the full political spectrum from socialism to authoritarianism, left to right, and anarchy to suppression. Occurring in concert with German reawakening in Europe, and as a proxy for gathering differences between Germany and Russia, it would set one of a number of pathways to World War II. After the war, and into the following century, it would resound in literature, in subsequent conflicts between those deemed oppressors or oppressed, and in the internal politics of nations that had not been party to the original conflict.

It appeared, however, that when Bert Acosta and his associates arrived in Valencia to fly on the side of the Loyalists, or Republicans, against the Nationalist forces of Francisco Franco, it was not primarily under any great political motivation. They had met tough qualifications for the work and would be paid $1,500 per month, plus $1,000 per plane shot down and be given a $2,000 insurance policy.[1] They worked effectively on the Republican side, and Acosta was believed to be an unnamed Ace who led very successful air battles against Nationalist planes over crucial supply lines early in December 1936.

The recruitment of Acosta, and other American flyers, had been administered by Col. C.W. Kerwood, formerly of Lafayette Escadrille. At the same time, socialist efforts around the world, including the Socialist Party of New York, were doing their own recruiting for what came to be called the "International Brigades" in Spain. Therein lay the opening of the same debates that had accompanied American enlistment in foreign forces during World War I, though some of them would take a more perilous tone. Two days before Christmas 1936, the New York Socialists announced that they had recruited 500 Americans to the Spanish conflict, and had hundreds more on a waiting list. Two days after Christmas, the matter was up for discussion in the U.S. Senate. Members of the Foreign Relations Committee expressed concern that the Socialist recruiting violated American Neutrality Law, or, at least, the spirit of the law, which did not actually apply to civil wars. Neutrality laws had not changed much, if at all, since the confusions of the First World War and accommodations made in support of Americans who had fought it in foreign forces. The senators proposed the loss of citizenship for Americans who volunteered to fight in foreign forces, and that it take effect retroactively in the case of Spain. The New York Times reported that "a proposal of that kind would hit scores of Americans reported to be fighting for Spain today, including Bert Acosta, transatlantic flyer."[2]

Senate deliberations on the matter seemed eventually to become lost in the larger discussions that developed as the problems in Europe increased the debate about American participation in the coming war. In January 1937, however, the U.S. State Department got into the matter with full force. The U.S. consul in Barcelona claimed that it had just become aware of 76 Americans in Spain who had come to the country to serve with Loyalist forces. That was followed by a declaration from the acting Secretary of State, R. Walton Moore, that such service would be "unpatriotically inconsistent"[3] with American neutrality law. As in World War I, the Citizenship Act of 1907 was cited as the determinant of what was not permissible, but was limited to the taking of an oath of allegiance to another nation rather than, more simply, to a foreign armed force. It seemed that all of the twists and turns of working through citizenship status for those Americans in foreign forces in World War I had been forgotten.

At the beginning of 1937, the State Department was in the business of trying to remove the United States from Madrid. The consul was directed to advise any Americans who had come to Spain to fight in the Civil War that they should turn around and leave. Further, the department urged the same for all Americans in Spain for any reason. Many had already done so, but a core group of more than 100 stayed in place. For the most part, they were those with business interests that required their attention. Two of those who did return from Spain, and rather quickly, were the American flyers Bert Acosta and Edward Schneider. They were met by federal subpoenas upon their arrival in New York on the ocean liner Paris, and they had a variety of stories to tell.

Each said that they had left the fight in response to American neutrality law. In a separate interview, however, Schneider let slip that the flyers had initially been hired for the fight by a New York attorney, but not been paid for their work as contracted. His lawyer quickly brought the conversation back to a patriotic response to American law, and a federal investigation of those who had gone to fly for the Loyalists apparently came to nothing. The stories the men told, however, offered a glimpse into the sketchy beginnings of the Spanish Civil War. The bombers they flew were domestic sport planes with holes cut in their floors for the dropping of bombs; and the planes of their adversaries weren't much better. Sometimes the only guns available were those the pilots carried in their own pockets, though the Spanish pilots in particular seemed to be heedless of any danger. Food was not reliably available, and one could never be sure of the true loyalties of those one spoke with, so it was best to remain quiet.

What was coming to be called the "Yankee Squadron" in Spain had a lifetime of about three months. In February 1937, Acosta was briefly jailed in Nassau County, Long Island, for failure to pay child support to his second wife. He next appeared in the news in 1943 after an arrest for sleeping in a New York subway station, and died of tuberculosis in 1954.

It was the Abraham Lincoln Battalion, one of the International Brigades, however, that became the most important American presence in the Spanish Civil War, and in the following years of developing anti-communism in American politics. One of those who traveled through that time, then through the worst of World War II as a member of the Royal Canadian Regiment was Joseph Grigas. He was born into the Lithuanian community of Worcester, Massachusetts, on February 15, 1915. Grigas would describe himself as a loner in life, probably coming out of a difficult childhood. He joined the U.S. army probably at age 18, and ended up in the 14th Infantry Regiment. The regiment had been created in the Civil War, and continued with distinction in the Indian Wars of 1866–1878. It had participated in the capture of Manila during the Spanish American War of 1898, and in the Chinese Boxer Rebellion of 1900, from which it gained the nickname "Golden Dragons," given by the Chinese government. In 1933, the Regiment's job was to protect the Gatun Locks of the Panama Canal. Grigas more than likely gained experience there in the jungle operations for which the regiment became famous, and admitted later in life to enjoying the inexpensive availability in Panama of women and marijuana. At some point, he left the service. Those who knew him later in life suspected that it might not have been a friendly split (records on Grigas may have been among the 16–18 million lost in a 1973 fire at the National Personnel Records Center in St. Louis).

By 1937, the proxy nature of the Spanish Civil War had taken on the specter of a world struggle between harsh authoritarianism that some referred to as fascism and a freedom to work together for economic and personal fulfillment that some referred to as communism. In the United States, as elsewhere, the struggle was fueled by the economic turmoil of the Great Depression. An attraction to the civil war in Spain seemed a natural result for some, as it was for Joe Grigas. A friend later in life, Duncan MacMillan of the Royal Canadian Regiment, had heard Grigas say that he had once been a card-carrying communist. "But I don't know if he was an ideological communist. I think it all went part and parcel with however he became aware of the call for volunteers for Spain. And I believe that men who volunteered didn't have to pay their way over. There was a committee to raise funds to send them over, and somewhere in that he probably did sign up with the Communist party. He was well read, aware, and liked to talk about current affairs. He may well have thought that the fight against fascism was a good fight."[4]

For whatever mix of reasons, 2,800 Americans entered the 15th International Brigade on the side of the Loyalists, part of an international group estimated at 40,000 to 60,000.[5]

Thirteen hundred Canadians also volunteered, defying a Foreign Enlistment Act of 1937, and a mix of Americans and Canadians eventually filled the American George Washington and Abraham Lincoln Battalions and the Canadian Mackenzie-Papineau Battalion.

As in the prelude to American involvement in World War I, they were fighters and nurses, ambulance drivers and engineers. And, as before, many enlisted in the cause under ambiguous identities. They may have been seen as the leading edge out of the American neutrality that was increasingly debated as conflict in Europe escalated. By 1937, Germany had continued its return to previous territories with the apparent acquiescence of former enemies. It had made promises of non-aggression that wouldn't be kept. The Italian dictator Benito Mussolini had also been on the move in North Africa, and the two nations became allies. Mussolini had then joined with what were perceived to be the fascist goals of Francisco Franco. It seemed that the stage was fully set in Europe for another war, but some believed that it could be avoided if Franco could be defeated in Spain. Their numbers increased as the fork in the European road became more apparent, and their movement became increasingly intellectual, personified in America by the writers Ernest Hemingway, John Dos Passos and others. As Russian assistance to the Republican Loyalists increased through the Spanish Communist Party, those who flocked to the war against fascism were increasingly associated with socialism and communism, though these were not associations then as onerous as they would become in the 1940s.

Joe Grigas' first of just eight days fighting with the Lincolns began in early April 1938. He had joined a battalion led by brigade commissar Fred Keller that had killed 400 insurgents near Gandesa on April 1, then been ordered to retreat. At Gandesa, they were met with a machine gun defense, suffered heavy casualties, and joined with other brigades to hold a hill northwest of the city. Though Keller had taken a shot in the leg, he led a renewed effort at retreat that met with continued resistance. At one point, he and 17 others, including Grigas, came to the fast flowing Ebro River. With a bullet still in his leg, Keller was the first to swim across the river to show his men that it could be done. He swam back across the river a second time to assist them, but they were discovered and attacked. Some died and some were taken prisoner. Others, including Grigas, escaped the attack, but were captured the next day. After a 38 hour march back to Gandesa without water, they were imprisoned in a wine cistern. At that point, Grigas' active service in the Spanish Civil War came to an end. He would, however, gain the nickname of "International Joe" that would follow him later in life, perhaps most by his own encouragement. His actions at one moment in the coming European war would prove extraordinary.

Among those Americans attracted to the fight against fascism in Spain was a group of approximately 90 African Americans. The black experience in America after World War I had been perhaps more frustrating than before a war that was supposed to relieve the world of oppression. Segregation and discrimination were no less virulent, and lynchings were still commonplace. For many blacks, communism, which promised that the oppressed would prevail over the ruling classes, was an attractive idea. During the Depression, communism in America was active in assisting those in lower socioeconomic classes of whatever race in dealing with problems of discrimination and fair employment. The struggle between socialism and fascism in Spain seemed to be a logical extension of the struggle in America. And lurking in the background was the sense that Germany's attempts at destruction of the Jews could very easily continue on to the destruction of the Africans. It did not help that Hitler's ally Mussolini had begun his own course of war with a successful invasion of Ethiopia in 1935. Support for the Spanish Republicans was especially found in Harlem, and among notable African Americans of the time like Lena Horne, W.C. Handy and the Rev. Adam Clayton Powell. The writer Langston Hughes reported from the trenches, and, with the singer Paul Robeson, raised funds on behalf of the cause.

The invasion of Ethiopia was felt in African American communities, and among those arrested in demonstrations against it was Oliver Law, born in West Texas in 1900. He had served in a segregated unit of the U.S. army in Mexico from 1919 to 1925, and worked afterwards in a cement factory, and as a Chicago cab driver. He tried to open a small restaurant at the outset of the Depression, then moved on to the Works Project Administration. Unemployed in 1932, he joined the American Communist Party whose demonstrations in Chicago led to beating and arrest by the police department's Red Squad. With passport in hand, he left for France and Spain early in January 1937.

Law's army and work background made him valuable in Spain, first as the section leader of a machine gun company. He continued to rise in rank until he became the first known African American to lead an integrated military force, the full Abraham Lincoln Battalion at the outset of the crucial Battle of Brunete in 1937. The Republicans hoped that the battle would be a turning point in the war. It was well planned and practiced to divert the Nationalist effort near Madrid and open up territory in the North. Despite a force of 50,000 men and several hundred pieces of artillery, tanks and aircraft, it gained minimal ground, and Oliver Law was killed on July 9 while leading his battalion over a ridge. All around him witnessed his death, but, by the end of the 20th century, it was still controversial. Officially, he was a strong, black man beloved by his troops, shot down in the full forward movement of

Many African Americans were drawn to fight against fascism in the Spanish Civil War. Oliver Law, left, became the first known black American to lead an integrated military unit in war. His life and death were controversial, but he was honored with "Oliver Law and Abraham Lincoln Brigade Day" in his hometown of Chicago as late as 1987 (Tamiment Library & Robert F. Wagner Labor Archives).

battle. But there were a few who described him as a coward, probably shot by one of his own men.

The former version was almost certainly correct. There was only one known contemporaneous written description of the event, a letter written by battalion member Harry Fischer, dated July 29, 1937, excerpted:

> Once again Law was upfront urging us on. Then the fascists started running back. They were retreating. Law would not drop for cover. True, he was exhausted as we all were. We had no food or water that day and it was hot. He wanted to keep the fascists on the run and take the high hill. "Come on, comrades, they are running," he shouted. "Let's keep them running." All this time he was under machine-gun fire. Finally he was hit. Two comrades brought him in in spite of the machine guns. His wound was dressed. As he was being carried on a stretcher to the ambulance, he clenched his fist and said, "Carry on boys." Then he died.[6]

On November 21, 1987, mayor Harold Washington declared "Oliver Law and Abraham Lincoln Brigade Day" in the city of Chicago. The true nature of the death of the first black American to lead integrated troops was still being debated in the following century.

The Spanish Civil War was won by Francisco Franco and the Nationalists in 1939. Spain was physically and morally devastated, and recriminations would follow for years. Internationally, it brought Europe closer to World War II, and planted seeds of distrust between Russia and the West that would grow into the following decades. As a prelude to his novel about the war *For Whom the Bell Tolls*, Ernest Hemingway wrote an elegy *On the American Dead in Spain*:

> Our dead live in the hearts and the minds of the Spanish peasants, of the Spanish workers, of all the good simple honest people who believed in and fought for the Spanish republic. And as long as our dead live in the Spanish earth, and they will live as long as the earth lives, no system of tyranny will ever prevail in Spain.[7]

The presence of American volunteers in the Spanish Civil War was, and would remain for decades, the most controversial example of the presence of Americans in foreign forces. It was part of a larger and timeless debate over soldiers of their country and conscience vs. mercenaries and soldiers of fortune.

In 1935, the question was provoked by a small literary kerfuffle in which one poem was written to decry the message of another. In 1922, the English poet A.E. Housman, writing of the aftermath of the World War I Battle of Ypres, published the poem "Epitaph on an Army of Mercenaries."

> These, in the day when heaven was falling,
> The hour when earth's foundations fled,
> Followed their mercenary calling
> And took their wages and are dead.
>
> Their shoulders held the sky suspended;
> They stood, and earth's foundations stay;
> What God abandoned, these defended,
> And saved the sum of things for pay.[8]

In 1935, the Scottish poet Hugh McDiarmid, wrote "Another Epitaph on an Army of Mercenaries."

> It is a God-damned lie to say that these
> Saved, or knew, anything worth any man's pride.

> They were professional murderers and they took
> Their blood money and impious risks and died.
> In spite of all their kind some elements of worth
> With difficulty persist here and there on earth.[9]

Detractors of each would point out either that Housman was never a soldier, but a scholar (and homosexual, if that was a consideration in understanding his work), or that McDiarmid in 1935 was an avowed communist, under watch by British Intelligence.

The Housman poem was a favorite of American Claire Chennault, and often quoted by him as he went about setting up a force of American flyers in China, beginning in 1938. If the Spanish Civil War was a precursor to the European theatre of World War II, events in China were the opening strikes in its Asian theatre, and they had begun in the early 1930s. Japan had been recognized as an effective ally against Germany in World War I, especially in its actions against German supplies and supply lines in the Pacific. It had taken the occasion to expand its influence in the region. Then, as its economic fortunes deteriorated after the war, it had become increasingly nationalistic. In addition, it had been rebuffed when it sought a declaration of racial equality between Asian and Western nations in the Treaty of Versailles. A majority of the participating nations had voted in favor of the proposal, but it was overturned by chief signatories to the treaty under the premise that such an important question would require unanimous consent. Japan acquiesced to the insult in fact, but not in spirit, and racial discord between East and West grew into the 1920s.

China had also been an ally in the war, and 140,000 Chinese had worked as civilian laborers on the Western Front. They had done the hardest work in the trenches and burial corps, and on the docks of the Allied nations. But China did not turn out to be a beneficiary of the Treaty of Versailles. Rather than return to the nation a portion of Chinese land that had been owned by Germany, it was given to Japan, and allegations of the involvement of bribery in the move only served to increase Chinese unrest.

By the 1930s, the Japanese need for natural resources had increased as its government became more fascist. Looking further into the resources of the rest of Asia to support its economy, it found a China that was engaged in its own civil war between nationalist and communist forces, and ripe for the taking. The province of Manchuria was occupied by Japan without much resistance from forces paying more attention to a civil war. Western protestations and attempted sanctions against the occupation were to no avail. The following years saw increasing Japanese dominance in China as the Japanese government evolved from civilian to military control.

Claire Chennault had been born in Texas in 1890 or 1894 and discovered flying too late in life to participate in World War I. After the war, though, he joined the U.S. Army Air Corps and formed its first precision flying team to demonstrate his (some perceived as obstinate) belief that aerial fighting, combined with better intelligence, was more effective than heavy bombing. Eventually, he lost the debate, and not with notable grace. By 1937, he left the army in poor health, partially deaf from years in high-speed aerobatics, and not in favor with his superiors. The day after his departure, he was on a steamer headed for Japan, on his way to China. His passport identified him as a farmer, and he and an associate managed to drive all over Japan gathering intelligence from a flyer's perspective. He used cameras and binoculars to study the airfields, harbors and cities. His own observation, some years later, was that he had gathered more intelligence than the War Department on these aspects of Japan.[10]

Moving on to China, Chennault conducted the same kind of intelligence. Happenstance had placed a general of the Chinese Nationalist Air Force in the audience of one of his last air shows, eventually leading to his hiring as a consultant for the force, working with the wife of Generalissimo Chiang Kai-shek, who spoke English fluently and took on the job of reorganizing the air force with Chennault's assistance. He was able to gather more intelligence about Japan by studying its aircraft that had been shot down in China, and sometimes by flying up into a Japanese attack to study its tactics firsthand. Among his initial successes was a fighting tactic that exploited the weaknesses of Japan's superior air force while enhancing the few strengths of the Chinese force, but the initial going was difficult and confused. In his own view of things, he tried to share what he was learning and thinking with those who could act upon it in America, but to no avail. In the meantime, he developed an early warning system against Japanese air incursion over China. He described it as "a vast spider net of people, radios, telephones, and telegraph lines that covered all of free China accessible to enemy aircraft."[11] Chennault found the Chinese to be hard working in defense of their country, but many of the young men who would eventually be fighter pilots were in no way prepared. He was able to send some Chinese flyers back to America for training, and to import new planes into the force, but their casualty rate was high.

At the same time, a strain of the history of Chinese immigrants in America was taking a new turn in Portland, Oregon. The first known powered airplane to fly on the West Coast of America had been built and piloted, in 1911, by Fung (sometimes spelled as Feng, or Fong) Joe Guey. He was the son, or paper son (a young Chinese man with legal but fraudulent status as the son of a Chinese American citizen) of a wealthy San Francisco businessman, and he had a vision of returning to his native China with a complement of inventions that would contribute to its industrialization. He was not an American citizen and thus could not seek American patents, but the inventions in electricity, hydropower and electronics that streamed out of his small room in Oakland were astonishing for the day. They were written about with much respect in newspapers across the country, though article headlines variously referred to him as a Chink or a Mongolian as much as they called him a Chinaman. But it was the airplane he created through various versions that might crash, only to prompt him forward, that brought him his greatest recognition. One evening in late September 1911 he took the finished plane to a rural area near Oakland and rode it into the sky, though not above 20 feet.

> Leaving the earth with the grace of a bird, its engines throbbing and eager, the aeroplane swung upward near Oakland and glided away across field and stream, pulsing with the strength and life of a living thing. Strapped to the seat, satisfied, sat Fung Guey making history.... The graceful machine in which he sped through the air across the country, each delicate mechanism faultlessly responding to every touch, was not the crude handiwork of an eager amateur. It represented ingenuity and tireless energy and it was perfect in mechanical detail, and a thing of beauty in the symmetry of its lines.[12]

Due to a suddenly broken propeller, the plane fell to the ground just a few feet short of its landing, but it and the pilot were not badly damaged. Fung Guey never sought fame, only the development of technology for China. The flight excited the Chinese government, and he and his airplane returned to the country he had left as a very small child. Eventually, he would be recognized as the father of Chinese aviation and the inspiration for the development of a Chinese Air Force, but he was killed in a crash there in 1912.

Fung Guey's accomplishment in 1911 energized the West Coast Chinese community. During the 1920s, Portland, Oregon, became an aviation capital in America, and by the time that Charles Lindbergh arrived in 1927 on a flying tour to evangelize for aviation, the Chinese had formed a small but significant portion of the flying community. In 1930, eight Chinese

American students graduated from Portland flight schools, and the Chinese Aeronautical School was established on Swan Island in the Willamette River in 1931. Chinese investment in Portland aviation continued during the country's troubled decade of the 1930s, accompanied by the financial attention of wealthy Chinese Americans.[13]

The Portland aviation community produced the first acknowledged air fighting Ace of World War II. Arthur Chin had been born in Portland in 1913 of a Chinese father and Peruvian mother. He was still in high school when Japan first invaded China in 1932. A student of the Chinese Aeronautical School, he already knew how to fly, and he left with more than 30 fellow graduates of the school to volunteer in the Chinese Air Force. Two of those graduates were women, one who was denied a combat role because of her gender, and another who died of malaria soon after arriving in China.

After contract training in aerial gunnery with the German Luftwaffe, Arthur Chin was fearless in combat, and at one point knocked a Japanese bomber out of the sky by purposefully crashing into it and parachuting out of his own plane. Injuries from a jump out of a plane on fire in December 1939 effectively kept him out of the air until service flying transports over Burma late in World War II. Though an American volunteer for the Chinese Nationalist Air Force, credited with eight and a half victories, he received a Distinguished Flying Cross as an American veteran from the U.S. Congress in 2008. A post office was named in his honor in Beaverton, Oregon.

The conflict between China and Japan escalated to all out war on July 7, 1937, and the subsequent official American response seemed as ambiguous as it had been to the German invasion of France in 1914 and the outbreak of the Spanish Civil War of 1936. American cit-

A Chinese soldier guards a line of American P-40 fighter planes, painted with the shark-face emblem of the "Flying Tigers," at an unknown field in China (U.S. Army).

izens and industry, however, were drawn to the fight. While Claire Chennault increased his attempts at recruitment from China, an American soldier of fortune, Russell L. Hearn, was said to have recruited enough pilots, crew and mechanics in Los Angeles to support almost 400 planes. It is not clear whether any or all of those recruits actually made it to China. North American Aviation, also in Los Angeles, also was in the business of recruiting American pilots for the cause. Learning of these efforts, Japan complained about American intervention in its war with China. The United States had been supplying mostly arms matériel to Japan, and mostly airplanes to China until President Franklin Roosevelt imposed an arms embargo on both nations on September 14, 1937. The basis for the action was the Neutrality Act of 1937, which had been passed by Congress in response to the civil war in Spain. Furthermore, the federal government forbade American volunteers from going to China, and, as before, it wasn't a fully effective prohibition.

In response to Japan's complaint about American intervention, the American State Department proclaimed that the prohibition against travel to China was firmly in place. In the rare instances that it would issue passports for China, they were endorsed with the statement "This passport is not valid for travel to or in any foreign state in connection with entrance into or service in foreign military or naval forces."[14] As before, however, prohibitions against American travelers to foreign wars were open to interpretation and varying degrees of enforcement. In this case, Madam Chiang Kai-shek complained to the American ambassador to China that a prohibition against American pilots going to China to train Chinese flyers using American airplanes was not logical.

The response of the State Department was that the policy was directed at both warring countries and not intended to single out China. Recruitment continued, however, as the sentiment of the American public grew to favor China in the face of Japanese aggression. In 1939, Japan had escalated its effort to constant bombing of major cities, and, in 1940, Claire Chennault was directed to return to America to obtain more planes and better flyers with the specific task of ending the bombing. He would need official American help, but could not find much sympathy in the American military.

His goal was to create a small, but well-equipped air force in China that would succeed by focusing on the Pacific supply lines of the island nation. It was not an attractive idea to American military leaders in 1941, but Chennault found that China had a small, quiet advocacy group in Washington and the White House, including two of President Roosevelt's closest advisors. They helped Chennault to form what came to be called the American Volunteer Group (AVG). In April 1941, Roosevelt issued an executive order allowing enlisted men and reserve officers in the flying corps of the various services to resign for the purpose of enlisting in the AVG. They would not lose rank in the U.S. military. The nature of Roosevelt's order would remain controversial into the 21st century. It was written but not officially published.[15] Some who would later choose to interpret Roosevelt's actions before Pearl Harbor as secretly intended to undercut American isolationism and get the country into the war would point to the stealth creation of the AVG as an attempt to place a foothold in China. It had followed by one month the implementation of Lend-Lease aid, which provided matériel to the Allied nations already at war, although the United States was still neutral in the conflict.

Those 300 who joined initially were required to sign a one-year contract with the Central Aircraft Manufacturing Company (CAMCO) to manufacture, repair and operate airplanes at monthly salaries ranging from $250 to $750 ($11,500 in 2014 dollars), plus 30 days leave, traveling expenses and some rations. An unstated understanding added $500 for every destroyed Japanese plane, whether in the air or on the ground. The first AVG group left for China in July 1941, and soon thereafter, Roosevelt authorized the creation of a second group that would arrive one month before the eventual American declaration of war. Upon their arrivals in China, they were noted as tourists, acrobats and artists.[16] They quickly came to be known as the "Flying Tigers." One member of the first group, Pak On Lee, came from the Portland aviation schools. Lee was probably in the United States as a paper son. He had seen an ad for CAMCO in a Chinatown newspaper, and quickly became an AVG mechanic in Burma.

Arthur Chin was a member of a community of Chinese aviators in Portland, Oregon. Though he was a fearless pilot for the Chinese Nationalist Air Force, he received a Distinguished Flying Cross as an American veteran from the U.S. Congress in 2008 (various sources).

ELEVEN

World War II

We are often machine-gunned, too. The planes come so close down. Damn them!—Elizabeth Adams

Notwithstanding Canada's placement of its Cross of Sacrifice in America's Arlington Cemetery on Armistice Day 1927, postwar relations between the two nations seemed to have some hidden agendas and missed connections. American participation in Canadian forces during World War I did not rise near the top of the consideration of historians about that period, if it was mentioned at all. The official history of the two nations stretched as far back as pre–Revolutionary War years. Its first real conflict was in the War of 1812, and the perception that the United States was using that war to gain Canadian territory. In terms of military actions, there had not been much actual American-Canadian cooperation in World War I, and there was a lingering public attitude in Canada that the United States had taken too much credit for its role in the outcome, to say nothing of its delay in entering the war during years when American participation might really have mattered.

Nor was it forgotten that, though they shared a peaceful existence, these were two separate nations sharing the world's longest shared border. Prudence required that they have plans in place to go to war against each other if necessary. Who knew what could happen between the two countries, or what the results would be if one of them were taken over by another hostile force? Canadian planning accounted for a scenario in which the United States and Great Britain went to war, and the result for Canada. American planning took into account a British incursion through Canada. One Canadian war plan put flying battalions in place to bomb strategic American cities south of the border, from Seattle to Albany, in the event of an American invasion. The plan included information already gained through military reconnaissance flights deep into American territory.

It was not until 1974 that a declassified American plan to invade Canada emerged from the archives of the interwar era. "War Plan Red," developed through the 1920s and 1930s, foresaw the British Empire as an aggressor. Its first version, in 1927, was coincidental with the Geneva Naval Conference of that year. The conference was intended for the Big Five powers after the war, but France and Italy declined to attend, leaving the United States, Great Britain and Japan. The goal of the event was to balance out the world's naval powers, but the former two nations could not come to an agreement on the formulae for determining parity. The U.S. wanted to use the criteria of tonnage applied to the tonnage of other nations, while the UK measured its naval effectiveness in numbers of ships. Reasons for the discrepancies were complicated, and related to the different natures of their missions of protection of either a continental nation or a far-flung empire. They could not reach a compromise, and there were some in the American military who could see the potential of a future armed conflict between the two nations.

The problems of the 1927 conference were lessened by the subsequent London Naval Conference of 1930, but Secretary of War Henry Lewis Stimson approved the defensive War Plan Red in that same year. It was re-affirmed in 1935, and accompanied by a thorough description of Canada's geology, geography, infrastructure, industry, natural resources and combat readiness, as well as geographic strategies for reaching targets. Halifax and Quebec City were prominent in the planning because of their strategic positions on the Atlantic coast.[1]

Adding further to the mixed messages of 1927 was a gaffe on the part of American president Calvin Coolidge that seemed to represent the disparate knowledge that each country had of the other. The decision had been made to open the first Canadian legation in Washington, representing a further movement toward Canadian independence from Great Britain. But when the new Canadian ambassador, Vincent Massey, presented his credentials to the president, Coolidge noted that Massey had been born in Toronto and asked if that city were anywhere near Lake Ontario. At least Coolidge seemed to know that Ottawa was the Canadian capital, but he compounded his slight by initially refusing to send an American ambassador there, for the reason that he would probably have nothing to do.[2] The decision was reversed in the same year and diplomatic relations between the two nations were set on a new footing, though other perceived diplomatic slights by America were not helpful.

There were other problems. An increasing number of Canadians emigrated to the U.S. during the 1920s, and their fellow Canadians resented the movement. By the 1930 U.S. census, 1.3 million of those in America were Canadian born. Only Germans and Italians formed larger immigrant groups. Underlying Canadian resentment was the feeling that U.S. industry should invest more in Canada rather than pulling Canadian workers across the border. Over the decade the labor drain began to turn to a brain drain, and, by 1927, 600 Canadians were teaching in American universities.[3] The decade also saw a social integration of the two nations that could be seen as good or bad, depending on one's viewpoint. American social organizations like the Rotary club and the Junior League began to extend their influences from American states south of the border to provinces north of the line. American media, popular culture and sports took the same route, and could not be stopped at the border by those who feared the loss of their country's cultural identity.

American Prohibition from 1919 to 1933 was another complicating factor. Canada had preceded the United States in attempts to restrict the use of alcohol, from 1918 through 1927. Different provinces, however, had different ideas about the validity, enforcement and exception to the laws, and it could be said that it was actually a good time for the alcohol industry in Canada. That was in large part due to the thriving American market for illicit Canadian beer, wine and liquor. The largest point of trade was the Canadian American nexus at Detroit-Windsor. In 1920, Ontario supported 45 active distilleries. The water border at Detroit-Windsor was 28 miles long, and included numerous hidden coves, inlets and boathouses. Tunnels between the two cities were also used, and it was possible to drive cars across the frozen water in the dead of winter. It was estimated that 75 percent of imported alcohol products during Prohibition had come across the Detroit and St. Clair rivers and Lake St. Clair. In 1929, liquor was the second largest business in Detroit, after automobiles.[4] The trade became a sore point in official relations between the two nations. It turned out that there was eventually a lot to do in Ottawa, after all, as the United States repeatedly demanded Canadian help in stemming the illegal trade. Canada's position was that alcohol production and trade was legal in the country, and what became of the alcohol was none of Canada's concern. Occasional attempts by Canada to accede to American wishes were ultimately ineffective.

Over the same period, the Canadian penchant for emigration south began to meet the resistance of American immigration policy. In 1921, American immigration quotas did not include Canadians, but, by 1930, regulations related to those who would come from Canada were no different from those for those who came from anywhere else in the world. Canadians who had been used to casual travel back and forth were now subject to stiff rules and contact with immigration officers who seemed not to be very friendly. Detroit's labor force of 15,000 citizens of Ontario became unemployed.[5] Naturalized Canadian citizens caught up in the American immigration bureaucracy could find themselves deported not to Canada, but to their country of origin.

Tariff disputes between the two neighbors were perhaps the most complicated sources of dispute, but could be expected during a time of increasing economic interaction through the boom of the 1920s and bust of the 1930s. At one point, President Herbert Hoover offered the reduction of American tariffs as a quid pro quo for Canadian cooperation in the development of the St. Lawrence Seaway as a transportation route from the Atlantic to the Great Lakes. The Seaway was not favored by Canadian railroads, and the country's response was to increase tariffs against American imports. In 1930, the liberal government of Canada became conservative and more nationalistic, moving its alliance energies away from America and back to Great Britain.

At the level of the citizen going about his or her daily life, social interaction between the two countries became more pronounced into the 1930s, though not without misgivings. The automobile and the economy of the Roaring Twenties allowed American tourism into the largely unknown country north of the border, and it continued to grow despite the limitations of the Great Depression. It was mostly a one-sided exchange. 1932 saw 730,000 American automobiles enter Ontario alone, but the following year counted just 417,000 Canadian cars coming to American from all provinces. The travel was enhanced by the cheaper Canadian dollar, and was appreciated in Canada as an economic boon.[6] As ever, there were often differences between Canadian self-perception and what Americans seemed to see in Canada, a rugged and rural country infused with Indians and Canadian Mounties. The birth of the Dionne Quintuplets in a small town in northern Ontario contributed greatly to American tourism in the country, but also to the sense that it was an odd place. Canadians appreciated the economic results of tourism, but it brought them in contact with what they saw as American ignorance about the true nature of their modern country. Academic studies and conferences of the time about Canadian American relations, however, often concluded that the ignorance was shared on both sides of the border, accompanied by a good degree of ambivalence.

The coming war would require the development of better understandings. The inauguration of President Franklin Delano Roosevelt in March 1933 brought with it a more enlightened official American policy toward Canada. In the long picture of the Roosevelt presidency, one of its most important missions was to evolve the country out of isolationism to heroic participation in World War II. Bringing Canada into the national conscience was a good place to start, and it was a country with which Roosevelt had had some experience, though limited. The family estate, and a formative location in Roosevelt's biography, was at Campobello Island, just across the border with Maine in the province of New Brunswick, Canada.

After his First Hundred Days of setting in motion laws designed to bring America practically and psychologically out of the Depression, Roosevelt seemed to make Canada his second order of business. He returned to Campobello Island for a visit, and was met with the enthusiasm of Canadians and the warm glow of renewing old friendships. That led eventually to a reduction in tariff quarrels and policies that were beneficial to both countries as they struggled to rejuvenate their economies. Even those Canadian voices that could be relied upon since the War of 1812 to warn against American territorial designs seemed uncharacteristically quiet.

Roosevelt next visited Canada on July 31, 1936, the first state visit to the country by an American president. Misperceptions, trade problems, even contingency plans to invade each other had been made pretty much irrelevant by events in the larger world. Germany, Italy and Japan were about to formalize relationships that would put them on one side of the brewing war. As in World War I, England, Canada and the United States would eventually become allies on the other side. Roosevelt's trip to Quebec City, though not the national capitol of Ottawa, became a celebration of the two North American neighbors, and, by extension, their common ally, Great Britain. Encomiums to and from each were given all around in public ceremonies on Terrasse Dufferin overlooking the St. Lawrence, and in the shadow of the majestic Chateau Frontenac hotel. Roosevelt, speaking occasionally in French, recalled his days at Campobello and the delights of a cruise he had just taken in the Bay of Fundy. His narration of the common history of the three nations and France in the twists and turns of history of this part of the world, and with good results, was seen as an allusion to current developments in Europe with hopes for the same.

Reporting on the event, the *New York Times*, recalled the importance of Quebec City in American history. It had been the site of a battle of the Revolutionary War that had been decisive for the British, fatal for the American General Richard Montgomery and a loss for his comrade Benedict Arnold. "From its portals," wrote the *Times*, "sallied forth Marquette to discover the Mississippi, La Salle to take possession of it for France, De Bienville to found New Orleans, La Motte Cadillac to sow the seeds of Detroit. Du Lhut to give a name and existence to Duluth."[7]

In the present day, however, Roosevelt's visit had come at an auspicious time, "when war clouds threaten the European horizon, and Canadians, dismayed by the spectacle, seem disposed to turn their eyes back to their own continent, where they have enjoyed a century and more of peace."[8]

Two weeks later and in following years, Roosevelt followed the warm words of his Canadian visit with specific pledges about the protection of Canada. The United States, he said in a wide-ranging speech at Chautauqua, New York, on August 14, 1936, would continue to try to influence all parties in conflict toward peaceful resolution, but would not be isolationist, and would protect its neighbors against aggression without hesitation. Two years later he told an audience at Kingston, Ontario, "The Dominion of Canada is part of the sisterhood of the British Empire. I give to you the assurance that the people of the United States will not stand idly by if domination of Canadian soil is threatened by any other empire."[9] Roosevelt's assurances were followed two days later with a complementary assurance by Canadian prime minister Mackenzie King that his country had an obligation in return to ensure that it would prepare to be immune from attack or invasion, and that "should the occasion ever arise, enemy forces would not be able to pursue their way either by land, sea or air, to the United States across Canadian territory."[10]

On August 17, 1940, Roosevelt and King met once again in upstate New York to sign the Ogdensburg Agreement. Canada had already declared itself in the war though it seemed certainly safe from physical jeopardy. But Germany had been so successful that the notion Great Britain would not be invaded, and that the Atlantic Ocean would be an effective barrier against its aggression seemed no longer fully certain. Canada was, after all, at war with Germany, and now it had to take steps to be ready to defend itself, if necessary. Aside from its willingness to be helpful to its northern neighbor, the United States also had to be vigilant about an attack on Canada that could easily move south. The resulting agreement led to the formation of the Permanent Joint Board on Defense. It had its operational roots in the successful International Joint Commission, which had been set up in 1909 to deal with boundary issues between the two nations. Some Canadians and Britons angrily opposed the agreement as giving the U.S. too heavy a hand in Canadian affairs while lessening British influence, but the Board would continue into the 21st century with an active agenda pursued by military and civilian officials of both nations.

On September 1, 1939, German troops quickly took control of Poland, and, on September 3, England and France declared war against Germany in response. On that same day, the British passenger liner SS *Athenia* was off the coast of Ireland on its usual journey from Glasgow to Montreal, with 1,100 passengers aboard, when she was hit by two torpedoes from a German submarine. The event was confusing and ambiguous. Had the submarine captain mistaken her for an armed merchant ship? Had there actually been a German submarine in the region? Was it secretly torpedoed by friendly forces to incite American and British sentiments for war? Whatever actually occurred, it was loosely covered up by Germany, and the truth of the matter didn't finally emerge until the Nuremburg war trials of 1946. Even then, it was not clear whether the attack was a deliberate and illegal act against a passenger ship, or a genuine case of mistaken identity.

No matter the cause, the *Athenia* was the first British ship to be sunk by Germany in World War II, and occasioned the war's first death of a Canadian citizen. The ship had taken more than half a day to sink, allowing the rescue of most of her passengers, but among the 117 killed was 10-year-old Margaret Hayworth of 240 Province Street, Hamilton, Ontario. Her body was returned to Hamilton where it was met with public ceremonies attended by Canadian dignitaries. The war was on, and the child's death would remain a rallying cry throughout its duration.

This was not 1914, and former British dominions were now free to conduct their own foreign policy. Canada was not anxious to get involved in another war, but, in debate, its place now as an independent nation engendered its responsibilities to the rest of the world, and Great Britain was still its spiritual partner. Other considerations for Canada included its relationship with a potentially fallen France, and the seeking of a way out of the lingering Depression. More significantly, there was an almost unspoken question in Canada that derived from the difference between its historic ties to England and its geographic proximity to America. If it went with America, would it become just another dependent of its southern neighbor?[11]

Though the outcome had not really been in doubt, the time between the British declaration of war on September 3 and the Canadian declaration on September 10 had contributed to the country's sense of self-determination before it committed its people and treasure to what would become a horrific war. As in World War I, it would be more than two years before the United States would follow suit. And, as in the previous war, Canada was not fully prepared for what was to come. Its active military personnel included less than 10,000 on land, sea and in the air, though there were plans already in place to quickly develop those numbers if needed. In the first month of the war, Canada enlisted more than 58,000 in the cause. By December, the first units of the First Canadian Infantry were on their way across the Atlantic.

Just more than 3,000 of the 10,000 active military in place were aviators. The Canadian Air Force of World War I had gained status as the Royal Canadian Air Force during the 1920s, but, in the early 1930s, it had fallen under the knife of budget cutting, and could only begin to regain its strength beginning in 1935. In 1939, the anticipation of war had set a number of steps in place that would have the force prepared for what would be a larger and more complex use of aviation and aviators in the fight. And, as in the previous war, it would consider aviators as members of an international talent pool that was not necessarily divided by country of origin.

Following the Canadian declaration of war, the RCAF was authorized to develop a reserve force that any man "of pure European descent" could join, and through which he could move on to service in the Royal Air Force in England. The potential pass through was a feature of the British Commonwealth Air Training Plan (BCATP), sometimes called the Empire Air Training Scheme (EATS), or, in Canada, the Joint Air Training Plan (JATP). The training program was begun in 1939 and designed to prepare enlistees from Great Britain, Canada, Australia and New Zealand with initial training in their home country and advanced training in Canada before going or returning to England for service in the war. Training facilities and trainees in the small country of England would be easy targets, while Canada would give them safety and the wide open spaces to experiment with their airplanes. The goal was to prepare 50,000 aviators per year, and, at first, recruiting and enlistment exceeded the capacity to absorb them.

Among those involved in the recruitment for a revitalized Canadian air force was the World War I Ace Billy Bishop. As a pilot of both the Royal Flying Corps and the Royal Air Force, he had shot down 75 German aircraft during the war, five of them within a two-hour period. For a time, he led a squadron made up of his own recruits among Britons, Canadians and Americans. The remainder of his years would seem both restless and substantial. After the war, he had tried exhibition flying and trading on his status as a lecturer in Canada and the United States, then returned to England as a businessman. A fortune made in the selling of iron pipe was lost in the stock market crash of 1929, and he started over again in the oil industry in Montreal. A flying accident during his sojourn in England had left him nearly blind until corrected by surgery some years later. He took up flying again in the 1930s, admitting that it was a skill that had to be relearned in a more modern time. As Canada headed toward war in 1938, he was among a handful of distinguished Canadian aviators to be appointed to an Air Advisory Committee that would counsel the government on matters pertaining to the RCAF. He had felt that the force had been drifting in the interwar years, and needed the invigoration of new training and technology.

Upon the Canadian declaration of war, Bishop was appointed to active service in the RCAF and made Director of Air Force Recruiting. He did not hesitate to look toward America for new personnel. As in the previous war, the legalities were tricky, but Bishop met the challenge head-on with a visit to the White House in March 1939, from which he returned with confidence that American aviators would once again serve in Canadian and British flying forces.

In August 1939, another veteran of World War I appeared in Paris to repeat one of the recruiting dynamics of that war. Colonel Charles Sweeny had been a member of the French

Foreign Legion, then of the American Expeditionary Forces in the first war. Then he had become a brigadier general in the Polish-Soviet War, and followed as commander of the Escadrille Chérifienne in the Rif War. In the interwar years, he had been a journalist specializing in military affairs. Now he was in Paris with a colleague, Brigadier General Henry J. Reilly, to announce that if war did indeed come about, they would be creating an American division under their own command. It was reported that planning for the division by members of the American Legion, the Veterans of Foreign Wars, and former members of the French Foreign Legion and the Lafayette Escadrille had been under way since late in the previous year. It would include an infantry brigade and the Prince Brigade, an aviation force named in honor of Norman Prince, who had lost his life in Escadrille fighting of 1916.

Once again, recruitment would try to respect American law by taking place in Canada through the French consular service. The movement of Americans into World War I starting in 1914 had never really been disapproved, in Sweeny's view, and there was no reason not to do it once more.

> It has seemed to us that apart from what the United States Government may or may not do provision should be made so those young Americans who feel deeply that the cause of freedom is at stake will have an opportunity to enlist in its defense. We have thought that the response which we are certain of getting may make those in Germany, who by their pressure on Poland, are endangering the peace of the world, reflect before they commit an irreparable act.[12]

Sweeny's surmise about sober reflection was not realized, but the beginnings of an infantry were reported from Paris the following month. Three hundred Americans had offered their services to France in the first week of September, and 2,000 more had registered for consideration, according to Sweeny, 250 of them from Texas.[13] Infantry enlistments were converted into a French ambulance corps, and no more was heard about them. Two months after the announcement in Paris, Reilly was reported to have arrived in America on the flying boat *American Clipper*. Soon thereafter, he was named a war correspondent for NBC News. A version of the Prince Brigade would come to pass, however, and Charles Sweeny would become a key player in the coming air war.

Just before the turn of the 1940s, reports began to emerge of Americans showing up in Canada to enlist in its army. In September, the premier of British Columbia said that he envisioned an expeditionary force of 2 million Canadians and Americans that "would soon end the war." His office had already received "scores of inquiries" from residents of the United States.[14] In April 1940, the United Press reported that thousands of Americans had already enlisted, or tried to enlist, and described the fairly easy path an American needed to take to reach that goal. He need only say that he had come to Canada before September 1, 1939, knowing that the claim would not be investigated. If he did not have an American passport, he could probably obtain a foreign passport from one of various consular offices in Canada. Any illegality involved was not the responsibility of Canada, but of the foreign country.[15]

Questions of the legality of enlistment by Americans in foreign conflicts were compounded by a contemporaneous event in Finland. In one of the first skirmishes of World War II, the Soviet Union had opened an invasion of its northern neighbor on November 30, 1939. The stated goal of the invasion was the recovery of land lost to Finland during the Russian Civil War of 1917, territory that was now needed to protect nearby Leningrad. It was met with worldwide condemnation and Russia's quick expulsion from the League of Nations, and, for all of that, it did not go well for Russia. There was, of course, no match in military resources between the Soviet Union and tiny Finland, but, large as the Russian force was, its morale and leadership had been hollowed out by Josef Stalin's Red Army purges of

1937. In contrast, the Finns were clever and more motivated in defense of their country and managed to keep the upper hand in the conflict until the following February.

The attempted oppression of the small country by its larger neighbor did not go unnoticed among those who monitored social justice internationally. It was pretty much agreed that when winter turned to spring in that part of the world, Russia would be able to finish the task. Once again, a strain of Americans became determined to join in the fight and pressed against the limitations of what it was legal for them to do. And, once again, the discussion was very public in newspapers and in Washington, and bent toward finding the legal paths through which an American could follow his or her convictions in a foreign war.

On September 6, 1939, President Roosevelt had greeted the beginning of the European war with a declaration and reminder of American neutrality law. It proscribed American citizens from serving with a belligerent force in various ways, and from serving against a force that was officially at peace with America—if said American joined that force, or was hired, from within the United States.[16] It did not apply to Americans who acted outside of American borders, and, though not stated in the review of neutrality law, it was generally accepted that such a citizen would not be in danger of losing his or her citizenship. Also accepted was the ability of the U.S. State Department to exercise individual discretion in perhaps not asking if an applicant for a passport intended to go to Finland, for example. And of course, Americans could go to Canada without a passport and out of American jurisdiction as they took whatever steps were needed to continue their journeys elsewhere. And it was pointed out that earlier State Department attempts to restrict American travel in relation to the Spanish Civil War and the Japan-China War had not ultimately been effective. It would seem unfair to try to apply them in this case.[17]

Ultimately, 400–500 Finnish Americans, naturalized and un-naturalized, were estimated to have traveled from New York to fight for their homeland. In addition, Kermit Roosevelt, the son of former President Teddy Roosevelt, formed a Finnish Legion in London. What came to be called the Winter War ended on March 12, 1940, with the ceding of relatively small, but important, portions of the border area to Russia. In its aftermath, however, confidence in Russian and Allied forces was shaken at the beginning of the Second World War.

The opening of the European war also brought about the revitalization of the American Field Service. During the interwar years, the AFS had maintained a mission in France to build upon the good feelings between the two countries that had derived in part from its work in World War I. The effort was assisted by Myron T. Herrick, who remained the American ambassador to France until his death in 1929, but was limited by the economics of the Depression. It managed to create only a handful of student exchanges between the two countries, but the organization was kept alive. The declaration of war brought an immediate attempt to restart the ambulance service, and a tendency for bureaucratic resistance in France was out-balanced, in this case, by lingering memories of the effectiveness of the AFS in the previous war. Offices in New York and Paris were opened in November 1939, and quick word came from the U.S. State Department that it would expedite all matters related to passports and international travel. Other Americans in France started a few similar ambulance services, but AFS would predominate.

The first order of business was to determine what cars would be used. They would need to be light so they could move at speed, but sturdy enough for conversion to war use by the French army. Most were General Motors products. Each ambulance unit would include 27 vehicles, including a kitchen truck and trailer and a staff car. By mid–1940, however, the need was so urgent that ambulances and personnel were sent to a general pool in France as quickly as they could be produced. American personnel would work for AFS and not have to sign any agreements with the French army, but, as the enlistment of American volunteer drivers began to accelerate at that time, the appeal included the words of those at the highest levels of French government and defense. Marshall Philipe Petain remembered the work of the AFS in World War I and expressed "infinite gratitude" for the effort already underway in the current war. "I beg of you to thank our friends in America with all my heart and to express to them all my good wishes for the entire success of your undertaking so valuable to France."[18]

Volunteers were required to be experienced automobile drivers under the age of 30. They had to pay for their own uniforms and travel expenses to and from France, where they were required to serve for a minimum of six months. The first of them sailed for France in March 1940. Many were students of the most prestigious colleges and universities, predominantly Harvard University. For the most part, they were recruited and sent on their way with best wishes by AFS volunteers who had distinguished themselves in World War I. By May, nine members of the first group were missing in action in northern France, and one wounded. All were eventually found to be in German custody, from which they were released on the condition that they be sent home. Those lost and found included members of an AFS unit known as the Polish American Volunteer Ambulance, which used vehicles donated by, and named for, individual American Poles. The unit worked with the Polish army in France, which had been formed under General Wladyslaw Sikorski after the German invasion of Poland.

AFS volunteers faced the constant possibility of capture, and could not be confident that they would be treated well. Among those who escaped near capture was Anne Morgan, daughter of financier J.P. Morgan, and, by 1940, 66 years of age. She had been a fierce advocate for women since her twenties, and a resident of France at the time of the German invasion of Belgium in 1914. A visit to the Marne battlefields set her on a life's course of using her influence to enhance the effect of the work that women did in war, especially in the healing arts and assistance to families caught up in war. In addition, she served as a go-between for transatlantic development of French American methods and philosophies in those regards. Among the organizations within the AFS that she helped to put in place was the Committee for a Devastated France (CARD). Between the wars she lived in a 17th century estate in Blérancourt, continuing the cultural exchange between the two countries.

When Germany once again invaded Belgium in 1940, Blérancourt became a home for Belgian refugees and regional medical center for those affected by the war. Anne Morgan was instrumental in the quick start-up of AFS in the new war, and she was working with the ambulance service perhaps within a mile of the German advance at Laon, France. The capture of an ambulance and its personnel led to speculation in the *New York Times* by one of those interviewed in a German prison camp that her safety might have been jeopardized, though it appeared that she had escaped from danger. Morgan would have welcomed the speculation in an American newspaper because her method had always included publicity in America for the work and the cause. She died in Mt. Kisco, New York, in 1952, and Blérancourt remained a museum dedicated to Franco American relations into the 21st century.

In May 1940, one of the ambulance drivers under her direction, Elizabeth Adams of Providence, Rhode island wrote at length to her parents, excerpted:

> At 1:30 A.M. one black early morning we were awakened with "Get out!—find your cars! evacuate all the children!—there isn't time to wait for the old and sick!—but save the children!"

Without lights, airplanes zooming overhead—bombs dropping about—we drove about evacuating people. When we left that town the enemy was very close. We are following the refugees—trying to give them food when we can find any—and care for them on their dreadful journey.

We are now in another town farther away, but bombs drop here just as much. One went down just this second.

I know what it is like to be driving twenty people in a truck—see the planes—because when planes are coming people's faces turn upwards to look and the truck makes so much noise I can't hear them—so I watch the refugee's faces on the roadside. Anyway-it is hell to get those twenty people out of the truck and into a ditch and lie down and wait. We are often machine-gunned, too. The planes come so close down. Damn them!

Elizabeth Adams ended her letter with the plea: "Please have America help. We need her."[19] She had been a social worker and teacher before joining the AFS, and after her service, for which she received the *Croix de Guerre*, she became a lecturer on conditions in Europe, and traveled the United States for the Treasury Department in support of U.S. war bonds. Upon the Japanese attack in Pearl Harbor, she joined the Women's Auxiliary Air Corps (WAAC) as a second lieutenant.

The American Field Service would continue to meet conditions like those described in her letter home, its work extending across the Mediterranean to North Africa.

TWELVE

In the Sky and on the Sea

I said to myself: "That's me. I'll have some of that." I waited no longer.
—Alex H. Cherry

The 1932 Winter Olympics in Lake Placid, New York, were opened on February 4 by New York Governor Franklin Delano Roosevelt and came to a conclusion 11 days later with just one piece of unfinished business. One round of four-man bobsled competition had already taken place on a very fast track, and trial runs since then had built anticipation for a dramatic final run. But sunny days had made the track at Saranac Lake difficult and the competition had been put off a number of times. Previous accidents born of excessive speed while the track was still frozen had whittled down the real competition to just two teams, both American. The favorite was led by Harry Homberger, a local civil engineer who had designed and built the track. The other sled was driven by 21-year-old Billy Fiske, a native of Brooklyn, New York, who had carried the American flag in the opening ceremonies.

William Meade Lindsley Fiske III was a child of wealth and distinguished ancestors reaching back to the Revolutionary War. After serving as a general under Ulysses S. Grant in the Civil War, Clinton Fisk (the family used both spellings of Fiske and Fisk) was appointed to the Freedman's Bureau, created to assist freed slaves after the war, and was credited with founding what became the predominantly African American Fisk University. Rear Admiral Bradley Allen Fiske graduated from the U.S. Naval Academy in 1874, and went on to invent a number of the tools of naval combat that would have an effect well into World War II: electrically powered gun turrets, telescopic sighting, electromagnetic torpedo detonators, and airplanes designed to drop torpedoes into the path of oncoming ships. Other ancestors included historian and philosopher John Fiske, and, by marriage, Minnie Maddern Fiske, known at the turn of the 20th century as the "First Lady of the American Stage."

Young Billy had spent much of his childhood in France, where he discovered that his inherent skills were especially suited to bobsledding. At age 16, he moved to Cambridge University in England and participated in the 1928 Winter Olympics in St. Moritz, Switzerland. There, he drove the U.S. bobsled and became the youngest person at that time to win a gold medal in Winter Olympics. Now, on the last day of the 1932 Olympics, he and his fellow bobsledders were in a foul mood. The first two of four runs had come sluggishly down the slushy track, and the competitors finally insisted that the day's racing be stopped. Although the Olympics would be officially over, they agreed among themselves to finish the event the following day if the track was in better condition.

It was, and, soon after, Fiske and his team bore down for the final run, exceeding speeds

Billy Fiske and his team exceeded speeds of 60 miles per hour in the winning American bobsled run of the 1932 Winter Olympics. He died in combat for the Royal Air Force, and was memorialized in services at St. Paul's Cathedral, London, on July 4, 1941 (Lake Placid Olympics Museum).

of 60 mph. Fiske needed to steer away from the ruts and find the fastest surface for his sled without getting too wide of the safe margins. The runners rose up to an inch of the track's lip, and the four bobsledders leaned into the curves, barely holding on to their leather straps. The sled found greater speed in the straightaways, then rose through a curve that had already shattered the dreams of a number of competitors, before reaching a final zigzag. It bucked left and right, occasionally lifting entirely from the track, and crossed the line with the best time of the race, 1:56:59. Once again, Billy Fiske won the gold medal. He might have been expected to seek similar glory in the 1936 Winter Olympics in Bavaria, but he felt that it would be disrespectful of his sport to offer it as an entertainment for Adolf Hitler, and he refused to enter the competition.[1]

Between the Olympics, Fiske had followed his education in economics and history at Cambridge with work in the London office of his father's firm, Dillon, Read & Co. And he had taken time out to enter the occasional automobile race, driving a Stutz Bearcat in the 24 hour Le Mans race of 1930, and setting the road speed record between London and Cambridge in his supercharged Bentley. Through all of that time, Fiske developed a dual image as a character who might have stepped out of a novel by F. Scott Fitzgerald, and as a serious young man with certain values and integrity. The decision to stay away from the 1936

Olympics seemed not to be difficult for him. He had lived a life of exquisite freedom and believed that it was worth fighting for.

In 1938, Fiske cemented his love of England with marriage to Rose Bingham, the Countess of Warwick. Then he began the course that would take him through the last two years of his life. In August 1939, he returned from England on the flying boat *Dixie Clipper* for work at Dillon, Read in New York but two weeks later he was aboard the British liner *Aquitania* as she slipped away from the city with anti-submarine guns on her deck and blackout paper in her portholes. His well-traveled American passport contained a rubber stamped condition of use, "This passport is not valid for travel to or in any foreign state in connection with entrance into or service in foreign military or naval forces." No matter; his goal was to become the first American to join the British Royal Air Force in time of war. He would simply convince the well-informed air chief marshal, Sir William Elliott, that he, the two-time American gold medalist and husband of the Countess of Warwick, was a Canadian citizen. For whatever reason, he succeeded.

Fiske may or may not have been the first American to join the RAF, and, although he seemed to be particularly talented at steering machines at treacherous speeds, he was not a flyer. He was not alone in a rush by American flyers and would-be flyers to get into a war that had not yet been declared by their own country. A number of them immediately followed him at their own expense. Soon, they began showing up in traditional points of enlistment like Windsor, Ontario, and they were entering a process that had been carefully and quietly developed to accept them.

After Canadian Director of Air Force Recruiting Billy Bishop left the U.S. White House in March 1939, he began to recruit those who would assist in the creation of a substantial screening and recruitment plan that would bring Americans into the RCAF. The effort was joined by Homer Smith, who had flown in the Royal Naval Air Service in the previous war, and was now a wealthy Canadian living in America. His portfolio would include airline presidents, aviation educators and flying school owners, and members of the Civil Aeronautics Authority. Bishop then sought out Clayton Knight, who was well known in the circles of American aviation.

In the fullness of his lifetime, Knight would most enduringly be known as an aviation artist. Born in Rochester, New York, in 1891, he was determined to be an artist, and would study at the Chicago Institute of Art under distinguished artists of the time such as the American realist George Bellows, and Robert Henri, a leader of the Ashcan School. In 1917, Knight was a young artist in New York's Greenwich Village and caught up in the prelude to the American declaration of war. He was most inspired by the photographs that were coming from Europe of the work of the Lafayette Escadrille. He would have liked to have joined the Escadrille, but, as America entered the war, he managed to gain entrance into the U.S. Air Service and ended up heading toward service in Italy under Captain Fiorello LaGuardia. A snafu in Liverpool, however, diverted him to continued training in Oxford, England, under British command. Eventually, he was moved to France where he became the only American member of a British intelligence squadron that examined the battlefields from a base just west of Ypres, Belgium. Occasionally, the assignment required flight at the upper levels of possible altitude in those days and the literal drinking from bottles of oxygen to keep a clear head.

It was on a rare bombing run in a de Havilland 9 that Knight experienced his first injuries and imprisonment. He had been given an airplane with a faulty engine, and it had left him straggling beneath and behind his formation. A German Fokker, piloted by Ace Oberleutnant Harald Auffarth found him an easy target.

I could see him gradually getting bigger and bigger, filling the sight: it seemed like a slow-motion picture. I had a very clear view of the pilot in the cockpit, and painted on the side of his Fokker was a yellow comet design. Firing at him, I could see my bullets stitching right up to where he was sitting and yet he wouldn't fall. I closed my eyes and thought, "This is the end, but I'll crash into him!" He went down underneath me and as he did, I got hit in the leg. It went in beside my knee, exploded, and went out the hip. I didn't know how bad it was—it didn't hurt at that time—but it jammed me back in the seat and felt like a hot iron scorching me.

I looked over the side and the Fokker seemed to be going down and out of control. Another Fokker fired at me from the other side and I turned and sprayed him. I had been trying to find which way was home—low clouds blotted out the rising sun and the compass was whirling madly in the spin. Every time I'd fly straight—for just a few seconds to the let the compass settle—another Fokker attacked. I might have been flying into Germany for all I knew! After I'd flown straight to get my bearings, and got sprayed every time, I was getting more and more desperate. I'd never heard the bullets so close; it was like crackling whips on the wings, and a stream of tracers would zip past my head; I was sure that's what was going to happen.

Suddenly the racket stopped and there was absolute silence. The engine had quit and for the moment nobody was firing at me. I looked down at the ground. We were only about 300 feet high at that time because I had to keep my nose down to get speed to fight these fast Fokkers. I didn't know which way the wind was blowing, but there was a nice green field underneath and I wanted like hell to get on the ground—but quick![2]

The crisp description of a few moments in a World War I biplane while under attack, given in an oral history interview to aviation writer Peter Kilduff, reflected the work that Knight would go in to in his own art and writing about aviation. He returned to that pursuit after German imprisonment through the end of the war.

Billy Bishop had looked at the history of American aviators who preceded their government into World War I and decided that history could certainly repeat itself in World War II. The British Commonwealth Air Training Plan was up and running and it remained to create a mechanism by which Americans could be blended into its mix of nationalities. In the previous war, the process had sometimes been seat-of-the-pants and impromptu; now it would be streamlined and methodical. It would find the best American candidates for the Commonwealth air forces, and, almost as important, prevent those who were not qualified from investing in the time and dislocation of a futile trip across the border.

The period between late 1939 and early 1940 was sometimes called the Phoney War. Though the war had been declared by all sides in Europe, not much had happened in the way of movement or fighting. The most significant event of the time may have been the Winter War between Finland and Russia. On May 10, 1940, however, Germany successfully invaded Belgium, Luxembourg and the Netherlands, and, phony or not, the quiet time had ended. The quick acceleration of events presented a challenge to the BCATP. Was the methodical movement of trained pilots into the war now too slow to keep up with events? Should planes and pilots now be funneled into the war as soon as they became available? Should the certain, planned needs of the future be sacrificed to the uncertain needs of the present? One choice was to suspend the deliberate process of BCATP altogether, but the choice that was made was to double down on the scope and speed of the plan. The need for American participation became more urgent.

Somewhere along the line, Clayton Knight and Billy Bishop had become friends, and, as Bishop began his program of American recruitment to the RCAF, he found Knight at the 1939 Cleveland Air Show. The annual Labor Day event at the edge of Lake Erie had become famous for its air races, but, as the prospect of war loomed, this year would also showcase the extent of American military might in the sky. Knight was the guest of a friend, Ohio attorney general Tommy Herbert, who had himself flown with the Canadian Royal Flying Corps in World War I. Knight described Bishop's appeal as more serious than seemed usual from the normally exuberant Billy Bishop. "You've heard," he had said, "we, in Canada are at war again. I'm convinced that history will repeat itself. American boys will want to help Canada as they did in the first war. But this time they must have direction and be screened. We need someone in the States to sort them out before they come across the border. You are in an ideal position to take on the job." Bishop's tone had turned apologetic. "We have no fund for this sort of thing ... but that may be worked out someway—later."[3]

His presence at the national air show gave Knight the opportunity to talk to a number of professional pilots about the Canadian plan. Not surprisingly, he found the younger pilots more open to the idea than those who were older, but the war had just begun in Europe and not many people had clearly formed opinions about it. His friend the attorney general pronounced the plan illegal without question, but hesitated to tell Knight what he should do. The legality of allowing Americans to be instructors of Canadian pilots was perhaps another matter. Knight decided to sign on to the project, and the Clayton Knight Committee would hide its work in plain sight. At the same time, the first rattling of opposition to American involvement in the war came, as it had in the previous war, from German Americans. Perhaps more important as Clayton Knight began to travel the country to gauge potential access to American flyers, he had to keep in mind the potential disapproval of a powerful American voice: Charles Lindbergh.

Lindbergh, the first man to fly solo across the Atlantic, was an opponent of American involvement in the European war, and of President Roosevelt. His father had been a Minnesota congressman, and one of the few in Congress to vote against the American declaration in World War I. On September 15, 1939, Lindbergh was in Tokyo to give a speech that was broadcast across most radio networks in the United States. America, he said was still protected by the Atlantic and Pacific oceans, even in the age of modern aircraft. There was no need to get involved in wars beyond those buffers. His predictions of what would happen were both accurate and not so in retrospect: "We are likely to lose a million men, possibly several million—the best of American youth. We will be staggering under the burden of recovery during the rest of our lives. And our children will be fortunate if they see the end in their lives...."[4] He argued that if Europe was returned to the Dark Ages, it would fall to a powerful America to bring the world back to order. And he warned that America should not now be listening to "insidious" propaganda designed to take it to war.

The speech was immediately controversial in the United States, and the first of a number of similar radio addresses by the aviator. In the broadcast for October 13, and in subsequent utterances, Lindbergh was heard to warn Canada that it should not try to involve the U.S. in the war. In England, the editorial reaction of the *Sunday Express* blazed on the front page, referring to a medal given to him on behalf of Adolf Hitler in 1938.

> Colonel Lindbergh, honored and decorated visitor of Hitler's, fervent admirer of Nazi strength, is now apparently developing the Hitler mind.
> He declares that Canada has no right to go to war unless with the permission of the United States.[5]

In Canada, newspapers reported the receipt of hundreds of letters from Americans across the border saying that Lindbergh did not speak for them. The *Toronto Telegram* editorialized that:

> ... nobody has compared for fatuous effrontery with this airman who has come forth as an amateur statesman to tell Canada what she should do and what she should not do. He does not, we

imagine, suggest that the United States should conquer Canada in order to prove that the republic is a good neighbor bent only on peace.[6]

The *Montreal Gazette* suggested that Lindbergh's words were tantamount to saying that the U.S. should enter the war on the side of the Third Reich. Other effects of the speech were to rekindle discussion about the good and bad of the long history of the two countries: America as the good neighbor vs. America as the arrogant neighbor. And it had the effect of bringing together, somewhat, those in Canada who had been debating the war themselves.

Lindbergh's pronouncements had the ironic effect of recalling the significant actions of Americans who had gone to Europe before their own country had declared its participation in World War I. The actions of the Lafayette Escadrille in France had resounded into the 1920s in the form of an international Lafayette Escadrille Association. In the United States, it was represented by the comprehensively named Trench and Air Association of American Volunteer Combatants in the French army, 1914 to 1918. In the excitement of Lindbergh's transatlantic flight in 1927, the association had named Lindbergh as an honorary member. It now called that naming "mistaken but understandable." Lindbergh's words were "opposed to the spirit which inspired the American volunteers of the Lafayette Escadrille and the Foreign Legion who rushed to the defense of France in 1914...."[7] The flyer's name was stricken from the list of association members.

Charles Lindbergh was a distraction in pre-war America, but one that Clayton Knight had to pay attention to as he traveled the nation. The colonel had many friends in the aviation community, and perhaps some who shared his views. On the whole, though, Knight was well received. The Operations Manager of United Airlines volunteered a list of 1,000 pilot applicants who had not been able to meet the airline's minimum requirements, as did the president of Western Airlines. Delicately, Knight approached those in American military commands who seemed willing to provide similar information. Visits were made to local aviation officials who knew of local candidates, airplane manufacturers and repairers, aviation schools, former aviation war heroes and potential hires.

Initially, the operation sometimes operated on a casually deceptive premise. Recruits were ostensibly for work with a non-military civil agency. "That was legal subterfuge really," Knight later admitted. "They went up as civilians and reported to the Dominion Aeronautical Company in Ottawa and it just so happened that the office of the RCAF was right next door. So after they reported to the Dominion Aeronautical they said, we really haven't anything for you right now but maybe the RCAF have."[8]

From the outset, the most significant initial opposition to the undertaking had actually come from Canadian prime minister Mackenzie King, who was properly worried about the effect of his country's potential flouting of the neutrality laws of its neighboring ally.

An early event in Ottawa, however, demonstrated the depth of Canada's problem. Knight and Homer Smith met with members of the RCAF Air Council, the heads of all of the country's commercial airlines, representatives of the many bush pilots who were vital participants in Canadian aviation, administrators of the BCATP and assorted other representatives of the United Kingdom. The meeting's agenda was primarily the need for instructors, and it was finally determined that only 25 candidates could be identified; the rest were already flying for the RCAF.

> In the heavy silence that followed this grim evaluation, heads were turned curiously in my direction when I stated, "Homer Smith and I have an initial list of slightly over three hundred pilots who are willing to come up to help." The number seemed to produce a profound shock. Some

skepticism was expressed as to the fitness of the volunteers, but the conclusion—of desperation—was reached that the scheme should be given a try.[9]

The Clayton Knight Committee was now fully engaged, and the decision was made to bring it out of the shadows of questionable legality. It would require publicity to succeed, and Homer Smith decided that one of the best ways to accomplish that would be to set it up auspiciously in a suite of rooms at the Waldorf Astoria Hotel in New York City. Knight went immediately to Washington where he met with the heads of army and navy air forces. They had few objections as long as there wasn't an active attempt to recruit those already in their forces, except for airplane mechanics who were in very short supply. It was also understood that physical (and marriage—American flyers could not be married) requirements for Canadian and British recruits were something less than for American aviators. Those who failed in U.S. recruitment could still offer much-needed talent to the war effort through the Commonwealth nations.

One of Knight's commanding officers in the previous war had been Fiorello LaGuardia, now the mayor of New York City. During a private dinner, Knight received LaGuardia's moral support for the plan. LaGuardia was thinking ahead to the probable American entry into the war, and the groundwork that the Clayton Knight Committee could have in place for that event. During a ride to open a new playground in downtown Manhattan, LaGuardia suggested that it would be important to get the U.S. State Department on board, and the mayor had connections in Washington to get that going. The meeting with an unnamed official was not overtly friendly, however, and it produced the same old conundrums of World War I, perhaps more succinctly described by Knight than in numerous pages of any book on the topic.

> ... he was icily and correctly non-committal, and simply quoted the phrasing of the U.S. law which said, among other things: "Hiring or retaining another person to enlist or enter himself in the service of a belligerent as a soldier, or as a marine, or a seaman on board of any ship of war...." (It is interesting to note that there was not mention of "airmen" inasmuch as the law dated back to a time before the Wright brothers' contraption had been taken seriously, and incidentally was originally drawn up against the British.) Title 18m Section 21 and 22, U.S. Code, R.S. Section 5282, March 4, 1909, then went on to state the consequences for breaking this law: "...he shall be fined not more than $2,000 and imprisoned not more than three years."
>
> An additional phrase in an earlier ruling (March 2, 1907) was equally explicit on another point: "That any American citizen shall be deemed to have expatriated himself ... when he has taken an oath of allegiance to any foreign state."
>
> This recalled the plight of Americans who had joined the French Foreign Legion, the Lafayette groups and the British or Canadian air services in WW-1. Fired by the rashness of youth, very few of them gave the danger of losing their citizenship a second thought until after the Armistice when all sorts of legal complications irked them: retrieving their lost right to vote, inheritance problems, and a number of other annoyances that took them years to straighten out.[10]

The German invasion of the Benelux countries in early May had been followed by the Battle of Dunkirk, which had brought mixed results for the Allies. As Germany continued its push into Western Europe, more than 300,000 French and British troops became isolated on the beaches of Dunkirk, on the English Channel and west of the border between Belgium and France. The British port of Dover sat less than 100 miles across the Channel, and the only solution that seemed available to the Allies was the evacuation of troops across the water from France to England. It was accomplished with the help of boats, sailors and fishermen of all sizes and sorts, and considered an accomplishment of war committed by the grass roots of England. Though a boost to morale, it was an acknowledgment of the limitations of the Allied forces against the German war machine.

The bittersweet evacuation of Dunkirk became a factor in the full American consideration of its place in the growing war. "The temper of our country at this period," wrote Clayton Knight, "in its vastness from the Atlantic to the Pacific, from the Gulf to Canada, presented a bewildering turmoil of divided sentiment."[11] He believed that the young men of America who formed his target group for recruitment were impatient to do what they needed to do, no matter the risk. And Canada's need for their help was painfully obvious. All that remained to ease the path to enlistment was an agreement by Canada to change the rule of the time that those fighting for the country swear an oath of allegiance to the King of England. The requirement was reduced to an oath made only to the recruit's commanding officer. That accomplished, basic requirements were an age between 18 and 45 (18 to 21 with parental permission), an equivalent of high-school education, and a license from the Civil Aeronautics Authority, with 300 hours of flying time. Each individual was also subject to a thorough background and temperament check by the Hooper-Holmes Bureau, a leading insurance investigator of the time. A recruit who passed medical and flying tests in America would be sent on to Canada for further testing with a per diem of $5 daily and lodging in a good hotel. He was given the choice of civilian employment as an instructor or staff pilot, or joining the RCAF to become an instructor in more rigorous bombing and gunnery training. He could also ferry planes to the war across the Atlantic. Recruits were not, at first, intended to be fighter pilots, but much needed support personnel. And many Americans who joined were husbands and fathers who wanted to stay near their families on the American continent.

The BCATP and the Clayton Knight Committee were the starting point for what would become a well-known and much-storied continuation of the entrance of a large number of Americans in the Canadian and British air forces over the course of the war, and long after their own country entered the war at the end of 1941. Barely known at all, both at the time and in the following decades, was the much smaller presence of Americans in British naval forces. Of the American dead in Commonwealth forces for World War I, approximately 30 were associated with a naval force. Nearly twice that number was listed as naval deaths among the American fatalities in World War II. Many of those were in the Canadian Merchant Navy, but most were in the Canadian Naval Reserve.

The naval reserve traced its beginnings to the mid–18th century as a force for sorting out the rules and practices of shipping on the Great Lakes, Lake Champlain and the St. Lawrence River. Its importance and development rosè and fell with the swells of following history, and in relation to the presence of the British Royal Navy in Canadian affairs. By the turn of the 20th century, it was in place to meet a decision that Canada ought to have its own navy. Great Britain was still the predominant military force for the country, but its efforts were stretched over much of the world, and it would not hurt to leave Canada more in charge of its own defenses. Its largest potential enemy was the United States, but there were no prospects of war between the two countries on anyone's horizon.

The most difficult conflicts between the U.S. and Canada, however, had to do with fishing on the Great Lakes, and, while a Fisheries Protection Fleet was expanded, the development of a larger navy did not come to pass. There were those who continued to advocate for a strong naval force for their country, but a fact of life for Canada was that it was a nation of vast lands and prairies, more than the lakes and coasts that connected it with the rest of the world. The people did not necessarily look about them and think about the need for naval defenses. By 1912, thinking began to focus on the idea of a Royal Naval Volunteer Reserve (RNVR) that would place citizen units across the full country of coasts and lakes, cities and prairies. As World War I began to evolve, the Royal Naval Canadian Volunteer Reserve (RNCVR) was formed. It was to include 3,600 men who were seafarers or otherwise suitable, and be organized into three regional divisions with 100 man companies located throughout each region.[12] Propelled by the war, the force had more volunteers than it could handle, and, in 1917, more than a thousand were moved to the Royal Navy in England.

The interwar years maintained minimal naval and reserve forces. In 1923, the Royal Canadian Naval Reserve (RCNR) was formed to operate in five port divisions of the country with a collective 70 officers and 430 men, and the Royal Canadian Naval Volunteer Reserve (RCNVR) was formed to include 70 officers and 930 men in both port and plains divisions. Members were required to attend 39 drills per year, whether in Montreal or Winnipeg, and two weeks of training in Halifax on the east coast, or Esquimalt, Vancouver Island, British Columbia, on the west coast. During that time they were in reserve for a limited Royal Canadian Navy (RCN). At the outbreak of World War II, the navy consisted of, by one of a number of varying accounts, six ocean-going warships and a total force, reserve force and staff of 3,500. By the end of the war the fleet would include 270 warships and 95,000 personnel.[13]

On May 13, 1940, Prime Minister Winston Churchill spoke to the British House of Commons. The subject was the gathering war:

> I would say to the House as I said to those who have joined this government: I have nothing to offer but blood, toil, tears and sweat. We have before us an ordeal of the most grievous kind. We have before us many, many long months of struggle and of suffering.
>
> You ask, what is our aim? I can answer in one word: Victory. Victory at all costs—Victory in spite of all terror—Victory, however long and hard the road may be, for without victory there is no survival.[14]

"...it was as if an electric current had just been applied to my spinal cord," wrote Allen H. Cherry. "Now I knew where I stood. Up til now few would have dared to throw in their lot with Britain. The risk of capitulation would have been too great, the uncertainty, the not knowing how the next blow would be taken, standing up or lying down. Here, however, was something different. A man knew where he stood, whose side he was on, and if he went down fighting he would go down not as one man but a team.... My heart warmed, and with the voice still ringing in my ears, 'I have nothing to offer but blood, toil, tears and sweat,' I said to myself: 'That's me. I'll have some of that.' I waited no longer."[15]

Cherry was a wealthy stockbroker with the New York brokerage Struthers and Dean. He was a child of Latvian immigrants, and, at age 38, in a position to uproot his life quickly and at will. As a young man, he had been inspired by the actions of the Lafayette Escadrille and the gratitude offered to them by France. At first, he determined that he would join the Royal Air Force, and set himself on the quietly prescribed track for enlistment, beginning with a discrete interview. He had flying experience, but he found a friend at Flushing Airport on Long Island to help him sharpen his skills. The next step would be a move to Ottawa for further training. The he received a letter from the British consulate-general in New York, dated April 29, 1941. It said only:

> Sir,
>   I should be glad if you would call at this office at your earliest convenience on a matter of personal interest. (Room 1141.)

In the event of your being prevented from calling, kindly inform me by letter.
I am, Sir,
Your obedient servant,
etc.[16]

A lot had occurred very quickly in the time since Cherry's initial interview for RAF service. An American step in the direction of war declaration had taken place in the form of the Lend-Lease Act of March 11, 1941. It was designed to provide American war matériel to the Allied nations currently fighting Germany, particularly Great Britain, and included 50 destroyers for the Royal Navy. The ships required staffing that was not fully available in England after years of austerity. Cherry also had maritime and wireless experience, and the consul suggested that he consider joining the Royal Navy instead of the RAF. It was Cherry's decision to make, which he did quickly during a respite of walking in New York's Battery Park. It was accomplished with a coin toss that pointed him to the sea.

> ...I sat down in a seat gazing at the towering beacon of freedom that stood out in the harbour ... the Statue of Liberty. I thought about the reports of Isolationists ranting against President Roosevelt on account of his Lease-Lend Act, and the old arguments that Britain was licked. "But what did that matter?" they said. "No one would ever dare to attack us. We could live with Germany if we learnt how. Germany is a powerful country, let's not antagonize her.... My Gawd! Is America coming to this? Has the time come when we have to learn through fright, to live a life poles part from our heritage? Frankly I'd rather not live that way. I'd rather fight, even a losing fight, midst friends, than live like a rabbit in a hole.[17]

After signing papers in the consul's office, Cherry was on a train to Boston. Even with all of his resolve, and the tacit understanding that American citizens were being recruited into British forces, he had to consider the implications of what he was doing. He would be taking an overnight steamer to Yarmouth, Nova Scotia, but he would have to face U.S. Customs with the claim that he was simply going on vacation. It was a lie and a crime, a violation of the Neutrality Act that Cherry knew could have serious consequences. He was irritated that one would have to worry about such things while going off to do the right thing, but thought of it as just another risk of war.

At the pier in Boston, he found himself in the presence of a Customs man "who gave me the impression he lived in a constant state of annoyance, and that he didn't like me. He looked at me with cold sharp eyes."

The man ordered him to open his bag, and asked Cherry the purpose of his voyage. "A sea voyage and see if I can find 'Evangeline,'" Cherry replied, referring to the Longfellow poem about an Acadian woman in constant search for her lost love. The poem was also interpreted as a narrative of the relationship between the Acadians of Louisiana and their role in the founding of Halifax, Nova Scotia. It was evidently well enough known, by Cherry's telling, that the gruff Customs man allowed a bare smile, and said: "Go ahead, wise guy."[18]

At Yarmouth, Cherry caught the train for Halifax, where he found a room waiting for him at the Royal Nova Scotia Hotel, adjoining the train station. There, his narrative pauses for a sidetrack into a perhaps unconsummated relationship with an intriguing woman named Ginger, one of a few women, or their intimate attire, who would show up in his book, *Yankee R.N.*, about his journey from the shock to his spine upon hearing Winston Churchill, to the end of the war.

After a meeting in Halifax with Royal Navy Vice Admiral Sir Stuart Bonham Carter, he was accepted into the RNVR and crossed the ocean to Scotland, then by train to London and the Royal Naval College. There, he wrote a letter to President Roosevelt telling him that he had joined Nelson's Navy, as per his understanding of what Roosevelt really wanted as he walked the fine line between isolationism and war. It is not known whether the two men actually knew each other, or if Cherry received a response to his note.

Among the 22 Americans who initially joined the Royal Navy through the RNVR, A.H. Cherry was preceded by John Stanley Parker. In 1940, Parker was, like others who would precede their countrymen to war, alarmed at the potential he saw for Hitler's designs on Europe. He was also a restless man who had grown up in the best schools, gone to Harvard, and enjoyed the country and yacht clubs of Boston and Bedford, though his family was not of exceeding wealth. He had served in the U.S. Navy in the previous war, but he was now 50 years old. The stock market crash of 1929 had set back his own business ambitions, and reduced him to a job he hated as a "customers man" in a Boston brokerage house. An attempt to rejoin the Navy at the Charleston Navy Yard was rebuffed, and Parker continued on north. His son Frank had preceded him into Commonwealth service by joining the Canadian Black Watch in October 1940, but the elder Parker was turned away from that group. Then he heard that the Royal Navy was in search of experienced yachtsmen to serve as naval officers. Back in Boston, he was referred to the British consul in Washington. There, he was met with bureaucratic indifference and traveled to Halifax to meet with Vice Admiral Bonham-Carter. In another indication of the confusion between different sources with different agendas about the legality of such enlistments, Parker carried with him a personal letter from Undersecretary of State Sumner Welles, which said that Americans would not lose their citizenship in such cases as long as they enlisted outside of American borders, but were liable to be punished if they then went into a war zone. Parker's efforts remained frustrated.[19]

What followed was a months' long dance between himself and various British consular officers in America who seemed only to respond to Parker and similar others in patronizing ways; a sense in Whitehall, London, that it would be desirable to have such Americans in the fold; and the real-world need by Bonham Carter for good men, nationality and age, evidently, be damned. The Vice Admiral won the day and, on June 7, 1941, Parker was commissioned as a (Temporary) Lieutenant in the RNVR. It seemed not to be noticed that this by now very well known man gave his age as 40 years. With two confederates, he was one of the first three World War II Americans to enter the Royal Naval College at Greenwich, London. Later he would write to his wife, Violet:

> All I can say is that at long last I'm doing exactly what I was made for, in what I have always wanted ... doing what has to be done and all I'm fit for any more. Am absolutely fit, tired and happy. I'm learning all the time—every hour something. But it's not diagrams on a blackboard. If only I could tell you what I've heard and seen.... It's a queer sensation this life. It is as if I've always lived this way ... and as if I were to always so live.[20]

John Parker sailed into the war on the ship HMS *Broadwater*, which was herself an old American enlistee in the British navy. She had been launched as the USS *Mason* from Newport News Shipbuilding and Drydock in 1919, then decommissioned after the war in 1922. She was turned over to the British Navy under Lend-Lease and commissioned in Halifax as the *Broadwater*. Her new name denoted her as a Town Class ship, one of those given a town name that was common to both the U.S. and UK. In this case it was Broadwater, Sussex and Broadwater, Virginia. The Virginia town, on an island in the lower Chesapeake Bay, had been virtually wiped out by a hurricane in 1933, and the new British ship's badge contained an image of clouds and rain in honor of that event. From Halifax, she took up the job of convoy escort on the North Atlantic and around the tip of Africa to the Middle East.

When Parker stepped aboard as a lieutenant, the *Broadwater* was a hunter of submarine wolf packs in the North Atlantic. On October 18, 1941, she was south of Iceland when she was attacked and sunk by a German submarine. Forty-four officers and crew were lost, including John Parker, believed to be the first World War II American to die in service to the Royal Navy.

Of his two sons, John, Jr., would be killed as a member of the U.S. Navy at Okinawa, and Frank would be the only war survivor of the three. Like his father, he had been a seeker of something more than life as it was given to him. He had dropped out of Harvard in 1937 and moved to Paris to become a young artist. He fled the city during the German invasion of June 1940, but stayed in France for a while in ambulance service before moving into Spain, where he was imprisoned for a time before being allowed to sail home from Portugal. It was not long before the continuing oppression of France prompted him to go back to Europe by joining the Black Watch in Montreal. His education would have allowed him to enter at a higher rank, but he preferred to start as a private. Like the artist that he was, he would see his following experiences in the shades of gray and color that would stay with him for the rest of his life.[21]

THIRTEEN

Americans in London

On arrival in England you should show this letter to the Immigration Authorities. You should come to London, call at 50 Queen Anne Gate, S.W. 1 and ask for Mr. Hoffman who would tell you where to go.—A letter from the Royal Navy

In 1940, Emporia, Kansas, was just a small town of 13,000, halfway between Kansas City and Wichita. But it projected an influential voice to the rest of the nation in the person of William Allen White, editor of the *Emporia Gazette* and known as The Sage of Emporia. He was a friend and adviser to presidents, a leader of the Progressive movement as it appeared in the liberal wing of the Republican Party, and a winner of two Pulitzer Prizes, one posthumously. His editorials and other writing reflected "small town" common sense, and a sense of humor that cut through pontification and bluster. At the time of the controversy over the participation of Americans in the Winter War, he wrote an editorial that might be applied to one aspect of the full history of Americans fighting with foreign forces.

> The urge to fight for what youth calls liberty is a normal and wholesome manifestation. Not that it is highly sensible—it is not. But it is the way of youth. If it hadn't been for that urge in young Jefferson and Washington, Patrick Henry and our ragtag and bobtail young grandfathers who fought the American Revolution, Kansas would today be singing "God Save the King," gasping for her Bill of Rights and fearing a ration of butter and coal.
>
> Probably a few, 50 or 75 a month, young Americans are scooting up to Canada to enlist for Finland and points east, and the answer [*sic:* question?] is, what are we going to do about it?
>
> A lot of youngsters, three or four years ago, got warmed up about the Spanish loyalists and probably the so-called Lincoln brigade had a thousand, maybe more, American youths fighting the fascists. That was their royal American right if they wanted to.
>
> The only way the law is violated is when open, organized recruiting is established, and that won't do. But in the case of the boys today, the FBI had better keep its shirt on, take it easy and not try to post notices against the crashing avalanche in the hearts of youths to fight for the thing they call liberty.
>
> They may be mad as March hares, as youth often is, about the wisdom and justice of the causes they espouse. They may be entirely wrong in believing that enlisting and appealing to arms will settle anything. Of course they are! But the sap of spring is the sap of spring—even if it is a sap.[1]

White's prose was perceptive as far as it went. It was true that the Federal Bureau of Investigation worked in the background of these matters, but it had notably kept track of the development of the Clayton Knight Committee and ultimately found nothing wrong with it. And it was not just innocent youth going off to war, as was demonstrated by principled older men like A.H. Cherry and John Parker.

White's seeming ambivalence in April 1940 about the validity of young American saps going off to fight a foreign war was followed by well thought out ambivalence on his part the following month. He became the organizer of the Committee to Defend America by Aiding the Allies (CDAAA). It shared the belief with other influential Americans, including General John J. Pershing, Adlai Stevenson and Senator Claude Pepper, that if America did all it could to help Great Britain with the provision of war matériel, it would not have to actually join the war. It played a role in the development of Lend-Lease, and advocated for changes in neutrality laws that would allow American merchant ships to better defend themselves against Axis actions on the open seas. It did not seem to take a position on Americans who entered the war through Canada and Great Britain. White eventually resigned from the committee under a combination of policy disputes within the organization and the effects of worsening health. Events soon suggested that America was headed to inevitable war and the organization became, more simply, the Committee to Defend America. It was dissolved after the Japanese invasion of Pearl Harbor.

It was true, as White asserted, that young Americans were going to Canada in increasing numbers starting in 1939, but the

The Royal Highland Regiment, the Black Watch, of Canada, fought more than 30 battles across France, Belgium, the Netherlands and Germany in the last years of the war. American members seen in Beveland, Netherlands, on September 30, 1944, included, left to right, Private R.F. Gallahan, Sergeants F.J. Garvis and A. McGrail (Lieut. Ken Bell/Canada Dept. of National Defence/Library and Archives Canada).

movement wasn't as organized as it had been in World War I. It would not be until 1955 that Canada's Department of Veteran Affairs would officially note for the record that 18,848 members of the Canadian army in World War II had given the United States as their place of birth. It also noted that 4,725 men had given their home address as American, though they were not necessarily included in the larger number. Determining who was who was as problematic as it had been in World War I. They were of American addresses, but not necessarily of American birth, and many may have given Canadian addresses to hide their American backgrounds.[2]

Not as much can be known about these Americans in the second war as is knowable about those in the first. Canadian law only allows access to their records individually and by request, and perhaps the largest grouping of them can be found in the listings of those with American next of kin buried in the cemeteries of the Commonwealth War Graves Commission. That list of just less than 800 people does not reflect death in proportion to the numbers of Americans in each of the Canadian services. Estimates of Americans in flying services like the RCAF, RAF, ferrying squadrons and others seem to rest near 9,000 or one-third of all Americans. But the cemeteries hold twice that percentage—more than 500 men—of air force dead. Of the remainder, seven percent—less than 60 men—were sailors, and the rest were members of land-bound forces. The skewed percentages would be partially explained by later events as the war was played out, and in the sorting out of bodies after the war, but they were also driven by the large role taken by American aviators in Commonwealth forces.

Ground forces were still important however. Col. Charles Sweeny's efforts to recruit Americans to a new Lafayette Escadrille in 1939 France continued as the Clayton Knight Committee began its recruitment effort for Great Britain. When Sweeny's efforts in France were stopped by the fall of that country in June 1940, seven of the pilots recruited for France crossed the Channel to enlist in the RAF. Sweeny followed and continued his recruiting effort on behalf of the RAF, though without consultation with the air force or the CKC. The RAF needed as many American pilots as it could get, but Sweeny was as flamboyant as ever, perhaps a loose cannon in the field of the more deliberative process of the CKC. The matter seemed to be resolved by taking Sweeny into the RAF as an officer, which would prohibit him from recruitment activities while the CKC absorbed those activities into its own effort.

At this point, another Charles Sweeny entered the picture. He was the nephew of the colonel, and had grown up as an American child in London. He returned to America to graduate from Yale University, then returned to London to work in the family's business interests there.

(Note: As in other narratives of this complicated family involvement in the war, this one will from this point refer to the elder Sweeny as Col. and the younger by name only. Note: Compounding upon problems with the spelling of the Sweeny name sometimes as Sweeney, noted in Chapter One, there is also a Charles Sweeney associated with the aviation history of the war as the pilot who dropped the nuclear bomb over Nagasaki. He is not part of this story.)

One of the results of the civilian participation in the evacuation of Dunkirk had been the formation of a British Home Guard to be composed of those who would not see regular service because of age or infirmity. It was conceived not as a crack military operation, but as an expression of the best effort of the British people to protect their country at the grassroots level. It seemed only natural to Charles Sweeny that an American Home Guard of U.S. citizens living in London should be formed, and he had the friends and associates with whom to begin. It became the First American Motorized Squadron, 100 men strong. It did not meet with the approval of then American Ambassador to England Joseph P. Kennedy, who believed that Britain would be lost to Germany in any case. But Kennedy was replaced with John Winant, who had the opposite view and supported any American effort in the cause.

Resources were scarce in England, and the many Home Guard units were likely not to have the tools they needed for effective drills and practice, to say nothing of what might be required if they were pressed into genuine service. Some units literally practiced with sticks in lieu of rifles. The American unit, however, had only to appeal to relatives and associates in the United States for help with supplies. It was reported that when Charles Sweeny wired his father in New York to inquire whether he might be able to obtain some machine guns, his father wired back that 100 Tommy Guns and 100,000 rounds of ammunition were on the way from the Thompson Company. The guard members contributed their own automobiles to the effort, including one very fast Mercedes Benz, and repainted them olive drab or in camouflage at their own expense.

The unit was placed under the command of Brigadier General Wade Hampton Hayes, who had been in the Spanish American War and served with General Pershing in World War I. Hayes then appeared in the newsreels of American movie theatres to explain that the men of the American Home Guard lived in England and shared the responsibility of defending the nation with their British hosts. "We would have felt ashamed of ourselves if we had sat on the sidelines and done nothing."[3] The group had been encouraged, he said, by numerous letters and telegrams from Americans urging an American effort to save England in any way short of actual war.

The First Motorized Squadron was not a thing just of vanity and good intentions by wealthy Americans. It was a well-organized participant in training exercises for Home Guard units, at one point tricking members of the British Coldstream Guards, who were playing Germans in an exercise, into believing they had captured an important general while the Americans effected the real general's escape. In January 1941, Winston Churchill, who at that point was paying a lot of attention to America as a desired ally in the war, chose the squadron for a special review in St. James Park.

> His progress down the ranks of the Americans was punctuated by at least a half dozen pauses for words with the men. They looked more like marines than business men, engineers, lawyers, etc. They had worn khaki greatcoats and steel helmets and gripped Winchester automatic rifles. They had the regular British Home Guard insignia except on the left shoulder they wore a badge bearing the red eagle [that had become their insignia].
>
> Following Mr. Churchill's tour along the ranks the squadron members broke away independently to man their cars—all of which were of American make except for a powerful German roadster.[4]

The *New York Times* article describing the event continued on with General Hayes' words about the unit, then arrived at a provocative paragraph.

> They have received no assignments for patrol duty since they are among the few motorized Home Guard outfits and General Sergiso-Brook [commander of the London Home Guard district] wants them to escort him in case of an emergency. There may have been more reasons that General Hayes was not inclined to mention.[5]

No hint of what those reasons might be was offered, but some months later a training exercise was described in the *Times* in which "a score of middle-aged American business men 'cap-

Unlike his predecessor, Joseph Kennedy, American Ambassador to England John G. Winant (1941–1946), was fully supportive of Americans who wanted to help Great Britain in the absence of an American declaration of war. On July 2, 1942, he inspected American and Canadian members of the British Home Guard at the Wellington Barracks in London (Lieut. C.E. Nye/Canada Dept. of National Defence/Library and Archives Canada).

tured' the heavily manned general headquarters of a brigade defending an important [British] airdrome."[6] The event involved the use of a dog chasing a stick to reveal the strategy of a hidden machine-gun position and a golfer who made practice shots for the same purpose. The Americans/Germans were able to overcome a sentry and enter the headquarters building, from which they took maps and strategic documents. The British participants were reported to have complained that the Americans had broken the rules of the exercise, to which the Americans responded that the Germans would not have played by the rules either. It did not help that an imitation grenade used by the Americans set a real fire to the headquarters building. The issues were resolved, and "The Americans withdrew, whistling 'Yankee Doodle.'"[7]

As always, the question of citizenship was at play in relation to the American Home Guard and other efforts by Americans to play a role in the war. At the time of the training exercise with a golfer and a dog, there seemed to be a determined effort on all sides to finesse the conflicts between oaths of allegiance to England and loyalty to America. In the case of the Home Guard, there was a tacit agreement to not raise the question. The case of more pronounced participation in the battle, as in the Royal Navy and Royal Air Force, could not be as easily ignored. A year earlier, and after much back and forth within the British government, King George VI approved a decision that an oath of allegiance to Britain would not be required of these Americans. And, lest there be any uncertainties on the matter, it was promised that any American who lost the citizenship of his country would be offered British citizenship in its place.[8]

On the other side of the Atlantic, the king's action was met with an unpublicized decision on the part of General Lewis B. Hershey, director of the U.S. Selective Service. Decades later, Hershey would become a focus of protest against America's participation in the Vietnam war, but he was a strong manager of the draft during the years of World War II. In July 1941, a story that barely circulated in Ohio newspapers reported that an unknown number of the state's young men had been classified by their draft boards as "lend-lease" material, and allowed to enlist in the military forces of Canada and Great Britain. All of the state's 330 local draft boards, it said, had received a directive from Hershey stating that it was national policy to "lend all aid to the Canadian and British governments."[9] Therefore, those who enlisted in those forces—whether military, medical or technical—were to be given the deferment classification of 11B for those who were engaged in crucial national defense work. Further, though the 11B deferment had to be renewed each six months, these particular deferments would renew in perpetuity as long as their holders remained in service, or until they were recalled for service in the defense of their own country.

The men who had already so enlisted had previously been noted as delinquents serving in the Commonwealth forces. The condition that they not be required to take an oath of allegiance to a foreign country, however, erased that notation and gave them full standing as Americans fulfilling an American policy. It was agreed on all sides that Canada and England would return the men to America if the need for them arose. Hershey said that Selective Service had a master list of all Americans in Commonwealth forces. If and when such an individual left the foreign force, he was required to notify his draft board for reclassification. The expectation, it was noted, was that most men already in the British forces would remain there for the duration of the war, irrespective of eventual American participation.

As always, the practices and pronouncements of one part of the U.S. government did not necessarily carry over to another part. The liberal Selective Service policy had followed a statement by President Roosevelt on June 24, 1941, that the British were trying to recruit

15,000 to 30,000 American technicians for service in the war, and there would be no problem with that, providing they did not move into combat roles. And neutrality laws, he said, did not prevent Americans from going to Canada or elsewhere to sign up for British military service. But in other quarters and categories, such enlistment seemed to be still forbidden. Just three months after the president's declaration of safe passage of Americans to England, those who were recruiting for the Royal Navy air forces thought it necessary to continue their work as if they were the characters of spy novels.

Fitness reports, the equivalents of résumés, were moved surreptitiously from American to British files by third parties who would follow the prospective enlistee through the rest of the process. It was still the case that most passports carried a rubber stamp forbidding travel for the purpose of joining a foreign force at war. It did not apply to Americans who enlisted in the Canadian army and crossed the ocean in transports, but a clear passport was still necessary to obtain transatlantic passage on commercial shipping. A plan was devised in which the Canadian Pacific and Cunard White Star lines, in complicity with Canadian Immigration, agreed to take the passengers aboard as undocumented. Prospects traveled on the strength of a vague letter:

> I write to tell you that if you will come to England about (date) I think you will be able to find employment. You should visit one of the agents of either the Cunard Company or the Canadian Pacific Company in Canada. Show then this letter and arrange with them to come to England on one of their vessels. On arrival in England you should show this letter to the Immigration Authorities. You should come to London, call at 50 Queen Anne Gate, S.W. 1 and ask for Mr. Hoffman who would tell you where to go.[10]

As contrived as it was, and even with the quiet knowledge about it on the part of interested parties in the U.S. government, it did not seem to bring American flyers to the Royal Navy.

It was then that the Lend-Lease Act and the advent of alternative kinds of British service for Americans, like the Royal Naval Volunteer Reserve and the American Home Guard, began the era of more visible and proactive recruitment of Americans into the accelerating needs of Great Britain.

At the same time as the creation of the American Home Guard, the younger Charles Sweeny was perhaps paying greater attention to what might happen in the air. When he looked at the English Channel he saw the potential of a confident German air force coming across the water to meet a Royal Air Force that needed to be stronger. At the same time, he knew that there were many American men who wanted to fly in the war, but were not able to be absorbed by the Army Air Force, in large part because they couldn't meet minimum educational and physical requirements. It would be natural to match the two situations, and it could have an effect that many were seeking as the ultimate goal for their actions: the more involvement in the war by Americans, the more American public opinion would support an eventual U.S. declaration of war.

Sweeny's notion and its rationale quickly intrigued the Air Ministry, which, on July 2, 1940, told him to go ahead with the plan. The Undersecretary of State for Air, Harry Balfour, offered the only resistance to the plan out of concern that it would compete with the British Canadian Air Training Plan. Balfour and the BCATP, however, were seeking to recruit American pilots for the training of Canadian pilots while the Sweeny plan would take American pilots directly to England for actual combat flying. The concerns were overcome and the venture was named The Eagle Squadron. A patch was designed for placement on a Royal Air Force uniform that would denote an American with an Eagle, and that led to a final naming of the unit as the American Eagle Squadron (AES). Eventually, the insignia would be painted on the airplanes flown by AES flyers.

Until it was officially sanctioned by the British, the AES required significant funding as a startup operation. Recruitment of men who were required to have 250 hours of flying time, a current physical and good character would be expensive, and the time lag between recruitment and eventual service for an enlistee would last from his arrival in Canada through the practical and legal requirement of getting him across the Atlantic until entrance into the RAF. Most of the $100,000 that was initially raised came from members of the Sweeny family and the Woolworth heiress Barbara Hutton. Hutton was very much involved in the war as a contributor of funds to the Free French forces led by Charles de Gaulle, and of her yacht to the Royal Navy. The figure was large enough to pay the men at the second lieutenant rank, offer commissioning bonuses in some cases, put them up in first class hotels and add a daily per diem of $5.

A public announcement of the existence of the AES was not made until the first group of pilots was ready to go in October 1940. The announcement was accompanied by reporting that the group of 34 Americans "who joined up with Britain 'in all sorts of devious ways,' is in training at a secluded airdrome somewhere in Britain and will enter the war soon alongside squadrons of the Royal Air Force."[11] Its commander was William E.G. Taylor, whose career had included time as a pilot in the U.S. Naval Reserves, the Marine Corps Reserve, United Airlines, and the Fleet Air Arm of the Royal Navy. He led the AES as a member of the Royal Air Force Volunteer Reserve. The announcement was met with no discernible reaction from the United States government.

At the time, the American Eagle Squadron was a separate endeavor from the Clayton Knight Committee. The CKC's bold step of working out of the Waldorf Astoria in New York was continued as it set up office suites in 14 others of the country's prominent hotels, including the Statler in Cleveland, the St. Anthony in San Antonio, the Hollywood Roosevelt in Los Angeles and the Davenport in Spokane. Similar operations were settled in the Canadian cities of Montreal, Ottawa, Toronto, Windsor and Vancouver. As an example of the nature of their work, the Waldorf Astoria office included the constant presence of three trained interviewers, supported by typists, telephone operators and file clerks. A bookkeeping staff worked under the supervision of the accounting firm Price Waterhouse.

"Most of the branch offices," Knight wrote in an unpublished history of the CKC, "were in charge of local men who were sincerely dedicated to the overthrow of Nazism. Also, two or three offices were headed by equally earnest young women who sent us a surprising number of acceptable candidates. That the girls were young, attractive, sympathetic, and also efficient in sorting out the applicants might have helped."[12]

The CKC was a very disciplined operation, and took steps to contrast itself with the more flamboyant Sweeny efforts with the AES. It may have been the case that members of the BCATP and CKC had a back-channel role in the absorption of both Sweenys into efforts in England, where their actions were more constrained by various sanctions and censorship laws than they had been in freewheeling New York. There was no doubt that U.S. officials were aware of what was happening, but the less visible it was the more they could not see it occurring. The CKC's professionalism was bolstered by the efforts of a number of distinguished Americans. Harold Fowler had flown with the British at the beginning of World War I, then had been put in charge of all Americans in the Royal Flying Corps for the rest of the war. Now he was deputy police commissioner of New York under Fiorello LaGuardia. Pierpont "Pete" Hamilton, nephew of J.P. Morgan, had been the author of the organization's "bible," a stylebook of sorts, in New York, then entered the U.S. Air Force and assisted in the planning of the North African invasion. His actions in the invasion yielded the Congressional Medal of Honor. He had picked up a dead officer, flung him over his shoulder and walked through oncoming machine-gun fire to confront the gunner verbally about the death of his friend.

It was found that most prospective CKC candidates for service came from Texas and California, and when Knight was once asked why that was so, he noted very matter-of-factly that the Powers Modeling Agency in New York had determined that its prettiest girls came from the same two states and New York. It was not an odd observation. The CKC method, perhaps in keeping with the exalted images of those who fought with airplanes, was everything about what was attractive, elegant, manly and deluxe. It determined that every potential flyer it worked with would receive first class treatment and accommodation, even if he eventually fell out of the program due to lack of qualification.

Applicants came from all backgrounds and locations. George Hand was a seaplane pilot from Long Island, who wanted to ferry Hudson bombers across the ocean. William Hutcheson of Forest Hills, Long Island, washed out in training, but was noted as an excellent source for other prospects. Rayfield Walsh of Texarkana, Texas, was a crop duster and airport manager with two to three years of college education in engineering. He, too, was noted to have extensive connections among Texas flyers. Hines Metz was a naturalized immigrant who had been driven out of Germany with the rise of Adolf Hitler. He had, he said, raced motorcycles and automobiles in the Grand Prix of Europe, and organized sailplane clubs across Germany. He had owned his own firm in Germany and employed 200 people. In New York, he was assistant foreign manager at the international commodities broker Henry Hentz and Company.

> In the present struggle it is my earnest desire to serve the United States. More than most people, I realize what is behind the present struggle and the issues at stake. I had considered enlisting in the R.A.F. but decided to wait and see whether America would need my services.
>
> I have had a definite training and only hope that I can use it for benefit of America at this time.[13]

On June 24, 1941, the Joplin, Kansas, *News Herald* reported that 19 Missourians were among more than 80 men from 13 Midwestern states to be recruited to Canada and England through the CKC. Eight would be going to service in Canada, 10 to British aviation refresher courses and one to the transatlantic ferry service. Some had been driven to Chicago for trains directly to Ottawa; some would go to Tulsa, Oklahoma, for training; others directly to England. They would end up flying either for the RAF or RCAF.

In May 1941, Knight took a tour through the CKC's offices in the western half of the continent. It gave a good picture of the basics of its operation, and began with a visit to a training facility already opened in Regina, Saskatchewan. It was commanded by an RCAF Air Commodore, with 21 American fliers in residence. From there, he flew to Vancouver where the training leaders suggested that recruits be given printed manuals relating to training planes to be studied before arriving in camp, and that confidential credit checks be administered to all recruits. In Seattle, he visited the Boeing Aircraft Factory, Plant No. 2 as it was preparing for production of the B17 Flying Fortress. The following day in Spokane, he met with the city's two newspapers, and with representatives of United and Northwest Airlines, both of which offered advice and support. None of the four applicants at the Davenport Hotel that day had sufficient flying hours to be accepted, but they were happy to recommend others who might. An office stenographer was hired that day, and Knight moved on to Oakland, California, arriving at 3:45 a.m. The Oakland stenographer suggested to Knight that intelligence tests be used in lieu of the required high school diplomas of applicants. The suggestion was taken under advisement. Other staff was hired, and, the office flight surgeon told Knight that applicants were not always up to standards in the matter of color blindness, but they were otherwise of good enough quality that they ought to be considered.

Landing in Los Angeles the following afternoon, Knight stepped off the plane and into the camera flash of United Airlines Public Relations, which distributed a press release about his arrival. The Los Angeles CKC office was small and disorganized, and the decision was made to rent more space. A discussion with a few distinguished Los Angelinos led to a suggestion that each office of the CKC bring on board as advisors and liaison those of the given city who had been members of the RAF during World War I. The group included Bogart Rogers, an American who had fought with the RCAF in the previous war, and the author of a number of books and articles based on that experience. A public relations strategy was furthered that would use larger newspapers to promote the quality and operational standards of the Committee, and smaller newspapers to promote "local boy makes good" stories. The only paid advertising would be inexpensive and minimal in aviation trade journals, along with attempts to place articles in popular magazines targeted at similar audiences.

The following day in Dallas was mostly taken up with meetings between a large number of American and British military aviation officers and enlistees who seemed to be constellated in the region. There was discussion of the creation of recreational facilities designed specifically for the young British flyers in Dallas. Two days later in Kansas City, Knight met with a member of the British Air Commission who was in residence there to oversee a training program for overseas pilots conducted by Transcontinental and Western Air (TWA).

The TWA operation was known as the TWA Scheme. It was one of a number of "schemes" in operation at the time that were designed to take on various tasks in America to prepare aviators for the war in Europe during a time when the Allies needed all the help that they could get, and the American response to the war seemed increasingly open-ended. There was a Pan American Airways Scheme devoted to navigation training, and a Refresher Scheme that brought American pilots who might join the RAF up to speed, eventually producing almost 600 flyers for the RAF and the American Eagle Squadron. The All Through Training Scheme was created to match British commanders with American airplanes and support staff. The Towers Scheme was an operation of the U.S. Navy that trained key personnel for British air forces. Some of the schemes continued after the American declaration as valuable resources for American flyers.

The most important of them was the Arnold Scheme, conceived by General Henry Harland "Hap" Arnold. Arnold had learned to fly at the Wright Brothers school in Dayton, Ohio, and gone on to set altitude records with the nascent Aeronautical Division of the Army Signal Corps, and to become the first pilot to fly the U.S. Mail, before a series of crashes and near crashes caused him to give up flying out of admitted fear. In 1916, however, he was able to overcome his fear, and went on from there to become one of the most influential forces in the creation of the U.S. Air Force. He retired after World War II with the highest medals for service from the United States and eight other nations.

The Arnold Scheme was similar to, but separate from, other efforts like the BCATP and the CKC. All were directed at dealing with the current war and its possible evolution by developing air forces and their matériel to respond to German aggression. Officially, in late 1940, Arnold was head of the U.S. Army Air Corps and overseeing the production of American airplanes for potential U.S. use and export to Commonwealth forces. It was estimated that 800 planes were being produced each month, and that half were going to England. He was also overseeing the training of pilots for American forces, planned to eventually produce 12,000 per month, and the Arnold Scheme's part of that effort was to help England train its own aviators. An enlistee in the RAF in 1941 was likely to find himself first in Cambridge for initial testing, then on a ship across the Atlantic to Halifax, and a train from there to Albany, New York, for more training before moving on to a facility in Kansas, or some other place in America, before returning to England. It was a rigorous journey: almost half of those who came out of England for training did not return home as qualified flyers.

High as the standards of enlistee acceptance had to be, however, Arnold knew that the coming air wars were going to require all sort and stripe of flyers—at least in the recollection of Clayton Knight. In the early days of the CKC, said Knight, Arnold described his own challenge, and made a suggestion. "We need all the people we can get, but we have to wash some of them out for getting drunk or flying low or we find out they are married. Those are the ones I'd want if I had a fighting job to do because often they're really good, you know."[14] He urged Knight to continue to work with those he had to reject, and provided their names

Arnold's advice and actions seemed to be representative of the more realistic side of a constant and quiet quarrel within the U.S. government. Some agencies and departments had it within their legitimate purviews to prevent American citizens from crossing the border to fight with foreign forces, and others had diplomatic and military agendas that may have been more abstract. Conflicts bubbled beneath the surface of the development of the CKC, as they always had with similar programs and projects, but the committee always prevailed. On one occasion in Clayton Knight's memory, New York mayor Fiorello LaGuardia reappeared in the story. "He called me down to the summer City Hall one day and announced with disarming calm. 'Two or three weeks ago I got orders from my friend at the State Department to close you people up.' Then, with a 'Little Flower' smile, he continued, 'I told him to file the order in a desk drawer and call me after a week. I haven't heard any more— so far.'"[15] Knight was able to reciprocate when he received a worried call from a member of the Canadian Government on the day that Italy declared war on France. LaGuardia was scheduled to speak before a group in Ottawa the next day. "Your mayor," said the official, "he's an Italian isn't he? He may not be too welcome here considering today's declaration by Mussolini." Knight reassured the official and reminded him how important he had been to the committee's work, then he called LaGuardia, who he described as amused.

"So-ooo, they have no idea I'm just another Wop. Well, tell them to have the newspaper boys there when the plane lands, and I'll set them straight on that point ... and quick."[16]

Whatever the government's back and forth about the legalities of the CKC and similar efforts, it was trumped again by the human element of it all. There was a war to be fought, sides to be taken, justice to be sought, adventures and jobs to be had. Laws and borders were secondary to all of that.

That was perhaps no more ultimately recognized and accepted than in the CKC requirement that any American applying had to have a letter from his draft board that, in effect, gave him permission. The boards seemed willing to comply. The CKC's work had become so accepted that it was absorbed into the new Canadian Aviation Bureau (CAB) in September 1941, and its mission continued even after the American declaration of war on December 8, 1941. On December 18, Selective Service Local Board 8, Harris County, Texas, as an example, sent a memo to the CAB in Windsor, Ontario, in re Tom Edison Mahavier, described as an American citizen enlisted in the RCAF, excerpted:

It is our purpose, at this time, to ask that you prepare some statement which we can place in this registrant's file, after you have investigated and have definitely established the fact that he is a member of the R.C.A.F.

As you well know, the presence of an American Citizen in the R.C.A.F. at this time, under the circumstances, is highly desirable, and we wish to congratulate the registrant if he has been accepted, and the Canadian Government for his selection, as we feel that he will be a valuable asset to you.[17]

FOURTEEN

American Eagles ...

... trying to fight off that damnable misty curtain from my eyes while fairly hauling my plane around in the most sickening turns. —Arthur Donahue

Eight months after the Ogdensburg Agreement of August 1940, U.S. president Franklin Delano Roosevelt and Canadian prime minister Mackenzie King met at Hyde Park to affirm the work of the American-Canadian Joint Board of Defense. After its creation by the two North American leaders, the board had moved quickly to integrate the strengths against the weaknesses of each country to "coordinate the defense of the northern half of the Western Hemisphere."[1]

Its chief appointed American representative was New York Mayor Fiorello LaGuardia, then president of the U.S. Conference of Mayors. Representing Canada was retired army Colonel O.M. Biggar, an Ottawa attorney who had represented Canada in the Versailles Treaty negotiations after World War I.

On April 17, 1941, the two men announced the completion of a comprehensive plan to defend both coasts of the continent, and on April 20 Roosevelt and MacKenzie completed an agreement described as "a virtual merging of the of the economies of the United States and Canada for production of war materials for Great Britain and for hemisphere defense."[2] In it, the two countries would supply each other with defense matériel that each could not provide for itself. The U.S. further agreed to supply Canada the parts it needed to manufacture war matériel for Great Britain without cost. A stated goal of the agreement was to use the combined manufacturing capabilities of the two nations for the most efficient production of matériel. It was accompanied by reports, which did not prove to be accurate, that, in the spirit of hemispheric defense, the U.S. would send its own troops to Canada to replace Canadian troops that went to England. The plan was interpreted as an expansion of the American resolve to help Great Britain, but its effect on the enhancement of American preparation for potential entrance into the war was unstated.

The Hyde Park agreement was in sync with American public opinion. Even before the war had erupted in Europe, President Roosevelt had been speaking publicly about the importance to America of the defense of Canada. Nearly 70 percent of the public agreed with him at the time, and the number increased to 80 percent after the fall of France in May 1940. After the work of the Joint Defense Board, 90 percent of those surveyed in May 1941 answered in the affirmative to the question: if Canada is actually invaded by any European power, do you think the United States should use its army and navy to aid Canada?[3] In July

1941, the American Legion held its annual convention in Toronto, and used the occasion to give medals to two Americans enlisted in the RCAF and one in the Canadian army.[4]

As leadership worked to develop a common American-Canadian response to the war, Americans kept coming across the border to fight with Canada. In October, the Canadian army and air force noted a recent surge in American enlistments that seemed to be driven by the increasing conflict, but yet undeclared war, between the United States and the Axis powers. The army said that nearly 10,000 Americans were now within its ranks, and the RCAF claimed that eight percent of its force had come from the United States. In addition, the BCATP included 600 American instructors, and American women were beginning to show up in Canada to enlist in the Canadian Women's Auxiliary Air Force.[5] Included in the army numbers were a number of Belgian Americans who had responded to a plea from the Belgian Minister to Canada Baron Robert Silvercruys, and been taken into a Belgian unit of the Canadian army.

"...I was always amazed at how many of these fellows showed up drunk, half-drunk or with a hangover. And an awful lot did," an unnamed Canadian told an oral history project on the war years. It did not seem to be an unkind observation. The speaker had been involved in recruiting in Toronto, and estimated that 90 percent of the 300 or 400 Americans he had met were headed to the air force. He thought they were "good chaps," educated and "officer class" perhaps more motivated by the prospects of action than by a determination to save the world.[6] He repeated a conversation he had had with one recruit who told him that the trip to Canada had begun during a party in Mississippi. When talk turned to whether the U.S. should be in the war, it was mentioned that Canada was already involved and it wasn't too far away.

> One of the fellows had a plane, and they spent the night and part of the next morning toodling along, stopped at this cornfield and that one for gas, and they had two or three quarts of bourbon with them, and that was about it. Here they were, looking like death warmed over, but ready to do or die. We put them through, of course, and that's the last we'd see of them.[7]

The recruiter speculated that a number of them had probably been killed in action. One of them would be Billy Fiske. Fiske had careened down the bobsled run of the 1932 Winter Olympics, refused to enter the 1936 Olympics with Adolf Hitler as chief spectator, and been perhaps the first American-as-Canadian to join the RAF, right into the thick of the Battle of Britain. In July 1940, Germany was two months past its defeat of France and was now training its sights on England with supreme confidence. It would be an air war, pitting the Luftwaffe against an RAF that had suffered significant losses in the defense of France, and which was still scrambling to gain full force in airplanes and pilots. Hitler may have believed that England would surrender rather than suffer the power of his air forces, but England saw it otherwise, and its resolve had increasingly reached across the Atlantic to men like Billy Fiske. The German onslaught was relentless and seemed to be overwhelming. It was intended to be demoralizing and destructive, and to prepare England to succumb to a land invasion from across the Channel if it came to that. The fight in the air was between any kind of airplane that could assert itself in the battle. It attacked water-borne shipping and terror-bombed British cities.

For those American men who followed every moment of the battle as would be flyers, a few things seemed inevitable: the United States would soon be entering the war, and they would probably be drafted into the army, though many had already washed out of air force enlistment for various reasons; so they would attempt to get into the air war by going directly to England. Americans would be found throughout the RCAF and RAF, but some would be concentrated in the American Eagle Squadrons. As Billy Bishop developed the AES, he talked with Billy Fiske as its potential first commander, and the RAF had agreed to the idea.

After training, Fiske had entered the 601 Squadron of the RAF just as the squadron was taking a lead role in the Battle of Britain. He saw his first significant action on July 20, 1940, flying a single seat Hawker Hurricane, and flew 47 sorties in the following 27 days. A 601 sortie on August 13 was typical: in the air at 0630 to a patrol altitude of 10,000 feet, the sighting of German bomber squadrons with escorts above and beneath, a climb at 180 mph to 500 feet above the highest squadron, a dogfight and the resulting inability of the bombers to hit any discernible targets, 10 enemy planes destroyed and everyone back on the ground by 0715.

Fiske had his first kill on August 11, taking down a Messerschmitt Bf 110, a two-engine heavy fighter, which he described in his report as "Terrific fight. Terrified but fun. Had to lead the sqdn in. Willie's engine failed!"[8] In total, he had claimed six kills and the forcing of a German bomber into a barrage balloon by August 15. On the following day, his plane was damaged in a second operation, and caught fire as he tried to get it back to base. His engine stopped, but he was able to glide to a belly-flop landing, though the fuel tank exploded. Fisk was badly burned and died of shock in a Chichester hospital on August 17. Perhaps the first American to join the RAF in World War II, he was also perhaps the first American to be killed in action in the war, and described as the first American member of the RAF to be killed in some accounts of his death. He was buried as a pilot officer in the Royal Air Force Reserve in the Boxgrove Churchyard, Sussex.

On July 4, 1941, the city of London devoted the day to a celebration of the signing of the American Declaration of Independence. The Union Jack and American flag were hung side by side in the streets and railroad stations, and in the midst of buildings that had already been damaged by German bombing. England still awaited the hoped for American declaration of war. Pictures of President Roosevelt were all about, and he would be giving a speech on British radios in the evening that was as eagerly anticipated as any given by Winston Churchill. Restaurants gave some of their selections American names like Baltimore Fried Chicken and Boston Baked Beans. At a luncheon held at the American Society in London, Americans and citizens of all the Commonwealth nations toasted to a common heritage and faith in the future.

The most solemn event took place at St. Paul's Cathedral where England's Secretary for Air, Sir Archibald Sinclair, unveiled a tablet in the memory of Pilot Officer William M.L. Fiske the Third, "An American citizen who died that England might live." It was placed in a wall near a bust of George Washington. Approximately 100 people in attendance heard the secretary continue with a remarkable encomium for a man who was a bobsled racer at heart:

> Under no kind of compulsion he came and fought for Britain and, fighting, died. So he gave his life for his friends and for the great cause, the common cause of free men everywhere, the cause of liberty. That is why we honor his brave spirit today. That is why we have written the chronicle of his deed in letters of bronze in the shrine of the empire's capital. He has joined the company of those who from Socrates to John Brown have died in freedom's name and for freedom's cause.[9]

St. Paul's had seen a similar event in World War I, on the American Memorial Day in 1917, but it had taken place after the United States had entered the war, not as England still hoped for an American declaration. The 1917 memorial had honored Americans in U.S. and

Canadian forces for sacrifices already made, but the memorial for Billy Fiske seemed to be an offering for what was yet to come. The Royal Air Force band played the patriotic music of both nations, and prayers were said for both the king of England and the president of the United States, who "being united in singleness of purpose and endurance unto the end may obtain at last the blessings of victory and a righteous and abiding peace." In a following luncheon, the American ambassador to Great Britain, John Winant, offered what he called "a few serious words to my fellow-countrymen."

The writing of the Declaration of Independence, he said, had been described by Thomas Jefferson not as a new idea, but as a declaration of the inevitable. The American flag represented "the universal ideal that lives within our land and beyond our frontiers, is an ideal that reaches out to all mankind." A British official offered that it was "natural and inevitable that in this great contest for the victory of humane and democratic values the United States and the British Commonwealth should draw ever closer."[10]

Much had occurred by the time of Fiske's memorial service in 1941. He had been a member of the RAF's Fighter Command, one of three divisions of the Air Force, along with Bomber Command and Coastal Command, each designated to focus efforts on specific tasks. England was judged to have won the Battle of Britain, but at great cost. After the battle, Winston Churchill gave the Fighter Command the name "The Few," relative to the many of the Luftwaffe. Throughout the defense of its nation, the Command suffered losses that kept it on the edge of effectiveness, and the average age of its flyers was just 20 years. Where one came from seemed the least concern in the face of considerable need for men who could fight with airplanes. They would not be required to swear allegiance to the king. Fiske had been one of 11 Americans in the Battle of Britain, according to the records of the Royal Air Force (the number is variously given from seven to 12).[11] All but one of them would be killed over the course of the war.

Vernon "Shorty" Keough was less than five feet tall, used cushions to give him enough height in a cockpit, and had been a professional parachute jumper. Born in Brooklyn, he had flown in the French Air Force until the fall of France, survived the Battle of Britain, but later disappeared in a non-combat accident over the English Channel as a founding member of the American Eagle Squadron 71. Andrew Mamedoff of Thompson, Connecticut, survived the Battle of Britain, but was lost in bad weather over Ireland in October 1941, believed by some to be the first Jewish American to be killed in the war. De Peyster Brown of Pennsylvania had claimed Canadian nationality and entered the Royal Canadian Air Force in 1939. He moved to the United States Air Force when the U.S. entered the war, served in the Berlin Airlift postwar and retired with the rank of major. Carl Raymond Davis had been born of American parents in South Africa, but joined the RAF as a British citizen and was killed in combat over England on September 6, 1940. He had shot down, destroyed or damaged 17 enemy aircraft before his death.

Eugene Tobin, a native of Los Angeles, had arrived in Finland too late to fly in the Winter War. He moved on to the French Air Force just before the German occupation, then to the 609 Squadron of the RAF in August 1940. He would be killed as a member of the American Eagle Squadron in September 1941. Shot down in a dogfight over northern France, he is buried in Boulogne Eastern Cemetery. John Kenneth Haviland, of Mt. Kisco, New York, was the child of an English mother and a U.S. Navy father. He grew up in England, and joined the RAF in September 1940. Injured in a training collision, he spent the rest of the war in non-combat air support. A retired professor of engineering, he died in Charlottesville, Virginia, in 2002. Otto John Peterson, of Atlanta, Georgia, had joined the RAF in 1938 and was shot down over England in September 1940. He is buried in the Brookwood Cemetery outside of London. Philip Howard Leckrone, of Salem, Illinois, flew through the Battle of Britain as a tail gunner, but was killed in formation exercises with the AES in January 1941. Alexander Natonski was born in Philadelphia, the child of Polish immigrants. The family had moved to Ontario in 1926, and Natonski had tried to join the Polish Air Force before the German invasion of that country. He parachuted into the English Channel with burns and an injured leg in August 1940, and disappeared in fighting over North Africa in December 1941. He was never found.

Arthur Donahue had grown up on a Minnesota dairy farm and taken his first flying lessons at age 15. His career ambitions ranged from the clergy to aviation, and took the latter turn as he began barnstorming around Minnesota and supplementing his income as a mechanic. By the time of the first German invasions, he was a remarkably qualified pilot and instructor, and wanted to go directly to England to join the RAF. To assuage his parents' fears, however, he tried to join the U.S. Army Air Corps Reserve, but nothing came of the effort. When he heard of the evacuation of Dunkirk, he took the route created by the Clayton Knight Committee, and went to Canada to apply for a non-combat job with the RAF. After a physical in Windsor, Ontario, the journey began with a slow trip up the St. Lawrence River and across the ocean in his own spacious cabin on a passenger liner that had been painted in camouflage. Donahue's book about his experiences, *Tally Ho! Yankee in a Spitfire*, describes languorous days in July sailing past icebergs, good food and a quiet time to prepare for what was to come.

In England, Donahue was picked up by a Royal Air Force car and taken to a train to London. He described England as a mystery with its strange money, left-hand driving and the unlit darkness of its cities at night. He noted that most of those out walking carried lit cigarettes, which seemed to prevent them from bumping into each other. The train ride to London was in a first-class compartment, and when he arrived the following morning he found the city to be beautiful in bright sunlight. But the barrage balloons meant to interfere with expected German bombing hung all over the sky, and the people seemed to Donahue to know what would eventually be coming. He felt "drawn into the struggle like a moth to the candle."

> Knowing that one of England's greatest problems was inferiority in numbers in the air, I felt it a duty as a follower of the civilized way of life to throw my lot in if they would take me. To fight side by side with these people against the enemies of civilization would be the greatest of all privileges. I had never done any military flying, but was confident of my ability to adapt myself.[12]

Within four days of his arrival, Donahue was a commissioned officer in His Majesty's Royal Air Force. Coming upon two non-commissioned RAF members on the sidewalk, he was saluted but realized that he did not know the proper way to return the salute, nor much else about the person he had become. In a café, a member of the Women's Auxiliary Air Force taught him the proper rules of procedure, and he was on his way again. At his assigned airdrome, he found comfortable accommodations and his own valet, a "batman" who pressed his clothes and made his bed, among other tasks.

The plane he was given to fly was one of the incentives for those who joined the RAF. It was a single seat, low-wing monoplane with a twelve-cylinder Rolls Royce engine. The Supermarine Spitfire had a top speed of 400 mph and a cruising speed of 300 mph; Donahue had spent the previous year flying 60 mph trainers. The practicing of acrobatics in this plane brought new challenges, not just to strategic thinking, but in the effects it had on the body and the brain. He had to find the edge at which vision could turn to blindness and blackout, and keep pushing those limits to increase his body's tolerance against g forces. He found that the more he could lean forward the shorter the distance that blood needed to be pumped from heart to head, and the more control of his faculties he had.

> ...I was leaning forward as far as my straps would permit, taking big gasps of air and holding them, and tensing my body muscles in the desperation one feels when his life is at stake, trying to fight off that damnable misty curtain from my eyes while fairly hauling my plane around in the most sickening turns. It invariably worked, too, and when I "came up for air" after a few seconds and looked around I usually found that my enemy had lost his advantage and it was my turn to take the offensive.[13]

Donahue's lengthy description of what followed, paraphrased, offers a fine evocation of the experience of an aerial dogfight:

The "misty curtain" reappeared during his first encounter with a German plane over the English Channel. Its demands on his cognition were mixed with incredulity at the experiences that had come to him one after the other. He had been required to push the plane's engine into full throttle, an acceleration that took him above 400 mph and 15,000 feet, then to 20,000 feet. He saw occupied France for the first time as enemy planes flew beneath in an opposite direction. Like flocks of birds, the formation in which he flew banked right and left, charged up and down in search of the small, black dots that became airplanes as they came closer. He saw a plane in front of him that might have been the enemy and not one of his own. It was perhaps his first actual sighting of a Nazi fighter in flight, and he pushed every piece of power and tilt of propeller the plane could muster into a dive toward the target. To be sure it was German, he closed in behind it and raised his nose slightly so that he could look down on its wings from above. Until that time, the enemy had seemed to be an abstract notion, but now the Swastikas on blue-gray wings with squared tips made the enemy real. He checked his rearview mirror to be sure he wasn't being followed, dropped back into firing position and pulled the firing button on his stick for just a second, 160 bullets.

The plane shuddered and seemed pushed backward by the recoil. Then, it was jostled sideways by the turbulence of the target's wake as it took evasive action and momentarily disappeared. He rolled over and descended until the German came back into sight, and he realized that he had just tried to kill another man without giving it much of a thought. In pursuit, he crossed into France for the first time, above Cape Gris Nez, but he had forgotten his rear view. His plane had nearly been hit by an exploding shell from a Messerschmitt behind him, which now wheeled around and above to dive at him head on.

It was not enough that he was now engaged in his first dogfight with two enemy planes, but the coast of France now presented him with anti-aircraft fire from below. The intricate fight continued for seemingly endless minutes. Donahue's gun sight had failed, and the flying had to compensate. At a point he realized he was exhausted and just wanted to rest. The sun bore down on him and he felt imprisoned by the straps and confines of the cockpit. He had begun to blackout in the constant turns, which also set his compass spinning so that he could not find a direction for escape. Then he saw a line of white across the water, and he remembered "The White Cliffs of Dover." The decision to fly in that direction was a retreat, but he thought it the best move to make. The Germans chased him to a point just short of the English coast, then turned away: a draw. Later examination of the fight determined that he may have shot down or significantly damaged one of the enemy planes.

On a patrol flight above the Channel one week later, Donahue came upon the largest group of enemy planes he had ever seen. They seemed to be flying in a holding pattern as more and more planes ascended to complete a formation. What Donahue thought to be a black cloud, in one instance, revealed itself to be a group of bombers. Then, halfway across the Channel, the formation headed for England. Before he could head back to base in advance of the formation, he was set upon by two German fighters. His control stick was damaged. It could only take him higher, but not lower, and his pedals moved too easily, without result. An incendiary bullet smoldered in the airframe beside him. He prepared to bail out if necessary, but a third fighter appeared and shot out his instrument panel and fuel tank. He would remember that moment as one in which all fear left him. The plane was now fully afire, and he could only leave the cockpit, falling into a 200 mph wind. He pulled the ripcord on his parachute, and suddenly all was calm. The parachute held him firmly as he drifted. His body was bruised and burned, and his clothes torn.

> I sighed and said aloud, feeling that the occasion demanded some recognition, "Well, Art, this is what you asked for. How do you like it?"[14]

Donahue was placed out of action for six weeks. The British Air Ministry reported that 61 aircraft of the enemy formation had been destroyed in action over the coast. Thirteen RAF fighters were lost, and just one of their pilots had returned home.

The conclusion of the Battle of Britain in October 1940 was followed by the introduction of the American Eagle Squadron. Its pilots had come to the squadron either through the Clayton Knight Committee, the recruiting efforts of Charles Sweeny, or through their own initiative in enlisting in the RCAF and RAF. One of those was the aviator and writer Len Morgan. He had been born in Indiana in 1923, and found himself in Detroit soon after graduating from high school. He had always wanted to fly, and set himself upon a course that started on a bus that took him through the tunnel beneath the Detroit River to Windsor, where he was let off in front of an RCAF recruiting station. He was surprised at how easily he could transform his desire to fly into the prospects of flight training in Canada. The only requirement of the recruiter was that he show a high school diploma and two letters of reference. Those who had not thought to bring such documents along could have them created at a print shop next door. That accomplished, he and the other American recruits of the day were assembled in a single room. An officer entered and closed the door behind him. They were reminded that Canada was at war, and that they were volunteering to fight in that war. "You must understand the seriousness of what you are doing," said the officer. "Anyone wishing to reconsider may do so now."[15] No one was discouraged, and by midnight each man was trying to sleep in a bunk 200 miles away in Toronto.

In Morgan's perception, young men like him who wanted to fly were subject to perhaps unfair limitations. Flying was still an exotic pursuit, made difficult to attain by the years of the Great Depression and the requirement of college education for those who would be accepted into army and navy flight schools. The 1938 beginning of the war in Europe didn't change those circumstances much in the United States, but whatever barriers may have existed in England had fallen. Word got out in American newspapers that the British were recruiting American high school graduates. It seemed inevitable to Morgan that his country would soon enter the war, and he figured that if he waited to attempt to join an American air force, he could just as easily "end up peeling potatoes at Fort Dix." The decision he made to enter the RCAF as a preemptive measure, however, put him on a troop ship leaving Halifax on December 7, 1941. His outcome might have been different had he waited, but he never came to regret his time in the RCAF, which he described as fun but serious, and not harmful to his American citizenship. He would be able to transfer to U.S. forces later in the war, and he ended his flying career as a pilot for Braniff International Airways, rated to fly a Boeing 747.

The first of three Eagle Squadrons, number 71, was formed within the RAF in September 1940. Its core members were Battle of Britain pilots Eugene Tobin, Andrew Mamedoff and Vernon Keough. Arthur Donahue was a member for just one month, and left to join another RAF squadron out of impatience with the startup time required for the AES. He would move on to be wounded in the Battle of Singapore a year later. After recuperation back in America, he returned to England to rejoin the RAF and was lost over the English Channel on September 11, 1942.

Donahue's impatience had been understandable. The pause at the end of the Battle of Britain, publicity about American participation in the battle, the arrival in England of American war matériel, and anticipation of what would happen next all seemed to come together in confusion. Part of the problem was the perceived quality of the airplanes involved. American Squadron 71 had been equipped by the RAF with American built Brewster Buffaloes, but the planes proved themselves to be inferior to the Spitfires and Hurricanes of the Battle of Britain. They were underpowered and not well armored. Pilots complained that they were perhaps well suited for landing on the long concrete runways of America, but dangerous in the cow pastures and cratered battlefields of Europe. Experience had shown that the way a plane was landed was as potentially dangerous as its vulnerability to enemy fighters in the air. It seemed to be no secret that pilots were told to land their Buffaloes in a way that would lead to non-lethal damage to the planes, which would then have to be taken out of service and replaced with Hurricanes.[16]

The AES pilots themselves were a point of some controversy, even within their own group. A report that also seemed to be part commentary in the *New York Times* noted that many of them had come from the West Coast, and, though they had not yet flown as members of the AES, there was already a suggestion that they would be returning to Hollywood as cinematic heroes. Not so fast, said the reporter. The AES "contains some excellent fliers. It contains others who are not quite so excellent. Some of these just maybe had the idea that after smacking down a couple of Messerschmitts they would drift on back to the Coast and step into that big Hollywood contract."[17] The article went on to report that the average British fighter pilot received pay of $3 per day, and the life expectancy of a Spitfire pilot was just less than six months. "You must be very deeply serious about why you are up there and what you are fighting for."[18] Some of the Eagles were said to wish for less attention to an effort that might or might not prove to be successful in the larger scheme of things.

The concern was underscored by the marketing of the Eagles within England. They were feted at the London Overseas Club in December. British Undersecretary for Air Harold Balfour called them ambassadors of goodwill who would also help the American people to further understand England's struggle against Germany. The following month, another British air official told a Washington news conference that his country's need for airmen was not desperate, but the Americans offered a symbolic value. After the squadron was declared ready for combat, its first assignment was only to fly escorts of shipping in the North Sea, and it didn't see combat until February 1941. The first of the Eagles to be killed in action, and the third American flyer to be killed in the war was Edwin Orbison of Sacramento, California. He had been preceded by Billy Fiske and Edward Leckrone. Leckrone was killed in a training collision with Orbison, and, soon thereafter, Orbison came upon a German fighter while on a training exercise and was apparently overcome by vertigo while in pursuit, crashing into the water. Vernon Keough was lost in a similar but separate incident. The bodies of both were never recovered.

In February and March, Squadron 71 blended into the work of the full RAF on the defensive side and not at the level of action its members desired, though, by April, it had been supplied with two generations of the desirable Hurricanes. In that month, Major General "Hap" Arnold and Charles Sweeny met in England. After a review, Arnold exclaimed that to the extent that the AES was still in training and defensive status, it should be sent full force into combat, or be disbanded. That was followed by an exhibition of the brashness for which the Americans were both criticized and admired when pilot Chesley Peterson, of Santaquin, Utah, broke protocol, not worrying that the Americans were seen by some as prima donnas, and demanded of a commander that the squadrons see more action. The admonishments and requests were answered and, by May, the AES was flying in full combat. Its first notable encounter with the enemy took place in a May 15 dogfight over the Channel with no major losses.

The first significant victories for the AES were not recorded until July 2. Squadron 71 planes were part of a larger canopy of fighters escorting a bomber force of 12. The purpose of the mission was the bombing of an electricity plant in France, and to draw German fighters into combat. More than 25 German planes showed up for the fight, and the squadron was credited with five enemy shot down or significantly damaged, suffering just one loss of a plane themselves. The pilot managed to parachute away, but was captured and taken prisoner-of-war.

In total, the AES would be comprised of 244 Americans, commanded by 116 English members. One hundred and nine of them would be killed in action. Squadron number 71 was followed by Squadron 121, which was put in operation on May 14. By this time, the Clayton Knight Committee was functioning at optimum efficiency, and the British Commonwealth Air Training Plan (BCATP), known as the Empire Air Training Scheme (EATS) in England had 70 of 85 planned aerodromes in full operation. Visiting London in July 1941, Canadian Air Minister C.G. Power told a reporter that the plan's capacity had been increased to accommodate volunteers from all of the Commonwealth nations and the seven to 10 percent of recruits that came from the United States. The number of enlistees was so great, in fact, that a number of them would be placed in reserve status.

A problem for the 71st American Eagle Squadron had been the bogging down of training when its members arrived in England; now they would be extensively trained before crossing the ocean, and the new squadron would be commanded by those who had already had experience with number 71. The third and final squadron, number 133, was in place on August 1 and one of the original American pilots, Andrew Mamedoff, became a co-commander with an English Flight Lieutenant. The 133 settled in Eglinton, Ireland in October, but, in the transfer there from a base in Norwich, four pilots were lost as they flew into a mountain in bad weather, Mamedoff among them.

In November, Squadron 71 led all squadrons of the RAF in the number of enemy aircraft "killed," and its leadership came under the command of now 21 year old American Chesley Peterson. It was now an RAF squadron made up entirely of American members. The appointment of Peterson occasioned significant coverage in the British and American press, to the extent that he took the step of closing the squadron's doors to press coverage so that it could stay focused on the mission. An element of that coverage was the notion that the British war and the American Eagle Squadron had blended into an effort that was not about where one came from or for whom one was fighting, but about the job that had to be done.

On November 20, 1941, an event in honor of the AES was held in Piccadilly with the attendance of American Ambassador John Winant, Prince Bernhard of the Netherlands, and British Secretary for Air Sinclair who continued on the theme he had set down in the earlier memorial at St. Paul's Cathedral. He recalled his first visit from both Charles Sweenys telling him that Americans were ready to fight with the RAF. Since that time, a lot of Americans had joined the force and fought splendidly and the only regret was that when those already in the RAF had moved into the AES, it was a loss to the units they had left. In their time so far, said Sinclair, they had definitely destroyed 28 enemy aircraft, probably destroyed 10 and damaged seven more with a corresponding loss of only 11 of their own.[19] On November 28, a slightly different view of things was offered by the Commander of the Royal Canadian Air Force in Britain who told a news conference that Americans were "coming over in droves" to join the Canadians. "We have a real problem in handling them."[20]

Then, on December 7, the Japanese attacked Pearl Harbor, and the question presented itself to the AES, and every other American already fighting: how much would things change, and how much would they stay the same?

FIFTEEN

... and Flying Tigers

I've chased the shouting wind along, and flung
My eager craft through footless halls of air....
—John Magee

In March 1941, the London Bureau of the Toronto *Star* reported on the American presence already in place in a war it had not yet entered. It had taken two full days to compile the list, and, even then, by the *Star's* admission, it wasn't complete.

The British War Relief Society (BWRS) was an umbrella organization for charities that provided food, clothes and medical supplies directly to the people of England whose cities were being regularly devastated by German bombing. Its best-known effort was Bundles for Britain, which had begun in a New York knitting circle in 1939 and made warm apparel for British sailors. As the war went on, city storefronts became collection points for clothing, which would be repaired if necessary, and other supplies that could be picked up at distribution points in cities like London and Plymouth. By 1941, BWRS had brought $2 million cash and $4 million worth of supplies to England. It supplied 135 truck convoys, known as Queen's Messengers, that brought food to the small bombed out towns of England, often operated by young women who had come from the United States. BWRS also assisted in services to British children, who were frequently removed from targeted cities to safety in smaller towns outside of the range of German bombers.

The American Field Service developed in World War I was operating in countries extending to the Middle East and Africa, including England, in World War II. It was supplemented by American Ambulance Great Britain, which received ambulances and supplies through British Relief. It had four centers of operation in London. The Field Service also sponsored the American Eagle Club on Charing Cross Road, supported by funds raised in American social and country clubs. It was designed to be a home away from home for the 10,000 Americans estimated to be in the British army and air force as of June 1941. A fundraising effort that month brought Britain's Lord Marley, a naval officer who had distinguished himself in World War I, to stand before American audiences to thank them for their charities. "The American supplies," he said, "are going right into the hearts and homes of the British people. A love for Americans is growing up in their hearts which will never die and will lay the foundation for us to shape together a reconstructed world."[1] He went on to say that Lady Marley was an assistant cook and dishwasher in a London canteen, which was badly in need of modern kitchen equipment.

Specific American fighting units in England included the First American Motorized

Squadron devoted to the defense of London, and the American Eagle Squadron, which had just become an official part of the Fighter Command. "History has given them a blank page in the R.A.F.'s glorious book, and no doubt it will soon be filled," said the *Star*.[2] Along with 200 ambulances and 200 mobile canteens, the American Red Cross in Britain had supplied 10 million surgical dressings, to say nothing of x-ray and surgical equipment, and the equipping of the Harvard Red Cross Field Hospital. The hospital was an operation of the Harvard Medical School, staffed by Harvard professors and Red Cross nurses and conceived to study communicable diseases in wartime. That mission extended to cases of food poisoning in London, an outbreak of scarlet fever, diphtheria and meningitis in Halifax, Nova Scotia, and the development of a medical inventory for England to be supplied under the terms of Lend-Lease. It took the form of a portable, 22 room field hospital based in Salisbury, England. Its wartime research would be applied to the larger international study of communicable disease.

Another defensive unit not widely known and not mentioned in the *Star* article was the Civilian Technical Corps (CTC). The corps was created by President Roosevelt to provide technical American support to the development of British weaponry, especially in electronics. Its recruitment effort was begun in the summer of 1941, based in the British consulate in New York City and administered in Canada. Among its American supporters were Mayor Fiorello LaGuardia, who was then the director of the Office of Civilian Defense, and Wendell Willkie who had lost a presidential election to Roosevelt in the previous year. Enlistment was open to any American male of sufficient character and qualification for work in a list of categories ranging from radio engineers to watch makers and automobile mechanics, but it was understood that a larger goal of the CTC was the development of radar and radiolocator technologies. They would work closely with the British military, but not be subject to military discipline and combat, and they would have to sign up for three years, or the duration of the war if it was less than that. Salaries ranged from $24 to $39 per week with a 50 percent premium for dependent wives and children, and other benefits were similar to those given to members of the Royal Canadian Air Force.

Roosevelt intended that the CTC be a way for qualified Americans to volunteer in the British war effort with clear legality. They were told that they would not forfeit citizenship because they would not be taking an oath of allegiance to the king, and that England had agreed to immediately release them from duty if they were needed by their own country. American Selective Service had been instructed to defer a CTC volunteer from call-up, and all of his travel expenses to and from England would be fully supported. By August 1941, 8,000 men had applied for the corps. Earlier reporting suggested that a number of women with experience as radio technicians had also applied, but no traces of women can be found in available histories of the effort. Testing of applicants was conducted by a number of organizations, including the Radiomarine Corporation of America (RCA), which offered 20 locations around the country, and the New York City Civil Service Commission.

Two of those who went to England were featured in a *New York Times* article about the CTC as notable exceptions to the rules. Age limits for enlistment were 18 to 55, or to 45 in occupations that required hard physical labor. Edwin S. Savage, Jr., of Teaneck, New Jersey, was a 16-year-old son of a Bell Telephone Laboratories engineer and already an expert in radio technology. His enlistment was briefly noted in the December 1941 issue of *Boy's Life* magazine. Fifty-two year old John Rhoads, of Philadelphia, had been a radio operator on the horse transports that sailed between England and Canada in World War I.

After acceptance into the corps, enlistees were taken to Montreal and given a last meal of filet mignon, lemon meringue pie and all the beer they could drink before being transported to food-rationing England. The first group of 25 to head across the ocean in July was sent off with newsreels running and flashbulbs popping. When they got to England, a number found that promises made weren't always fulfilled, particularly in the matter of military discipline. Some British officers could not see a way in which men working with those under discipline could not be subjected to it themselves, but the matter was later resolved. In total, 899 men were reported to have arrived in England for service. Twenty had been lost at sea or otherwise killed before arriving, and, after the American declaration of war, 287 had returned to America, presumably to enlist in U.S. forces, although almost all Americans in the CTC were exempted from military service because they were already engaged in vital work for the common defense. In May 1944, British Secretary for Air Archibald Sinclair awarded two of them with the Order of the British Empire: Donald Lee Gill of Brooklyn was Commandant of the CTC, and William Henry Manning of Del Rio, Texas, was one of its first volunteers.

The Toronto *Star* article could only make passing reference to "many American volunteers in the British army," because so little was known about them. On August 1, 1941, it was reported that a large contingent of the Third Division of the Canadian army had arrived in England, the largest single convoy of men since the beginning of the war, ready to engage in the Battle of Britain or the invasion of Europe, if it came to that.

> ... they were a cheerful, boisterous lot, eager to "wipe Hitler off the face of the earth." ... Among them were some Americans. One of them, Gunner W.R. Goldfein of the Bronx, New York, enlisted at Montreal five months ago. Asked why he wanted to join the Canadian Army, he answered: "Well, my number was due to come up and this is one way to beat the draft." Another American, who is known in his outfit as "Pop." Is Gunner J.W. Doyle, a member of the Air Service with the American Army in France in the last war. He says he is 41 years old.[3]

While the flow of American men into the Canadian army continued without much notice, the enlistment of air personnel seemed perhaps as negligible, though it sustained a constant back and forth of negotiations between the American and Canadian governments in which both countries sought to accommodate to changing conditions. By the first months of 1941, the RCAF's need for American pilots and instructors had lessened and its response was to increase the standards that applied to new recruits. As a result, there was less need for the work of Clayton Knight Committee. At the same time, the developing certainty that the United States would eventually enter the war was increasing preparation for participation of an American air force, while American isolationists were becoming increasingly agitated and vocal about what they saw coming.

In July, a decision was made by the RCAF to change the focus of Canadian enlistment from air pilots to supporting aircrew, and, through the CKC, to have 2,500 in place by September 1. In effect, it would bring about a dramatic expansion of the Canadian Air Force through the use of a large number of American citizens. The plan needed to be mindful of the continuing uncertainty about the fine points of American law in this regard, and of an isolationist movement that could be harmful both to the effort and to American-Canadian relations and public opinion. Once again, safety seemed to lie in the mechanism by which Americans were recruited and moved to Canada, though the plan would be used to directly recruit those who had succeeded in a training program run by the American government.

The Civilian Pilot Training Program (CPTP) had been created in 1938 to develop the nation's labor of commercial aviators, with a secondary goal of increasing military preparedness. It came under the purview of the Civil Aeronautics Authority (CAA) and ultimately worked with more than 400 colleges and universities to develop a body of 9,000 students by the end of 1939, and 98,000 trained pilots in 1942 (including the famed African American Corps the Tuskegee Airmen, and female pilots). The Canadian plan was presented to officials of the two American agencies, who agreed that it could be executed with some tweaking of its process and American blessing. It was agreed that the CPTP would provide names of its graduates and staff, and recommend a path of recruitment that would not break American law. Across the border, the American acceptance of the plan led to a reformulation of Canadian aviation agencies into the umbrella Canadian Aviation Bureau (CAB) so that it would operate in better conformity with American law.

The predicted agitation of American isolationism came to pass in the form of an Oregon congressman who demanded that the State Department produce a full investigation of RCAF recruiting in America. The demand had apparently derived from an ill-conceived letter from the CAB seeking American recruits to the Canadian Coast Guard. The effect of the response of both the U.S. State and Justice departments was to re-assert the legality of Canada's actions, and also to head off a threatened investigation of the Clayton Knight Committee.

The CKC, however, was not by far the largest source of Americans for the RCAF. By December 7, 1941, most estimates put more than 6,000 Americans in the Canadian force. Most had arrived there on their own by slipping across the border and applying on their own credentials. One of them would be killed early in the war, and leave behind a poem that would become an anthem to combat flight. It would also be recited by an American president on the occasion of a national tragedy at the end of the century. Like many in World War I, and more still in World War II, John Gillespie Magee, Jr., was an American of confused heritage. Born in Shanghai, China, he was the son of an English mother and an American father; thus an American citizen. His parents were missionaries during a time of intense Christian expansion in China. His first nine years were spent in Shanghai, before being sent to schools in England where, at age 12, he emerged as a poet and was taken under the wing of the British war poet P.H.B. Lyon.

Magee's father, John Sr., was an Episcopal priest from a wealthy Pittsburgh family who had chosen the life of a missionary after graduation from Yale University. John Jr. was the oldest of four sons, and when the mother and sons returned to England for the children's educations, the father stayed behind, moving to Nanking. In 1937, he was head of the Nanking Committee of the American Red Cross as Japan opened what came to be called the Nanking Massacre, or the Rape of Nanking. The city had been a target in the expanding Japanese takeover of China, and, in December 1937, Japanese troops asserted the force of their entrance into the city in what some would later consider to be the second Holocaust of World War II. Fifty thousand Japanese soldiers participated in the murder of 200,000–300,000 soldiers and civilians. Death was by torture, bayonet, mass execution and burning alive. Twenty to eighty thousand women, from age seven or eight to old age, were gang raped and often then murdered. Chinese men were forced to rape their own daughters and mothers. Stores were looted and buildings destroyed.

Though John Magee, Sr., worked in a safe zone of Nanking, he coursed the streets of the city with others to do what he could in the face of remarkable atrocity. As important, he took with him a movie camera that produced several hours of visual record of the massacre and its effects. At the time, the rest of the official world seemed unwilling to recognize the gravity of Japan's ambitions in China. Magee's films were smuggled out of China, but had little obvious effect in both the German and American governments. Nor was stray reporting on the events in American media much noticed or believed. It was not until stills from the Magee footage were published in *Life* Magazine in spring 1938, followed by attention in other magazines, that the floodgates of anti–Japanese feeling seemed to open in the United States. They were still fresh in the American mind at the time of the Japanese attack on Pearl Harbor in 1941, but Magee's films did not show up in American newsreels until 1942.

At the time of his father's hardest work in China, the young John Magee was finding much to contemplate in the gathering of war in Europe. It was expressed in a 10-page, blank verse treatise "The Brave New World," which, though youthful at his age of 16, won a poetry prize that had been received by one of his heroes, the poet Rupert Brooke, 34 years earlier. Brooke had been a contemporary of Alan Seeger, and identified with England as much as Seeger was identified with America. Both had been energized by their own fatal visions and the inevitabilities of war, and both had died young: Seeger perhaps by his own hand after a fatal wound, and Brooke, more strangely, from an infected mosquito bite as he headed toward the Gallipoli Landings. He was buried on the Greek island of Skyros.

The first of Magee's mature poems was *Sonnet to Rupert Brooke*, excerpted:

> We laid him in a cool and shadowed grove
> One evening in the dreamy scent of thyme
> Where leaves were green,
> And whispered high above–
> A grave as humble as it was sublime[4];
> ...

In 1939, Magee moved to America to attend a Yale prep school in Hartford, Connecticut. He was not happy there, and felt out of place. As his family finally reunited to live in Washington, he declined a Yale scholarship and went to Canada in October 1940 to join the RCAF. Training brought about a conversion from a loosely disciplined and slightly overweight young poet to a purposeful, mustachioed graduate of the flying school at St. Catherines, Ontario, and ahead of his classmates in flying skill. In England, he joined the 412 Squadron of the RCAF, and flew Spitfires as a bomber interceptor over Holland and the North Sea. Between flights, he made model airplanes and continued to write poetry. In December 1941, his plane collided with another over England and he was killed at age 19. He was said to have been seen pulling back his airplane's canopy as it sped toward the ground and setting foot on the wing, but it was too late to use his parachute.

Before his death, Magee had sent his parents a poem he had written in haste, starting it while 30,000 feet above the earth and finishing when he landed. Upon his death, his father published it in the bulletin of the Washington church of which he was now an assistant pastor. It would come to be considered a World War II equivalent of John McRae's World War I poem "In Flanders Field."

> "High Flight"
> Oh! I have slipped the surly bonds of Earth
> And danced the skies on laughter-silvered wings;
> Sunward I've climbed, and joined the tumbling mirth
> of sun-split clouds,—and done a hundred things
> You have not dreamed of—wheeled and soared and swung
> High in the sunlit silence. Hov'ring there,
> I've chased the shouting wind along, and flung
> My eager craft through footless halls of air....

Up, up the long, delirious, burning blue
I've topped the wind-swept heights with easy grace.
Where never lark, or even eagle flew—
And, while with silent, lifting mind I've trod
The high untrespassed sanctity of space,
—Put out my hand, and touched the face of God.[5]

"High Flight" became a centerpiece of memorials in various air forces, and a theme of pieces of music, including modern masses, and writing in books and magazines. In the 1960s, it entered the culture of the U.S. National Aeronautics and Space Administration, and was often taken into manned space flight. In 1988, the poem was quoted to the nation by President Ronald Reagan after the explosion of the space shuttle *Challenger* on January 28.

When nearly 400 Japanese aircraft attacked the U.S. Navy base at Pearl Harbor, Hawaii, on December 7, 1941, it took only one day for all of the country's pent up pro-war sentiment to result in an American declaration of war. The December 8 declaration against Japan by President Roosevelt was followed by declarations against Germany and Italy on December 11. America was now entering the war, but many Americans had been at war for previous months and years. The often-stated figure of 10,000 Americans already in the Canadian army may actually have been larger, given the official number of 18,848 stated by Canadian Veterans Affairs in 1955. The number of Americans in British or Canadian air forces was derived from a mix of sources that may have overlapped in some cases. The true number was always elusive in reporting over the course of the war. Also fluid, and sometimes depending on who was making the estimate, was the number of Americans believed to be in the RCAF. The reported number hovered around 9,000, and was confused by statistics from sources like the Clayton Knight Committee and other programs and "schemes." Smaller groups of Americans already at war could be found in places like the Royal Naval Volunteer Reserve, and the American Volunteer Group, or Flying Tigers, which was already in place in China.

The Flying Tigers would be the first group of American fighters to be brought into American forces at war, with gratitude for their state of experience and preparation. At the time of Pearl Harbor, they consisted of 82 pilots flying 79 Curtiss P-40s to protect cities and transportation routes in Burma, most notably the Burma Road from Rangoon to Chongquing, China. In December, it could be said that the Tigers were relatively successful against Japanese attacks on China and Burma. Their loss/kill ratio seemed often better than that for the enemy (later years would revisit action reports and suggest otherwise), but they were outnumbered by Japanese aircraft and severely reduced in force in the opening months of the Japanese Burma Campaign. By the end of February, and after the Japanese taking of Rangoon, the Tigers removed themselves to Magwe in Northern Burma, then across the border into China, with just four remaining P-40s, in late March.

During this time, the Tigers' creator and commander, Claire Chennault, had been in negotiation with the U.S. army, which wanted to incorporate his organization into its Air Force. As the first American to lead a strike against the hated Japanese Air Force, he had briefly become an American hero. Chennault was disposed to re-join the army he had left in 1937, but it would have to be at a rank higher than the army envisioned. Dutifully, he wrote to Madame Chiang Kai-shek asking for the thoughts of her husband. Chennault suggested that the pay his men would receive would be reduced in the deal but that China might want to still supplement their pay as the change would be very much to China's economic advantage. His only real concern, he told her, was that the army might replace him as head of the AVG with someone who did not understand China.

China agreed to the plan with gratitude that would extend into post-war memorials to Chennault and the Flying Tigers. The airman was brought back into the U.S. Army Air Force in the spring as a colonel who would distinguish himself in the remainder of the war and become major general of the 14th Air Force. On July 2, 1942, the American Volunteer Group became the 23d USAAF Fighter Group. Most of its members returned home, or scattered into other branches of service. One who stayed in the AVG, however, was Pak On Lee of Portland, Oregon. The "paper son" of China was now a member of the USAAF, and would serve through the duration of the war, becoming a U.S. citizen in 1947. He returned to Portland and a successful career as a mechanic for high performance engines. His war service was honored by the state of Oregon in 1977.

Another flyer to join Chennault had been last seen most visibly trying to remove a large gorilla from the top of the Empire State Building. Since the debut of *King Kong* in 1933, Merian Cooper had re-enlisted in the U.S. Army Air Force with the stripes of a colonel. He had come to China to assist in the Doolittle Raid, the first direct American attack on the Japanese Islands, then become Chennault's Chief of Staff and master tactician in July 1942. In 1943, Cooper became chief of staff for the Fifth Air Force Bomber Command in the South Pacific. He ended the war as a Brigadier General, and a witness to the Japanese surrender aboard the USS *Missouri*.

On the occasion of their 50th reunion in 1992, the Flying Tigers were recognized by Congress as having been full members of the U.S. military while they were in service to China. The AVG was awarded a Presidential Unit Citation. Each of its pilots was given the Distinguished Flying Cross and each crewmember the Bronze Star. Chennault had never been fully accepted by his military peers and betters, but he had Roosevelt's support, and served as a go-between for the American president and Chiang Kai-shek during the course of the war.

The aftermath of the attack on Pearl Harbor made it obvious to Clayton Knight that his committee had done its job and was no longer needed, but to the extent that the word got out to its potential recruits they didn't seem to agree. There were still young men who didn't see a possibility of enlisting in American air forces for a variety of reasons mostly related to vision standards that were more strict than those of the RAF or RCAF. The Waldorf Astoria office closed in February 1942, though the CKC continued to correspond with disappointed applicants for some months after that. Knight became an historian and artist for the U.S. Air Force, but it would be just the beginning of the next era in his life. In 1946, he was awarded the Order of the British Empire for his service in both world wars. A requirement of the award was that it be given on British territory, and that was accomplished when the *Queen Mary* came to a stop in New York Harbor.

The Arnold Scheme to train Canadian and British pilots in USAAF schools came to an end with graduation ceremonies in Washington on February 26, 1943. It had produced more than 4,000 pilots, and would continue with five training schools remaining in the U.S. for both RAF and USAAF pilots. General Hap Arnold noted the event with the conclusion that the men of different countries and forces who had trained together would now fight together more effectively, and he thanked those Americans who lived near the training bases for the hospitality they had shown to those from other countries.[7]

The British Commonwealth Air Training Plan would continue until the end of the war, and train 16,000 members of the RAF of all nationalities in the United States over

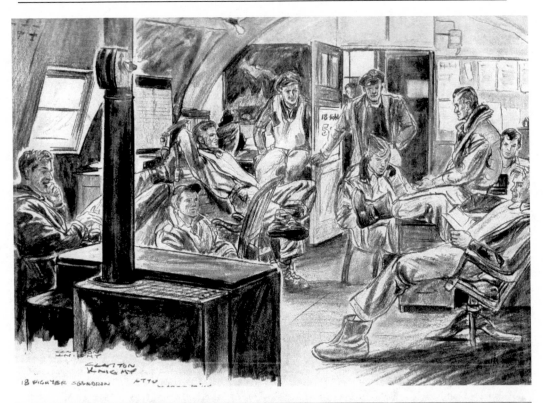

After the dissolution of the Clayton Knight Committee, Clayton Knight continued work as a writer and artist. In the 1980s, he created a series of untitled drawings about World War II for the Department of Defense (National Archives).

General Hap Arnold, center, meets with General George Patton, left, and General Mark Clark, right, in December 1943 (National Archives).

those years. It received its greatest fame in the U.S., however, just at the time it was no longer relevant to the country. In the spring of 1941, some in Hollywood were looking for a way to bring a movie about a war that was taking place elsewhere in the world to an American audience, and with all the trappings of patriotic sentiment. The solution was proposed to Warner Bros. by the Canadian American actor Raymond Massey. Massey had been born in Toronto of an American mother and a father who owned the Massey-Ferguson tractor company. During World War I, Massey had served on the front lines of the Canadian army, then as a military instructor at Yale University, and an entertainer to Canadian troops in Siberia in 1918. His film career began in the 1920s, and by 1940 he was a very popular cross-border movie star.

Massey's proposal was a natural for the movies and told a story that was not well known. There were American citizens in Canada training to fly against the German enemy for the Canadian Air Force. Canada was still a mystery to most Americans, a rough and tumble place, in this case inhabited by bush pilots and other adventurers who were always ready for a fight and the pursuit of a beautiful woman. As thinking for the movie developed, the identity of its flinty hero came into sight in the form of the actor James Cagney. *Captains of the Clouds* would be the first American film to be shot almost entirely in Canada, the first Technicolor film for Cagney, and the first major studio film about the war. The script was full of every cliché and situation that might be imagined in such a venture; even James Cagney didn't like it, but he was reportedly drawn to its patriotic appeal even though the U.S. was not yet at war.

The making of the film was preceded by a much-publicized 60 vehicle "Cavalcade to

Canada" of production equipment and crew, from Hollywood to Ontario where it was shot in various BCATP training camps and the wilderness territory around North Bay. *Captains of the Clouds* was, basically, a complicated soap opera about grizzled bush pilots, one of them (Cagney) an unscrupulous, womanizing opportunist, and two beautiful women, one good and one bad. One of the pilots joins the RCAF, but the others continue their roughhouse ways until they hear the Winston Churchill "We shall fight on the beaches..." speech, and determine that they, too, will go off to war. Upon enlistment, they are shocked to learn that they are too old for action, but just ripe enough to be flight instructors. Cagney's character, however, rebels and the plot becomes even more complicated, ending with Cagney's eventual redemption by ferrying bombers across the Atlantic.

The film was premiered not in Hollywood, but in a simultaneous release in New York, the major Canadian cities, London, Cairo and Melbourne, Australia. A publicity stunt had the reels delivered to their premiers around the world by RCAF airplanes. The *New Yorker* magazine reviewed it briefly as "about 45 percent superb Technicolor photography; stunt flying, 20 percent; detailed information on the training methods of the R.C.A.F., 15 percent; acting, 3 percent; technical effects, 2 percent; and of plot a trace."[8] It would, however, remain a classic of filmed aviation, and it was, at the very least, a powerful introduction to the American public of the concept of Americans at war before the war, and the role of their northern neighbor. One of its goals had been to act as a recruiting tool for the RCAF, but the point was moot by the time of its release in February 1942.

At the same time, the three American Eagle Squadrons seemed caught between two allegiances. Soon after Pearl Harbor, leaders of Squadrons 71 and 121 met with American Ambassador John Winant to request that they be absorbed into the USAAF. The 71st, in particular, wanted to be sent to the Pacific to fight the Japanese. It was understood that the squadrons would eventually join their American brethren, but there were tactical and procedural reasons to keep them where they were. The 71st was already scheduled to make a normal rotation to less active service, and the RAF insisted that the move take place. Its commander, Chesley Peterson, never reluctant to challenge his higher ups, went over the head of his immediate superior, and demanded that the squadron stay in the heart of the action. All three AES squadrons were kept in place in proximity to the North Sea, and they would prove to be well placed for what was to come.

At the opening of 1942, the RAF was as strong as it had ever been, with 100 squadrons. Thirty-four of them were specific to other nations, including Canada, New Zealand, Australia, Newfoundland, Poland, Czechoslovakia, Belgium, France and the United States in the form of the AES. But the Luftwaffe had generated a wave of fighter planes that could outmaneuver and out-fire the RAF's Spitfires. In March, the RAF undertook a renewed four-month offensive. An average of 180 fighter sorties per day protected bomber strikes on targets in France and Belgium. Even then, the loss of British aircraft exceeded that of Germany, but the effort limited the Luftwaffe's efforts in other parts of the war. On August 19, the Allies launched an attempt to open another front with Germany with a raid on the French port of Dieppe. Its secondary goal was to unnerve the enemy and to gain intelligence through whatever contact could be gained with people on the ground in the occupied city. Though it was ultimately unsuccessful, all three American Eagle Squadrons fought together for a rare time and contributed to a large portion of German air losses.

Among the AES flyers who distinguished themselves in what was called Operation Jubilee was Flight Lieutenant Donald Blakeslee who had grown up near the Cleveland air races during World War I, and flown with the RCAF before joining the AES and continuing on to the USAAF. He was reputed to have flown more missions against the Luftwaffe than any other American. Dominic Gentile was also a child of Ohio and followed the same career course as Blakeslee. He was said to have exceeded Eddie Rickenbacker's accomplishment in World War I with 26 kills. Both men received the British Distinguished Flying Cross.

It was only by August that the USAAF could begin to play an active role in the air war. The first American bombers began to arrive in England in July, followed by the development of four fighter groups based in England, which flew Spitfires and P-38s. The Eagles had put America immediately into the battle after its declaration of war, and now it was time to transition them into their own Air Force. The first discussions between the U.S. and UK paid attention to an obvious desire by AES flyers to maintain RAF ranking in the USAAF. As a result, all transferees would be interviewed and assigned a rank based on qualifications and experience. And Chesley Peterson successfully asserted the need to maintain fighter cohesion by transferring the three squadrons intact.

The transfer was initiated in mid–September. It was noted that the 50 flyers would be bringing to the USAAF a seasoned experience in German fighting tactics and with the terrain beneath their wings. Chesley Peterson, now age 22, would lead them. The transfer would take place on September 29, but on September 26, the 133 squadron set out on a fateful, final mission as the AES. The unit was assigned to escort 24 bombers over targets in France. Weather briefings warned them of 35 mph winds aloft, but when they arrived at altitude the winds were 100 mph and visibility was poor. The bombers, which had already completed parts of their mission, could not be found. Then radio contact was lost, but the RAF squadrons came across another bomber group in need of escort to home base. As fuel was running low, the squadron dipped beneath the clouds to get what were thought to be bearings over England. Instead, they found that the winds had drifted them off-course to France. All 12 planes of the squadron were lost, and all but one of the pilots, were killed or taken prisoner.

The transfer ceremonies took place three days later at RAF Debden, Essex. The squadron transfers from the RAF to USAAF were 71 men to Squadron 344, 121 to 335 and 133 to 356 as parts of the Fourth Fighter Group, which would go on to become one of the most successful air units in the war. Upon the transfer, British Air Chief Marshall Sholto Douglas remarked upon the RAFs loss of its American squadrons:

> It is with deep personal regret that I today say "Goodbye" to you whom it has been my privilege to command. You joined us readily and of your own free will when our need was greatest.
>
> There are those of your number who are not here today—those sons of the United States who were first to give their lives for their country. We of the RAF no less than yourselves will always remember them with pride.[9]

The Eagles did not lose their identity after the transfer. First Lady Eleanor Roosevelt came to England in November 1942 and was treated to an air show by AES pilots who received her gratitude for what they had accomplished. They were described as wearing RAF wings on the right sides of their tunics and USAAF wings on the left side.[10]

As with the BCATP, the story of the AES would be told from a Hollywood perspective. The July 1942 film *Eagle Squadron* starred Robert Stack, Diana Barrymore and Eddie Albert. But it was seen as a corruption of the true story. A number of AES members who saw it walked out of the theater in disgust before the film's end. The first notable book about the AES was *War Eagles* by USAAF Colonel James Saxon Childers, published in 1943. It was respectful and laudatory of the group, and presented the flyers as they really were by their own lights rather than by the drumbeat of patriotism. They were in it as much for the adventure as for any other reason, according to the author. Some had sought relief from otherwise troubled lives. They were exceedingly young and prone to mischief when they were bored. The book calculated that of the 112 of them 34 were dead, missing or prisoner of war, but only eight of them had actually been killed in combat. They had destroyed or probably destroyed 60 German airplanes, and damaged 24 more. They were certainly worthy of equation with the fighters of the Lafayette Escadrille, but about that Major G.A. Daymond, 22 years old, said "They're going to keep on telling us that hero rot until we believe it ourselves."[11]

SIXTEEN

Transitions and Transfers

We talk to them and if we think it is to their advantage to stay in Canada, we tell them so.—Major-General Henry Guy

Upon the attack on Pearl Harbor on December 7, 1941, and the American declaration of war on December 8, Americans who were already in Commonwealth forces in England began trying to enlist in their own nation's defense on December 9. The American declaration of war against Germany was made on December 11.

The overall number of Americans already in British forces, including those in the army, Royal Canadian Air Force, Royal Air Force and Royal Naval Reserve, was now estimated between 15,000 and 20,000. Statistics developed after the war put the number of Americans in the RCAF on December 7 at 6,129, with 3,886 of them still in BCATP training in Canada. RCAF recruitment of Americans was stopped as of January 30, 1942, and by that time, 8,864 American nationals had joined with the Canadian flyers, and 5,067 of them would stay with the Canadian force until the end of the war. Of those, 704 would be killed in training or combat. As per the recruiting patterns of the Clayton Knight Committee, the four states that sacrificed the most of their sons to the RCAF war were New York, California and Texas, with the addition of Michigan.[1] Overall, it was estimated that more than 49,000 Americans had responded in some way to the need for aviators and crew in Canada between 1940–1942.[2]

As usual, the precise number of Americans in the British and Canadian armies was unknown. Reporting on events at the American embassy in London in March 1942 referred again to the 15,000—20,000 Americans in all British and Canadian forces, but added an estimate of 10,000 more still in Canada.[3] At that time, the embassy and the American Expeditionary Forces, London were beginning to administer transfers from Commonwealth to American forces.

The United States and Great Britain had not been prepared for the press of American fighters at the doors of the London embassy beginning December 9, nor for the American civilians in England who would also seek to enlist. Whether and how each would be enlisted would have to be figured out by the two countries together, but other matters seemed more pressing. A good faith attempt was made, however, and, on January 17, 1942, President Roosevelt recognized the demand of Americans to enlist in England, with assurances that the problem of transition would be solved over time. As in World War I, the considerations of the Allies had to take into account the effect of such transfers on the larger Allied effort rather than each nation's individual services. Roosevelt acknowledged the many Americans already at war and their natural desires to join their own forces.

While the interested governments are expediting as much as possible work on the necessary arrangements, the importance of the subject and the numerous technical problems involved will undoubtedly cause considerable delay before final agreement can be reached. Until these transfers can be arranged, however, I cannot emphasize too strongly that the American citizens involved can best serve the interests of their country through contributing loyal and effective service in the units in which they are now enlisted.[4]

Things moved quickly. On March 20, an exchange of documents between Canadian prime minister King and the American ambassador to Canada, Pierrepont Moffatt, set out an agreement that all Americans in Canadian forces could file for transfer within the window of April 1–20. It would not be a compulsory move for these Americans, though those who had lost their American citizenship by enlisting in Canada would see it fully restored. All Americans—army, navy or marine, officer or enlisted—would retain their rank and grade in the transfer if they met American physical requirements. The agreement further required that all Americans in Canadian services be made known of the agreement and be given the opportunity to file their applications if that was their choice.[5] In addition, a February 27 agreement allowed those Americans not eligible for the U.S. draft to enlist in Canadian forces if they wished.

An embassy office devoted solely to transfers and their procedure was created in London. It handled an average of 50 applications per day, and most potential transferees sought to maintain their rank and occupation from one nation's service to the other. Some would be returned to the United States for further training, and others, mostly those with direct fighting responsibilities, would make immediate lateral transfers. Flyers were treated a bit differently. They would be allowed to *apply* for the air services of the army, navy or marines. They were reminded, however, that they were fighting a common enemy no matter the uniform they wore and were urged not to seek transfer at that time. Though many wanted to move from the European to the Pacific war, some ultimately adopted Roosevelt's attitude that the force they fought with wasn't as important as the defeat of the enemy they faced.

Another group of American flyers was certain to stay in place, however. By the end of March, 25 female aviators had come to England to fly under contract for the British Air Transport Auxiliary. They would ferry light aircraft within England, a more effective contribution, they thought, than the Civil Air Patrol duties they were limited to in the U.S. They would be trained in Canada and sign up for terms of 18 months with pay of $400 monthly.

On May 4, a remarkable 15-car train set out from Washington's Union Station for a month-long journey into the Canadian north, and then to the west. The window for transfer from Canadian to American forces had closed, but, as per the March agreement by the two countries, a final sweep of Canadian military bases would give any remaining Americans the opportunity to make the change. Passengers included officers and staff of the army, navy and marines, headed by Army Brig. Gen. Henry V. Guy. Guy had been born in an army tent in Fort Robinson, Nebraska, in 1875, and into a family of distinguished military and political leaders, including Vice President Daniel D. Tompkins (1817–1825). He had been awarded the Silver Star in the Spanish American War, and would go on to serve in various ways in the two world wars.

Perhaps Henry Guy's unique contribution to American military history came from his interest in horses. He had won a Bronze Medal for horsemanship in the 1912 Stockholm Olympics. After the Spanish American War he studied with the French Cavalry School, and brought out of that experience a revolution in the use and treatment of horses in the American army. It could be characterized as a change from the notion of "breaking" a horse to bringing it more naturally to accommodating its human rider, along with the use of riding implements that were less painful and more humane.

The train was met at each base by Canadian officers permitted to immediately release members from service and give them any pay not yet received, and carried with it officials of the U.S. State Department empowered to immediately reinstate citizenship when necessary. The effort was supported by a clinic, and a bureaucracy of more than 100. In Winnipeg alone, it converted 175 men to U.S. service, more than half of them flyers. "We don't take all of the men who apply," said Major-General Guy. "We talk to them and if we think it is to their advantage to stay in Canada, we tell them so."[6] It had been a good trip for all, according to the American officers. The Canadians had extended wonderful hospitality, and Ottawa was the most beautiful city one of them had ever seen. The train moved on to Regina and Calgary, and ended its trip in Vancouver.

On June 11, 1942, the War Department announced that all Americans who wished to transfer from Canadian forces had applied to do so. Transfers were effected individually, but on July 1, Canada's Dominion Day, a U.S. military depot outside of London, England saw a ceremony involving a mass transfer of 30 Americans, including the taking of an oath of repatriation of those who needed to be returned to American citizenship.

Transfers accomplished, it remained for the two Allies to work together on the drafting of their own citizens who were resident in the other country. In June, the Canadian government was able to set up seven recruiting stations within the United States to cover those Canadian nationals in America still in the process of obtaining U.S. citizenship, or those who were eligible for the American draft for various reasons. In addition, those Canadians who were called up in the U.S. draft could request to be transferred to Canadian forces. In September, Canada widened the scope its own draft to any capable resident man age 19 or older of any non-enemy nationality. By October, it was no longer possible for a citizen of either country to avoid the draft through residence in the other country. The United States agreed that its own citizens living in Canada, and not applying for citizenship there, could be subject to the Canadian draft, with the option of joining the U.S. army instead. A man opting for U.S. service would start the induction process in Canada by meeting that country's lower qualifications. He would then be sent to an American induction point where, if he didn't meet American qualifications, he would be immediately required to continue his enrollment in the Canadian army. The American government sent a pamphlet explaining the process to all such Americans in Canada.[7]

On August 19, 1942, the U.S. State Department announced that 2,058 of 16,000 Americans who had enlisted in the Canadian army and navy had made the transition back to American forces. Secretary of State Cordell Hull offered a thank you to the Canadian government for its assistance in the transfers, and spoke to its effect on the relationship between the two countries. "These young men," he said, "who have now returned to serve in the American forces will constitute a group of ambassadors of good-will to spread throughout the United States the story of Canada's great contribution to the common war effort." In return, the Canadian ambassador to the United States, Leighton McCarthy, expressed the gratitude of the Canadian government for their service. It was "sorry" to lose them, but could understand their desire to serve under their own flag.[8] At the bottom line, most Americans who had joined Canadian and British forces before December 8, 1941, stayed where they were. In a number of cases, they would not have been able to meet the more stringent qualifications of American service, but, in general, there seemed to be no imperative on the part of either of three governments to regain their own nationals.

Among those who stayed in the Canadian army was Ben Brinkworth of Oak Park, Illinois. Brinkworth's life would be followed by his hometown newspaper, the *Oak Leaves*, beginning nearly from his birth in 1917 until his retirement years in California. At age six months, he was the subject of an article headlined "CHAMPION BABY BOY ... Forrest Ben Brinkworth, Six Months Old, Claims Belt in Infant Welfare Contests—He Breaks Records." The article reported that the infant had been the most notable participant in the city's Infant Welfare Campaign, despite the handicap of having lost his mother in childbirth. It pointed out that, among other things, "By holding to someone's fingers, he can pull himself erect. He is as intelligent as the average child of twelve. He has two teeth. He has never been ill a day in his life." He had been given a 100 percent score in infant welfare, and, perhaps revealing its true skepticism of the welfare campaign, the newspaper reported that Brinkworth had visited their offices and "said a few words which sounded to the uninitiated like 'goo' and 'da,' but were no doubt in reality a significant revelation of the process by which Forrest has attained his record smashing place in Infant Welfare circle annals."[9]

Two years later, Ben Brinkworth was in the news again under the headline "AN INFANT HERCULES ... Ben Brinkworth, Famous Local Phenomenon, Rides Bicycle at Age of Two Years and Seven Months." The article described his method of bicycle riding accompanied by a picture of the act, and continued with descriptions of the child, which may or may not have been tongue in cheek. The *Leaves* kept track of the child's growing up years, including his adventures in baseball and summer camp, and, on February 13, 1941, it reported that he was now in the Canadian army. In a letter to the newspaper he had offered a description of England at the time that he insisted was not as gloomy as the reporting he had found in the British and Canadian press. The bombing raids, by his telling, had not done that much damage, and morale was good.

> I was of the opinion, that [*sic*] of all peoples, the English would be in most difficulty, in attempting to adjust themselves to conditions as they are, but watching some of the celebrations sixty feet below ground in the tube station shelters on Christmas Eve I'll readily admit that I was completely wrong. They're the best.[10]

A sense both of purpose and adventure had prompted Brinkworth to attempt to join the U.S. army at the outbreak of the war in Europe in 1939. Though 100 percent on the Infant Welfare Scale at age six months, his vision at age 22 could not meet army specifications, so he went to Windsor, gave up his American citizenship, and was among a number of Americans to join the Essex Scottish Regiment. In the 1860s, the Windsor region had been one of the parts of Canada under attack by an offshoot of an American-based group of Irish radicals, the Fenians, who were trying to leverage Canada to change British policy toward Ireland. The origins of the Essex Scottish derived from the defense of Windsor during those years, and, by 1939, the Regiment was poised to join World War II. It set sail for England in August 1940, but, unfortunately, its first significant action was in the fated raid on Dieppe, France, on August 19, 1942. Brinkman was an intelligence officer for the Regiment in an effort that was specifically designed to gather intelligence on the ground. Sadly, a miscommunication in the command structure of the raid left the Essex Scottish under attack on a beach. It lost 121 men, and a number taken as prisoners of war, Ben Brinkworth among them. He would live in the German stalags for nearly three years.

In August 1945, the *Oak Leaves* reported that Cpl. Brinkworth was back in town for a visit after liberation from the prison camps.

> At first stationed at stalag 8-B, and later stalag 2-D, near the Baltic sea [*sic*], the prisoners were marched through the country for two months. Marching prisoners were poorly fed, receiving

potato peeling soup and short rations of black bread, and en route, he sold a sweater and trousers for food.[11]

Brinkworth described the first year of captivity as a time of constant hunger, and cold in winter months. He was handcuffed each day between 8 a.m. and 7 p.m. He would later describe himself as "bitter for years at the British and Canadian officials. Dieppe was incredibly stupid."[12] He left Canadian forces after the war, regained U.S. citizenship, and joined the U.S. Army Transportation Corps, serving most notably in the Berlin Airlift of 1948–49, and retiring after service all over the world as a lieutenant-colonel in 1967. As late as 2006, the failed raid at Dieppe was still on his mind. "They did a terrible job, they didn't do a job at all," he told the *Windsor* (Ontario) *Star*. "We were hoping to get some air cover or some real support and we didn't get either."[13] He had returned to the beach at Dieppe three times since then, and was about to take his fourth trip. "I want to relive the whole memory and the close the books on the entire thing. This is the last trip. It's all over."[14] He died in 2008, with honors received from both the Canadian and U.S. militaries, and was buried at Arlington National Cemetery. His tombstone listed World War II among the conflicts in which he had participated though he had fought with Canadian forces, and not been a U.S. citizen during that time.

The Dieppe Raid was acknowledged as perhaps the lowest point in Canada's participation in World War II. Nearly a thousand had died, and more than twice that number was taken prisoner. Like Ben Brinkworth, many of those who survived were haunted by it for the rest of their days. One of those was Frank Parker of Massachusetts who had served in the Black Watch of Canada. The Black Watch traced its origins to the American Civil War. While many Canadians were going over the border to fight on behalf of Union forces at that time, others were concerned about the potential danger to Canada of a stronger and more unified American military. The response was the formation of a regiment based on the Royal Highland Regiment of Scotland. The name Black Watch was of uncertain origin and dated to the early 18th century.

The Dieppe Raid was the first significant action for the Canadian regiment in World War II. Frank Parker stepped on to the beach east of Dieppe on August 19, 1942, and from that day would have a good but troubled life. In 2012, his youngest daughter Diantha wrote that he had told her of the sight at Dieppe of the bodies of those who had walked forward into relentless machine gun fire lying in a surf that grew increasingly red with blood.[15] Like Ben Brinkworth, Frank Parker ended up in German Stalag VIII B. His captors openly expressed consternation that the raid had even been attempted. He spent most of the rest of the war as a laborer on what he described as a gigantic feudal estate, and developed farming skills that he would bring home to his own garden after the war. That gentle pursuit, and resumption of his work as a painter and graphic artist, was accompanied, however, by alcoholism and the mood swings and nightmares that came to many men who had returned from war.

The Dieppe Canadian War Cemetery at Hautot-sur-Mer would take custody of the bodies of nine Americans killed on the day that Frank Parker first set foot on Dieppe.

Another American who stayed with Canadian forces after the U.S. declaration was Joe Grigas of Worcester, Massachusetts. After his capture as a member of the Lincoln Brigade of the Spanish Civil War, he had endured more than a year as a prisoner of war on a diet that consisted mainly of beans, and the sardines for which he developed a taste that would stay with him for the rest of his life. He returned to Worcester in 1939, and worked as a hospital orderly. For whatever reason, the war in Europe took him past the U.S. army and to Montreal in 1940. He asserted that he was a resident of Vancouver, and he chose the Church of England as his religion (telling a friend years later that his own Lithuanian ancestors had worshipped trees, so it made no difference to him). His experience in Spain had left him bitter about what he had perceived to be command cowardice and lack of organization in the Republican effort there, and he wanted to join up with a traditional, well-established fighting unit. He entered the Royal Canadian Regiment (RCR), not knowing the importance that enlistment would have until the last year of his life, 65 years later.

After World War I, the Canadian army had been reduced almost to the bare numbers of its pre-war strength. The RCR was retained as a training source for the Canadian Militia, with just 400 members, and, in 1939, it was remobilized as Canada's oldest Regular Infantry Regiment. The official focus of the Canadian army in the first years of the war was the protection of England, and preparation for future significant action on the Continent. As might be expected, a strategy that would keep troops essentially out of the fight was the source of tension between the command structure and the enlisted ranks. Further, the army's commander, Lieut. Gen. Andrew McNaughton, held the view that the Canadians would fight as a single unit or not at all, following the general and successful strategy of World War I. Subordinates and others wanted to send whatever division of Canadian troops to wherever they might be needed. The few times that they were allowed to prevail, however, led to heroic but deathly results.

The first Canadians to see action in the war were the Royal Rifles of Canada and the Winnipeg Grenadiers, sent to assist in the protection of Hong Kong. Eight hours after the attack on Pearl Harbor, the Japanese had moved on toward the British Crown Colony in full battle force. The Canadian role in the defense of the colony had been valiant and untiring, but the battle was lost by Christmas Day. Canadian dead included 293 in battle and 260 who would eventually perish in Japanese prison camps. That was followed in August 1942 by the failed raid on Dieppe, with the loss of 900. More than twice that number was taken prisoner. Back in England, the Canadians became increasingly restless, some with the feeling that they were no more significant than the British Home Guard of volunteers and old soldiers. Their first chance to fight together came in July 1943 at the outset of the Italian Campaign and the Allied invasion of Sicily.

It was barely a secret that British general Bernard Montgomery held little love for the leadership of the Canadian general McNaughton who had insisted his men fight together or not at all. While they waited to fight, Montgomery had managed to have the Canadians subjected to the kind of rigorous training he felt they were not getting under McNaughton. Especially after Dieppe, McNaughton had wanted to take the time to be certain of the soundness of the plan to invade Sicily, known as Operation Husky. Eventually, each of the two arrived at a point of satisfaction that Canada was ready to fight, and their confidence would prove out. The Allied invasion of Sicily removed the island from Axis holdings and helped to open the sea-lanes of the Mediterranean for the successful Italian campaign. The Royal Canadian Regiment was among the first of those to hit the beach near Pachino, Sicily, on July 10, and, for his part, Joe Grigas seemed to take on the task on his own terms, in much the way that he lived his own life. He would be honored with the RCR's first battlefield citation of the war.

On 10 Jul 43 in vicinity of PACHINO Airfield "A" Coy The Royal Canadian regiment of which Pte Grigas was a soldier was operating against enemy coastal defences. At 1000 hours the Coy commenced an assault on a coast defence battery immediately north of Pachino Airfield. Pte

Grigas took command of the section and, advancing under heavy fire managed to reach the perimeter wire. The remainder of the Coy was by this time pinned to the ground. Pte Grigas breached a gap in the wire and led his section through to assault the enemy concrete posts which were knocked out in quick succession. Although Pte Grigas' section was the only section of the Coy to enter the battery position the attack was led with such determination that it caused the surrender of the garrison of approximately two hundred men and the capture of four 4.2" how-itzers and large quantities of ammunition, small arms and stores. The personal gallantry, deter-mination and leadership of Pte Grigas was largely responsible for the success of this operation.[16]

The action was reported in the Canadian press, identifying Grigas as a soldier from Montreal. The citation was the basis of Grigas' receipt of the Canadian Distinguished Con-duct Medal, second only to the Victoria Cross for enlisted men. Though it was a medal of the sort that might have been awarded directly by the king if he had been nearby, Grigas never received it, and did not know about it at the time. Decades later, Capt. Sherry Atkinson, who had also participated Operation Husky, would offer, with great affection, the observation that "Joe was a lousy soldier, but a great fighter," and that he had probably been in the brig when the medal arrived. Atkinson also believed that Grigas had been offered a promotion to lance corporal, but turned it down because he was not interested in the increased respon-sibility it would entail.

Grigas' most beloved companion was his Bren gun, a simply constructed light machine gun that seemed to work as an extension of his arm. At one point in the battle for Sicily, Grigas' unit was resting in an olive grove that formed an indentation in the land. Without warning, a German plane appeared over the slope and started firing on the group, though its nose was not far enough down to give the fire an angle into the grove. A British Spitfire was on its tail. Capt. Atkinson was one of those under attack.

> Our reaction was instantaneous—hit the ground—all but Joe Grigas. Joe loved his Bren gun and considered himself a good shot. He always kept his Bren gun within reach. Without missing a beat he took his Bren gun, took a long lead on the FW 190 and was rewarded with a trail of smoke as the enemy plane flew out of sight. The Spitfire pilot was a true gentleman and sent a message back that the FW 190 had crashed a few miles away, and he gave credit for the kill to the ground fire.[17]

Atkinson pointed out that one does not simply fire a gun at an oncoming jet fighter without accounting for the closure speed between bullet and plane. In standard practice, every fifth bullet in a Bren gun was a tracer that told the shooter where the bullet was going. But Grigas had begged, borrowed or stolen enough tracer bullets to load his gun with one of every three it shot, giving him an enhanced ability to aim and shoot more effectively, especially at a speeding airplane.

The Royal Canadian Regiment and other Canadian units continued to press into Sicily, and reached the city of Regalbuto on July 30, 1943. From there they would go on to the decisive battles that would begin Germany's retreat from the island, but Grigas was captured as his unit was cut off and isolated. His Bren gun was on a tripod, but he was wounded in the wrist by a German submachine gun before he could get to it. Taken captive, he and the soldier who had charge of him came under Canadian mortar fire behind German lines. For whatever reason, the soldier pushed him into the protection of a trench and lay above him. Then, in a prison hospital that had been bombed by the Allies despite the white cross on its roof, he was given the option of moving on with his captors or staying behind to await either the further destruction of the hospital, or eventual liberation by his comrades. The second choice was obvious, and he returned to an RCR anti-tank platoon as the Canadians moved from Sicily to the Italian mainland. He was medically discharged in Halifax in mid–1944, and returned to Worcester, Massachusetts.

At the time of his return to America as an unidentified Canadian war hero, and in perhaps another realm of the world that Joe Grigas might not known or cared about, his name was on a document of the Special Committee on Un-American Activities of the House of Representatives of the 78th Congress. He had appeared in a list with the heading "American Communists and Sympathizers who Fought for Loyalist Spain."[18] It had taken just a few years for the taint of perceived Communist influence in the Spanish Civil War to catch up with those Americans who had gone off to fight with the Lincoln Brigade. Many of them, including Grigas, had returned without the passports they had been required to give up when joining the Brigade. The House committee's resolution placed Grigas, among 1,600 other Americans, under the heading of a scheme by Soviet Russia to secure American passports for later use in espionage. It asserted in particular that 500 of these "comrades" were part of a plan by the New York based American party of Communist International to set up its own espionage program in America's industrial centers. Many of them were added to another list kept by the FBI of "individuals deemed most dangerous" to national security, and subject to immediate arrest in the event of a national emergency.

The scrutiny of American volunteers in the Lincoln Brigade only increased in the anti–Communist years following the war. In December 1947, the U.S. attorney general released a list of "subversive" organizations in America, including the Veterans of the Abraham Lincoln Brigade (VALB), which was forced to register as a foreign agency, specifically one which was associated with underground trade unions in Spain.[19] The purposes and intentions of the Lincoln Brigade and its members would continue into the 21st century as a touchstone of controversies over Communism, Fascism, anti–Americanism and politics of the right and left, among many others. It may have been that one of the reasons Joe Grigas went to Montreal in 1940 was because, as a Lincoln Brigade veteran, he would have been accepted into the U.S. army, but with a mark already against him, and subject to policy that limited such veterans to the lowest ranks.

It is not known whether Grigas' listing by a congressional committee as a potential subversive had any effect on his life following the war, or whether he was even aware of the designation. In whichever case, after his service in Canada, he disappeared into decades of what one of those who found him many years later would describe as "living in the weeds" in America.

At the time of the announcement of the Japanese attack on Pearl Harbor, Wall Street Broker turned member of the Royal Naval Volunteer Reserve (RNVR) First Lieutenant Allen H. Cherry was sharing gin with fellow officers at HMS Osprey, an anti-submarine training base on the River Clyde in Scotland. Upon hearing the news, the wardroom in which he sat was first stunned and silent, then full of toasts and huzzahs to America. Before his glass was drained, Cherry thought his next steps were clear. The next day he and a number of his fellow Americans in the RNVR made official calls to offer themselves to the U.S. Navy. Some of them would transfer to the Navy and other American forces over the next couple of years, but, for whatever reason, Cherry remained with the British. He passed through command positions on a number of British ships, and sometimes acted as liaison between British and American naval operations. He was popular and successful in the RNVR, but at one point a British officer who, Cherry believed, just did not like Americans, gave him a bad evaluation that may have come in part from Cherry's relative disinhibition about saying what he thought.

When it was his gun on the HMS *Wren* that brought forth the sinking of an enemy submarine, he was not given the commendation received by his shipmates, and he would chafe at the omission, though retaining affection for the RNVR, for years after the war.

It was from the *Wren* that Cherry would witness the full seaborn drama of the Normandy invasion on June 6, 1944. On the evening before, he had prepared for the worst possible outcome of his ship's participation in the invasion. He went through his cabin, destroying letters he would not want to be read in the event of his death, and putting other possessions in order either for destruction or forwarding. The opening of the last footlocker, as he would describe it in the facile storytelling of his book, *Yankee R.N.*, took him back to an evening in New York with one of the women in his life, this one with the nickname Redcoat. The two had been gambling over games of Gin Rummy and he had added one of his Navy pins to the pot. The pin was especially coveted by Redcoat, and he demanded that it be matched on her part by a pair of her panties.

"One day when I'm going into battle," he told her, "I'll wear them like the knights of old."[20]

At first she demurred, but then returned with a pair of red woolen ice skating panties. She had doused them with a splash of the perfume "My Sin," and she asked him to swear to his vow that they would be worn in battle. Now, in his small cabin on the morning of D Day, he considered them to be an omen and put them on. They were tight, and some adjustment was required, but he covered them with his long pants and headed for the bridge.

The news was not good. The *Wren* had been assigned a position far behind the action that was about to take place, and would never reach "the box seats," in Cherry's words. But his view of one of the most important invasions in military history was splendid. "The drone of hundreds of aircraft suddenly filled the sky, giving one the feeling that a giant nest of wasps had been let loose. The buzzing sound was all we heard in the night air." Then the sky fell silent.

> I never will forget that morning. Junior and I were standing this watch together. We were expecting Germans from sea and sky. It was the hour before dawn and things were a bit creepy. An unusual quietness had reigned for more than an hour. Our troopships must be creeping up the Normandy coast now, I told myself. I stood on the port wing of the bridge holding a pair of binoculars to my eyes with one hand and scratching in the dark with the other. I was feeling some discomfort. The red woolen panties were itching like hell. I heard footsteps. Junior was coming over from the other wing of the bridge to make the hourly entry in the ship's log. He had just put the pencil down when he turned and began prowling about the bridge sniffing the air like a pedigree hound.
>
> Christ! I thought to myself, he's smelling Redcoat's panties! He came back to my corner like a beagle hound on the scent. I waited for his remark.
>
> "Good Lord! We must be getting awfully close to the French coast. I'll swear I smell perfume." He kept sniffing the air.
>
> "Don't be silly. You couldn't possibly. We're too far off," I said.

Junior concluded that perhaps a perfume factory had been bombed on the coast, but Cherry finally confessed to the nature of his apparel.

> "What?" exclaimed Junior again. For a moment I thought I heard his eyes click like a couple of billiard balls. "A girl's panties!" he whispered incredulously. "Really! How interesting! How very interesting! Is it possible!"[21]

When the war in Europe was won, Cherry was given a conditional release from the RNVR and applied to transfer to the U.S. Navy for service in the Pacific. He was turned down, with the given reason that the USN was over quota with officers, and welcomed back into the RNVR where he served in the demobilization of the German navy and its fortifications, and occupation supply logistics in Berlin. He worked briefly for the American government in a similar capacity in 1947. In New York, he returned to very successful work as an investor and real estate broker, and became historian of the Naval Order of the United States which, though an organization of those who had commanded American naval forces, welcomed him as a recipient of the Order of the British Empire (OBE) and perhaps the first American to have reached a command position in the Royal Navy. *Yankee R.N.*, published in 1951, sold through seven editions. A.H. Cherry died in Florida in 1987.

SEVENTEEN

Sorting the Dead

We tried to give him a proper send off. And we had an American flag there as well.—Duncan MacMillan

In the years immediately following World War II, the most visible sign that Americans had fought with the British Commonwealth Forces could be found hidden in the cemeteries of the Imperial War Graves Commission, now the Commonwealth War Graves Commission (CWGC). Americans were buried in 33 of the 150 CWGC countries or other jurisdictions, alphabetically from Algeria to the United Kingdom. Most of them were the dead of the Royal Air Force or the Royal Canadian Air Force buried in Canada, France and England, but many rested in the farthest corners of the world.

RCAF Flying Officer Roger Wallace Haven of Malden, Massachusetts, for example, was buried in El Alia Cemetery in Algiers after his Hudson bomber crashed into a mountain while returning from submarine patrol.[1] RCAF pilot Lawrence Robert Maguire had hitch-hiked from Long Branch, New Jersey, to enlistment in Ottawa, been shot down over Aden in July 1942 and was buried in Djibouti. RAF Volunteer Reserve pilot Sidney Muhart of Lorain, Ohio, had reportedly had tea with the British royal family at one point during his time in England, before dying as the result of a dogfight over Egypt in December 1941. He was buried at Heliopolis War Cemetery in Cairo.[2] Pilot Lloyd Duncan Thomas of Detroit had joined the RCAF in Toronto and was struck down by Japanese ground fire over Burma in April 1944. He was buried in the Taukkyan War Cemetery in Burma/Myanmar.

The exact numbers of American flyers and aircrew killed in Commonwealth forces cannot be known. As in World War I, though less so, misleading information given upon enlistment may have obscured some American identities, and transfers from British to American forces upon American declarations of war further confused the numbers. Unlike World War I, how-ever, the numbers of Americans in CWGC cemeteries could not be used to proof estimates of the numbers of Americans in Commonwealth forces. If it was the case, as the Canadian Department of Veterans Affairs stated in 1955, that more than 23,000 of their army members were American born, or from American addresses, less than 300 of them still rested in CWGC cemeteries as of 2009. Many or most may have been returned for burial in America, as was probably the case for American dead in air forces. The Bomber Command crews comprised of the RAF, RCAF and the Royal Australian Air Force (RAAF) and Royal New Zealand Air Forces (RNZAF) lost, by various estimates, approximately 55,000 members, a death rate of 44 percent. The RCAF, for one example, listed 10,659 dead, 379 of them Americans, but years after the war less than 500 flying Americans of all services remained in CWGC cemeteries.

Royal Canadian Air Force flyer Roger Wallace Haven was killed in a crash while returning from the Mediterranean, and is buried in the Commonwealth War Graves Cemetery at El Alia, Algiers (Commonwealth War Graves Commission).

As in the previous world war, the Commonwealth War Graves Commission followed procedures designed to deal with war dead in an efficient and compassionate way, was challenged in some cases post-war, and changed policy in response to American law. Late in 1941, the CWGC began a review of where it stood. Sir Fabian Ware was once again its vice-chairman, and offered that review in a letter to the High Commissioner for Canada in London, dated December 23, 1941. It was his expectation that the policies of "the late war" would continue in the current war: the removal and transport of bodies during hostilities was prohibited, and that after hostilities they should remain buried in the lands in which they fell (or, as was often the case of those buried in England and Canada, where they died of wounds, or other causes not directly the result of combat).

As early as 1941, however, Ware was concerned that the policy would be challenged, particularly in the case of Americans in Commonwealth forces. The Americans had come mostly from Canada, thus his letter to the chief Canadian consul in London to ask if Canada would hold to the policy. He reminded the commissioner that it had been America's own policy to bring its dead home freely, and he suggested that the policy had not worked well.

> There is reason to believe, from information in the possession of this Commission and of its Agency in Canada, that the procedure then adopted led to much difficulty and dissatisfaction that the United States may not wish it repeated in this War. But at present the United States representatives here are making provisional arrangements for the bodies of members of the American Forces, who may be buried in this country, to be embalmed and buried in coffins of a particularly protective kind, so that they may be ultimately returned to their own country.[3]

The discussion that followed in letters back and forth, and summaries of various meetings and committees, seemed to confirm the idea that those killed in combat abroad would not be returned during hostilities, and there could be no exception for Americans. The same would hold after hostilities. Britons and Canadians would not be exhumed and transported back to their home countries, and the prohibition would extend to Americans fighting with those forces. There were always those who would attempt to create exceptions to the rules, and perhaps be able to spend a lot of money to do so, but such exceptions, in the views of Lt. Col. H.C. Osborne, a Canadian who was secretary general of the CWGC, would create resentment in those who could not afford similar exceptions. Americans should be treated as Canadians in the matter, he warned, though he could envision the Americans sending their own ships to collect their own bodies, or otherwise effecting exceptions. He thought they would probably not do so "in view of the most undignified and scandalous situation which arose in the last war as a result of President Wilson's pledge and the subsequent attempt to return the bodies of all American soldiers from France."[4]

Osborne's view of an undignified response by President Wilson to the reluctance of the French to give up bodies after World War I may or may not have been shared by others, and Ware's intelligence that the Americans were rethinking the policy of right of repatriation may or may not have been accurate, but exceptions were bound to occur and by the end of the war they would become the rule. They were undergirded by American Public Law 66-175 in 1920 that allowed American citizens who had fought and died in the forces of American Allies to be buried in American national cemeteries. The law was reaffirmed in various forms after World War II, and held that among those eligible for burial in Veterans Administration cemeteries were "U.S. citizens who may have served in the armed forces of a U.S. ally during a time of war (service must have been terminated honorably by death or otherwise)."[5] If the bodies of Americans who fought with other forces could be brought home, there would be a place to bury them.

One of those bodies was that of RCAF Flight Sergeant Richard Elmer Stageman of Chicago. Stageman was a technical school graduate with a private flying license. He had enlisted in the force in April 1941 in Windsor and trained in Saskatchewan. He returned to his home in the Park Manor community of Chicago where 100 friends and family gave him a send off reception before he traveled on to Halifax for transport to England in December. In the week of July 26, 1942, his parents received a letter from him telling them not to worry. "I'm fine, but tired. We have been flying day and night."

That week had found British air forces focusing on the area of Hamburg, Germany. On the 26th and 27th, 403 aircraft were sent over the city in a general bombing. They had encountered clouds and some wing icing on the way, but clear skies over the target. After-action reports tallied 823 houses destroyed, more than 14,000 people bombed out of their homes, and 337 killed. Twenty-nine Allied aircraft were lost, though the raid had not much affected industrial and dock areas. In the following two days, a much larger force was intended to continue the attack on more vital targets. Much of it was held back because of weather, however, and many planes were recalled for the same reason. Just 68 scattered bombers were left to cover the city, and, though the damage done was minimal, casualties were described as heavy, Stageman among them. He was buried three days later in the Hamburg Ohlsdorf Cemetery.

After World War I, the Hamburg Cemetery had held 300 Allied bodies interred by Germany during the war, and another 408 interred after the consolidation of German war cemeteries, including two men married to American wives, and who may or may not have been citizens themselves. World War II brought 1,466 Allied burials to the cemetery, including airmen lost in raids over Germany. Two of those, John Heffernan of Los Angeles and Lawrence McGee of Fort Wayne, Indiana, would remain in the cemetery into the 21st century, but the family of Richard Stageman wanted his body returned. It began the process in the summer of 1946 through the American Graves Registration Command.

The first response to the request came in strong, but diplomatic terms from the Air Attaché at the Canadian Embassy in Paris. A decision had been made by all member nations of the British Empire that War Graves Commission policies of World War I would be continued. Those who had died in service to His Majesty overseas would not be returned to their home countries at government expense, nor would there be exceptions for those who could be brought home with private resources, due to the guiding principal of equality of treatment for all. By December, however, it was acknowledged within the commission that it was a difficult question, and the history of similar situations after World War I began to be revisited. At the same time, more requests for transfer were coming from America.

The case of Richard Stageman was taken up, at the request of the Canadian government, in a meeting of the Commission on January 16, 1947. A review of correspondence on the matter included the first denials of repatriation, followed by an escalated correspondence between the Counselor of the American Embassy in Ottawa and the Canadian Secretary of State for External Affairs. Reference was made to a written acceptance of British policy by the quartermaster general of the United States in 1921:

> ... it is recognized here that an American who entered the British Service and was killed therein, may be considered by the British as subject to their rules governing military dead and if they decide that notwithstanding his American citizenship, prior to entering the British service, his body must remain buried with his British comrades, they are within their rights so deciding.[6]

It was noted that the American Embassy in London had agreed with the conclusion and approved a letter to an American family so stating. But the report of the 1947 meeting turned the page to a "However."

> ... under United States Public Law No. 383 of May 16, 1946, it is now the responsibility of the United States Government, upon application of next-of-kin, to return to the United States for interment remains of American citizens who died or were killed in the services of the Armed Forces of any Government at war with Germany, Italy or Japan. In this case, the father of Flight Sergeant Stageman has expressed the wish that his son's remains be repatriated.[7]

As in the aftermath of the previous war, the decision was made that American law would trump commission policy. That being accomplished, however, the case of Richard Stageman then took a much more complicated turn into one of the largest problems presented by fallen aircrews: the commingling of remains and ashes. Stageman had been one of a crew of seven who had crashed together and burned beyond recognition. It was practice to not attempt to differentiate between remains in such cases, but to bury all remains together in fewer graves than there were dead. The Commission noted that, though the American request for disinterment and transfer specified the remains in one particular grave in Hamburg, the remains of all seven crew were commingled in three graves, and it would probably be impossible to isolate those of the American.

The problem was further complicated by the international nature of the commingled remains. The American body was buried with six British bodies, and that presented two more problems. It was RAF policy that unidentified crewmembers be buried with their fallen comrades, and of course no one would agree that it would be permissible to send possible

Briton remains to America. The setting of that kind of precedent would open a floodgate of similar requests, to say nothing of national anger in England. A further complication, as discussed in the commission meeting, was the contemporary reverse case of a single Canadian killed and commingled with five American airmen and buried in England. The American government was requesting that the six bodies be returned to the United States for reburial, even though one of them was a national of Canada. The Commission came to the conclusion that it would not be possible to release the body of Richard Stageman to American Graves Registration, though the matter was still not concluded.

In April 1946, America began to concentrate more fully on bringing home its fallen in Europe and Asia. The effort was budgeted at $200 million and initially targeted as many as 250,000 bodies in more than 350 cemeteries worldwide whose families requested their return to American cemeteries.[8] The matter of American bodies in foreign forces did not seem to be part of the national discussion. Of the major veterans organizations at the time, including the American Legion and the Veterans of Foreign Wars (VFW), only one recognized that such Americans existed. The 65,000 members of the American Veterans Committee (AVC) tended to be more liberal and freethinking than those of their brother organizations. Until its dissolution in 2008, the AVC would champion civil and human rights, and go through a period of suspected communist influence during a time when many American institutions faced similar accusations. Whether or not the policy was derived from its political viewpoint, its membership was open to any American, black or white, male or female, who had served in the forces of the United States or any of its Allies.

American law at the time also firmly recognized these Americans, though without much ado. Public laws like 383, and 526 in 1948 echoed the law of 1920 in their statement of the right of Americans in Allied forces to rest in American cemeteries. And the reach of the post World War II laws extended to Americans who had joined foreign forces before the American declaration of war; even to those who had not taken the opportunity to transfer from British to American forces after the declaration.

There was a strain of argument within the CWGC that was skeptical of American policy in this regard. In an internal document dated April 18, 1947, an author whose identity cannot be determined recounted U.S./CWGC history at length and warned about a rush to comply with American law. "Discussions between the American authorities and the United Kingdom Foreign Office have already taken place on the matter and there is danger that the Commission be faced with a 'fait accompli' unless strong action is speedily taken to resist the American request, (or perhaps it would be more correct to say *demand*), for repatriation of the bodies concerned."[9] The document went on to suggest that the legal situation now faced by the commission was brought about by "influential 'mortician' organizations in the United States."[10] It stated that the difference between the aftermath of World War I and this one was that there was no relevant American law after the first war, and "the present request is backed by a Public Law of a mandatory nature and by what appears to be a much stronger desire on the part of the United States Government to force the matter through."[11]

The document's author did not prevail in his warning against easy compliance with the United States, and the CWGC's conclusion of the primacy of American law opened a persistent flood of requests through American Graves Registration that loved ones be brought home from what had been permanent burials in cemeteries all over the world. Graves Registration seemed to deal with those requests equally with the rest of its work. By the end of 1947, the CWGC had reached the efficiency of very gracious and individually tailored form letters. Letters of request received directly from the families of the Americans within its cemeteries returned a response reflecting the commission's willingness to comply according to American law. But it often included an assurance to the family that if the loved one was allowed to remain with his comrades he would be treated with full care in perpetuity. Families of flyers were reminded of the RAF's belief and wish that fallen comrades should be buried in unity.

Most of the completed repatriations reflected in the commission archives appeared to be American members of the RAF or RCAF, though exact figures of how many were returned could not be determined, and less could be learned about army soldiers. The numbers seemed large enough, however, that the CWGC eventually had to adopt a policy that would allow emptied graves to remain as unused space, thus working against the spirit of the intent of burial with one's comrades in war.

In the Australian government, it became accepted by early 1947 that all Americans in Commonwealth forces buried in the country would be repatriated to their home country. Their remains were thus concentrated in two cemeteries and placed in caskets that would be suitable for shipment as needed with sufficient proof developed by American Graves Registration that they were indeed American.

On December 1, 1949, a letter was sent from George Springer of the American Graves Registration Command to Oliver Holt of the Imperial War Graves Commission, excerpted:

> After many months of planning we have finally successfully completed our mission as it pertains to the removal from your cemeteries of certain American deceased killed while serving with the British Armed Forces. Our work in this regard was greatly facilitated by the sincere cooperation of your office and the Imperial War Graves office at High Wycombe. Reports I have received indicate that no difficulties were encountered and throughout the entire mission the cemetery caretakers were fully informed and most helpful.[12]

In the case of Richard Stageman, his grave was opened in Hamburg in July 1949 and his remains were found to be discernible from those of his gravemate, RCAF Flight Sergeant F.B. Andrews of London, England. He was re-buried on April 29, 1950, in Cedar Park Cemetery in Calumet Park, Illinois, attended by his surviving parents, Mr. and Mrs. Elmer Stageman.

It would not be until 2005 that "International" Joe Grigas of Worcester, Massachusetts, would find a final resting place in Plot 527 of the military section of Woodland Cemetery in London, Ontario. A writer of a book about Americans who fought with foreign forces in war could find many of the themes and questions of that story in Grigas' life. Were they soldiers of fortune or simply men in need of work? Were they mostly adventurers and outsiders; partisans, patriots, or apolitical; citizens of America or of the world; fearless in some cases and properly cautious in others; men of full substance or men who lived at loose ends when not at war? And how did others perceive them? Were they patriots, or traitors of a sort who would take up wars that their own country did not agree with? Were they American or un–American; exploited or thoughtfully enlisted by other countries; as worthy of remembrance as their fellows in Americans forces, less so, or even deserving of being ignored? And what of their post-war lives in America as veterans of service with other countries?

A particular aspect of Grigas' military career, his receipt of a Distinguished Conduct Medal (DCM), puts his story into the larger context of an era of warfare that is often seen as beginning with the Crimean War of 1853–1856. Called the Russian War by the British, it was a conflict between Russia and an alliance of England, France and others over the territories of the declining Ottoman Empire. The developing technologies of telegraphy, photography and steamship travel made it the first major war that could be reported upon across distances in near real-time. That led indirectly to the writing of classic war poem "The Charge of the Light Brigade," by Alfred Lord Tennyson.

The war had been one of tragic errors in tactics and decisions, which could be easily reported through newspapers back home. The Battle of Balaclava on October 25, 1854, had been part of an attempt to wrest the Black Sea port of Sevastopol from Russian forces. A charge of light brigade forces was intended to accomplish the relatively minor work of attending to a retreating enemy. An error in command, however, directed the brigade to charge headlong into a fully armed offensive battalion. In the lore of the battle, it was believed that the members of the Light Brigade were fully aware of the mistake that had been made and the fate that would await them, but followed orders as it was their duty to do. The effort was valiant, but with devastating results. A full account of the battle appeared in the *London Times* on November 13, and following days. Tennyson is believed to have read the accounts on December 2, and written the first version of the poem immediately, excerpted:

> Cannon to right of them,
> Cannon to left of them,
> Cannon in front of them
> Volley'd & thunder'd;
> Storm'd at with shot and shell,
> Boldly they rode and well,
> Into the jaws of Death,
> Into the mouth of Hell
> Rode the six hundred.[13]

The concept of the Distinguished Conduct Medal was first articulated by Queen Victoria on December 4. It was intended to be a military award that would recognize the valor of lesser rank officers and men, and not to be awarded casually. It recipients were entitled to append the initials DCM to their names. The first DCM was not actually awarded until 1901, and its exclusive nature was purposefully maintained into World War I, when a lesser Military Medal was created to honor most cases of extraordinary valor as a more available alternative to the more prestigious DCM.

Grigas' actions in Sicily had been similar to those of the members of the Light Brigade in Tennyson's poem. After the landing at Pachino, he had charged forward into certain gunfire with "such determination that it caused the surrender of the garrison of approximately two hundred men."[14] For that he was awarded the DCM, one of only five to be gained by the entire Royal Canadian Regiment in World War II. But he never received it. After the war, he disappeared back into America. In 1950, it was determined that he could not be found and the medal was destroyed.

Almost 60 years later, Capt. Duncan MacMillan, CD (*Canadian Forces Decoration*, for long and good service), retired, president of the London, Ontario branch of the Royal Canadian Regiment Association, would suggest that Joe Grigas presented another theme in the life of war veterans that was not considered in the 1940s. "He lived basically as a vagrant," he said of Grigas' life from the end of the war to the end of the century. "Today we would be talking about PTSD."[15]

After action in Sicily for which Grigas had been awarded the DCM, the RCR had fought up the boot of Italy to join the British Eighth Army, then the First Canadian Army in Northwest Europe at the outset of 1945 and, finally, the liberation of the Netherlands on May 5 of that year. It was the Canadian Lt. Gen. Charles Foulkes who formally accepted the surrender of 117,000 German troops in Wageningen on that day. The regiment then fought in the Korean War, losing 107 of its own, and was part of NATO deterrent forces in Cold War Germany. Since its beginning in 1883 and into the 21st century, the RCR and its Regiment Association conducted itself as a "family" in the service of its motto "Pro Patria," For Country.

One day in 2002, the RCRA's website received an email from Bill McCarrick, an American who advocated for veterans in Massachusetts, saying that he had befriended an old veteran in a nursing home named Joe Grigas who claimed to have been a member of the RCR in World War II. The message made its way to Capt. S.E. "Sherry" Atkinson of the Association. Atkinson had fought with Grigas in the Pachino landing in 1943, then been medically discharged after serious wounds received in subsequent fighting in Sicily. Before the war was over, he had taken employment with the Department of Veterans Affairs, rising to become District Director of Veterans Welfare Services for Western Ontario before his retirement in 1974. He knew veterans' issues well, and remained active in the development of Canada's social and governmental policies toward those who had fought on its behalf. He, and others who had known the American, received the message about a still living Joe Grigas with surprise and skepticism. They had thought he was probably dead, and, even upon a trip to visit the man in Massachusetts, Atkinson wasn't sure.

"He didn't look like the Joe I knew and remembered. Same disposition, but he didn't look like Joe at all."[16] Atkinson finally asked the man questions about the Pachino landing that could only have been answered by someone with Grigas' experience at the time, and was convinced by the answers he received. As their realization about the identity of the man who had reappeared in their midst took hold, they began to see more fully the disposition that Atkinson had remembered. Always the outsider except in the flint of battle, Grigas had lived his last 50 years, in the view of Duncan MacMillan, "on the edge of society."

"He was a vagrant. He lived in the weeds and he would come into a shelter when it was cold."[17] MacMillan thought that he had probably done some traveling in those years, but probably not returned to Canada, finally returning to Worcester as a heavy drinker. "I think a lot of guys dealt with memories and experiences by using a bottle. A lot of the guys who served in World War II and still stayed in the military and were successful were nevertheless heavy drinkers." Starting in 1994, Grigas had come to the attention of a social worker in Worcester who would try to help him maintain his health in the winter months, but see very little of him in the spring and summer. He was hit by a car at one point, perhaps as a drunken pedestrian, and the resulting surgery left a knee fused in the open position.

During those years on the bottle and the minimal supports of social work and charity, he had also been a veteran without a country. If there had been an attempt to seek benefits from his service with the U.S. army in Panama, the St. Louis fire of 1973 had probably destroyed his records; and it could not be known whether those records would reflect his inclusion in the lists of the House Un-American Activities Committee. He was a decorated Canadian war hero, but had disappeared from the country after the war. Canada treated its veterans well, and Sherry Atkinson had played a role in developing its services, but it was a system that required proactive participant by a veteran, and it was not in Grigas' nature to act that way. A reciprocal agreement between the veteran agencies of both nations provided shared services for each other's veterans in some cases, but was not activated in this case. Those who had supported Grigas in Massachusetts became aware of his service in Canada, but knew little about its true nature. In addition, Canada's largest veterans organization, the Royal Canadian Legion, maintained branches in 13 communities throughout the United

States, including one not far from Worcester, but could not know about veterans who did not speak up for themselves.

Eventually, Grigas was finally prompted by the circumstances of his life in the Worcester nursing home to seek some recognition for his past. He asked his social worker to find his service record so that he could show others in the home that "he wasn't a worthless bum." As the fact of military service in his life became more apparent, she was able to move him into a slightly better facility for homeless veterans, mainly of the Vietnam era, and Bill Carrick's investigation was begun. After the visit by Sherry Atkinson and others of the RCRA, the decision was made that this was a man who should not be forced to end his days as a charity case in America, but as a family member of the RCR living in Canada. Grigas' own voiced plan had been to move to Arizona, perhaps with the funding of bunch of un-cashed Social Security checks found after his death, and take up life with good vodka and a good woman. The attention of the RCRA was not unwelcome, however, and the work was begun that would bring him into the care of the Association and the Department of Veterans Affairs.

Sherry Atkinson's first hand knowledge of the DVA helped to steer the effort through the twists and turns of bureaucracy, and he was at least able to obtain a letter from Parkwood Hospital in London, Ontario, that Grigas would be temporarily accepted as a patient although he was not a permanent resident. On a spring day in 2003, he was brought on the train by friends to meet Atkinson at the Lewiston, New York, border crossing, but Atkinson was not sure that he had the papers needed to get Grigas to the other side. After a "reconnaissance" of the situation he joined in a line of those waiting to be interviewed by border agents, but, perhaps by virtue of his military bearing, was able to get the friendly attention of a supervisor.

> He said, "There something I can do for you." And I said, "There sure is, but I think we should sit down and talk about this." We went into his office and I told him the story about Joe in terms of what he had done for us during the war, the medal he had, what shape he was in, that he would be accepted at Parkwood hospital, and everything else.
>
> And I said to him "Do you want to go out in the car and talk to him?" And he said, "Don't ask me that." He slipped Atkinson a piece of paper. "That's how we got him across the border. I couldn't believe it."[18]

Across the border and in Parkwood Hospital, the RCRA could take up the task of converting his temporary visa to permanent. It was determined that he had not known about the award of the DCM, and, in fact, did not know what a DCM was; the process was begun to have it reissued to him. An account for him was set up with the Bank of Montreal, and a stream of monthly income was opened with redirected U.S. Social Security Checks, and DVA supplements for hearing loss and the valor indicated by the DCM, which yielded just more than $4 extra each month.

At Parkwood, he could smoke a pack of cigarettes a day, and was allowed a ration of two beers each day in the hospital's pub. He chugged them both down in rapid succession for full effect. Once each week, the Tim Horton's franchise in the hospital offered free coffee and donuts, a favorite time for him. He was conversant in current affairs and popular poetry, but his vision would no longer allow him to read, so he watched television. He would exercise as best he could, with a walker and a rigid leg, with the avowed purpose of rebuilding his strength for the day he could be independent again. The men of the RCRA would take him on drives out into the world and to appointments.

The day before a planned celebration of his birthday on February 15, 2005, Grigas fell

Joseph Grigas of Worcester, Massachusetts, served with the U.S. Army in Panama, the Lincoln Brigade in the Spanish Civil War and the Royal Canadian Regiment in World War II. His ashes were interred in Woodland Cemetery in London, Ontario. William McCarrick, who had discovered Grigas in a Worcester nursing home, stood behind Capt. Sheridan Atkinson of the Royal Canadian Regiment Association as he added sand from the beach at Pachino, Sicily, to Grigas' grave (Royal Canadian Regiment Association).

ill. He died on March 8, and was buried July 10. The RCRA broke its own rule against holding memorial services on Sundays, because the anniversary of the Pachino Landing in Sicily fell on that date and it seemed an appropriate day. Approximately 50 people were in attendance at Woodland Cemetery, including Bill Carrick who came from Massachusetts, and who, because of his efforts on Grigas' behalf, had been made an honorary member of the RCRA family.

"We tried to give him a proper send off," said Duncan MacMillan. "And we had an American flag there as well."[19] Grigas might have reminded them that he had once been known as International Joe because of his service in Spain. It had made him an honorary citizen of that nation as well.

A year later, the same group convened at the same time and place to finally give to the American Joe Grigas the Distinguished Conduct Medal of the British Empire. It had finally been re-struck from original molds and sent from London, England, to London, Ontario.

Afterword

Others may fix it differently, but, for me, the human and geographic centers of this story converge on Le Place des États Unis on the Rue de Lubeck in Paris.

The American who may be most at the center of the story poetically, Alan Seeger, also has a history with the small park that continues into the 21st century. He was to have recited his poem "Ode in Memory of the American Volunteers Fallen for France" during the dedication of Bartholdi's statue of Washington and Jefferson at the northwest end of Le Place on May 30, 1916. Duties in the Foreign Legion, however, kept him away from that event, and he died at Belloy-en-Santerre the following July 4. Thus, seven years later, on July 4, 1923, Seeger was memorialized himself, with others, by his own poem. Excerpts were included on a memorial set back from the Rue de Lubeck, that also included the names of 23 other Americans who had been killed in service to the Foreign Legion, and a rendering of an American and French soldier shaking hands. It was topped by a bronze statue of Alan Seeger in salute to the cause. Complimented by the statue of Lafayette and Washington at the other end of the park, Le Place des États Unis became an important symbol of the history of the United States and France as Allies in war.

Years have passed, of course, and the threads of history have become frayed and forgotten. I had to admit that, even though I had written about Le Place in a previous book and was yet to write about it again in this book, it was pretty much out of my mind as my partner and I walked down the Rue de Lubeck one blustery day in May 2012 on our way to the Eiffel Tower, which sat on a near horizon. I would have gone right past it, but the memorial to the American volunteers caught the corner of her eye and she called me back. She asked, "What's wrong with this?"

I quickly realized what I was looking at, and began to examine it in a light rain. A portion had been spray painted with a common epithet. The list of names was stained with old moss and a darkness that seemed to be the result of decades of rain. A stencil of a giraffe unaccountably covered one of the lists, and other squiggles of spray paint were found here and there. Most striking, the statue of Alan Seeger that had been atop the monument was gone, so much so that if you had not known it was supposed to be there you would not have known it was missing.

American War Memorials Overseas is a Paris-based nonprofit devoted to information and advocacy about the hundreds, perhaps thousands, of war memorials devoted to the United States that are all over Europe. I had coffee with its executive director, Lil Pfluke, an American living in Paris, and asked if we could find an explanation for what I had seen. She forwarded to me this email from the city's public information office, roughly translated:

The Monument to the American Volunteers in France was dedicated in the Place des États Unis in Paris on July 4, 1923. It was topped by a statue of the American poet Alan Seeger, who had been killed in the French Foreign Legion and was considered a dear friend of France.

The monument became a target of vandalism beginning in 2010, and the statue was torn away, though it was not lost.

Hello,

You need more information about the restoration of the monument to volunteers.

Following your email, we inform you that the monument to the American volunteers was vandalized in 2010, the bronze statue was thrown to the ground, which was severely damaged.

Restoration of this work has been carried out in 2012. Relocation of the base is currently subject to a broader discussion about securing bronze works in the Paris area. Once the security method chosen, a maintenance of the lower part of the monument carved stone may be incurred in respect of the replacement of the statue.

Recall that the City of Paris manages more than 600 statues spread over the Parisian public.

Sincerely,

Team Posts Parisians.

All of us have lived among war memorials all of our lives, and, like most of us, I've never paid much attention to them—until I started writing books about the human results, particularly for Americans, of past wars. The damaged monument at Le Place des États Unis and the city's obviously good faith effort to fix it in the larger context of the 600 statues of Paris is representative of the subject of this book.

In 2013, the monument was restored; the following year the statue of Alan Seeger was returned to its rightful place (American War Memorials Overseas).

When I was shown the graves of Americans that "nobody knows anything about" by the official of the Brookwood Cemetery outside of London I had no idea of the journey I was about to take to find out who they were. Physically, it took me to the great cities of London and Paris, among others, but mentally it took me to understandings of war and the reasons that men and women fight in them, or drive their necessary ambulances, that had not yet been part of my experience.

These Americans who fought war in the uniforms of other countries were no more noble than those who fought directly on behalf of the United States. Their motivations and circumstances were similar and universal. But I hope I've been able to suggest that they were also no *less* noble, and their contributions were no less profound. In fact, they were Americans who played an intricate role in the conflicts and geopolitics of the first half of the 20th century. Like the damaged monument in Paris, however, their spirit has been lost to time and their existence forgotten—to the extent that it was ever known.

One of the most interesting things I discovered in my research for this book was hard to find, and, for me, a quiet revelation about a quiet decision made by the U.S. government in 1920 and reaffirmed in following years. American citizens who had fought in the uniforms of Allied forces in the two world wars had just as much of a right and honor to be buried in an American military cemetery as their fellows who had died in the uniforms of their own country. And what happens in death, it seems to me, is the ultimate response to what has happened in life.

I hope that in Memorial Days to come the Americans whose stories have been told in this book can be remembered with the same light and force as all Americans who have fought in war.

Chapter Notes

Chapter One

1. Samuel Lorenzo Knapp, *Memoirs of General Lafayette: With an Account of His Visit to America, and of His Reception by the People of the United States; from His Arrival, August 15th, to the Celebration at Yorktown, October 19th, 1824* (Boston: E.G. House, 1824), 168.

2. Ibid.

3. Ibid., 16.

4. Ibid., 17.

5. Ibid., 95.

6. "Jusserand Lauds Our 'Lafayettes.'" *New York Times*, September 7, 1916.

7. Ibid.

8. John Bowe and Charles L. MacGregor, *Soldiers of the Legion: Trench Etched by Legionnaire Bowe, Who Is John Bowe of Canby, Minnesota, and Charles L. Mac-Gregor, Collaborator* (Chicago: Peterson Linotyping, 1918), 8.

9. Ibid., 41.

10. Ibid., 45.

11. As an example: "...we rejoice that we are at last to pay our debt to France, for Lafayette, Rochambeau and the Army and the Navy she sent us when we needed them sorely." Spoken at the Lafayette Day ceremony in Saratoga, NY, September 6, 1917. *Report of the Fortieth Annual Meeting of the American Bar Association, Volume 42* (Baltimore: Lord Baltimore Press, 1917), 101.

12. "Kiffin Y. Rockwell, World War I Aviator, Lafayette Escadrille, Biography & Photographs," *Virginia Military Institute*, http://www.vmi.edu/archives.aspx?id=12371.

13. William Archer, introduction to *Poems by Alan Seeger* (New York: Scribner's, 1916).

14. Mark Anthony DeWolfe Howe, *Memoirs of the Harvard Dead in the War Against Germany, Volume 1* (Cambridge, MA: Harvard University Press, 1920), 118.

15. Ibid, various pages.

16. John Joseph Casey, "The New 'Old Guard' in France," *New York Times Current History, Volume 5* (1917), 856.

17. Christopher Charles," *St. Petersburg [Florida] Independent*, September 10, 1966, 14a.

18. Paul Ayres Rockwell, *American Fighters in the Foreign Legion* (Boston: Houghton Mifflin, 1930), 173.

19. Ibid., 175.

20. "Hug American Recruits," *New York Times*, August 26, 1914, 4.

21. Albert N. Depew, *Gunner Depew* (Chicago: Reilly & Britton, 1918), 33.

22. Ibid., 40.

23. Ibid., 193.

24. Anonymous, *The Bookman, Volume 47* (New York: Dodd, Mead, 1918), 311.

25. George William Hau, ed., *War Echoes: or Germany and Austria in the Crisis* (Chicago: Morton M. Malone, 1915), 252.

26. Depew, *Gunner Depew*, 301.

27. *The Bookseller, Newsdealer and Stationer*, March 15, 1918, 245.

28. Ibid.

29. "63 Americans Aboard Two of Sunken Ships," *New York Times*, January 18, 1917.

30. "Huntington Campaign for Red Cross Is On," *Fort Wayne [Indiana] Journal Gazette*, December 17, 1917, 9.

31. "Gunner Depew," *Lorain County [Ohio] Chronicle-Telegram*, March 5, 1917, 7.

32. Edwin Wilson Morse, *The Vanguard of American Volunteers* (New York: Scribner's, 1918), 178.

33. Edward Dale Toland, *The Aftermath of Battle* (New York: Macmillan, 1916), x.

34. Ibid., 3.

35. Ibid., 22.

36. Morse, *The Vanguard of American Volunteers*, 160.

37. "Nine Americans Get the French War Cross," *New York Times*, February 9, 1917.

38. James William Davenport Seymour, *History of the American Field Service in France* (Boston: Houghton Mifflin, 1920), 305.

39. Morse, *The Vanguard of American Volunteers*, 138.

40. "Saw War at Its Worse," *New York Times*, March 3, 191, 3.

41. "An Urgent Request." *New York Times*, March 31, 1915, 10.

42. "Queen Mary Thanks American Red Cross," *New York Times*, November 1, 1914, 10.

43. *Modern Hospital, Volume Six, No. 1* (Chicago: Modern Hospital Publishing, 1916), 48.

Chapter Two

1. Col. T. Bentley Mott, *Myron T. Herrick, Friend of France* (Garden City, NY: Doubleday, Doran, 1929), 143.

2. Ibid.

3. The Citizenship Act of 1907, Pub. L. No. 2, 5–7, title 8, ch. 12, 3, 3, § 1481.

4. "President Wilson Proclaims our Strict Neutrality," *New York Times*, August 5, 1914.

5. Convention (V) respecting the Rights and Duties of Neutral Powers and Persons in Case of War on Land, The Hague, October 18, 1907, ch. 3, 17, § B.

6. "Alan Seeger, Poet, Terribly Wounded, Ended Own Life," *New York Tribune*, May 14, 1917, 1.

7. John Jay Chapman, Victor Chapman's Letters from France (New York: Macmillan, 1917), 4.

8. Ibid., 36.

9. *Gail Lumet Buckley, American Patriots: The Story of Blacks in the Military from the Revolution to Desert Storm* (New York: Random House, 2001).

10. James Norman Hall, Charles Nordhoff, and Edgar G. Hamilton, eds., *The Lafayette Flying Corps, Volume 2* (New York: Houghton Mifflin, 1920), 326.

11. "The Foundation," *Lafayette Flying Corps Memorial Foundation*, http://rdisa.pagesperso-orange.fr/html/Frames/lafayette.html.

12. James J. Hudson, Clouds of Glory (Fayetteville, AR: University of Arkansas Press, 1990), 6.

13. *The Royal Flying Corps 1914–1918*, http://www.airwar1.org.uk.

14. "Uncle Sam's Adopted Nephews," *Harper's Magazine, Volume 137*, 1918, 289.

15. Frederick C. Croxton, *Statistical Review of Immigration, 1820–1910, Distribution of Immigrants, 1850–1900* (Washington, DC: Government Printing Office, 1911), 44.

16. "Court House Crater Easy for British Tank," *New York Times*, March 1, 1918.

17. "Zionists Plan Big Army," *New York Times*, June 28, 1918, 14.

18. "Jewish Legion Losses," *New York Times*, December 28, 1918.

19. W. Todd Knowles, *The Knowles Collection*, http://knowlescollection.blogspot.com/search/label/Jewish%20Legion.

20. "Poles Form a Legion," *New York Times*, January 13, 1915, 2.

21. "Record Audience Hears Paderewski," *Indianapolis Star*, November 24, 1916, 5.

22. "Poles Here to Enlist for Army in France," *New York Times*, October 7, 1917.

23. "Many Here Join Polish Legion," *New North Rhinelander* (Wisconsin), March 28, 1918, 12.

Chapter Three

1. H.C. Osborne, Report for the Minister (Americans in Canadian Forces), International War Graves Commission, October 14, 1927, Library and Archives Canada.

2. "France in Protest to United States," *New York Times*, September 26, 1914.

3. "American Weakened by a Failure to Protest," *Toronto Star*, January 14, 1915, 5.

4. "The United States and the War," *Toronto Star*, February 11, 1915, 6.

5. "250,000 to Unite in Army League," *New York Times*, March 1, 1915, 1, 4.

6. "Garrison Demands Inquiry into Legion," *New York Times*, March 2, 1915, 7.

7. "Gen. Wood Defends American Legion," *New York Times*, March 4, 1915, 15.

8. "Hints Treason in Attack on Reserve Army," *The Washington Herald*, March 4, 1915, 1.

9. "Gen. Wood Defends American Legion," *New York Times*, March 4, 1915, 15.

10. "Wood Told to Shun American Legion," *New York Times*, March 12, 1915, 9.

11. Winston S. Churchill, *The World Crisis, 1911–1914, 2nd ed. Vol. 1* (New York: Scribner's, 1923), 272.

12. Ibid.

13. James Norman Hall, *Kitchener's Mob, The Adventures of an American in the British Army* (Boston: Houghton Mifflin, 1916), 201.

14. Harry White Wilmer, West Sandling Camp, Devonshire. Letter to Jack Mathews, La Plata, Maryland, September 5, 1915, http://21stbattalion.ca/tributetz/wilmer_hw.html.

15. 1st Lt. Joseph S. Smith, *Over There and Back in Three Uniforms* (New York: E.P. Dutton, 1918), 11.

16. Ibid., 51.

17. Edwin Austin Abbey, *An American Soldier* (New York: Houghton Mifflin, 1918), 3.

18. Ibid.

19. Ibid.

20. Ibid., 10.

21. Ibid., 65.

22. Martin Thornton, *Churchill, Borden and Anglo-Canadian Naval Relations, 1911–14* (London: Palgrave Macmillan, 2013), 7.

23. Richard F. Selcer, *Civil War America, 1850 to 1875* (New York: Infobase Publishing, 2006), 232.

24. Robin W. Winks, *Civil War Years, Canada and the United States* (Montreal: McGill-Queen's University Press, 1998) offers a very thorough discussion of this topic, and estimates of Canadian participation in the Civil War that are less than these figures.

25. Danny Jenkins, "British North Americans Who Fought in the American Civil War, 1861–1865" (thesis, University of Ottawa, 1993), 21.

26. Paul R. Magocsi, ed., *Encyclopedia of Canada's Peoples* (Toronto: University of Toronto Press, 1999), 190. Also see Forging Our Legacy, *Citizenship and Immigration Canada* (website), accessed August 8, 2013, http://www.cic.gc.ca/english/resources/publications/legacy/chap-2.asp.

27. Ibid.

28. Magocsi, *Encyclopedia of Canada's People's*, 191.

29. "The 'Machine Gun Man of the Princess Pats,'" *New York Times*, October 31, 1915.

30. "Enlisting Young Men for the War," *Toronto Star*, January 26, 1915, 6.

31. Serge Durlinger, "French Canada and Recruitment During the First World War," *Canadian War Museum*, http://www.warmuseum.ca/education/online-educational-resources/dispatches/french-canada-and-recruitment-during-the-first-world-war/.

32. Ibid.

33. "Has Enough Men Says Hughes for Fourth Contingent," *Toronto Star*, April 10, 1915, 1.

34. "Lavergne," *Detroit Free Press*, November 15, 1916, 1.

35. "Home Town Helps," *Oelwein (Iowa) Daily Register*, July 18, 1913, 2.

36. "American Minister Furls U.S. Flag," *Winnipeg Free Press*, May 11, 1915, 1.

37. "Nation Gets Roster of American Legion," *New York Times*, December 26, 1916.

Chapter Four

1. "Sexless, Soulless, Spineless," *Toronto Star*, May 13, 1915, 7.

2. "Roosevelt Urges the U.S.," *Toronto Star*, January 11, 1915, 6.

3. "Roosevelt to Join Canadian Force?," *Toronto Star*, November 19, 1915, 7.

4. "Colonel Refuses to Speak," *New York Times*, December 9, 1915, 6.

5. "Americans Join Legion," *New York Times*, December 12, 1915, 3.

6. Ibid.

7. Ibid.

8. Ibid.

9. "An American Legion," *The Middletown (NY) Daily Times Press*, January 3, 1916.

10. "Battle of Ideals," *The London Times*, January 25, 1916, 7.

11. "American Legion," *Manitoba Free Press*, February 28, 1916, 2.

12. "Leaves the U.S. Navy for American Legion," *Toronto Star*, January 25, 1916, 13.

13. "97th Am. Legion Going Overseas in Near Future," *Toronto Star*, March 30, 1916, 1.

14. Gregory Mason, "Crusaders of Today," *The Outlook*, vol. 113 (1916), 502.

15. Ibid., 509.

16. Ibid., 502.

17. "First of American Legion Off for Flanders," *New York Times*, May 28, 1916.

18. Ibid.

19. Ibid.

20. Rudolf Cronau, *German Achievements in America* (New York: Rudolf Cronau, 1916), 230.

21. Major Edward C. Boynton, *General Orders of George Washington* (Newburgh: New York: E.M. Ruttenber, 1883), 86.

22. Cronau, 231.

23. Ibid., 231.

24. Francis Whiting Halsey, ed., *The Literary Digest History of the World War* (New York: Funk & Wagnalls, 1919), 107.

25. Neil Baldwin, *Henry Ford and the Jews* (New York: Public Affairs, 2001), 59.

26. "Jewish Jazz—Moron Music—Becomes Our National Music," *The Dearborn (Michigan) Independent*, August 6, 1921, 1.

27. "Roosevelt," *The Detroit Free Press*, May 5, 1917, 1.

28. "Roosevelt to Visit Detroit," *New York Times*, May 14, 1916, 6.

29. "Roosevelt Urges Unity in America," *New York Times*, May 20, 1916, 1.

30. Ibid., 4.

31. "Ford Answers Roosevelt," *New York Times*, May 21, 1916, 3.

Chapter Five

1. George Sylvester Vierick, *The Fatherland, Volume IV* (New York: The Fatherland Corporation, 1916), 131.

2. Ibid.

3. Ibid., 133.

4. "Americans May Be Shot," *The Gettysburg Times*, August 4, 1916, 2.

5. "Hun Threats Do Not Daunt," *The Brandon (Manitoba) Daily Sun*, August 5, 1916, 2.

6. "First of the American Legion Off for Flanders," *New York Times*, May 28, 1916.

7. "213th wants Grant," *Toronto Star*, June 15, 1916, 18.

8. "Daniels Scolds His Editor for War 'Ad,'" *New York Sun*, February 26, 1916, 1.

9. "Says Canadians Hoot Americans," *El Paso Herald*, September 29, 1916, 4.

10. "Comforts of the American Legion," *New York Times*, August 11, 1916, 8.

11. "Germans Spiteful at American Legion," *Toronto Star*, September 9, 1916, 11.

12. "Big Ocean Ferry Between Halifax and Ally Posts," *The Attica [Indiana] Daily Tribune*, December 21, 1916, 5.

13. Russell Anthony Kelly, *Kelly of the Legion* (New York: Mitchell Kennerly, 1917), 59.

14. Ibid., 92.

15. "Kelly of the Foreign Legion Sought Honors on Battlefield," *Princeton (Minnesota) Union*, January 20, 1916, 2.

16. Alan Seeger, "Ode in Memory of the American Volunteers Fallen for France," The Project Gutenberg Ebook of Poems, prod. Alan Light, http://gutenberg.org/cache/epub/617/pg617.html.

17. "'Lost' American Legion Found on the Somme Front," *The (New York) Evening World*, November 23, 1916, 2

18. Ibid.

19. "American Corps in War to Lose Name," *New York Sun*, November 3, 1916, 1.

20. Ibid.

21. "American Airmen on the Somme," *The Times*, London, November 7, 1916, 7.

22. "21 German Machines Toll of Americans," *New York Times*, November 19, 1916.

23. Ibid.

24. Georges Thenault, *The Story of the Lafayette Escadrille* (Kirkland, WA: Tale Ends Press, 2012), ch. 5.

25. "Days Spent in a Land of Death...," *New York Sun*, November 12, 1916, supplement 2.

26. Ibid.

27. "'Lost' American Legion Is Found on Battle Front," *The Xenia (Ohio) Daily Gazette*, November 25, 1916, 7.

28. Theodore Marburg, *A League of Nations* (New York: Macmillan, 1919), 142.

29. Ibid., 145.

30. Captain Theodore Marburg (statue), Inscription (Baltimore: Druid Ridge Cemetery).

Chapter Six

1. Glenn Hyatt collection.

2. "Lost American Legion Found," *Oakland Tribune*, November 23, 1916, 5.

3. Ibid.

4. "Iowan Returns from Trenches," *Renwick (Iowa) Times*, January 25, 1917, 3.

5. "Many Americans Are Killed on the Battlefields of Europe," *The Sumner (Iowa) Gazette*, February 15, 1917, 6.

6. "The American Soldiers in France," *The Times*, London, February 2, 1917, 5.

7. Ibid.

8. Issac Frederick Marcosson, *Leonard Wood: Prophet of Preparedness* (New York: John Lane, 1917).

9. "Role of the United States," *The Times*, London, March 3, 1917, 3.

10. "France, Our Oldest Friend," *The Evening Independent*, Massilon, Ohio, February 17, 1917.

11. "Patriotism Is Personal," *The New-York Tribune*, April 1, 1917, 2.

12. Ibid.

13. "Nation's Leaders Active in Preparations for War," *The New-York Tribune*, March 21, 1917, 7.

14. J.J. McMahon, Jr., Letter to Mrs. S. P. Kennedy, May 4, 1918.

15. *American Military History* (Office of the Chief of Military History, United States Army), 372.

16. Ibid., 373.

17. Ibid., 374.

18. "Fourth of July in Paris," *Philadelphia Evening-Ledger*, July 28, 1917, 8.

19. Ibid.

20. Ibid.

21. Ibid.

22. William J. Bennett, *America: The Last Best Hope* (Nashville: Thomas Nelson, 2007), 26.

23. "Lafayette Flyers Get Official Flag," *New York Times*, July 10, 1917, 2.

24. Bowe and MacGregor, *Soldiers of the Legion*, 36.

25. "American Soldiers Under American Flag," *Fort Wayne News*, May 25, 1917, 17.

26. "Fighting Battles with Stretchers," *The Ogden Standard*, May 12, 1917, Magazine Section, 24.

27. "Americans Launch Mad Raid to Mark Nation's War Entry," *Philadelphia Evening-Ledger*, May 28, 1917, 5.

28. Ibid.

29. Lt. Col. W.M. Sage, Commanding 211th Overseas Battalion, Letter to the Officer Commanding the 14th Canadian Infantry Training Brigade, February 6, 1917.

30. Ibid.

31. "Plans to Organize U.S. Citizens Now Fighting Abroad Into One Fighting Unit," *The (New York) Evening World*, April 25, 1917, final, extra, 2.

32. "Americans Abroad May Fight as a Unit," *The Washington Times*, April 25, 1917, 4.

33. "Repatriation of Americans," *The Evening Tribune*, Albert Lea, Minnesota, July 7, 1917, 2.

34. "Americans at Front May Save Citizenship," *New York Times*, April 23, 1917, 8.

35. "For the Freedom of the World" (advertisement), *The Wilmar (NM) Tribune*, February 20, 1918, 1.

36. "Screen Play Based Upon Army Tragedy," *Philadelphia Evening-Ledger*, November 7, 1917, 20.

Chapter Seven

1. "Military Schools to Give Officers," *Adams County (Iowa) Union Republican*, February 28, 1917, 10.

2. "Americans Win Glory in France," *Washington Times*, April 28, 1917, 6.

3. "American Legion Proves Its Breed," *Philadelphia Evening-Ledger*, April 24, 1917.

4. Charles R. Thompson, Letter to Mrs. S.P. Kennedy, December 16, 1917.

5. Tom Hiney, *Raymond Chandler: A Biography* (New York: Grove Press, 1997), 42.

6. Frank Mac Shane, *The Life of Raymond Chandler* (New York: E.P. Dutton, 1976), 29.

7. Ibid.

8. U.S. Naval Institute, *Proceedings*, Vol. 44 (Annapolis: U.S. Naval Institute, 1918), 459.

9. "Military Pay for CEF," *Canadian Expeditionary Force Study Group*, http://www.cefresearch.ca/phpBB3/viewtopic.php?f=3&t=88.

10. Couvi, "Pay Tables for 1917," *Couvi's Blog* http://couvisblog.blogspot.com/2007/04/pay-tables-for-1917.html.

11. "Foreign Legion Won Glory at Verdun," *New York Sun*, September 5, 1917, 2.

12. Rockwell, *American Fighters in the Foreign Legion*, 258.

13. Ibid.

14. Ibid., 259.

15. Ibid., 267.

16. Ibid., 268.

17. Ibid., 312.

18. "Christopher Charles: Humble Hero," *The (St. Petersburg) Evening Independent*, September 10, 1966, 14a.

19. Rockwell, *American Fighters in the Foreign Legion*, 301.

20. Ibid., 298.

21. Ibid., 299.

22. "Lion Mascot Knew Him," *New York Times*, July 12, 1919, 3.

Chapter Eight

1. Veterans Affairs Canada, http://www.veterans.gc.ca/eng/remembrance/history/first-world-war/canada/canada8.

2. Fred James, *Canada's Triumph from Amiens to Mons: August to November 1918* (London, Canadian War Records Office, 1918), 6.

3. Ibid., 14.

4. Ibid., 28.

5. Ibid., 37.

6. Ibid., 54.

7. J.F.B. Livesey, *Canada's Hundred Days* (Toronto: Thomas Allen, 1919), 400.

8. "Canadian Benefit for 'Honor Legion,'" *New York Times*, May 6, 1918.

9. Ibid.

10. "War Veterans to Convene to Form 'Legion,'" *New York Tribune*, April 9, 1919, 7.

11. "2600 Who Fought in British Army Demobilized Here," *New York Times*, April 10, 1919.

12. "Ruling of Immigration Officials Keeps Them on Board Mauretania," *New York Times*, April 8, 1919.

13. Ibid.

14. Glenn Hyatt collection.

15. Ibid.

16. Ibid.

17. Commonwealth War Graves Commission Archive.

18. Mike Hanlon, "Trench Report," *St. Mihiel Trip-Wire*, http://www.worldwar1.com/tripwire/smtw1006.htm.

19. Commonwealth War Graves Commission Archive.

20. Commonwealth War Graves Commission Archive.

21. Ibid.

22. Ibid.

23. Ibid.

24. Ibid.

Chapter Nine

1. "Soldiers Finish a Drive for the American Legion," *New York Tribune*, September 21, 1919, 6.

2. *Ontario's Historic Plaques*, http://www.ontarioplaques.com/Plaques_JKL/Plaque_Kawartha15.html.

3. "The American Legion in the Canadian Expeditionary Force, 1914–1917: A Study in Failure," *The Canadian Historical Review—Volume 61* (Toronto: University of Toronto Press, 1980), 262.

4. "Nations Honor War Dead," *New York Times*, November 12, 1927, 1.

5. Ibid.

6. "Poincare Grateful for Our Aid in War," *New York Times*, July 5, 1923, 17.

7. "Paris Celebrated Independence Day," *New York Times*, July 5, 192, Business Opportunities 20.

8. Ibid.

9. Janus Ciseck, *Koscziusko, We Are Here* (Jefferson, NC: McFarland, 2002) 8.

10. Ibid., 10.

11. Public Law 111-94, 111 U.S. Congress, November 6, 2009.

12. Ibid.

13. Kenneth Malcolm Murray, *Wings Over Poland* (New York: D. Appleton, 1932), 358.

14. "Polish Army Outfitted with American Uniforms," *New York Times*, February 2, 1920.

15. "Sweeney of the Legion Goes to War Again," *New York Times*, July 26, 1925, SM 9.

16. Ibid.

17. "13 Americans Quit Fighting for Spain," *New York Times*, November 25, 1921.

Chapter Ten

1. "Personalities in Today's News," *Salt Lake City Tribune*, November 27, 1936, 6.

2. "Seek to Penalize U.S. Volunteers," *New York Times*, December 27, 1936.

3. "U.S. Bans Service in Spanish Force," *New York Times*, January 14, 1937, 10.

4. Author interview with Duncan MacMillan.

5. Arthur H. Landis, *The Abraham Lincoln Brigade* (New York: Citadel Press, 1967), vii.

6. Cary Nelson and Jefferson Hendricks, *Madrid 1937* (New York: Routledge Press, 1996), 187.

7. Ernest Hemingway, "On the American Dead in Spain," *New Masses*, February 14, 1939.

8. Michael Harrison and Christopher Stuart-Clark, *Peace and War: A Collection of Poems* (Oxford: Oxford University Press, 1989), 88.

9. Ibid.

10. "Claire Lee Chennault and the Problem of Intelligence in China," *Studies in Intelligence* 54, no. 2 (June 2010), 3.

11. Ibid., 4.

12. "He Will Fit Wings to the Chinese Dragon," *San Francisco Sunday Call*, undated 1911.

13. Ann Wetherell, "Salvation Through Aviation: Chinese and Chinese American Aviators in Portland, 1918–1945" (paper, Portland State University, 2011), 10.

14. Walter L. Hixson, *The American Experience in World War II* (New York: Routledge, 2003), 21.

15. Daniel Ford, "FDR's Secret Order," *The Warbird's Forum*, http://www.warbirdforum.com/fdrnote.htm.

16. "Flying Tigers in Burma," *Life Magazine*, March 30, 1942.

Chapter Eleven

1. F. W. Rudmin, "A 1935 U.S. Plan for Invasion of Canada," *Glasnost Archive*, http://www.glasnost.de/hist/usa/1935invasion.html.

2. John Herd Thompson, Stephen J. Randall, *Canada and the United States: Ambivalent Allies* (Atlanta: University of Georgia Press, 2002), 106.

3. Ibid.

4. "Mobsters, Mayhem & Murder," *Magazine Times*, http://www.walkervilletimes.com/34/mobsters1.html.

5. Thompson and Randall, *Canada and the United States: Ambivalent Allies*, 129.

6. Ibid., 140.

7. "Roosevelt Visit Links Three Nations," *New York Times*, August 1, 1936, 5.

8. Ibid.

9. Thompson and Randall, *Canada and the United States: Ambivalent Allies*, 147.

10. Stanley W. Dziuban, *Military Relations Between the United States and Canada—1939–1945* (Washington, DC: Center of Military History, United States Army, 1990), 4.

11. Thompson and Randall, *Canada and the United States: Ambivalent Allies*, p. 149.

12. "U.S. Volunteers Sought in France," *New York Times*, August 26, 1939, 5.

13. "Americans Enlist," *Miami [Oklahoma]Daily News Record*, September 6, 1939, 1.

14. "Americans Seek to Enlist," *New York Times*, September 21, 1939.

15. "Americans Join Canadian Army," *Hammond (Indiana) Times*, April 5, 1940, 4.

16. "Text of President Roosevelt's Proclamation on American Neutrality," *New York Times*, September 6, 1939.

17. *San Antonio Express*, February 24, 1940, 4.

18. "American Field Service Also Appeals for Funds," *New York Times*, May 25, 1940.

19. "U.S. Ambulances Rushed to Front," *New York Times*, May 29, 1940, 6.

Chapter Twelve

1. Andy Bull, "The Forgotten Story of ... Those Magnificent Men and Their Fllying Bobsled," *Talking Sport*, http://www.guardian.co.uk/sport/blog/2010/feb/25/forgotten-story-magnificent-men-flying-machine.

2. Clayton Knight Papers, An Interview with Clayton Knight, Library and Archives Canada, 37.

3. Draft: Clayton Knight, O.B.E., *Contribution to Victory 1939–1942*, July 1965, 2, Library and Archives Canada.

4. "Lindbergh Urges We Shun the War," *New York Times*, September 16, 1939, 1.

5. "Lindbergh Scored by Press in London," *New York Times*, October 16, 1939.

6. "Canadian Press Scores Lindbergh; Opposing War Stand," *New York Times*, October 22, 1939, 74.

7. "Lafayette Escadrille Ousts Lindbergh as Honorary Member," *New York Times*, May 29, 1940, 6.

8. Interview ofClayton Knight by Robert Hays, Major USAF, June 17, 1965, 5, Library and Archives Canada.

9. Ibid., 6.

10. Ibid., 9.

11. Draft: Clayton Knight, O.B.E., *Contribution to Victory 1939–1942*, July 1965, 2, Library and Archives Canada.

12. Richard Gimblett and Michael Hadley, eds., *Citizen Sailors: Chronicles of Canada's Naval Reserve, 1910–2010* (Toronto: Dundurn, 2010).

13. Roger Sarty, "The Royal Canadian Navy and the Battle of the Atlantic, 1939–1945," *Canadian War Museum*, http://www.warmuseum.ca/education/online-educational-resources/dispatches/the-royal-canadian-navy-and-the-battle-of-the-atlantic-1939–1945.

14. Winston Churchill, speech before the House of Commons, May 13, 1940. "Blood, Toils, Tears and Sweat," http://www.winstonchurchill.org/learn/speeches/speeches-of-winston-churchill/92-blood-toil-tears-and-sweat.

15. A. H. Cherry, *Yankee R.N.* (London: Jarrolds Publisher, 1951), 14.

16. Ibid., 16.

17. Ibid., 17.

18. Ibid., 18.

19. Eric Dietrich-Berryman, Charlotte Hammond, and Ronald E. White, *Passport Not Required* (Annapolis, Naval Institute Press, 2010), 45.

20. Ibid., 1.

21. Diantha Parker, "In a Little-Known WWII Battle, a Father's Experience Becomes a Daughter's Journey," *At War*, http://atwar.blogs.nytimes.com/2012/08/22/in-a-little-known-wwii-battle-a-fathers-experience-becomes-a-daughters-journey/ .

Chapter Thirteen

1. "The Young Recruits," *Joplin News Herald*, March 7, 1940, 4.

2. "Recruiting in the United States of America" (unpublished narrative, 1945), Library and Archives Canada.

3. Eric Dietrich-Berryman, Charlotte Hammond, and Ronald E. White, *Passport Not Required* (Annapolis: Naval Institute Press, 2010), 22.

4. "Churchill Inspects American Unit," *New York Times*, January 10, 1941.

5. Ibid.

6. "Home Guard Unit Embarrasses Defense," *New York Times*, July 22, 1941.

7. Ibid.

8. Dietrich-Berryman, Hammond, and White, *Passport Not Required*, 35.

9. "Ohioans Serving with British, Canadian Units Given Official Ranking," *Sandusky Register Star News*, July 22, 1941, 12.

10. Dietrich-Berryman, Hammond, and White, *Passport Not Required*, 39.

11. "U.S. Pilots Join to Fight for Britain," *The Wisconsin State Journal* (Madison), October 9, 1940, 9.

12. Clayton Knight Papers, Interview of Clayton Knight by Robert Hays, Major USAF, June 17, 1965, 5, Library and Archives Canada.

13. Clayton Knight Papers, undated letter, Library and Archives Canada.

14. Clayton Knight Papers, Interview of Clayton Knight by Robert Hays, Major USAF, June 17, 1965, 17, Library and Archives Canada.

15. Clayton Knight Papers, Draft: Clayton Knight, O.B.E., *Contribution to Victory 1939–1942*, July 1965, 23, Library and Archives Canada.

16. Ibid.

17. Clayton Knight Papers, U.S. Selective Service memo as described in text, Library and Archives Canada.

Chapter Fourteen

1. "Two Capitals Act," *New York Times*, August 23, 1940, 1.

2. "Economies Merged," *New York Times*, April 21, 1941, 1.

3. "90% of U.S. Voters Would Fight If Canada Is Invaded," *New York Times*, May 19, 1941, 2.

4. "Three Get Legion Medals," *Toronto Star*, July 4, 1941, 2.

5. "Canada Reports Brisk Increase in Army and Air Force Recruits," *New York Times*, October 26, 1941, 15.

6. Barry Broadfoot, *Six War Years 1939–1945* (Toronto: Doubleday Canada Limited, 1974), 284.

7. Ibid., 285.

8. Battle of Britain, http://www.rafmuseum.org.uk/research/online-exhibitions/americans-in-the-royal-air-force/pilot-officer-billy-fiske/battle-of-britain.aspx.

9. "All Britain Honors Independence Day," *New York Times*, July 5, 1941, 1.

10. Ibid.

11. Royal Air Force, "Battle of Britain—Role of Honour," *Royal Air Force*, http://www.raf.mod.uk/history/BattleofBritainRollofHonour.cfm.

12. Arthur Gerald Donahue, *Tally Ho! Yankee in a Spitfire* (New York: Macmillan, 1941), 9.

13. Ibid., 19.

14. Ibid., 73.

15. Len Morgan, "Eagle Squadron," *Flying*, January 1993, 88.

16. Kenneth C. Kan, *First in the Air The Eagle Squadrons of World War II* (Washington, DC: Air Force History and Museums Program, 2007), 8.

17. "Eagle Squadron Disturbed by 'Ballyhoo,'" *New York Times*, November 20, 1940, 3.

18. Ibid.

19. "3 Eagle Squadrons of the R.A.F.," *The Times* (London), November 20, 1941, 2.

20. "U.S. Recruits a Problem," *New York Times*, November 29, 1941.

Chapter Fifteen

1. "U.S. Club at Call of 10,000 Americans," *New York Times*, June 25, 1941.

2. "London's U.S. Guard Unit Imports Its Own Tommy Guns," *Toronto Star*, March 29, 1941, 3.

3. "Big Canadian Unit Crosses Atlantic," *New York Times*, August 2, 1941, 2.

4. John Gillespie Magee, Jr., http://blogs.loc.gov/catbird/2013/09/john-gillespie-magees-high-flight/.

5. Ibid.

6. "The Americans in the RCAF," *The Bomber Command Museum of Canada*, http://www.bombercommandmuseum.ca/americansrcaf.html.

7. "4,000 R.A.F. Pilots Trained in U.S.," *The Times* (London), February 27, 1943, 3.

8. "The Current Cinema," *The New Yorker*, February 21, 1942, 49.

9. Kan, *First in the Air: The Eagle Squadrons of World War II*, 25.

10. "First Lady Sees Spitfire Circus," *New York Times*, November 5, 1942, 13.

11. "Eagles with Talons," *New York Times*, May 9, 1943, BR 4.

Chapter Sixteen

1. Clarence Simonsen, "The Clayton Knight Committee," *The Bomber Command Museum of Canada*, http://www.bombercommandmuseum.ca/s,claytonknight.html.

2. Rachel Lea Heide, "Allies in Complicity," *Journal of the Canadian Historical Association*, 15, no. 1 (2004), 207.

3. "Recruit File Kept by AEF in London," *New York Times*, March 17, 1942, 3.

4. "To Let Americans Shift to Our Army," *New York Times*, January 18, 1942, 20.

5. "Americans in Canada's Army Can Transfer in Like Rank and Grade," *New York Times*, March 21, 1942, 7.

6. "U.S. Forces Stage Friendly Invasion," *Winnipeg Free Press*, May 25, 1942, 5.

7. "Lets Canada Draft American Citizens," *New York Times*, October 2, 1942, 9.

8. "2,058 Transferred to American Forces," *New York Times*, August 20, 1942, 3.

9. "Champion Baby Boy," *Oak Park (Illinois) Oak Leaves*, May 18, 1918, 30.

10. "Letter to the Editor," *Oak Park (Illinois) Oak Leaves*, February 13, 1941, 8.

11. "Ben Brinkworth," *Oak Park (Illinois) Oak Leaves*, August 16, 1945, 10.

12. Fred Gaffen, *Cross Border Warriors* (Toronto: Dundurn Press, 1995), 62.

13. "Ben Brinkworth," *The Windsor Star* (Ontario), August 11, 2006.

14. Ibid.

15. Parker, "In a Little-Known WWII Battle, a Father's Experience Becomes a Daughter's Journey," http://atwar.blogs.nytimes.com/2012/08/22/in-a-little-known-wwii-battle-a-fathers-experience-becomes-a-daughters-journey/.

16. Canadian Infantry Corps application for DCM (Distinguished Combat Medal), originated July 24, 1943, passed August 14, 1943. Copy retained by Royal Canadian Regiment.

17. Interview with author.

18. *Investigation of Un-American Propaganda Activities in the United States*, 78th Congress, House Resolution 282, Committee Print, Appendix—part IX, 1944.

19. Peter N. Carroll, *The Odyssey of the Abraham Lincoln Brigade: Americans in the Spanish Civil War* (Stanford: Stanford University Press, 1994), 287.

20. Cherry, *Yankee R.N.*, 434.

21. Ibid., 435.

Chapter Seventeen

1. Chris Dickon, *The Foreign Burial of American War Dead* (Jefferson, NC: McFarland, 2011), 265.

2. "Pilot Officer Sidney Nicholas Muhart," *Find a Grave*, http://www.findagrave.com/cgi-bin/fg.cgi?page=gr&GRid=59420853, accessed August 9, 2013.

3. Fabian Ware, Letter to the High Commissioner for Canada in London, dated December 23, 1941, Commonwealth War Graves Commission Archive.

4. H. C. Osborne, *Disposal of the Bodies of Americans Killed When Serving with the British Armed Forces*, Commonwealth War Graves Commission Archive.

5. Christine Scott, *Veterans' Benefits: Burial Benefits and National Cemeteries* (Washington, DC: Congressional Research Service, 2013), http://www.fas.org/sgp/crs/misc/R41386.pdf.

6. Imperial War Graves Commission, 288th Meeting, Thursday, January 16, 1947. *Graves of American Citizens Killed While Serving in Empire Forces*, Commonwealth War Graves Commission Archive.

7. Ibid.

8. "Army Prepares to Return Dead," *New York Times*, April 14, 1946.

9. Untitled Memo, April 18, 1947, Commonwealth War Graves Commission Archive.

10. Ibid.

11. Ibid.

12. George E. Springer, American Graves Registration Command, European Area, Letter to Oliver Holt, Imperial War Graves Commission, dated December 1, 1949, Commonwealth War Graves Commission Archive.

13. Stanley Applebaum, ed., *Alfred Lord Tennyson Selected Poems* (Mineola, NY: Dover, 1992), 52.

14. Canadian Infantry Corps applicated for DCM.

15. Interview with author.

16. Ibid.

17. Ibid.

18. Ibid.

19. Ibid.

Bibliography

Abbey, Edwin Austin. *An American Soldier*. New York: Houghton Mifflin, 1918.

"Alan Seeger, Poet, Terribly Wounded, Ended Own Life." *New York Tribune*, May 14, 1917, 1.

"All Britain Honors Independence Day." *New York Times*, July 5, 1941, 1.

"American Airmen on the Somme." *The Times*, London, November 7, 1916, 7.

American Bar Association. *Report of the Fortieth Annual Meeting of the American Bar Association, Volume 42*, Baltimore: Lord Baltimore Press, 1917, 101.

"American Corps in War to Lose Name." *New York Sun*, November 3, 1916, 1.

"American Field Service Also Appeals for Funds." *New York Times*, May 25, 1940.

"American Legion." *Manitoba Free Press*, February 28, 1916, 2.

"An American Legion." *The Middletown (NY) Daily Times Press*, January 3, 1916.

"American Legion Proves Its Breed." *Philadelphia Evening-Ledger*, April 24, 1917.

American Military History. http://www.history.army.mil/books/AMH/AMH-17.htm. Office of the Chief of Military History, United States Army, 372.

"American Minister Furls U.S. Flag." *Winnipeg Free Press*, May 11, 1915, 1.

"The American Soldiers in France." *The Times*, London, February 2, 1917, 5.

"American Soldiers Under American Flag." *Fort Wayne News*, May 25, 1917, 17.

"American Weakened by a Failure to Protest." *Toronto Star*, January 14, 1915, 5.

"Americans Abroad May Fight as a Unit." *Washington Times*, April 25, 1917, 4.

"Americans at Front May Save Citizenship." *New York Times*, April 23, 1917, 8

"Americans Enlist." *Miami [Oklahoma] Daily News Record*, September 6, 1939, 1.

"Americans in Canada's Army Can Transfer in Like Rank and Grade." *New York Times*, March 21, 1942, 7.

"The Americans in the RCAF." *The Bomber Command Museum of Canada* (website), accessed August 9, 2013, http://www.bombercommandmuseum.ca/americansrcaf.html.

"Americans Join Canadian Army." *Hammond (Indiana) Times*, April 5, 1940, 4.

"Americans Join Legion." *New York Times*, December 12, 1915, 3.

"Americans Launch Mad Raid to Mark Nation's War Entry." *Philadelphia Evening-Ledger*, May 28, 1917, 5.

"Americans May Be Shot." *The Gettysburg Times*, August 4, 1916, 2.

"Americans Seek to Enlist." *New York Times*, September 21, 1939.

"Americans Win Glory in France." *Washington Times*, April 28, 1917, 6.

Applebaum, Stanley, ed. *Alfred Lord Tennyson Selected Poems*. Mineola, NY: Dover, 1992.

Archer, William. Introduction to *Poems by Alan Seeger* by Alan Seeger. New York: Scribner's, 1916.

"Army Prepares to Return Dead." *New York Times*, April 14, 1946.

Baldwin, Neil. *Henry Ford and the Jews*. New York: Public Affairs, 2001.

"Battle of Ideals." *The Times*, London, January 25, 1916, 7.

"Ben Brinkworth." *Oak Park (Illinois) Oak Leaves*, August 16, 1945, 10.

"Ben Brinkworth." *The Windsor Star* (Ontario), August 11, 2006.

Bennett, William J. *America: The Last Best Hope*. Nashville: Thomas Nelson, 2007.

"Big Canadian Unit Crosses Atlantic." *New York Times*, August 2, 1941, 2.

"Big Ocean Ferry between Halifax and Ally Posts." *The Attica [Indiana] Daily Tribune*, December 21, 1916, 5.

The Bookman, Volume 47. New York: Dodd, Mead, 1918, 311.

The Bookseller, Newsdealer and Stationer. March 15, 1918, 245.

Boynton, Major Edward C. *General Orders of George Washington*. Newburgh, NY: E.M. Ruttenber & Son, 1883.

Broadfoot, Barry. *Six War Years 1939–1945*. Toronto: Doubleday Canada Limited, 1974.

Buckley, Gail Lumet. *American Patriots: The Story of Blacks in the Military from the Revolution to Desert Storm*. New York: Random House, 2001.

Bull, Andy. "The Forgotten Story of ... Those Magnificent Men and Their Flying Bobsled." *Talking Sport* (blog), *The Guardian*, last modified February 25, 2010, accessed August 8, 2013, http://www.guardian. co.uk/sport/blog/2010/feb/25/forgotten-story-magnificent-men-flying-machine.

"Canada Reports Brisk Increase in Army and Air Force Recruits." *New York Times*, October 26, 1941, 15.

"Canadian Benefit for 'Honor Legion.'" *New York Times*, May 6, 1918.

"Canadian Press Scores Lindbergh; Opposing War Stand." *New York Times*, October 22, 1939, 74.

Captain Theodore Marburg (statue). Inscription. Baltimore: Druid Ridge Cemetery, accessed August 8, 2013, http://www.flickr.com/photos/senoravetinari/7792623264/in/set-72157631020533052/lightbox/ (Photograph taken by Ashtray Girl, August 8, 2012, Flickr).

Carroll, Peter N. *The Odyssey of the Abraham Lincoln Brigade: Americans in the Spanish Civil War*. Palo Alto, CA: Stanford University Press, 1994.

Casey, John Joseph. "The New 'Old Guard' in France." *New York Times Current History*, 5 (1917), 856.

"Champion Baby Boy." *Oak Park (Illinois) Oak Leaves*, May 18, 1918, 30.

Cherry, A. H. *Yankee R.N.* London: Jarrolds Publisher, 1951.

"Christopher Charles: Humble Hero." *The (St. Petersburg) Evening Independent*, September 10, 1966, 14a.

Churchill, Winston S. *The World Crisis, 1911–1914, 2nd ed., Vol. 1*. New York: Scribner's, 1923.

"Churchill Inspects American Unit." *New York Times*, January 10, 1941, 4.

Ciseck, Janus. *Koscziusko, We Are Here*. Jefferson, NC: McFarland, 2002.

The Citizenship Act of 1907, Pub. L. No. 2, 5–7, title 8, ch. 12, 3, 3, § 1481.

"Claire Lee Chennault and the Problem of Intelligence in China." *Studies in Intelligence*, 54, no. 2 (June 2010), 3.

Clayton Knight Papers. Draft: Clayton Knight, O.B.E., *Contribution to Victory 1939–1942*, July 1965, 2, 23. Library and Archives Canada.

_____. An Interview with Clayton Knight No. 206 Squadron, RAF, Peter Kilduff, 37. Library and Archives Canada.

_____. Interview of Clayton Knight by Robert Hays, Major USAF, June 17, 1965, 5, 17. Library and Archives Canada.

Clayton Knight Papers. U.S. Selective Service memo. Library and Archives Canada.

"Colonel Refuses to Speak." *New York Times*, December 9, 1915, 6.

"Comforts of the American Legion." *New York Times*, August 11, 1916, 8.

Commonwealth War Graves Commission Archive. Untitled memo, dated April 18, 1947.

Convention (V): Respecting the Rights and Duties of Neutral Powers and Persons in Case of War on Land, The Hague, October 18, 1907, ch. 3, 17, § B.

"Court House Crater Easy for British Tank." *New York Times*, March 1, 1918.

Couvi. "Pay Tables for 1917." *Couvi's Blog* (blog), last modified April 14, 2001, accessed August 8, 2013, http://couvisblog.blogspot.com/2007/04/pay-tables-for-1917.html.

Cronau, Rudolf. *German Achievements in America*. New York: Rudolf Cronau, 1916.

Croxton, Frederick C. *Statistical Review of Immigration, 1820–1910, Distribution of Immigrants, 1850–1900*. Washington, DC: Government Printing Office, 1911.

"The Current Cinema." *The New Yorker*, February 21, 1942, 49.

"Daniels Scolds His Editor for War 'Ad.'" *New York Sun*, February 26, 1916, 1.

"Days Spent in a Land of Death..." *New York Sun*, November 12, 1916, Supplement 2.

Depew, Albert N. *Gunner Depew*. Chicago: Reilly & Britton, 1918.

Dickon, Chris. *The Foreign Burial of American War Dead*. Jefferson, NC: McFarland, 2011.

Dietrich-Berryman, Eric, Charlotte Hammond, and Ronald E. White. *Passport Not Required*. Annapolis: Naval Institute Press, 2010.

Donahue, Arthur Gerald. *Tally Ho! Yankee in a Spitfire*. New York: Macmillan, 1941.

Durflinger, Serge. "French Canada and Recruitment During the First World War." *Canadian War Museum* (website), accessed August 8, 2013, http://www.warmuseum.ca/education/online-educational-resources/dispatches/french-canada-and-recruitment-during-the-first-world-war/.

Dziuban, Stanley W. *Military Relations Between the United States and Canada, 1939–1945*. Washington, DC: Center of Military History, United States Army, 1990.

"Eagle Squadron Disturbed by 'Ballyhoo.'" *New York Times*, November 20, 1940, 3.

"Eagles with Talons." *New York Times*, May 9, 1943, BR 4.

"Economies Merged." *New York Times*, April 21, 1941, 1.

"Enlisting Young Men for the War." *Toronto Star*, January 26, 1915, 6.

"Enlistment for Foreign Wars." *San Antonio Express*, February 24, 1940, 4.

"Fighting Battles with Stretchers." *The Ogden Standard*, May 12, 1917, Magazine Section, 24.

"First Lady Sees Spitfire Circus." *New York Times*, November 5, 1942, 13.

"First of American Legion Off for Flanders." *New York Times*, May 28, 1916.

"Flying Tigers in Burma." *Life Magazine*, March 30, 1942.

"For the Freedom of the World" (advertisement). *The Wilmar (NM) Tribune*, February 20, 1918.

Ford, Daniel. "FDR's Secret Order." *The Warbird's Forum* (website), accessed August 8, 2013, http://www.warbirdforum.com/fdrnote.htm.

"Ford Answers Roosevelt." *New York Times*, May 21, 1916, 3.

"Foreign Legion Won Glory at Verdun." *New York Sun*, September 5, 1917, 2.

"The Foundation." *Lafayette Flying Corps. Memorial Foundation* (website), accessed August 9, 2013, http://rdisa.pagesperso-orange.fr/html/Frames/lafayette.html.

"4,000 R.A.F. Pilots Trained in U.S." *The Times*, London, February 27, 1943, 3.

"Fourth of July in Paris." *Philadelphia Evening-Ledger*, July 28, 1917, 8.

"France in Protest to United States." *New York Times*, September 26, 1914.

"France, Our Oldest Friend." *The Evening Independent*, Massilon, Ohio, February 17, 1917, 4.

Gaffen, Fred. *Cross Border Warriors*. Toronto: Dundurn Press, 1995.

"Garrison Demands Inquiry into Legion." *New York Times*, March 2, 1915, 7.

"Gen. Wood Defends American Legion." *New York Times*, March 4, 1915, 15.

"Germans Spiteful at American Legion." *Toronto Star*, September 9, 1916, 11.

Gimblett, Richard, and Michael Hadley, eds. *Citizen Sailors: Chronicles of Canada's Naval Reserve, 1910–2010*. Toronto: Dundurn, 2010.

"Gunner Depew." *Lorain County [Ohio] Chronicle-Telegram*, March 5, 1917, 7.

Hall, James Norman. *Kitchener's Mob: The Adventures of an American in the British Army*. Boston: Houghton Mifflin, 1916.

_____, Charles Nordhoff, and Edgar G. Hamilton, eds. *The Lafayette Flying Corps, Volume 2*. New York: Houghton Mifflin, 1920.

Halsey, Francis Whiting, ed. *The Literary Digest History of the World War*. New York: Funk & Wagnalls, 1919.

Hanlon, Mike. "Trench Report." *St. Mihiel Trip Wire* (website), last modified October 2006, accessed August 8, 2013, http://www.worldwar1.com/tripwire/smtw1006.htm.

Harrison, Michael, and Christopher Stuart-Clark. *Peace and War: A Collection of Poems*. Oxford: Oxford University Press, 1989.

"'Has Enough Men,' Says Hughes for Fourth Contingent." *Toronto Star*, April 10, 1915, 1.

Hau, George William, ed. *War Echoes: or Germany and Austria in the Crisis*. Chicago: Morton M. Malone, 1915.

Haycock, Ronald G. "The American Legion in the Canadian Expeditionary Force, 1914–1917: A Study in Failure." In *The Canadian Historical Review—Volume 61*, Toronto: University of Toronto Press, 1980, 262.

"He Will Fit Wings to the Chinese Dragon." *San Francisco Sunday Call*, n.d., 1911.

Heide, Rachel Lea. "Allies in Complicity." *Journal of the Canadian Historical Association*, 15, no. 1 (2004), 207.

Hemingway, Ernest. "On the American Dead in Spain." *New Masses*, February 14, 1939.

Hiney, Tom. *Raymond Chandler: A Biography*. New York: Grove Press, 1997.

"Hints Treason in Attack on Reserve Army." *Washington Herald*, March 4, 1915, 1.

Hixson, Walter L. *The American Experience in World War II*. New York: Routledge, 2003.

"Home Guard Unit Embarrasses Defense." *New York Times*, July 22, 1941.

"Home Town Helps." *Oelwein (Iowa) Daily Register*, July 18, 1913, 2.

Howe, Mark Anthony DeWolfe. *Memoirs of the Harvard Dead in the War Against Germany, Volume 1*. Cambridge, MA: Harvard University Press, 1920.

Hudson, James J. *Clouds of Glory*. Fayetteville: University of Arkansas Press, 1990.

"Hug American Recruits." *New York Times*, August 26, 1914, 4.

"Hun Threats Do Not Daunt." *The Brandon (Manitoba) Daily Sun*, August 5, 1916, 2.

"Huntington Campaign for Red Cross Is On." *Fort Wayne [Indiana] Journal Gazette*, December 17, 1917, 9.

Imperial War Graves Commission, 288th Meeting, Thursday, January 16, 1942. *Graves of American Citizens Killed While Serving in Empire Forces*. Commonwealth War Graves Commission Archive.

Investigation of Un-American Propaganda Activities in the United States, H.R. 282, 78th Cong. (1944), Appendix, § IX.

"Iowan Returns from Trenches." *Renwick (Iowa) Times*, January 25, 1917, 3.

James, Fred. *Canada's Triumph from Amiens to Mons: August to November 1918*. London: Canadian War Records Office, 1918, 6.

Jenkins, Danny. "British North Americans Who fought in the American Civil War, 1861–1865," master's thesis, University of Ottawa, 1993, 21.

"Jewish Jazz—Moron Music—Becomes Our National Music." *The Dearborn (Michigan) Independent*, August 6, 1921, 1.

"Jewish Legion Losses." *New York Times*, December 28, 1918.

"Jusserand Lauds Our 'Lafayettes.'" *New York Times*, September 7, 1916.

Kan, Kenneth, C. *First in the Air: The Eagle Squadrons of World War II*. Washington, DC: Air Force History and Museums Program, 2007, 8.

Kelly, Russell Anthony. *Kelly of the Legion*. New York: Mitchell Kennerly, 1917.

"Kelly of the Foreign Legion Sought Honors on Battlefield." *Princeton (Minnesota) Union*, January 20, 1916, 2.

"Kiffin Y. Rockwell, World War I Aviator, Lafayette Escadrille, Biography & Photographs." *Virginia Military Institute* (website), http://www.vmi.edu/archives.aspx?id=12371.

Knapp, Samuel Lorenzo. *Memoirs of General Lafayette: With an Account of His Visit to America, and of His Reception by the People of the United States; from His Arrival, August 15th, to the Celebration at Yorktown, October 19th, 1824*. Boston: E.G. House, 1824.

Knowles, W. Todd. "The Jewish Legion." *The Knowles Collection* (website), last modified October 27, 2010, accessed August 9, 2013, http://knowlescollection.blogspot.com/search/label/Jewish%20Legion.

"Lafayette Escadrille Ousts Lindbergh as Honorary Member." *New York Times*, May 29, 1940, 6.

"Lafayette Flyers Get Official Flag." *New York Times*, July 10, 1917, 2.

Landis, Arthur H. *The Abraham Lincoln Brigade*. New York: Citadel Press, 1967.

"Lavergne." *Detroit Free Press*, November 15, 1916, 1.

"Leaves the U.S. Navy for American Legion." *Toronto Star*, January 25, 1916, 13.

"Let Canada Draft American Citizens." *New York Times*, October 2, 1942, 9.

"Letter to the Editor." *Oak Park (Illinois) Oak Leaves*, February 13, 1941, 8.

"Lindbergh Scored by Press in London." *New York Times*, October 16, 1939.

"Lindbergh Urges We Shun the War." *New York Times*, September 16, 1939, 1.

"Lion Mascot Knew Him." *New York Times*, July 12, 1919, 3.

Livesey, J. F. B. *Canada's Hundred Days*. Toronto: Thomas Allen, 1919.

"London's U.S. Guard Unit Imports Its Own Tommy Guns." *Toronto Star*, March 29, 1941.

"Lost American Legion Found." *Oakland Tribune*, November 23, 1916, 5.

"'Lost' American Legion Found on the Somme Front." *The (New York) Evening World*, November 23, 1916, 2.

"'Lost' American Legion Is Found on Battle Front." *The Xenia (Ohio) Daily Gazette*, November 25, 1916, 7.

"The 'Machine Gun Man of the Princess Pats.'" *New York Times*, October 31, 1915.

Mac Shane, Frank. *The Life of Raymond Chandler*. New York: E. P. Dutton, 1976.

Magocsi, Paul R., ed. *Encyclopedia of Canada's Peoples*. Toronto: University of Toronto Press, 1999.

"Many Americans Are Killed on the Battlefields of Europe." *The Sumner (Iowa) Gazette*, February 15, 1917, 6.

"Many Here Join Polish Legion." *New North Rhinelander* (Wisconsin), March 28, 1918, 12.

Marburg, Theodore. *A League of Nations*. New York: Macmillan, 1919.

Marcosson, Issac Frederick. *Leonard Wood: Prophet of Preparedness*. New York: John Lane, 1917.

Mason, Gregory. "The Naval Plattsburgh." *The Outlook*, vol. 113 (1916), 501.

McMahon, J. J., Jr., Pvt. Letter to Mrs. S. P. Kennedy, dated May 4, 1918.

"Military Pay for CEF." *Canadian Expeditionary Force Study Group* (Bulletin Board), last modified April 18, 2005, accessed August 8, 2013, http://www.cefresearch.ca/phpBB3/viewtopic.php?f=3&t=88.

"Military Schools to Give Officers." *Adams County (Iowa) Union Republican*, February 28, 1917, 10.

"Mobsters, Mayhem, & Murder." *Magazine Times* (website), accessed September 5, 2013, http://www.walkervilletimes.com/34/mobsters1.html.

Modern Hospital, Volume Six, No. 1. Chicago: Modern Hospital Publishing, 1916, 48.

Morgan, Len. "Eagle Squadron." *Flying*, January 1993, 88.

Morse, Edwin Wilson. *The Vanguard of American Volunteers*. New York: Scribner's, 1918.

Mott, Col. T. Bentley. *Myron T. Herrick, Friend of France*. Garden City, New York: Doubleday, Doran, 1929.

Murray, Kenneth Malcolm. *Wings Over Poland*. New York: D. Appleton, 1932.

"Nation Gets Roster of American Legion." *New York Times*, December 26, 1916.

"Nations Honor War Dead." *New York Times*, November 12, 1927, 1.

"Nation's Leaders Active in Preparations for War." *The New-York Tribune*, March 21, 1917, 7.

Nelson, Cary, and Jefferson Hendricks. *Madrid 1937*. New York: Routledge, 1996.

"90% of U.S. Voters Would Fight If Canada Is Invaded." *New York Times*, May 19, 1941, 2.

"97th Am. Legion Going Overseas in Near Future." *Toronto Star*, March 30, 1916, 1.

"Ohioans Serving with British, Canadian Units Given Official Ranking." *Sandusky Register Star News*, July 22, 1941, 12.

Ontario's Historical Plaques (website), accessed August 8, 2013, http://www.ontarioplaques.com/Plaques_JKL/Plaque_Kawartha15.html.

Osborne, H. C. *Disposal of the Bodies of Americans Killed When Serving with the British Armed Forces*, undated. Commonwealth War Graves Commission Archive.

_____. Report for the Minister (Americans in Canadian Forces) dated October 14, 1927. Library and Archives Canada RG 24, vol. 6561.

Paquette, William A. "Canadian Immigrants." *Immigration in America* (website), last modified August 24, 2011, accessed August 8, 2013, http://immigration-online.org/402-canadian-immigrants.html.

"Paris Celebrates Independence Day." *New York Times*, July 5, 1924, Business Opportunities, 20.

Parker, Diantha. "In a Little-Known WWII Battle, a Father's Experience Becomes a Daughter's Journey." *At War* (blog), *New York Times*, last modified August 22, 2012, accessed August 6, 2013, http://atwar.blogs.nytimes.com/2012/08/22/in-a-little-known-wwii-battle-a-fathers-experience-becomes-a-daughters-journey/.

"Patriotism Is Personal." *The New-York Tribune*, April 1, 1917, 2.

"Personalities in Today's News." *Salt Lake City Tribune*, November 27, 1936, 6.

"Plans to Organize U.S. Citizens Now Fighting Abroad into One Fighting Unit." *The (New York) Evening World*, April 25, 1917, Final, Extra, 2.

"Poincare Grateful for Our Aid in War." *New York Times*, July 5, 1923, 17.

"Poles Form a Legion." *New York Times*, January 13, 1915, 2.

"Poles Here to Enlist for Army in France." *New York Times*, October 7, 1917.

"Polish Army Outfitted with American Uniforms." *New York Times*, February 2, 1920.

"President Wilson Proclaims our Strict Neutrality." *New York Times*, August 5, 1914.

"Queen Mary Thanks American Red Cross." *New York Times*, November 1, 1914, 10.

"Record Audience Hears Paderewski." *Indianapolis Star*, November 24, 1916, 5.

"Recruit File Kept by AEF in London." *New York Times*, March 17, 1942, 3.

"Repatriation of Americans." *The Evening Tribune*, Albert Lea, Minnesota, July 7, 1917, 2.

Rockwell, Paul Ayres. *American Fighters in the Foreign Legion*. Boston: Houghton Mifflin, 1930.

"Role of the United States." *The Times*, London, March 3, 1917, 3.

"Roosevelt." *Detroit Free Press*, May 5, 1917, 1.

"Roosevelt to Join Canadian Force?" *Toronto Star*, November 19, 1915, 7.

"Roosevelt to Visit Detroit." *New York Times*, May 14, 1916, 6.

"Roosevelt Urges the U.S." *Toronto Star*, January 11, 1915, 6.

"Roosevelt Urges Unity in America" *New York Times*, May 20, 1916, 1.

"Roosevelt Visit Links Three Nations." *New York Times*, August 1, 1936, 5.

Royal Air Force. "Battle of Britain—Role of Honour." *Royal Air Force* (website), last modified February 2012, accessed August 9, 2013, http://www.raf.mod.uk/history/BattleofBritainRollofHonour.cfm.

The Royal Flying Corps 1914–1918 (website), accessed August 9, 2013, http://www.airwar1.org.uk/.

Rudmin, F. W. "A 1935 U.S. Plan for Invasion of Canada." *Glasnost Archive* (website), last modified February 1, 1995, accessed August 8, 2013, http://www.glasnost.de/hist/usa/1935invasion.html.

"Ruling of Immigration Officials Keeps Them on Board Mauretania." *New York Times*, April 8, 1919.

Sage, Lt. Col. W. M., Commanding 211th Overseas Battalion. Letter to the Officer Commanding the 14th Canadian Infantry Training Brigade, dated February 6, 1917.

Sarty, Roger. "The Royal Canadian Navy and the Battle of the Atlantic, 1939–1945." *Canadian War Museum* (website), accessed August 9, 2013, http://www.warmuseum.ca/education/online-educational-resources/dispatches/the-royal-canadian-navy-and-the-battle-of-the-atlantic-1939–1945/.

"Saw War at Its Worse." *New York Times*, March 3, 1915, 3.

"Says Canadians Hoot Americans." *El Paso Herald*, September 29, 1916, 4.

Scott, Christine. *Veterans' Benefits: Burial Benefits and National Cemeteries*. Washington, DC: Congressional Research Service, 2013, accessed August 9, 2013, http://www.fas.org/sgp/crs/misc/R41386.pdf.

"Screen Play Based Upon Army Tragedy." *Philadelphia Evening-Ledger*, November 7, 1917, 20.

Seeger, Alan. "Ode in Memory of the American Volunteers Fallen for France," The Project Gutenberg Ebook of Poems, prod. Alan Light. http://gutenberg.org/cache/epub/617/pg617.html.

"Seek to Penalize U.S. Volunteers." *New York Times*, December 27, 1936.

Selcer, Richard F. *Civil War America, 1850 to 1875*. New York: Infobase Publishing, 2006.

"Sexless, Soulless, Spineless." *Toronto Star*, May 13, 1915, 7.

Seymour, James William Davenport. *History of the American Field Service in France*. Boston: Houghton Mifflin, 1920.

Simonsen, Clarence. "The Clayton Knight Committee." *The Bomber Command Museum of Canada* (website), accessed August 9, 2013, http://www.bombercommandmuseum.ca/s,claytonknight.html.

"63 Americans Aboard Two of Sunken Ships." *New York Times*, January 18, 1917.

Smith, 1st Lt. Joseph S. *Over There and Back in Three Uniforms*. New York: E.P. Dutton, 1918.

"Soldiers Finish a Drive for the American Legion." *New York Tribune*, September 21, 1919, 6.

Springer, George E., and Oliver Holt. Correspondence dated December 1, 1949. Commonwealth War Graves Commission Archive.

"Sweeney of the Legion Goes to War Again." *New York Times*, July 26, 1925, SM 9.

"Text of President Roosevelt's Proclamation on American Neutrality." *New York Times*, September 6, 1939.

Thenault, Georges. *The Story of the Lafayette Escadrille*. Kirkland, WA: Tale Ends Press, 2012.

"13 Americans Quit Fighting for Spain." *New York Times*, November 25, 1921.

Thompson, Charles R. Letter to Mrs. S. P. Kennedy, dated December 16, 1917.

Thompson, John Herd, and Stephen J. Randall. *Canada and the United States: Ambivalent Allies*. Atlanta: University of Georgia Press, 2002.

Thornton, Martin. *Churchill, Borden and Anglo-Canadian Relations, 1911–14*. London: Palgrave Macmillan, 2013.

"3 Eagle Squadrons of the R.A.F." *The Times* (London), November 20, 1941, 2.

"Three Get Legion Medals." *Toronto Star*, July 4, 1941, 2.

"To Let Americans Shift to Our Army." *New York Times*, January 18, 1942, 20.

Toland, Edward Dale. *The Aftermath of Battle*. New York: Macmillan, 1916.

"21 German Machines Toll of Americans." *New York Times*, November 19, 1916.

"Two Capitals Act." *New York Times*, August 23, 1940, 1.

"250,000 to Unite in Army League." *New York Times*, March 1, 1915, 1, 4

"213th Wants Grant." *Toronto Star*, June 15, 1916, 18.

"2,058 Transferred to American Forces." *New York Times*, August 20, 1942, 3.

"2,600 Who Fought in British Army Demobilized Here." *The New York Times*, April 10, 1919.

"Uncle Sam's Adopted Nephews." *Harper's Magazine*, Vol. 137 (1918), 289.

"The United States and the War." *Toronto Star*, February 11, 1915, 6.

"U.S. Ambulances Rushed to Front." *New York Times*, May 29, 1940, 6.

"U.S. Bans Service in Spanish Force." *New York Times*, January 14, 1937, 10.

"U.S. Club at Call of 10,000 Americans." *New York Times*, June 25, 1941.

"U.S. Forces Stage Friendly Invasion." *Winnipeg Free Press*, May 25, 1942, 5.

U.S. Naval Institute. *Proceedings*. Vol. 44. Annapolis: U.S. Naval Institute, 1918, 459.

"U.S. Pilots Join to Fight for Britain." *The Wisconsin State Journal* (Madison), October 9, 1940, 9.

"U.S. Recruits a Problem." *New York Times*, November 29, 1941.

"U.S. Volunteers Sought in France." *New York Times*, August 26, 1939, 5.

"An Urgent Request." *New York Times*, March 31, 1915, 10.

Veterans Affairs Canada. http://www.veterans.gc.ca/eng/remembrance/history/first-world-war/canada/canada8.

Vierick, George Sylvester. *The Fatherland, Volume IV*. New York: The Fatherland Corporation, 1916.

"War Veterans to Convene to Form 'Legion.'" *New York Tribune*, April 9, 1919, 7.

Ware, Fabian, and High Commissioner for Canada in London. Correspondence dated December 23, 1941. Commonwealth War Graves Commission Archive.

Wetherell, Ann. "Salvation through Aviation: Chinese and Chinese American Aviators in Portland, 1918–1945," paper, Portland State University, 2011, 10.

Wilmer, Harry White, West Sandling Camp, Devonshire. Letter to Jack Mathews, La Plata, Maryland, dated September 5, 1915, http://21stbattalion.ca/tributetz/wilmer_hw.html.

Winks, Robin W. *Civil War Years, Canada and the United States*. Montreal: McGill-Queen's University Press, 1998.

"Wood Told to Shun American Legion." *New York Times*, March 12, 1915, 9.

"The Young Recruits." *Joplin News Herald*, March 7, 1940, 4.

"Zionists Plan Big Army." *New York Times*, June 28, 1918, 14.

Index

Numbers in **_bold italics_** indicate pages with photographs.